*This book is dedicated to
Elizabeth*

Enticing the Learning
trainers in development

Enticing the Learning

trainers in development

John Staley

The University of Birmingham

Published in the United Kingdom by The University of Birmingham,
Edgbaston, Birmingham B15 2TT, UK in 2008
library@bham.ac.uk

Set in Garamond and Gil Sans Light,
printed and bound in Poland.
www. polskabook.pl

CONTENTS

CONTENTS *continued*

CONTENTS

FOREWORD

The Selly Oak Development Studies programme ran for almost 30 years and has benefited large numbers of professional development workers from nearly 100 countries around the world. The original programme was conducted by two leading figures in the development world, Laurence Taylor and John Staley. Laurence founded the programme and developed the content. John's contribution was to make the process of training as integral to learning as the content.

This important element increasingly informed the programme, and is the basis for this excellent training manual. John draws on the best material used frequently in the programme, as well as the experiences of the participants, to give a clear and eminently practical manual. This will be of immediate and immense usefulness to development work training throughout the world today and in the future. The manual is a tribute to all the participants in the programme over the years, leaving a valuable legacy, of benefit to current and future generations of development workers.

Though they would not say so, the publication is a fitting tribute too to John and to Laurence for the pioneering work they did, spurred on by the vision of a more socially just and environmentally thriving world. It also gives us a permanent record of an unusual and remarkable training programme.

Ralph Thomas
Director of Social Work Education
University of Birmingham
(*Former Head of Social Studies Department, Selly Oak Colleges*)

PREFACE

The purpose of this book is to increase the effectiveness of community workers and leaders by means of training. The book is a resource for trainers and would-be trainers.

It originated with the training of practitioners in development work, but the principles and methodology can be used in any setting where people work professionally with other people in community.

The book contains a wide variety of methods, together with appropriate interpersonal and group events. These should be viewed as components in an overall approach to training. The approach is person-centred, participatory, and experience-based. The starting point is the participants themselves, individually and as a group in training together. The focus is upon how they — as practitioners, leaders and managers — can work more effectively with others, whether in the training group or in organizations and communities back home.

There is an openness about this approach to training. Any contribution can become raw material for learning, and every participant makes contributions. What is required is experience and the willingness to examine and analyse it. Participants work together co-operatively, sharing in the experience which arises day-by-day — even moment-by-moment — during such training. Many also bring professional experience from back home, and all bring life experience. Seniority, certificates and amassed information are less important. To learn about working with human beings the main qualification is to be a human being.

The task of the trainer is to choose the methods, to organize the events, and to play the roles that create conditions favourable to the participants' reflection and learning — to 'entice' the learning. The further task for the trainer is to manage his or her own learning: as trainers we cannot support others in their learning unless we ourselves are learning.

The approach has a long reach. Attention shifts between the human scale of the group in training and the challenges of the wider world. Issues of the world are played out in the group. As participants consider their roles in the group they also consider their roles in the community. The individual is connected with the global through thought, feeling and action.

I have been committed to this kind of training for many years, both as a participant and as a trainer. I find it practical, egalitarian, broad in outlook and profound in effect. It encourages respect for people, and supports diversity and exploration. It can be deeply satisfying, exciting, and at times inspiring, as others also have found:

> *'this has been one of the best times of my life'*
> *'the most enjoyable two and a half months of education in my whole life'*
> *'a major event in my life'*
> *'it has been beautiful and a symbol of how the world might become'*
> *'the course touched me, I hope for ever ...'*

John Staley,
Malvern, UK, 2008

ACKNOWLEDGEMENTS

Enticing the Learning grew out of an unusual training course. The Development Studies Course at Selly Oak Colleges owed much to many people, but any appreciation must start with Laurence Taylor. Laurence launched the DSC in 1975, and he remained at its helm until 1999. It was his commitment, concern for people, breadth of experience and determination that kept the ship 'on course' in all weathers, and despite some uncharted seas.

I joined Laurence in 1982, and we worked together as tutors on the course between 1982 and 1998. The third permanent member of the team was Wendy Banner, who was course secretary during that period and in subsequent years. Throughout every course Wendy remained patient, reliable, cheerful and effective. I would like to thank Laurence and Wendy for their continued support while I have been preparing *Enticing the Learning*.

Laurence and I were joined on successive courses by Visiting Fellows from the so-called developing countries. Valli Seshan, Paul Siromoni, Regina Camargo and Juanita Paniamogan (Neneng) were able to join us full-time for two or more courses each. Those courses benefited directly from their work; while their perceptions, skills and concerns — and those of our other Visiting Fellows — contributed to the evolution of the DSC as a whole. In that sense every Visiting Fellow has a part in this manual, and I would like to thank them all for the contributions they have made.

The DSC was also supported by Visiting Tutors who joined us for a day, or several days, during each course, and who made their particular contribution on this regular basis. Denys Saunders and John Madeley played a part in more courses than I did. Sue Mayo's contribution came in later years. I believe that the DSC meant a lot, in different ways, to Denys, John and Sue. I also know how greatly each course and its members benefited from their work, and I thank them for that.

Chapter 7, A Fresh Look, is based on the innovative work which Sue developed for the DSC. Sue prepared the written material for the chapter, and I am especially grateful to her for this additional contribution.

I would also like to thank the course members themselves. Like the Visiting Fellows, members made their contributions, not only to particular courses, but also to the evolution of the DSC as a whole. In that sense all have contributed to this manual.

Many members have contributed in a more direct way too. After I began *Enticing the Learning* I realized that extracts from the course diaries would enrich and enliven the text, and would provide examples, insights and different points of view. While choosing such extracts I have — yet again — been struck by the humour, wisdom and commitment of the course members. I think this will be apparent to the reader too.

It was impractical to ask for permission to use each extract, but I have disguised names by using initials only, and I have not shown the dates of the extracts, so individuals cannot be identified. Otherwise I have edited this material very little, and I hope that members whose words are included will recognize them and be pleased. I have also included 10 case studies contributed by course members. These were in regular use in the DSC.

The DSC was housed, physically and organizationally, within the Social Studies Department of the Selly Oak Colleges. We were fortunate here too in our colleagues from other courses. They took a warm interest in our sometimes outlandish activities, and gave us cheerful encouragement. In particular I thank Ralph Thomas, who was Head of the Department during some difficult transitions, and who has encouraged me in the writing of *Enticing the Learning* from the beginning. Ralph is now Director of Social Work Education at the University of Birmingham, and Head of Academic Programmes at the Institute of Applied Social Studies, which has taken over the work of the Social Studies Department. In his new role Ralph has continued to offer support, and has made it possible for the University to publish the manual. He has also kindly written the Foreword. These continuing links provide an important sense of continuity with the work at Selly Oak.

The Geraldine and Barrow Cadbury Trust made a grant for publications related to the Development Studies Course. The money is given so that publications can be made available to former course members, and I would like to express thanks for this 'appropriate aid'.

The line drawings were kindly made by Carol Eden, and the photographs have been contributed by Anders Iversen, Eleanor Pritchard and Laurence Taylor.

Old friends, former colleagues and co-workers have given me permission to use their material. These include Laurence Taylor, Udai Pareek, Henry Volken and Peter Oakley. I am also grateful to The Commonwealth Youth Programme, Commonwealth Secretariat, London and to Vishwa Yuvak Kendra, New Delhi for permission to quote material. The case studies on pages 190 and 191—2 are taken from the British Association for Commercial and Industrial Education, *Bacie Case Studies*, London, with the permission of The Chartered Institute of Personnel and Development, London.

I am grateful to Sue Mayo, Elizabeth Staley, Ralph Staley, Clive Taylor and Mary Worthington who, between them, have checked the text for errors. Any errors which remain are my responsibility.

Finally I thank my wife Elizabeth, who has supported me throughout this work, and has given me so much timely help — practical, emotional and editorial. For me, writing *Enticing the Learning* has been a labour of love; it is Elizabeth who has made that possible.

CHAPTER 1

The Background

Enticing the Learning: Trainers in Development is a practitioners' manual for those who use, or want to use, an experience-based approach to training and learning.

The manual describes this approach and sets out the methodology which is appropriate to it. It introduces the methods themselves, together with additional and compatible resources for experience-based training. These include a variety of participatory events and person-centred topics, together with exercises, examples, handouts and other materials.

Each method, event or topic is described in a separate section. A few topics occupy two sections. Each section includes a brief introduction, with learning objectives, an explanation of how and where the method or event may fit in a course, and an indication of the time required for it. Links are also made to other methods and events which can be used to broaden or reinforce the learning.

The sections are grouped in chapters. The order of the chapters roughly corresponds to the unfolding of a course.[1]

Directions for the trainer on using each method or event are included in sequence from the beginning to the end, including final reflections. This more directive material is intended to make matters clear to those who are new to training, but it should not limit those who are already practised. In experience-based training it goes without saying that trainers are encouraged to work out their own style of training and their own ways of using methods and events.

Attention is given in each section to the role of the trainer — to what the trainer does — at each stage of the method, event or topic concerned. Attention is also given to the members of a course and to their roles, needs and learning. Members are assumed to be 'people who work with people' professionally in communities or in other settings.

Enticing the Learning is based upon the Development Studies Course (DSC) at Selly Oak Colleges, so the references, the examples and many of the materials relate to the community development work of the voluntary agencies.[2] The training model assumes a full-time course lasting about three months and a course group of 15—25 members.

However *Enticing the Learning* is not a manual of the DSC, nor does it deal with development in general. Much that was part of the DSC, especially course inputs and subject matter, is not included. Any future course which may be built around this manual, or

1. The best order for reading may be different. Readers interested in the methodology may want to start with Development Studies at Selly Oak Colleges (page 19); Approaches to Training (page 156); Introducing the Methodology (page 67); More about the Methodology (page 122) and. The Role of the Trainer (page 30).
2. See Development Studies at Selly Oak Colleges, (page 19).

which uses the resources included here, should incorporate its own topics and events, depending on the purpose and scope of that course.

The word 'student' was used at Selly Oak Colleges, but seemed inappropriate given the age, seniority and depth of experience of DSC members. Furthermore the word belongs to an academic approach and methodology. 'Course member' is used here.

The staff of courses at Selly Oak Colleges were known as 'tutors'. This too is an academic role which did not fit the DSC and its methodology. The word 'trainer' is more descriptive and is used here. Nonetheless, the words student and tutor — and class and classroom — appear in some of the illustrative material taken from the DSC.

Formats Used in the Text

Five formats are used in this manual in order to distinguish and identify different kinds of text.

Format One

The main text provides the overall framework and continuity of the manual. It is used in each section to introduce the material, to set out the objectives, and for information and commentary. It uses a serif typeface, and looks like this:

... Once their initial anxieties are allayed members may find that the first days of a course feel unexpectedly comfortable. The content, the methodology, the trainers, and the membership are all now known, and there can be a sense of anticipation and excitement ...

Format Two

A different format is used for direct instructions to the trainer. Where the trainer is being told what to do and how to do it — which method to use, how to conduct an particular session — the typeface is sans serif, like this:

■ Tell the members that they are going to work with photographs. Lay the photos separately, face up, on the floor in the centre of the group. Then invite the members to stand and walk slowly round all the photos, looking at them.

The change to such instructions is marked by a small black square. The square is repeated when the instructions continue over a page. The style of writing is itself more directive, and addresses the trainer as 'You ...'

Format Three

Members of successive DSC groups took turns to write a daily course diary. Short extracts from the diaries enrich and enliven the manual. These appear in italic typeface like this:

▶ *The fact that we sit in a circle is important. The circle is always intact, and we can see everyone, with everyone at ease to contribute. We are seventeen nations in one room ...*

Each diary extract is indicated by a small grey triangle.

Format Four

In some sections there are short quotations from published sources. Such quotations look like this:

> ... ever increasing knowledge of a subject is no substitute for adequate training skill; but neither is training skill a substitute for familiarity with the subject.

References for the quotations are provided in footnotes.

Format Five

Handouts, questionnaires and other training materials are included at the ends of some sections.[1] They appear in a typeface like this:

Questions require answers; and that is why they are such an effective tool. But some kinds of question are more useful in development work than others.

Each handout is indicated by a small blank square.

The Footnotes

These provide additional information about material in the main text. Each note is numbered and placed at the bottom of the relevant page.

The Glossary

Certain words tend to be used during experience-based training, and may have a particular meaning in that context. It is likely that some readers of this manual will be working in English as a second or foreign language, so definitions and clarifications of such words may be helpful. A selection of these words will be found in the glossary on page 471. A few terms from development work, which occur in the handouts and elsewhere in the manual, are also included for those who are unfamiliar with this work.

---

1. Such materials may be copied and distributed to course members for individual work or reading. Some material is protected by copyright, and should be used only for training. References and sources are given, and these should be included on copies.

▶ *I felt like a fish <u>in</u> the water when I joined the course here ...*

▶ *On my way to the class I opened my heart and mouth and I sang my songs.*

▶ *What is important is the idea that adult learning is a development process. The course is designed around that ...*

For twenty-five years the Selly Oak Colleges in Birmingham, UK, ran an international training course in development work and aid administration. The course ran for one academic term (eleven weeks), twice a year, and was known as the Development Studies Course or DSC. Those who attended the course were mostly on the staff of voluntary agencies and NGOs which were engaged in development. The DSC was widely known and much respected among such organizations throughout the world. In 1999, when the Selly Oak Colleges were dissolved, the course was taken over by the University of Birmingham.

This manual is based on the DSC during the later years of its life under the Selly Oak Colleges. The author, John Staley, was a full-time tutor or trainer for the course during that time. The manual covers the approach to training, the methodology, the methods themselves, and participatory events in the course of that time. It does not include content and subject matter as such.

The main purpose of the manual is to support the work of former participants who now have responsibility for training others. More especially it is for those who want to use the methodology which they experienced in the DSC. The manual is also a resource for anyone who is using or considering an experience-based approach to training, whether for development work or for other leadership roles.

While the author was working on the DSC, the daily demands of the course made writing about it impossible. Now, in retrospect, there is an opportunity to look beyond those demands and define what made it an unusual course. The fact that it was an unusual course, and was recognized as such, is another reason for writing this book.

 ## The Course

The Selly Oak Colleges ran a number of other courses, including training for social workers, teachers and community workers. The common theme was preparation for social responsibility. Where these courses related to professional work in Britain, they received formal accreditation. They then operated under the requirements of an appropriate professional authority.

The DSC had much in common with these courses, but its authority came from a different direction. The work to which it was linked is not in Britain, but in countries in Asia, Africa, South and Central America and the Pacific. Those who attended the course also came from those countries, or were working in them. The Colleges provided a physical base for the DSC, but authority for the way the course operated lay more with the individuals and organizations that used it. Our responsibility, as trainers, was to the members of each successive course group, and to those who had sent them. Beyond that, we felt a wider responsibility towards people in communities thousands of miles away, whose lives would later be touched by what course members learned while they were at Selly Oak. Ultimately, perhaps, authority for the work came from the imperative of development itself.

This carried a heavy responsibility, but it gave a certain freedom and flexibility. It allowed us to respond to the needs of each course group. The structure and the broad objectives of the course remained unchanged, but the content and the process could be attuned to the particular group. This enhanced the learning and allowed more 'real life' into the classroom.

We can say that the DSC was self-validating. In the last resort, as long as people continued to come, the course could continue to run. And they did keep coming. We also knew that levels of satisfaction were generally high, not only among the participants, but also among their employers and sponsors, and among the donor and scholarship agencies which paid the fees.

 ## The Course Members

Almost all course members were involved in development work in the so-called 'Third World' or 'South'. The number attending a course varied from 15 to 25. Among them there were never less than six nationalities, and sometimes 12 or more. The majority of the members came from Asia and Africa. Others were Western Europeans working in developing countries as expatriates, or working for donor agencies in their own countries. Smaller numbers came from Eastern Europe, South, Central and North America, the Pacific region and Australasia. By 1998 ninety countries had already been represented in the course.

Members' ages ranged from 20 to 65 and most were in mid-career. The proportion of women to men changed over the years, rising from 10—25% in the early 1980s to 50% or more 20 years later. Formal qualifications ranged from none to postgraduate. Some were technically qualified, and some had previous training in development work. Most already had several years' experience, but there were a few who were starting work or changing career. Some came from community groups and some from national or international organizations. There were members with every political view, and members of every religion and none. Their job descriptions were as varied as the members themselves.

In these and other ways the course groups were remarkably heterogeneous and diverse. This was made possible by the nature of the course and its methodology. The heterogeneity and diversity was a source of enrichment and learning for the course; it was also one of its challenges.

The number of full-time trainers was two or three. Two were on the permanent staff of the Selly Oak Colleges, and the third was a Visiting Fellow from Asia, Africa, South America or the Pacific region. Other specialists contributed by the day or week. Names and further information are included in the Acknowledgements (page 12).

The Course in Practice

The broad objectives of the DSC had evolved from years of experience of development work and training, but the final objectives for each course incorporated the expectations of the members of that course.[1] An example of the objectives for a course are given at the end of this section.

The course day started at 9.0 a.m. The first 30 minutes were allocated for the Course Diary and for any practical matters, announcements etc. Two sessions, each of 1½ hours, were taken during the morning, with a 30 minute break at mid-morning. A third session of 1½ hours followed in the afternoon.[2] Each session was filled by one or more events or inputs. These events and inputs were the raw material for the learning in the course, and were determined ultimately by the course's objectives. Every event and input included in a course related to one or more of the objectives.

The allocation of the events and inputs to sessions was indicated in a weekly timetable. As each new course began, timetables for the first two weeks were distributed to the members. After that timetables were planned week by week, as the course evolved. During Week 2 the trainers drafted the timetable for Week 3, and so on. As they planned the sequence of each week's work trainers took account of many factors, some practical or methodological, but others less predictable, such as the concerns and issues which were emerging among the members as a course proceeded, and the climate and growth of the group as this changed from one week and the next.[3]

---

1. See Why Have We Come? Sharing Expectations (page 77)
2. See Sessions and Breaks (page 53).
3. The following were considered as each weekly timetable was drafted: inputs and events which reinforce each other; changing the method and changing the trainer; choosing inputs, events and methods for the the time of day (lectures and films in the morning, case studies and exercises in the afternoon); the alternations of the methodology (individual work alternating with group work, small groups with the whole group, personal work with impersonal issues, action with reflection, discussing with reading, and so on); taking up topics which emerge as concerns among members; the growth, climate and cohesion in the course group; using the process in the course group to explore issues (such as communication, gender relations and leadership); increasing levels of challenge as the course progressed; and practical constraints (such as public holidays, visits by specialists, external visits, and the availability of extra rooms).

The course could thus evolve in a logical sequence, but also as a response to its members, individually and collectively, in a more flexible and creative way than is possible with a conventional predetermined timetable. This made for a closer and more timely match between the needs of the members and the resources of the course. This in turn supported the motivation and the learning. More important, it allowed the process and dynamics of the course to become a closer analogy — or mirror — for development itself. In other words, it strengthened the parallels between the process and learning in the course and the process and practice of development work. Such parallels are important in the methodology and in members' experience of the course.[4]

Nonetheless many components of successive courses were the same. The sequence may have been different, but by the end of each course much of the same ground had been covered.

Being able to take many factors into account, and choose the appropriate inputs, events and methods, is possible with a large repertoire of suitable alternatives. We had two or three times as many resources available for the DSC as could be fitted into any one course. The items which appear in this manual were used regularly.

Assessing the Learning

One of the principles of the DSC was that learning is not for knowing more, but for doing things differently. Such a course is to be judged by the impact it has on the work of course members in their own organizations and communities back home. Only if members become more effective in their roles, and improve the quality of their work, can we say that useful learning has taken place.

So success cannot be judged by an examination of knowledge before members depart. However extensive and deep that knowledge may be, it is only effective if it is acted upon. Furthermore, the conventional examination is an academic device which does not fit with an experience-based approach and methodology. Exams may make it easier to measure or to quantify, but our concern was with qualitative change. So course members were not examined or graded, and formal awards were not given.[5]

Nonetheless we used every opportunity to make informal assessments of the course, of the process, and of members' roles and learning. Assessments were made through:

● continuous observation by trainers, with daily discussion and review of the course, the group, and the roles of individual members;

● daily and weekly events, such as the Course Diary and Ending the Week;

---

4. See Introducing the Methodology (page 67). Constructing a course as it goes along may seem insecure — and even irresponsible — to those used to an academic approach, who may expect a plan for the whole of a course before it has even begun. In reality, with an evolving course, there is no less planning; the difference is that the planning continues until closer to implementation.

5. Certificates of Participation in the DSC were awarded (see Saying Farewell, page 469n).

- statements by individuals and small groups about their learning after course events;
- statements made in the final sessions at the end of a course;
- periodic meetings between trainers and individual members.

In addition there were two structured evaluations of each course and of the learning. One was arranged at the end of the third week. Members were asked to assess progress in the course, the usefulness of inputs and events, the functioning of the course group, their individual role and contribution, and their own learning. A similar but fuller evaluation took place at the end of every course.

We also received feedback from employing organizations, from sponsoring and funding agencies, from the colleagues and co-workers of course members, from the members themselves after their return back home, and by informal word-of-mouth through the development network.

For members the learning was often profound; for the trainers the results were often inspiring and inspiriting.

Postscript

The DSC at Selly Oak Colleges ran twice a year from 1974 until 1999, the year when the Colleges were dissolved. The course then continued for another five years as part of Birmingham University. That is a long life for any course. The course was closed by the University in 2004. The demise of the DSC is another reason for publishing a record of some of its features.

An Example of Objectives for the DSC

The following are the objectives set for one course with the participation of the members of that course:

1. To broaden and deepen our understanding of underdevelopment and development.
2. To exchange experience of development work, and to reflect upon that experience.
3. To raise awareness of how political, social, economic, technological, cultural and religious factors affect our work in development.
4. To consider the approaches and strategies of our own and other organizations in development work.
5. To explore the role of the development worker and to increase our own effectiveness in that role.
6. To deepen our understanding of the role relationships of women and men in development.
7. To increase our understanding of how the international economic and political system affects our work.

8. To become more aware of environmental considerations in development.

9. To improve understanding of principles, practices and skills in management applied to development work, including planning, budgeting, implementation, evaluation, organizational structures, personnel and training.

10. To examine our attitudes and improve our skills in encouraging participation, relf-reliance and development.

11. To increase our understanding of ourselves and others in order to improve our effectiveness in communicating and working with others; and to improve our leadership effectiveness, in order to encourage leadership among those we work with.

12. To consider the effects of aid on the development process; to examine our attitudes towards aid; and to explore the nature and practicalities of the relationship between donor agency and recipient agency.

▶ *You can't imagine how much use I have had from the Development Studies Course.*

▶ *A lot of good changes take place after the studies ...*

▶ *I have gone through a transformation here ...*

The Approach to Development

▶ *How does this course express development? What does the structure of this course tell us about development? What about methods? Working in the group? The attitudes of our tutors or members?*

▶ *We are beginning to see development not as an activity but as a <u>process</u>. We are learning to ask questions like, 'Who has power? How is it used?'*

▶ *We used to think that the question was, 'How can we change the world?' but now we realise that there is another question, 'How can <u>we</u> change?'*

The central subject in development studies is, naturally, the development process itself. This is as much a practical as an academic subject. Those who participated in the DSC were practitioners. Their main concern was to become more competent and more effective in their work.

Our main concern, as trainers, has been to provide opportunities for learning about the process and practice of development. The way that we, as trainers, approach development is therefore important when it comes to choosing events and methods to use in a course. Subject matter, approach, methodology, learning and practice must all interlock and reinforce each other. For these reasons a short discussion on the approach to development is included here as part of the background to this manual.[1] This will also help to explain the examples, diary extracts and course materials to readers who are not familiar with development work. It will also convey more of the 'flavour' of the DSC.

How Do We Understand the Problem?

The concern among NGOs for development begins with the chronic and degrading material poverty and physical suffering found in many communities in the world. The remedy being sought is changing such conditions through development.[2] The role of the development worker is to assist communities to achieve development.

What we understand by development, and the kind of assistance we offer, will depend on what we think are the reasons for poverty and suffering. Members of the DSC, and the organizations which employed them, were already being guided by varying ideas

---

1. A longer discussion is not possible because subjects and topics as such are beyond the scope of the manual. However two introductory exercises are included: Perceptions of Poverty and Poor People (page 298) and Factors in Underdevelopment (page 301).

2. To develop literally means to uncover. It is the opposite of envelop. Already, in the word itself, is the idea of potential within.

and assumptions. As members worked together in the course group, they discovered where their ideas and assumptions fitted in the spectrum of thinking, both within the course group, and within NGO development work generally. It soon became clear that some members, and some organizations, had a narrow approach, were using a limited analysis, and were making questionable assumptions.

We encouraged members to widen their enquiry beyond the strictly economic, and to recognize that there are other dimensions to development. We drew on the idea of 'underdevelopment'. Poverty is commonly thought of as an economic condition only; whereas underdevelopment implies active impoverishment, often associated with social, political, societal, psychological, cultural — and even spiritual — deprivation.

It became clear from members' interaction that the way we understand underdevelopment in one situation may, or may not, help us to understand it in another. Factors which are critical in one situation may be less important, less relevant, and even absent, somewhere else. Different situations require different analyses.

We looked at the experience of NGOs in development work during the last fifty years. Such work has not always been successful. When organizations examine the reasons for failure they often conclude that their analysis and understanding have been inadequate. In other words, they have misunderstood, and probably underestimated, the problem. They have usually found that the way forward has been to test their existing assumptions, to take more factors into account, and to broaden and deepen their understanding, not only of poverty, but also of underdevelopment.

As the NGOs learned from practical experience, they often found that their programmes needed to be broadened. To give an example from one community programme, an early evaluation of curative medicine led to nutrition education, which led, on the one hand, to health education and community health programmes and, on the other hand, to attempts to increase food production. The latter led to irrigation, which in turn led to water harvesting and environmental conservation. All these were interconnected, and in the growing understanding of development, all were recognized as necessary in that situation.

At a conceptual level, the early thinking after the Second World War had proposed that Development = Economic Growth, and this was the 'formula' generally accepted in the 1950s. By 1960, the NGOs of the time had found it inadequate. The formula was then extended to become Development = Economic Growth + Social Change. This was also found to be inadequate and, as experience grew, further dimensions were added, roughly one each decade, until the formula had become Development = Economic Growth + Social Change + Social Justice + Peoples' Participation + Sustainability.

As the understanding of underdevelopment has extended beyond the economic, so the vision and scope of development itself has become widened and diversified, until it sometimes seems to embrace much of human life. The agenda of development which NGOs are now advancing extends into every dimension, from human health to environmental protection, from economic livelihood to political awareness, from traditional culture to modern science, from human rights to global advocacy, from micro-savings to intergovernmental debt relief, from personal effectiveness to organizational capacity, and so on.

As course members became more aware of the wider NGO experience, they recognized that underdevelopment usually has multiple inter-related causes. As they reflected on their own work, and on the work of their organizations, they often concluded that they too might need to deepen their analysis and broaden their approach.

Yet this deeper and broader understanding among NGOs has remained rooted in practice. It has not been taken over by ideology. Our thinking about development has become more wholistic. It includes more diversity and complexity, and it is more realistic about the obstacles to change, but remains an agenda based on practical experience.

 ## Perspectives on Development

Practical work with the poorest people has led many NGOs to criticize 'official' thinking and policy, which usually concentrates on economic growth and 'modernization'. Some of those who arrived for the DSC were already questioning the prevailing assumptions and approaches. Those from societies where there are big inequalities had seen for themselves how economic growth reflects those inequalities, with the rich becoming richer and the poor poorer.

Modernization assumes that the process of development is the same everywhere, and that all will follow the same path, or 'climb the same ladder', but the experience of many in the course contradicted this immediately. Others did not accept the devaluation of tradition, history and culture which accompanies modernization. We drew attention to the political and commercial interests which promote modernization, and urged members to become more aware of vested interests and the workings of power. Yet all agreed that in some situations the need is for infrastructure and modernization.

We examined, and criticized, the approach which attributes poverty and suffering to social injustice and which asserts that people are made poor and made to suffer by the prevailing political and economic structures. We raised members' awareness about inequality within societies and between nations, and explored the dynamics of exploitation and marginalization at every level. Here too the issues crystallized around power, disparities, and values. We encouraged members to extend their own power horizons (see glossary page 471), and to explore the links between the local and the global.

We drew on experience of consciousness-raising, community organizing, gender awareness, popular participation and empowerment. We explored the change in the development worker's role: how, instead of 'bringing development' from outside, he or she becomes an enabler of development from within.

We gave importance to common-sense management as a tool to be made use of, but we questioned the assurances of managerialism. We drew attention to the impositions that accompany aid. We rejected the control of development by the powerful, the external, and the vested interest.

Over the years we have increasingly encouraged members to give attention to the physical environment. Much of the damage to the environment has been done in the name of development, and pressures on the environment already constrain development for the poorest. All development workers need a clear and comprehensive knowledge of natural forces and cycles, and how these are disrupted by inappropriate development.

We came to understand underdevelopment and development as universal processes, while recognizing that they vary according to context and situation. So there is underdevelopment even in the so-called developed countries, and the need exists for certain kinds of development there too. Just as there may be underdevelopment at any level — nation, community, group or individual — so there is potential at every level and in every human being.

As members worked and interacted together, the focus of attention shifted back and forth between the course and the communities back home, so that the processes of learning in the course group and of development in the community often mirrored one another. Individual learning, improved confidence and self-image, group growth and community development became merged in a wider process of transformation. Perhaps it is our own participation in this process — whether we describe the process as learning, growth, change or development — which gives *us*, as development workers, the moral right to expect others to make changes in *their* lives. At the very least we recognized the parallels between encouraging other people in the process of development and being sustained and extended ourselves, as persons, in the same process.

As their perspectives on development grew, members were able to recognize their own organization's assumptions and understanding more clearly, and were able to identify the position of their organization within the overall spectrum of thinking about underdevelopment and development. As trainers we encouraged them to reflect also on where their individual assumptions and values fit within this spectrum, how their attitudes were affecting their daily work, and whether there was any mismatch between themselves and their organizations.

Our approach was to examine varied practical experience, to explore differing perceptions of this, to compare these with other people's ideas and theories, and to encourage members to deepen their understanding of underdevelopment in their own contexts. In the light of this, we encouraged them to reconsider, and perhaps redirect, the responses which they and their organizations were making. We were not seeking to

---

3. Preconceived certainties, whether among politicians, aid administrators, programme managers, or development workers, have been a recurring obstacle to achieving appropriate development.

identify a 'correct' or consensual view of development.[3] On the contrary, we encouraged diverse thinking for diverse situations.

What brought all in the DSC together was our sense of outrage at the scale of underdevelopment, the avoidable suffering, and the wasted human potential. What united us were our shared assumptions about the worth of human life and the potential of all to take charge of their own lives. What gave us hope was the encounter with development in our own selves, in others, and in the groups and communities we have been working in.

▶ *There is a strong feeling that we have touched and felt the animal 'Development'.*

▶ *The consensus was that underdevelopment and development are linked in a dynamic process; and that we should understand all 'mechanisms' in this system (economic, politic, social, spiritual) and from the local level to the international ...*

▶ *... development can be defined differently according to culture, nation, society, but the real meaning will remain the same.*

▶ *For me, development is always about asking questions, particularly the questions that ask who benefits and who decides.*

▶ *I now see development as transformation — including myself. Unless we are prepared to change, it is useless to talk about and promote development.*

▶ *For me, this course has been a personalisation of development.*

▶ *It has been a special experience of ... building up the inner spirit.*

1.4   The Role of the Trainer

▶ *Even if our tutors are very careful not to tell us <u>what</u> to think, they quite clearly expect us to <u>think</u>.*

▶ *Our tutors have many times proven that they are pretty 'crafty' in designing the progression of our learning process.*

▶ *... tutors helped members to set up structure for their own learning.*

Preparing for the Role

Much of a trainer's authority and effectiveness depends upon the confidence that trainees and course members have in him or her. If they sense that the trainer is skillful, caring, committed and enthusiastic they will be disposed to trust him or her, and much can be done. Without that trust little can be done.

An essential requirement for anyone who seeks to become a trainer in a specialized field — such as development work — is to be knowledgeable and competent in that field.

> ... ever increasing knowledge of a subject is no substitute for adequate training skill; but neither is training skill a substitute for familiarity with the subject.[1]

In this section we assume the necessary specialized knowledge and competence, whether this is in development work or in some other professional field.

The first move towards becoming a trainer is to participate in training. Learning about experience-based training is best done by reflecting on our own experience of it! Attending training of the kind described in this manual — experience-based and directed towards professional work — would be a start. 'Laboratory' training provides deeper and more searching preparation.[2] This would be especially useful for the intricate work with process and conflict, and for inter-personal, group and community dynamics. Sensitivity or assertiveness training — according to personality — is often useful. Attending a formal programme of 'training for trainers' is another possibility: this usually includes supervision of practice and assessment of competence. Whatever the exact route, the need is to widen experience, increase awareness, sharpen and strengthen skills, and deepen learning and confidence.

Observing and working alongside experienced trainers, especially those skilled in facilitating process, is equally necessary. It is a principle of experience-based training that we learn most from those who are in similar roles to our own.

---

1. Rolf P. Lynton and Udai Pareek, *Training for Development*, Taraporevala, Bombay, page 275.
2. 'Laboratory' training is described briefly on pages 159—160.

Working in a training team can be especially rewarding if the other trainers, while sharing similar values and convictions, have different perspectives and styles. For example, if I myself have a tendency to dwell on future possibilities — on how global development might be and what the individual's role might become — I shall learn much from colleagues who focus on the reality of the present. If I usually apply my head to problems, I shall learn from someone who applies the heart. If I make judgements quickly, I shall learn from someone who takes a more careful and searching look first. Working with colleagues who share a commitment to experience-based learning, but whose way of setting about it is different, enriches us all.

The principle here is complementarity: the contributions of the trainers in a team complement each other, and strengthen the combined work of the team. Such colleagueship among the trainers is enriching for members of a course group too.

Enticing the Learning

The central task of the trainer is to support the course members' learning. Lynton and Pareek describe it like this:

> Learning takes place within the individual as a result of a confluence of diverse, intertwining, and occasionally opposing influences ... The function of the trainer is to entice this mysterious process to develop within the participants ...[3]

As we watch a trainer using experience-based methods with a group we see how his or her role seems to be repeatedly changing. Within the same day, even within the same session, the trainer may move from organizer of an event to facilitator of the group, from manager of learning opportunities to observer of process, from moderator of discussion to subject-matter specialist, from leader to follower, or from challenger to resource person. All of these, and more, are parts of the trainer's role. We can think of them as sub-roles.

The trainer's choice of sub-role at a particular moment depends on how he or she judges learning can best be achieved in the circumstances of that moment. Some of this assessment is objective. The topic or issue being considered, the method/s being used, the stage in the course, the growth in the group, the constraints of time, and so on — these are known already. But much of the assessment is more subjective, more intuitive.

The trainer observes the course members, listens thoughtfully to whatever they say, follows the dynamics and process of the group, and arrives at an understanding of 'where people are'. He or she then adjusts his/her own behaviour to the appropriate

3. Lynton and Pareek, page 275.
4. For the trainer's role with particular methods see the relevant sections, for example, The Trainer as Facilitator, page 167.

sub-role, and moves in the direction which seems likely to produce — or entice — the most learning.

One of the rewards of being a trainer is to see course members making changes — in understanding, in commitment, in statements, or in behaviour — not because the trainer has told them what they should think or say or do, but because they are using the opportunities and resources of the course to reach their own conclusions and learn for themselves. Significant learning which leads to change, whether in oneself or in others, is deeply satisfying.

Growth in the Course Group

Yet the trainer's attention is as much on the group as on individuals. Individuals learn and change: so does a group. As a course unfolds the progress of the group as a whole becomes one of the principal concerns of the trainer.

All being well, a course group follows a more or less predictable pathway, going at greater or lesser speed through certain stages of growth, from inception to maturity. One model suggests that there are seven stages in the growth of a group which is being accompanied by trainers.[5] In the case of a heterogeneous or international group we may add one more stage.

At each of these stages the trainers have an appropriate role or combination of sub-roles to play.

The eight stages can be summarised as follows:

1. Members become acquainted and oriented. Procedures, expectations and objectives are dealt with. There are anxieties among members: 'How will the group function?' 'Will they accept me?' 'Will my needs be met?' The trainers give introductions, make things known, explain and organize.

2. Conforming. Members clarify what is expected, and conform to that. Norms are established and initial anxieties are met. Members depend on the trainers. Trainers offer clarifications and reinforce the conformity.

3. Adjusting. Members adjust themselves to the training approach and to life in the course group. They engage with each other, and begin to work together. Trainers offer support, encourage interaction between members and emphasize members' responsibility.

4. Group members recognize their interdependence. Members begin to co-operate together, disclose themselves further to each other, build trust, and take responsibility. Trainers encourage trust, and emphasize mutuality and interdependence.

---

5 David W. Johnson and Frank P. Johnson, *Joining Together*, Prentice Hall, pages 423—429.

5. The members establish individual autonomy. They challenge the trainers' authority, disagree with each other, resist participation, and there may be conflicts. Trainers accept rebellion as normal, and use confrontation and negotiation to help the members to establish their independence.

6. The members sort out their own leadership. They commit themselves to goals, internalize norms, and take ownership of the course. They begin to refer to 'our group'. There is interdependence, support for each other, and taking responsibility for learning. The trainers facilitate this.

7. The group gains autonomy and functions maturely. There are improving relationships, collaboration, consensus decisions, and a sense of group identity. Conflict is dealt with, and there is productive work, with learning maximized. Trainers act as consultants, making arrangements and providing resources.

8. Closure and moving on.

Such a summary is neat and tidy, whereas the growth and dynamic of most groups — especially heterogeneous groups — is, in practice, less certain and less clear-cut. The stages are seldom so clearly defined.

Following the process of the course group, discerning how far it has reached, playing the appropriate role or sub-roles, and helping the group to move on — these are a central strand in the trainer's work with the group. The skills needed for this include sharp observation and listening, being sensitive to feelings, awareness of group dynamics and being able to unravel process.

The Early Stages of Growth

Once their initial anxieties are allayed members may find that the first two or three days in a three-month course feel unexpectedly comfortable. The content, the methodology, the trainers, and the membership are all now known, and there is often a sense of anticipation and excitement.

Extracts from course diaries reflect the optimism of these early days:

▶ *It was noticed with great compliment that students and tutors sit together and that there was no fear of expression among the students ...*

▶ *We were well and cheerful. Our faces were calm, showing very little anxiety. The beams of the sun shone through the windows and added additional warmth in our hearts.*

▶ *As each day goes by we are led into new experiences and face new challenges, which seem to be generating new awareness and creating a harmony within the group.*

▶ *We are all different but equal. We can exploit our distinctiveness to the best advantage, as we can use this to complement each other and have a richer experience.*

▶ *We are really coming closer to one another ... We are slowly becoming like a family of brothers and sisters. We have told each other about many things, but we did not yet mention anything about our inner life ...*

▶ *It is the last day of the first week, and our assembly of races, cultures and creeds are showing signs of community development. We are now greeting each other by name; there are fewer silences after tutors' questions; and more of the group are contributing comments, questions and humour to the general discussions. There is even a little open self-criticism.*

A few days later, however, and the mood may become more subdued. By now members are recognizing the demands which the course is going to make on them. They are beginning to engage with the content — and development, at least, is a challenging subject!

At the same time they must get to grips with the other course members. Meeting each other at a personal level has been one thing: working together, discussing together, deciding together, is another:

▶ *The mood in the room looked a bit different. I can't describe it much better, but it's like dull yet not dull. Anybody present can give his/her expression on how they judge such an atmosphere.*

▶ *... most members of the group seemed to be in a different world with their thoughts, and reactions came slowly ...*

▶ *So much to take in. I've never known sitting and talking to be so exhausting.*

▶ *Tired is one word I would use. I feel my brain is near to explosion with all the things I am learning. I never knew group participation would be so tiring.*

Most members enjoy the variety of methods, but at the beginning some members find that certain methods seem open-ended and inconclusive. At the same time they are being told that they must take responsibility for their own learning. Such responsibility can feel uncomfortable to those members who are more used to 'being taught'. Some are puzzled when the trainers do not act like the familiar teachers of formal education, do not say what members ought to know or think, and do not provide a neat conclusion at the end of an event or a discussion.

Trainers are not the figures of authority that members may have expected. They do not give 'answers;' indeed they probably offer more questions than answers. They may keep referring matters back to the group: 'What do you think is the answer?' They may even say, 'I don't know', or worse, 'No one knows'.

By the second week some members may feel that there is a lack of certainty, and perhaps some want of direction and leadership. The earlier optimism may give way to doubt, and even frustration. Diary entries during the second week may hint at this:

▶ *Y expressed her frustration and felt the need of a tutor in her small group. I was also in the same group and enjoyed the exercise. I wonder where things went wrong? Were there difficulties in understanding what the process was all about? Differences in language? Or dependency on the traditional way of learning? Is there a need to learn more to distinguish between content and process? Whatever the reason may be, to my mind, for obvious reasons, efforts to persuade our group to work independently have to continue.*

▶ *One couldn't help feeling a sense of being cautiously observed by the facilitators.*

▶ *A comment was made concerning the multitude of questions our tutors directed towards our group ...*

▶ *A suggestion to document conclusions at the end of each session prompted a lively debate. Some stated that studying the analysis was more important than the conclusion and others preferred to have questions remaining for further private thought.*

▶ *We are studying development, but I feel this is also a course about management and leadership. We also learn to listen and understand each other, how to relate to each other, how to motivate each other, attitudes, etc. This makes the course more interesting and challenging, but more difficult.*

All being well, the group will soon work through such initial doubts and dependence. Meanwhile however there may be some discomfort and dissatisfaction. To be able to identify the discomfort, accept the dissatisfaction, confront the dependence, and hold to the approach is another aspect of the trainer's role.

Further Growth

As the course proceeds the group members begin to take more responsibility, not only for themselves, but for the functioning of the group. Eventually — and ideally — they will share the authority and leadership of the course with the trainers. However there may be difficulties in the group, and even disagreements, to be worked through first, and perhaps some conflict between members and trainers:

▶ *In the end the task given to them was never done, as they could not agree. It was clear that people's attitudes and feelings towards each other hinder full attention to the task ...*

▶ *Our group started fine until everyone wanted to talk at the same time and forgot to listen. I was unhappy with its outcome. The other groups seemed to have difficulties too.*

▶ *After that, hot discussions started. ... I felt that the more we discussed, the more sensitive the issue became. That was why I asked our tutors to intervene. I felt challenged when J said that some wanted to escape by pushing the issue to the tutors ...*

▶ *... that issue again brought the temperature of discussion up to the level of arguing. People feel sore or hurt. Good, we are in touch with reality. Let us learn out of this sore reality-experience.*

Trainers expect difficulties and conflicts, but the members may not, and may be disturbed by them, especially when they had earlier begun to feel comfortable. All being well, the difficulties and conflicts are dealt with. Members discuss their perceptions, and even confront each other. Feelings are shared. Leadership and other issues are settled. Trust is re-established, perhaps at a deeper level. Then the members can combine and commit themselves to each other, to the course, and to the group as a whole:

▶ *Slowly members, one by one, start discussing and sharing their own feelings about the group. In the end, putting all the feelings together we generally accept that, even though we have lots of differences and diversities in the group, we find them quite healthy and decided to go on ...*

▶ *'Do you think the group has any difficulties at present?' ... 13 people out of 19 said the group had some difficulties. The group reacted well to this question and most of our hidden feelings were revealed.*

▶ *... concern was universally shown that some people were not participating fully ... It was felt that it was the group's responsibility to facilitate participation, and it was realised that we have gone a long way to solving the problem by acknowledging it.*

▶ *I wonder why after every reading of the diary there is a minute of silence or pause. I asked myself what that silence means? ... after the moderator asks for any reaction, everyone looks at each other, and if no one raises a hand I notice An or Ar make the initiative, then followed by everyone.*

▶ *The group process took a new turn as everybody put in resources and shared with one another ...*

Members may recognize such a change in group climate, but be unaware of its significance. They may recognize this later on:

▶ *... members of this group are becoming more interested, more creative, more co-operative, more caring and concerned, which makes us feel the absence of any member ...*

▶ *I had been absent from the group as it learned and grew together. I felt a substantial sense of loss of not being a part of most of the day's events.*

▶ *It was really very nice to see all of us — as groups — assuming our responsibilities ...*

▶ *The group process ... demonstrated in my view the impact the course has had on us. I was amazed with the ease in which we worked as a team to complete our task.*

▶ *We had a very high level of ownership of the course. When the course was a success it was our success. If it had failed it would have been our failure.*

It is a gratifying moment for trainers when they realize that they are providing more training opportunities and resources but less leadership.

Fitting the Content to the Process

The planning of a course already anticipates growth in the course group, even though the extent of the growth and the timing of the stages cannot be predicted beforehand. Yet learning will be strengthened if the course events and sessions are appropriate to the stage that the group has reached.

> What matters is not the event or the act but the meaning that participants see in it. And this meaning has a lot to do with the social process through which the particular training group develops its distinctive character and reaction ...[6]

6. Lynton and Pareek, page 277.

The members of a three-month course not only understand more by the eighth week than by the second week, but they can achieve much more as a group. Yet they will have needed time, and appropriate experiences, to have reached this point. Each group must go through the early stages of growth before it can come to the late stages. The growth, like the learning and the meaning, is progressive. Much has meaning by the end of a course which was meaningless at the beginning. Even the very skills of learning, such as shared reflection, have to be practised together.

So choosing or devising training events which are appropriate and meaningful to the group at a particular time, and at a certain stage in its growth, is another strand in the trainer's work. Perhaps we can describe this as 'fitting the content to the process'.

The benefit to learning is clearest when the work corresponds to current concerns, whether these are explicit or not. To give an extreme example, if members appear to be preoccupied with an inter-personal conflict within the group it may be more helpful to deal with that topic — and even to use the conflict as an example — rather than to introduce the scheduled topic, however important. Nothing favours learning more than a current and pressing concern with it. If the course is following a pre-planned timetable, the trainer has to weigh the advantages of 'following the moment' against any disruption and necessary re-adjustments later.

Seizing opportunities for learning calls not only for flexibility in the trainer, but also for clarity, a strong awareness of group process, and a sense of timing. Lynton and Pareek offer a helpful analogy:

> Circumspect timing of inputs of new data and of different kinds of activities and concerns is one of the trainer's most delicate tasks. The whole process has proper seasons. Some times are ripe for disturbing and questioning — ploughing, others for seeding and fostering growth. This farming language is far better for describing the trainer's orientation and activities than talk about 'making' or 'requiring' people to learn.[7]

Again there are obvious parallels with the process of development in the community.

Gratifying Moments

As a course progresses some groups achieve a memorable level of emotional interdependence and attachment. Members may make moving statements about this:

 How did our tutors bring us so close and help us become so fond of each other? Here we are like brothers and sisters. I feel so comfortable in this group. When I leave this room at the end of the day, already I feel anxious to be here again with all of you.

▶ *We are such a good company/group. We laugh, cry, dance, eat, shop, struggle with a topic*

---

7. Lynton and Pareek, page 276.

together, quarrel at times ...

▶ *We have achieved incredible openness between participants ...*

All this is gratifying to us, as trainers, but even as we listen to it we must question whether the group is becoming too cosy. Cosiness does not always support learning.[8]

At the end of a course, as the life of the group ends, tears can be expected. A member remarks,

▶ *This is the first time I have cried when leaving a group ...*

There may be tears at other times too. A member from a country which is riven by civil war tells the group,

▶ *Here I am laughing for the first time in years ...*

As we hear this, it may be we who shed tears in solidarity.

When course members and trainers affirm each other, take each other seriously, and respond to each other, not only as professional practitioners but as fellow human beings, it is an important achievement for all.

As trainers we shall welcome such solidarity within a group, both for its own sake and for the learning and growth which it makes possible. We shall welcome it also as a foundation upon which challenge and confrontation can be safely and usefully practised.

Before they leave members may make other statements which are gratifying:

▶ *I do not worry about forgetting what I have learned, because it has become part of me. I have changed ...*

▶ *Previously I have worked with people wanting to control others — the course has started to liberate me from this.*

▶ *I feel a growth in myself and others.*

▶ *I have learnt much, but I have also grown as a person. That gift will remain in me for the rest of my life.*

Trainers may allow for some exaggeration, but they will treasure such statements, and may draw upon them later in times of difficulty.

 ## Keeping the Learning Close

Experience-based learning embraces the whole person, not just the professional role or the academic interest. One of the trainer's tasks is to maintain the connection

---

8. See Cosy or Challenging? The Climate in The Group, (page 86).

between the members and the learning process by 'keeping the learning close' to the members as persons.

Sometimes the connection is disturbed. A course group may make progress for some weeks and reach a certain level of interdependence, and then seemingly revert to dependence. The members may appear to be working effectively and achieving results, and may report satisfactory learning. Yet there is a lack of energy and a lack of growth. Trainers may sense that members are 'going through the motions', meeting expectations but without depth or conviction, and without engaging with the course content or with each other as persons.

If there is no apparent cause, the trainers may ask themselves:

'Are we doing something that is contributing to this?'

'Has the course become unbalanced? Too much content? Not enough attention to process?'

'Is there an issue or conflict in the group which is not being addressed?'

'What are the members really concerned about at present?'

The trainers may create opportunities for members to share their current perceptions and feelings, and to discuss the situation:

'How do you think the group is functioning?'

'How is the level of motivation at present?'

'Are there issues or conflicts in the group that are not being dealt with?'

'What is it that you are not saying?'

A check on individual feelings, or an appropriate exercise, may be helpful.[9] It may be that the group is in a state of subdued rebellion. For example, members may have moved from Stage 3 in the model towards Stage 4, but without finding a way of expressing disagreement and resistance, or of acknowledging conflict. Questions and challenge from the trainers may help members to confront this and find their way forward as a group.

At other times some members may resort to statements which are so general that they contribute little to the matter being discussed. Some cultures encourage generalization before coming to the point, but it can be a way to avoid engaging with issues or with other people. When this happens the trainer's task is to encourage the members to anchor what they are saying in the reality of their own work and experience:

'How does that statement/question/opinion relate to you?'

'You say, "People always …" Does that include you …?'

'What is your evidence?'

'Can you give an example?'

'What is your own experience?'

'How does this connect with your work?'

Again the principle is to keep the learning close to the members.

---

9. See some of the exercises suggested in Ending the Week (page 247) or Where Am I in the Group? (page 146).

Sometimes the reality of development or group work is such that members find it difficult to acknowledge their own role, or to recognize their share of responsibility in relation to an issue. They may cast blame on others, or on 'the system', or on those in different roles, such as Governments and donor agencies — or, indeed, the trainers. This too may have to be confronted:

'How is that different from what you are doing yourself?'
'Are you benefiting from the system too?'
'How are you contributing to this situation?'
'Let's think about what we are doing, rather than what other people are doing.'
'Whose behaviour can we change? Other people's? Or our own?'
'Whose responsibility is it? What can you do about it?'

Such challenges help members to switch their attention from others 'out there,' and to focus instead on their own role and behaviour and the effects these are having.

Sometimes members gain new learning, and are enthusiastic about using this when they return back home, while failing to use it in the course group. Yet a group in training can be an ideal setting to try out and practise new behaviour, new roles and new skills:

'You have been talking about doing it with other people. Perhaps you should do it with some of the people here.'
'This is probably the most accepting and supportive group of colleagues that you could have to try something out ...'
'If you can't use your development skills in this group, how can you expect to use them in the community back home?'

Deliberate opportunities can be created for members to try out new behaviour and new approaches, perhaps through the use of role play. This too helps to keep the learning close.

Congruence and Confidence

There are contradictions in all fields of work — as in all human beings — but they can seem especially glaring in development work, with its lofty aspirations and endeavours. A training course provides opportunities for each of us, trainer or member, to work at some of our own contradictions and to become more congruent.

When we are congruent, our feelings, our thoughts, our words and our actions become consistent with one another, and reinforce one another. We say what we think, and we mean what we say. We say what we feel, and we do what we say. Congruence is an indicator of growth, and the trainer looks for it and encourages it, not only in individuals — including his or her own self — but in the life of the group.

Congruence is linked to self-confidence. Self-confidence is a component of the development process. It is also required by development workers. If we feel we do not control our own lives, how can we give confidence to others that they can gain more control over theirs?

Self-confidence is an elusive quality, yet members recognize it in themselves, whether during a course, or when writing about it afterwards:

▶ *The whole experience has given me a powerful new confidence in myself.*

▶ *The course increased my knowledge and understanding ... improved skills and competence ... but above all, strengthened my motivation and self-confidence ...*

▶ *I used to think I know a lot. Now I am more critical, more cautious. I have lost my false self-confidence in discovering a new and complex reality. I am now less willing to follow directions blindly, as I see there are no ready-made answers. My new self-confidence is the start of new self-development.*

▶ *I'm going to feel more at home in my situation.*

▶ *... the course has stirred in me greater confidence in what I do ...*

▶ *One aspect is the growing confidence that my boss puts in me.*

▶ *I am now enjoying my work more than I used to ... In short, I feel much more confident and relaxed in my work than before.*

The approach to training, the methodology used, members taking responsibility for themselves and their own learning — all these contribute to it. If trainers perform their roles effectively they too contribute, both to their own self-confidence and to the confidence of members.

The Person in the Role

There remains the question: Who is the trainer?

To begin with, those of us who work professionally with other people must sort out our own 'tangled motivations'. We must examine ourselves personally and professionally, especially in relation to power. We must recognize how we are meeting our own needs — and also where our own needs are not being met. We must become more sensitive to the impact we have on the individuals and groups we work with.

We can raise this awareness by undergoing further training ourselves. We shall always need further training. We have to go on learning and developing ourselves if we are to support the learning and development of others.

Lynton and Pareek answer the question by referring to feelings:

> Finally ... the nature, quality, and effectiveness of the interaction we call training depends primarily on the feelings that the trainer communicates to the participants through his behaviour ... We have always known, in our heart of hearts, that neither great erudition nor social skill was enough to make an effective trainer, that his

"personality" finally mattered, too ... To put it most simply, for a trainer to express the kinds of feeling that evoke an effective training climate, he first has to have them.[10]

Another answer might also refer to attitudes and values. The role of the trainer may be flexible, but it rests on a firm framework of attitudes and values.

These include:

- taking human beings seriously;
- respect for the dignity and potential of all, individually and collectively;
- belief in the possibility of learning and change;
- belief in people taking charge of their own lives, their own development, and their own learning;
- commitment to participation, social justice, cultural identity, self-reliance ...

Surviving in the Role

The role of trainer has many satisfactions, and even excitements, but it has difficulties and disappointments too. In an ideal self-reliant system the emotional demands made upon us are balanced by the support we receive. Sometimes such an emotional loop is completed by a course group, and the trainer finds that the demands and challenges of the course members are matched by their support and solidarity. But this is rare, and usually we shall need the support of colleagues in the training team.

Perhaps we complete the work of each day by reflecting with colleagues. We share observations, review the day's content, unravel some of the process, consider the roles of individual members, puzzle over the dynamic of the group, offer our own percep-tions of the learning ... Difficulties, anxieties and disappointments are discussed. Feedback and affirmation are offered. Much of this flows back later into the mainstream of the course.

One inevitable difficulty is the continuous demands which a course makes on our attention. As trainers we live in two worlds at once. The first is our usual world of home, with family and social life. The second is the world of the course group, with another set of relationships, roles and expectations, and a parallel life all its own. We are pulled between two reference points, two competing commitments, even two cultures. Moving from one to the other, and responding to both, demands energy — although it can also generate energy.

At the times when tension between these two worlds is high, or when we feel unsupported, or beset by uncertainty, one remedy is humour. We may be committed to the idealistic vision and earnest endeavours of work such as development, yet still accept that there is something absurd about wanting to transform the world.

---

10. Lynton and Pareek, pages 277—278.

A sense of fun, a sense of the ridiculous, a sense of history, a sense of humility — these can be our safeguards when we are fortunate enough to be engaged in the challenges of development and in the training of others for this work.

▶ *The way we have learnt has taught me new things about learning. The tutors have treated us all with respect, and this was a surprise to me.*

▶ *The trainers are largely facilitators and help the trainees to identify and fulfil their own training needs during the training, using a methodology that is highly participatory.*

▶ *... what we have been doing ... have been cleverly put together in an appropriate sequence by our Tutors, so that we gradually have become ready for the next stage in our own development ... Many of the things would have had no meaning for us if they had been presented in a different order. It is difficult to describe this essential progression, but it is quite clear that the composition and, not least, the sequence of the various elements of our course have been essential for the learning process. I see now the importance for the tutors to have the possibility to be flexible in the design, as they would have to make a continuous assessment of our progress as a group, before the next stage could be planned, and thereby have maximum learning effects.*

▶ *What has impressed me here is that the tutors are also learners. This will be important to me as a development worker in future ...*

▶ *Fun I am glad that things aren't taken too seriously ...*

CHAPTER 2

Before We Begin

The Sizes of Groups

▶ ... *the size of the group and the ideal form of participation are two poles that have to meet* ...

▶ *Discussion started in Whole Group → Small Groups → Whole Group → Pairs of Groups →*
Small Groups → Whole Group, enabling all to participate ...

The Whole Course Group

A group of sixteen members is probably ideal for a course which lasts for some weeks
or months, and which is using an experience-based methodology. A group of this size
contains enough experience — and enough variety of experience, and difference in
attitudes and views — for fruitful sharing and reciprocal learning. Yet it is small enough
to function as a community with a single focus of attention. When the whole group is
sitting in a circle, each member can see the faces of all the other members at the same
time, and can communicate directly with them. When the trainers are working with the
group as a whole they can, at the same time, relate to the members as individuals.
Sixteen members are enough to form effective smaller groups.

The lower limit for such a course is probably twelve members. A group which is
smaller than this may not contain enough resources and variety for reciprocal learning.
Moreover it may lack sufficient dynamic energy and interaction among its members.
There is less scope for work in smaller groups.

The upper limit is probably twenty. A group of this size has more resources, but may
have difficulty in making effective use of them. Some members may find it hard to
contribute in the whole group.

If the size goes beyond twenty, the dynamics change further. There may then be
difficulties in seeing, speaking and listening to every member, and in maintaining a
focus for the group's energy and attention. The group may no longer function as a
single community.

The physical arrangements for work in the whole course group are dealt with in Sitting
Together: The Course Room (page 49).

Working in Pairs

With experience-based methods members often 'work in pairs' while they are sitting in
the whole course group. This allows a quick exchange of reactions, experience or
examples between 'neighbours', who can simply turn towards each other but remain
where they are sitting. Each partner may have two or three minutes for the task. If the
total number of members is an odd number there can be a small group of three.

As well as being a quick means of exchange, working in pairs allows a quick change of
method and some limited physical movement. It allows every member to speak, but

does not take up much course time, and it calls on each member to make at least some response of their own to the matter being considered.

It is particularly useful as an alternation in method during a presentation.[1] It can be used at appropriate stages to explore and reinforce the current topic, perhaps after every 15 minutes. It can also help to change the mood and to re-invigorate a group.

Working in Small Groups

Many methods and events in experience-based training involve splitting up the whole course group so that members can work in separate small groups. 'Small group' normally means from three to eight members. The trainer usually decides on the size of the group, although the instructions for some simulations and exercises specify groups of a certain size.

The size of group that is appropriate will depend upon the task, the kind of interaction required, and the possible learning. The following provides a rough guide:

- to share feelings or interpersonal information — groups of three (or pairs);
- to share commitments and values — groups of three or four;
- to share opinions or experience, or compare notes — four or five;
- to reflect the diversity of the group — five to seven;
- to discuss situations or issues — six to eight.

In general a group of three or four seems more intimate and perhaps more comfortable, while a group of six or eight offers more interaction, more resources and more points of view. Some members will find it easier to contribute in the smaller groups than in the whole course group.

The simplest way to form small groups is to divide the whole group at random. The trainer asks members to count round the circle — 'one, two, three — one, two, three' — according to the number of small groups required. Random groups are suitable for many purposes and methods, including case studies. The members themselves usually find this the most natural and comfortable basis for splitting up. If counting round itself becomes tedious, trainers can devise other ways of forming 'random' groups: members who are wearing blue, those who are wearing sandals, and so on.

Another possibility is self-selected groups, where the trainer invites members to form groups of their own choice. This is appropriate for special interests, and when simultaneous but different tasks are to be done by small groups.

However for many tasks and purposes, especially with a heterogeneous course group, the trainer may allocate members to small groups. There are many reasons why a trainer may choose to do this, such as:

---

1. For alternations see Action-Reflection page 160.

- Members from certain parts of the world may benefit from working together.

- The task may be to share contrasting experience from different situations; or to bring together comparable experience from similar situations.

- The task or issue may be gender-related, so small groups of the same sex may be needed, or mixed groups may be needed.

- For some methods, such as role play, it can help if members who work well together are allocated to the same small group.

- Sometimes members who are having difficulty with each other may benefit from working together. For example, it may increase the learning if those with differing ideologies are invited to discuss certain issues together.

- Individual members may be allocated to particular groups because of their ability to perform a particular role or task. It is often helpful to a small group if a member with an aptitude for facilitating is included.

- Those with similar roles back home may be brought together. Members usually learn more from sharing experience with each other when their roles are similar.

- Small groups which combine members with different but related roles back home can be productive; e.g. professionals with clients, outside experts with local counterparts, donors of aid with recipients, development workers with community members. Hearing about the experience of those with different roles can be enlightening.

For such reasons the deliberate allocation of individuals to small groups can help members make better use of each other's resources, and so strengthen the learning.

When a trainer allocates individuals to small groups, he/she should be ready to explain the reasons. When the basis is geography or gender, this is easy. When the basis is the trainer's perception of personality or ability for a task, the decisions become more difficult to explain or justify. As members gain trust in their trainers, such decisions will be accepted without question.

▶ *I found it easier for me to share my ideas in the small discussion group but not in the large circle...*

▶ *People were very concerned about the 'passive' people in the group. How did you decide that some of us were passive? Are we judged as passive just because we do not manage to participate in the same way as you in the big group?*

▶ *One group changes to another. We work in the group of three, group of six, group of twenty-two, group of norms, group of review of our week, group at supper and lunch. It is hard to connect again and again, but it is the truth of our work.*

▶ *The fact that we sit in a circle is important. The circle is always intact, and we can see everyone, with everyone at ease to contribute. We are seventeen nations in one room ...*

A course room which is clean, cheerful, quiet and uncluttered does much for the life of a group and the motivation of its members. When resources are scarce, it may seem extravagant to give attention and care to a room. Yet most of us take care of our homes and offices, making them comfortable and suitable for our domestic needs and work. We recognize that this benefits our effectiveness as well as our enjoyment.

In the same way, a course room which is cared for will make the work of a course group more enjoyable and more effective. The reverse is also true, and most trainers will agree that learning needs all the support it can be given!

The Room and Its Furnishings

It helps if the size of the room is appropriate to the size of the course group. If the space is confined some members feel uncomfortable, and any tensions within the group may seem exaggerated. If the space is much larger than necessary, contributions and energies seem diluted or lost, and it is more difficult to maintain emotional warmth in the group.

Clear natural light, sun-blinds when needed, good artificial lighting, warm but calming colours, a comfortable temperature, suitable ventilation, and an absence of clutter are all important too.

Chairs should be upright, easily moved, and comfortable — if not too comfortable! Work tables, suitable for small groups of four to eight, should be available. When members are sitting in the whole group the chairs should be arranged in the centre of the room, while the tables can be kept against the walls.

In some institutions it is usual to arrange tables in a rectangle at the centre of the room, with chairs around the outside of the rectangle. The problem then is that the tables serve as barriers to keep people apart from one another instead of encouraging them to come together. Such an arrangement may suit meetings and formal study methods, but it will not do for informal and experience-based methods.

It may seem unnecessary to add that the number of chairs should match the number of people, yet in many institutional rooms there are stacks of spare chairs and other unused items. Surplus furniture should be removed if possible, and training equipment should be kept in storage until needed.

In some cultures tables and chairs are not used at all, and groups work on the floor.[1] The size of the room is again important. A floor surface which stretches away into

---

1. Even for groups which use chairs, an occasional session on the floor can be energizing.

distant corners may bring a sense of bleakness and dilution. A suitable floor covering is then helpful. For example, a comfortable carpet, of a size that allows all the members and trainers to sit on it together in a circle, sets a boundary around the group and helps to maintain a sense of unity and focus.[2]

Arranging the Chairs: Circle and Horseshoe

Assuming that chairs are being used, and that tables are kept against the walls, how should the chairs be arranged?

There are institutions where the usual practice is to put the chairs in rows in the centre of the room, facing the trainer and the boards or screens. This is the conventional classroom, but again it will not do for experience-based methods.[3]

For these methods the criterion for arranging the chairs is that every member, and the trainers, should be able to look directly at the face of everyone else. There should be the possibility of eye contact, of speaking directly to each and every other person, and of observing behaviour and facial expressions throughout the group, the whole time.

The obvious way to achieve this is with a circle. The circle also symbolizes our unity and equality as human beings.

In practice a circle can be used when the nature of the work is personal, for example:

● introducing ourselves and getting to know each other as persons;

● sharing personal material and personal history;

● expressing feelings, sharing values and motivation;

● farewells.

A circle in which individuals are physically close helps to create emotional closeness, and gives support to such delicate and sensitive work.

At other times, when the concern is more with professional work and roles, the circle can be opened up to form a U-shape or horseshoe. This shape enables the course group to focus its attention on the trainer who is leading the session at the open end of the U, yet it still allows all the members to see each other and to speak directly to one another and to the group as a whole. This is the usual arrangement for work in the whole course group.

Where Do the Trainers Sit?

The trainer who is to lead the session usually takes a chair at one end of the U. He/she can remain seated during any general discussions — after the diary, for example — but

---

2. If training is conducted out of doors, a raised platform, or the shade of a particular tree, or some other feature may provide the boundary needed.
3. While discussing training and methodology later in the course you can ask members to put their chairs in rows, give them a short lecture suitable for such a formal arrangement, and ask for reactions. Members may comment that it not only feels uncomfortable and inappropriate, but is top-down and disempowering.

is then free to stand if he/she chooses, without blocking anyone's view, while introducing an event or giving a briefing. From this position he/she can reach the board and screen, and has space to mobilize handouts or visual aids. He/she can sit again if the discussion becomes general, or his/her role changes to moderator. All the while the trainer is able to see members' faces and can also be seen by them.

The arrangement of chairs, and who sits where, come to symbolize the roles and relationships in a course. The chairs at the ends of the U become 'Top Chairs', and are used by the leadership of the moment.[4]

However the area at the ends of the U, in front of the board and screen, should not become the trainers' exclusive territory. It should be open to any member who is speaking to the group at length, or who wishes to use the board or screen. This demonstrates in a visible way that members of the group also contribute leadership to the course.

Additional Rooms

It is possible to organize some of a course using only one room, provided the room is large enough for members to work in small groups without disturbing each other. This is practicable when members break into small groups for a short time only, as happens with questionnaires, some simulations, and personal work.

However there are other tasks where a small group is hampered if it is within earshot and sight of others. Examples are the discussion of case studies, the preparation of role plays, and parts of some simulations. Then additional rooms will be necessary.

Additional rooms should be ready for immediate use, so that when a small group enters its members can settle quickly to their task. Scattered chairs and debris left by other users of the room are distracting, if not demotivating. If a room seems neglected, the work to be done there may be neglected too. The issue is not cleanliness — important though that is — but a sense of preparedness for what is to be done. In many institutions this is not understood by managers and maintenance staff, and trainers should be prepared to check rooms beforehand. This may seem a chore, but it is another way to facilitate the learning of a group.

When the work of the small groups could be done in the course room, but additional rooms are available, the trainer has a choice. He/she should then consider other pros and cons, such as the distance and time involved in moving, the advantage of a change of scene, and the climate prevailing in the group. If there is any tendency to become drowsy after lunch, a change of rooms may help to revive members' energy.

▶ *What is fascinating is that while in class we are usually in a circle, including the Tutors. This to my mind explains why we have quickly found the Tutors approachable and the discussion flowing all round.*

---

4. For 'Top Chair' see page 263. Additional trainers who are not leading can choose where to sit according to how they see their role at that time. If they sit at the open end of the U, this could represent support for the colleague who is leading. If they sit among the members, it could represent a facilitating role or solidarity with the members.

▶ *I have noted with interest that the members of this group sit in different positions every day giving us an opportunity to continue knowing each other better ...*

▶ *When we all gathered here on Monday the 20th of April, we were generously told by L that from now until the course ended, this room no. 101 was ours. Quite an ordinary room, fairly square, a double door, two windows, a wall-fixed blackboard, a free-standing blackboard, 12 black chairs, 11 red, 3 white ... 4 large tables, 2 notice boards ... plus a NO SMOKING sign! Not a particularly attractive room, but we were told that it was <u>ours</u> ...*

... And who were <u>we</u>, a group of strangers to each other, from a variety of cultural and educational backgrounds — with only one thing in common, the wish to learn more about Development Work. And what did we do? We did what a community normally do, we started working on our immediate environment in order to make it more 'ours' — we began a process to decorate the room, to give it some character and personal identity. The walls soon became covered with self-made posters, and from the ceiling we hung self-made mobiles. One of the wall boards gave basic information on what was going to happen next in our newly established community; the other gave information on where we all came from. We established a community kitchen, with a coffee-pot, various cups and the necessary consumables ...

... The decoration of room no. 101 gradually became more significant, we filled it with reflections, exchange of thoughts, feelings, compassion, informal and more personal chats, video sessions, lectures, group sculptures, role plays, case studies, games and so on ...

... When we part from each other ... we will think back to the 11 weeks we have spent together as an important period of our lives. We will remember each other with respect and love, we will remember each other in our prayers ... And we will remember room no. 101 as the place where we together created our own local and very special community for learning through equal and active participation.

2.3 Sessions and Breaks

Sessions of 1½ hours are appropriate for an experienced-based methodology.[1] This is long enough to explore a topic to some depth, and is convenient for many exercises. Two such sessions, with a 30 minute break between, fit comfortably into a morning or afternoon. Three or four sessions in a day provide for up to six hours of work in the course group. Much of that time involves interaction with other people, and six hours may be as much as some members can sustain. There may be one hour of additional work for members to do overnight, together with their own reading.

The breaks between sessions may vary from 30 minutes at mid-morning to one hour or more for the midday meal. Such breaks must be arranged according to institutional timings, local practice, culture and season.

Short breaks of a few minutes only during the sessions are at the trainer's discretion. Even if course members do not expect them, it is important to provide short breaks.

Some reasons for short breaks are:

- to provide relief after a period of continuous listening;[2]
- to allow members and trainers to have refreshments, smoke, use the toilet, etc;
- to give members an opportunity to stand, stretch, move about and energize themselves;
- to change trainers, or assist a trainer to 'change gear' and introduce a new subject or new event;
- to support the members in changing to a new subject, a new event, a new partner, or a smaller or larger group;
- to provide an opportunity for informal discussion and sharing among members who are not otherwise working together.

These breaks should not be long enough to distract attention from the work, or disrupt the process and divert energy elsewhere. They may last for one, two, three or four minutes only, but can be repeated after 20 or 30 minutes.

Movement is natural and necessary to human beings and mobilizes energy. Some trainers introduce action songs and games to raise energy levels and refresh members' interactions. This can be especially useful after lectures which tend to isolate and immobilize individuals. But if participatory methods are being used regularly, there may be enough movement and interaction in the course already.

---

1. It is assumed throughout this training manual that a session is 1½ hours.
2. Some say that no lecture or presentation should continue for more than 20 minutes without a break.

CHAPTER 3

Making A Start

3.1 Who Are We? Introducing Ourselves

▶ *The first day is possibly the most important event, as it sets the course agenda, mood and context.*

▶ *The day began with a feeling of excitement as we have started the first day of the course and, more than that, the participants are from different parts of the earth.*

Much happens in the first session of a new course. It is an exciting time. The course members gather together and greet each other. As they do so, they are already bringing the course group to life and setting it on its way towards formation and growth. Meanwhile the trainers make themselves known and begin to play their roles. The approach to training becomes apparent, the methodology takes effect, and the content begins to emerge.

Members are making individual transitions too, with departures from home and arrivals in the new setting. There is the sudden loss of familiar roles and routines, and the challenge of new demands. In an international course some may be contending with a second language, and perhaps with a new culture and a different climate.

After greetings and a brief formal welcome, trainers and members take turns to introduce themselves to the whole group. Then the trainers conduct some simple exercises to help members engage with each other and begin to work together.

The main focus of the session is the members themselves. The methods are already participatory and experience-based, and the intention is to provide a foretaste of the flavour and dynamic of the course as a whole.[1]

Linked events are The Course Begins: Expressing Our Anxieties (page 64); Photolanguage: Talking Through Pictures (page 101); Introducing The Methodology (page 67); The Course Diary (page 72); and Why Have We Come? Sharing Expectations (page 77).

Objectives

- to provide a welcome and an affirmation to the members of a new course;
- to provide the opportunity for members and trainers to introduce themselves as individual persons;
- to support members as they begin to co-operate and work together;
- to assist members in making the transitions from their culture, setting and role back home to the life of the course group and the demands of the course;
- to initiate processes which contribute to a climate of confidence, trust and learning within the new course group;
- to provide a foretaste of the methodology and content of the course.

---

1. Briefing about the course, or the training institution, and practicalities should be given in a later session.

Preparation and Arrival

■ Prepare the course room with the appropriate number of chairs in a circle before the members arrive. Do this in advance so that you and other trainers can give full attention to members as they arrive. An atmosphere of order, calm and attention will reassure them. If you are still arranging chairs as the members arrive, it will suggest incompetence, if not discourtesy.

As members enter the course room, meet them individually, greet them warmly and invite them to take a seat in the circle. All the full-time trainers should be present. They too should sit in the circle among the members, and should participate in the introductions and the first exercises.

The Formal Start

The session — and indeed the whole course — should be given a formal start with a brief speech of welcome to the members. This is usually the task of the course director or a leading trainer. It will help to meet the expectation of some members that every new venture should begin with a formal inauguration.

However the focus of attention should be shifted to the members themselves within a few minutes.

Who We Are

■ Invite everyone present to introduce themselves around the circle in turn.[2] Ask them to give only their formal or full names, the country or place where they live and work, and the familiar name by which they like to be addressed.

Acknowledge that there are many other things that members may want to say or hear — organization, role, and nature of work are obvious examples — but all of these must wait until later.

Start the procedure with yourself. Introduce yourself in the way proposed, which gives an example for others to follow.[3]

---

2. Some training manuals recommend that members work in pairs and introduce each other: 'My partner's name is A and he ...' 'This is B, and she ...' This procedure may cause unnecessary anxiety in a newly-assembled group where there are mixed cultures and languages.

3. Another procedure is sometimes recommended in training manuals. One member is asked to give his or her name. A second member is asked to repeat that name and then to add his or her own name, and so on. This goes round the group until those at the end may have to remember fifteen or more names, many of which may be unfamiliar in a multi-cultural group. This procedure may help members to learn each others' names, but it raises levels of anxiety about performance at the very time when trainers should be allaying such anxieties.

This procedure allows members to introduce themselves formally to the group, with full names as preferred; but requires other members to learn only the familiar name.[4] It allows trainers to introduce themselves in the same way, among the members, as their turn happens to come in the circle.

The procedure also discourages lengthy introductions and descriptions of role and work at a time when these cannot be absorbed or dealt with.

These introductions may take ten minutes.

A Foretaste of the Course

The session continues with some short exercises which are intended to give members a foretaste of the course. The exercises help members to meet and begin to talk with each other, and to work with their own experience rather than only listening to trainers. Members begin in pairs and then move into groups of increasing size. In each exercise members change partners or groups, so that they will soon have worked with every other member.[5] The content starts with the members themselves and gradually widens to touch on their work.

If the trainers take turns to introduce the exercises, it demonstrates their roles and team-work from the beginning. Trainers who are not leading at that moment should participate in some of the early exercises. This demonstrates how trainers change roles, allows them to participate in the interpersonal sharing, and makes them more accessible as persons.

The first four exercises make up a progressive sequence, and together may take about 45 minutes. If time is short The Decision to Come can be left until a day or two later.

■ Explain to the group that the remainder of the session is intended to give the flavour of the course. Tell them that the methodology will be informal. Acknowledge that some members may be used to a more formal style, and assure them that the informal or experience-based methods will be comfortable and easy.

Explain that the trainers will introduce a sequence of small exercises and tasks. Members will start by working in pairs with their neighbours. Then they will be asked to move about the room and meet other members and work in different pairs. After that they will work together in small groups.

---

4. This saves members from the complexities of full names which may belong to cultures, social systems and languages which are unfamiliar. Names can be explored later in team-building, in cultural exchanges, or in discussions about gender.
5. Some trainers believe that members should be encouraged to move physically because it symbolizes movement in other spheres, such as ideas and behaviour. Physical movement thus supports the process of change and learning.

Starting with Ourselves

This is an affirming exercise. It literally 'starts where people are', itself a basic principle of development work. The exercise recognizes that each of us already has his or her own thoughts and feelings, whatever these may be. Sharing them with another person can help us to move our attention onwards.

■ Ask the members to remain where they are sitting, to turn to one of their neighbours in pairs and begin by greeting each other. Additional trainers should participate and make up the numbers as required.

When the partners have sorted themselves out, invite them to share with each other whatever thoughts they have in their minds at this moment and which they feel comfortable to share:

'Whatever is on your mind at this moment ...'
'Whatever you are thinking about at present ...'
'Anything you are feeling just now ...'

This is likely to be an unexpected task, and some members may be mystified, so elaborate and explain the task as necessary.

The complete exercise should take five minutes only. Conclude by making the link with development work, but do not invite any reporting or discussion in the large group.

Individuals and Their Feelings

This exercise demonstrates that individuals and their feelings will be given attention. It deals with happy feelings first, because these are easily shared and spoken about. It then asks about anger, which is more problematic. Anger is often repressed or denied in development work, and needs to be recognized and acknowledged.

■ Tell the members to remain where they are sitting, but to turn to their neighbours on the other side. Ask the new partners to share with each other a happy occasion or experience from the last few weeks:

'Tell your neighbour about something that has made you feel happy.'

After they have done this, ask them to share in the same pairs something from the last few weeks that has made them angry. Some members may respond to this with anxious laughter, or claim that they have not been angry. If any member does deny anger, you should challenge him/her in a light-hearted way:

'I don't believe that is possible for a human being ...'

This may take ten minutes altogether. Explain that feelings will be given attention in the course, but do not invite any discussion in the whole group.

The Decision to Come

This touches on the central development issue of decision-making and how that affects motivation. If time is short this exercise can be postponed for a day or two. Additional trainers should sit out of this exercise.

■ Ask members to get up, move about the room, choose a different chair, and greet a different partner. Tell members that their task now is to explain briefly to their partner how it was decided that they should attend this course:

'Who was involved in deciding that you should come to this course?'
'How was that decision made? Who made the decision?'
'What was your own role in the decision?'
'How do you feel about it now?'
'How has that process affected your attitude towards being on the course?'

Make it clear that the purpose is to see how this process has affected the person concerned. The purpose is not to elaborate on career history or the decision-making structures of members' organizations.

After the sharing in pairs — which should not take more than five minutes — invite two or three members to summarize their experience briefly in the whole group. This may illustrate different decision-making processes, and lead into a discussion of the consequences for members' motivation. If all members have made the choice for themselves at some level, this can be compared with the imagined effect on people who are sent to attend courses against their will.[6]

Emphasize the link between the way a decision is made and the effect this has on the people concerned. Mention the parallel with decision-making processes and motivation in a community.

How Did I Get Here?

This exercise invites members to review the journeys which they have made from their homes to the course venue, however long or short those journeys may have been. It gives members an opportunity to share their feelings about leaving home, worries about their family while they are away, the difficulties of the journey itself, and the problems of arrival.

■ Ask all members to get up, move about the room, sit on a different chair, and form groups of three. Ask them to think about the journey from their home to the course, and to share two reactions:

'Share briefly something from the journey that was a pleasant surprise.'
'Share something that has been difficult to cope with.'

The sharing in groups of three may take up to ten minutes. If time permits, invite two or three members to report their experiences in the whole group.

It will help the course members to know that you recognize and acknowledge their difficulties in travelling and adapting, but do not dwell on these. If you identify any great difficulties you should meet the member concerned in private.

---

6. If any member has been sent for training against his or her will it is important that the trainers discover this, because it is likely to affect the member's willingness to be actively involved. This in turn will affect the climate in the group. If any members are attending unwillingly they should be given a chance to discuss this with trainers privately, and perhaps be offered the choice of staying or leaving.

This is the most suitable point in the sequence for a short break. During the break another small task can be given.

Pins in the Map

■ If the members come from different or distant places, put up appropriate maps during the break, for example, a world map for an international group. Invite every member to stick in a pin to indicate where he/she comes from, or works. This again indicates affirmation and acceptance. It also gives a quick visual display of the spread and diversity of the group, and contributes to the group-forming process.

If some members are citizens of one country, but live or work in another — perhaps as expatriates or refugees — invite them to put in the pin 'where your heart is ...' Later in the course this issue may be explored.

During the remainder of the session, attention moves from the members themselves towards the work that they are concerned with.[7] If time permits both the exercises given below can be used. If time is short, When I Am the Boss ... should be used, and Photolanguage left for another occasion.

Photolanguage

This exercise can be used to explore members' perceptions of a broad topic, such as development. The exercise also encourages members to recognize and discuss differences of perception, which is always an issue in a new group. It can help members to distinguish process from content, and encourages some self-disclosure.

It is a useful exercise at the beginning of a course because it allows members to speak to one another 'indirectly', through the medium of photographs or pictures, rather than wholly face-to-face. During the first sessions, and especially in an international group, members find that working with new people from other cultures, and listening to unfamiliar accents, is demanding. Being able to communicate 'through' the medium of pictures gives a respite.

■ The exercise is described in a separate section (page 101) and you should follow the instructions given there.

If you want members to focus on a broad topic, such as development, you can make your instructions for choosing pictures more specific:
   'Choose a picture that reminds you about development,'
   'Find a picture that you connect with development work,'
   'Do any of the pictures remind you of an experience in development?'

---

7. An alternative for the second half of the session is Expressing Our Anxieties (page 64). This would keep attention on the members themselves, instead of moving it towards their work.

■ Otherwise follow the procedure described, but do not spend more than 45 minutes altogether. Additional trainers should participate fully.

Used in this way, Photolanguage can give an indication of the range of attitudes within the group towards a topic such as development.

When I Am the Boss...

The final exercise encourages the use of the imagination and some sharing of ideas about organizations and training. Any issues raised can be taken up later.

■ Ask the members to move their chairs and sit in groups of four or five. Tell them to imagine that they are now in senior positions in their own organizations (which they may already be), and that they have the power and the opportunity to make changes. Tell them to imagine they want to improve the working of the organization, and to help it meet its goals more effectively:
    'Which aspects will you think of changing?'
    'What steps will you take?'
    'What will you do first?'

Ask them to think on their own for three or four minutes, and then to share some of their ideas in the small groups. After ten minutes discussion in the small groups, ask the members to remain sitting in their groups, but to give their attention to you.

Invite each small group in turn to mention one issue or topic which they have been discussing. Allow other members to clarify if necessary, although the issues themselves cannot be dealt with until later. As each issue is mentioned, ask if the other groups have also discussed it. Then move to the next group for another issue. In this way each small group contributes in turn until all their issues have been mentioned.

This exercise will give a useful indication of the attitudes and levels of awareness within the group towards organization, management and training.

Finish this exercise with a few questions about the process:
    'Did everyone in your small group share their ideas?'
    'How did you manage your discussion?'
    'Could you understand each other?'
    'Were there any difficulties?'

Conclusion

Bring the whole session to a conclusion by pointing out to members that they have already begun working with each other, in pairs, in threes, and in small groups. This is the way it will continue during the course.

If appropriate, you can also point out that the focus started on themselves, and then moved on to development (with Photolanguage), and then to organization and training. That may also be the sequence in the course as a whole.

Some course groups end their first session in a buzz of excitement and enthusiasm. Other groups are more hesitant, usually because they are new to informal methods. Nonetheless if course members feel that they are welcome and accepted as individuals, and if they sense that the trainers are caring and competent, they will have confidence in the course. If they feel comfortable with each other, they will begin to build trust in the group, even in this first session. If they see that they will be able to make their own contribution to the course, they will be further satisfied.

A group of course members with the author on the left

▶ *Before the official opening of the course, participants were quite busy greeting one another. The words 'how do you do' and 'where do you come from' could be heard everywhere in the room, although some participants were not familiar with the shaking of hands.*

▶ *I have to accept that I am here in a different country with different people, experiences and cultures; yet it has been difficult for me to accept the suggestion of calling the elders by their first names.*

▶ *Today the Development Studies Course started! Today teaching, learning, envisioning, community-building has started to become a reality! Homes and loved ones, work and colleagues were left behind for various reasons: grand, noble, petty ... In the various exercises, we shared ourselves: our thoughts, joys, anger, problems, expectations. Each one trying to reach out; some with ease, others with difficulty, hesitating and wanting ... In 2s, in 3s, in groups, we opened part of ourselves, voluntarily yet still with caution...*

▶ *As I think about the day and the group, it feels that we have said our hellos and welcomes, and we are now beginning to settle in together, gently testing and pushing to see how we bend and flow as a group. Are we flexible and elastic? Rigid and brittle? Or formless and without shape?*

The Course Begins: Expressing Our Anxieties

▶ *Everyone seemed to feel that speaking about our anxieties made them feel more trivial.*

This short exercise allows members to express the anxiety they feel at the beginning of a course and helps them through the emotional transition from back home. It contributes to a climate of openness and sharing during the formation of the course group. It also provides an experience of work at the interpersonal level.

It can be used immediately after Who Are We? Introducing Ourselves (page 56). If it is followed by briefings on the course, these may relieve some anxieties immediately. Why Have We Come? Sharing Expectations (page 77) and How Should we Behave? Norms for the Group (page 82) may relieve other anxieties.

Objectives

- to provide an opportunity for members to identify and express their personal and professional anxieties at the beginning of a new course;

- to assist members in making the emotional transition from their back home situation to the course;

- to encourage a climate in the course group for the recognition and acceptance of feelings, and the recognition and acceptance of each other (and trainers), as feeling human beings;

- to check for any major or unexpected anxieties (especially relating to back home) that may need additional attention.

Introducing the Topic

■ Point out briefly that our feelings are a natural and inevitable part of our life at every moment, although we do not always recognize or acknowledge them. At the beginning of a new course, with new challenges and new people — probably in a strange place, and perhaps in a different climate and culture — it will be natural for members to have strong feelings, including excitement and anxiety.

Tell members that they will work with their neighbours in pairs. Ask them to identify their partners, turn to them, and greet them if they have not already done so. Any additional trainers present should join the exercise and work with members.

Tell the members to start the work on their own, individually. The first step is for each individual to sit quietly and 'listen' to him/herself:

■ 'What are you feeling at this very moment?'
'Do you feel anxious about anything?'
'If you have any anxieties — or worries, or doubts, or fears — can you identify them?
What is causing them?'

After a minute or two ask members to decide which one is the greatest:
'My greatest anxiety at this moment is ...'
'The thing that is making me feel most anxious at present is ...'

When both partners are ready, they should share this anxiety with each other, and explain as much of the reasons for it as they choose.

After a few minutes bring attention back to the whole group and invite members — and trainers — to express any of their anxieties in the whole group.[1] Ask if any other members feel anxious for the same reason, but do not offer any reassurance, and do not allow discussion or reassurance by the group either. If you contribute your own anxiety, it can help course members to perceive you as a person as well as their trainer.

As members share their feelings and the causes, you may be able to put these into categories. As the sharing takes shape you can list some categories on the board. These may include:

● back home — my family, my children and their safety. my organization, my work in my absence;

● the course — content, methodology, academic level, language issues;

● the group — its size. the ratio of women to men, behaviour in the group, gender issues. 'Will I be accepted?'

● being in a new place — climate, culture, food, practical arrangements etc.

Make the point that such feelings are natural, and are to be expected. Many of them will be felt by other members of the group too.

After the anxieties have been expressed, and perhaps related to the listed categories, ask members to discuss with their partner how they feel now. Then bring attention back to the whole group:
'Has the sharing and discussion made any difference?'
'What happens if you discover that others have similar anxieties?'
'What happens if your anxiety seems to fit into a wider and predictable pattern?'
'Has talking about your anxiety helped to relieve it?'

Now ask members to consider in their pairs the effect of their anxieties:
'What effect are your anxieties having on the way you approach the course?'
'Are they helping you to prepare for the course, or distracting you from it?'

Invite any general comments or insights to be shared with the whole group. Each stage in the discussion is for a few minutes only. Do not over-work the material.

---

1. In such exercises it is sometimes suggested that partners should speak for each other, but in the early days of a multi-cultural group this is likely to lead to misunderstandings and difficulties.

■ Emphasize that the purpose has been to identify and express anxieties at a time of transition, but not necessarily to deal with them. If members have anxieties about how the group is going to be, they will have to wait and see. If they have anxieties about their situation back home they will have to live with those.

However, you may be able to deal with some of the anxieties by briefings on the course and other information. There may also be individual concerns that you can discuss with members privately.

Conclude by saying that feelings will be given attention during the course, so that we may become more aware of them, and better able to work constructively with them in our professional roles.

▶ *During the first hour of the course, I had so many anxieties, but they were reduced ... and I have felt comfortable because other course members have the same problems as me ...*

▶ *I noted with tremendous interest in the morning the easing of an atmosphere which I felt tight and unclear, to one of friendliness and comradeship as we learn of each other's background and names. When the group went on to express anxieties, commonalities emerged that only served to emphasise the humanity of all of us.*

3.3 Introducing the Methodology

▶ *...this course does not focus on lecturing theoretical knowledge to individual students, but is based on the whole group learning as one body ...*

▶ *I have the responsibility for learning. Nobody can learn on behalf of me.*

With an experience-based methodology the learning grows out of a cycle of action and reflection. The best way of understanding this is to experience and reflect upon it, rather than to hear someone talk about it.

Nonetheless a short briefing, as a part of the general introduction on the first day of the course, is helpful to members. It will satisfy those who already have an interest in training and want to know what methodology will be used. It will also alert others, who may be familiar only with academic and formal study methods, that experience-based learning is different, and that it may seem strange and even uncomfortable at first.

Additional material follows in More about the Methodology (page 122), and can be used to continue the briefing a day or two later. Links can be made with other introductory work such as The Course Diary (page 72) and Why Have We Come? Sharing Expectations (page 77).

Introducing the Topic

■ Give an introduction to the topic based on the points which follow. This should not take more than 20 minutes.

Training and Development

- Development itself is often thought of as a process of learning. There are strong parallels and similarities between the process of development among people in a community and the process of learning among the members of an experience-based training course, such as this.

- Much that applies to groups and communities generally applies to this training group. Many of the issues and forces which we will experience in this group are similar to the issues and forces which operate in any other group anywhere in the world. This includes members' own organizations and communities back home.

- Examples are communication, participation, gender relations, decision-making and leadership. These issues will become central to the life of this group as members begin to work together. The same issues are central in all development work.

- When these issues and forces emerge during our work together in this course, we can use them as raw material for analysis, reflection and learning, and can then apply that learning in other situations.

The Course Members

- The learning needs of members of a course such as this are to increase their effectiveness in work roles and improve professional practice. These are different from the needs of students in formal education.

- Members know what they want to learn. This course should be guided more by their needs, and by the trainers' perceptions, than by any pre-set syllabus.

- The members are adults who are used to running their own lives and taking responsibility for themselves. They are expected to take responsibility for their own learning. Self-reliance is a component of experience-based learning and of the development process.

- Course members are rich in experience of work and life, and rich in understanding, skills and insight. These are resources for the course. Members will learn most from each other, especially from those in similar roles.

Learning

- It is often assumed that learning is about information and knowledge only. An experience-based course is also about skills, attitudes, values, behaviour and action. We are less concerned with what we know, and more concerned with what we do, and how and why we do it.

- The most important resource or tool each of us has in our development work is our own self. To work more effectively we need to understand ourselves better. We need to understand our own values, motivation, behaviour, the way we play our roles, and the impact we have on other people.

- If we are to become more effective in our roles, more skilled and sensitive in working with others, and more competent in making decisions and contributing leadership, we need to develop ourselves. Some trainers say that, unless we ourselves are developing and changing, we shall not be able to encourage development and change among other people.

- Development is about change. As professional development workers we expect other people to change — to change food habits, to change farming practices, to learn this skill, to adopt that attitude — but what about us? Are we willing to change? If not, have we any right to expect others to change? Can we understand change and its difficulties unless we experience it in ourselves?

- 'Education is not for knowing more, but for behaving differently.'[1] If we attend a

---

1. Attributed to John Ruskin, British educationist and writer.

training course, and then go home and continue to do everything as before, can we say that we have learned?

The Learning Model

■ Present the following simple model of experience-based learning. It shows the learning process as a continuing spiral in six stages.

ACTION

REFLECTION

1. Action
- doing: 'What did we do?'
- the experience: 'What happened?'
- the implementation: 'How did we do it?'
- may refer to events in the course, or events back home.

2. Describing the experience
- reviewing what happened: talking about the experience;
- sharing with each other; comparing notes;
- identifying feelings;
- 'How was I involved? What did I say/do/feel?' 'What did others say/do/feel?' 'What did you experience?' 'Who did what?'

6. Further action

5. Doing differently
- applying the learning; making changes; new experience;
- further implementation; trying something new;
- doing better; improved effectiveness;
- further action ... and further reflection ...

3. Analyzing the experience
- analysing what happened;
- understanding how it happened; making sense of it;
- thinking critically; asking questions: 'Why did it happen like that?' 'How were decisions made?' 'Who had power?' 'How do we understand it?' 'What does it mean?' 'How does it relate to...?'
- seeing links and contradictions.

4. Identifying learning
- clarifying understanding; reaching conclusions;
- increasing our awareness;
- new perceptions and insights;
- 'What conclusions do we come to? 'What can we learn?' 'Does it fit our previous understanding?' 'What are the implications? Where does it lead? How shall we move on?'
- deciding on the next step; further planning for the future.

■ Build up the diagram on the board, using the headings and starting with 1. Action. Collect contributions from the group, adding in examples and questions at each stage in the spiral. After explaining the model, continue with the points below.

- The process summarized in the model is sometimes called Learning from Doing. The process is a continuing alternation of Action and Reflection.

- In normal life we often take action without reflecting on it afterwards. This is like food which we eat but which we do not digest. The food passes through our system without giving us any benefit. Action must be reflected upon if it is to result in learning.

- Action which is not reflected upon may be repeated over and over again. When we hear someone who says, 'I have 20 years' experience' we may find that he/she has one year's experience which has been repeated 19 times. It is the review and analysis of action, by means of reflection, that leads to learning, change, improvement — and development.

- During the course we shall constantly reflect on action, whether the action is something that happened in our work back home, or an experience which we share together in the course, or events elsewhere that someone has described in a case study. The Course Diary fits into this methodology as a reflection on the previous day's action.

- Reflection is a different process from evaluation. The difference will be further explained (see More About the Methodology, page 122).

The Variety of Methods

■ Conclude by referring to the methods themselves.[2]

- The principal methods of experience-based learning are discussions, group-work, exercises, simulations, role plays, case studies, visual materials, and field visits. Many of these methods are active, and they are often fun.

- Individual styles of learning vary, and so some members will like one kind of method and some will like another.

- The variety of methods allows for alternating opportunities in the training and learning process. For example, they make it possible to switch between individual work and group work, between small groups and large groups, between involvement and withdrawal, between doing and thinking. Such alternations are part of the methodology.

- The trainers will change their roles according to the method. A trainer may give a lecture, manage an exercise, chair a discussion, and participate in a role play, all in the same day. Members who expect staff only to lecture may be surprised by this.

---

2. Members may be more familiar with the methods of formal education, such as lectures, reading, writing assignments and so on. These are not dealt with here.

The members of a newly-gathered course may find it difficult to absorb more than this during the introductory sessions. The remainder of the material (see More About the Methodology, page 122) can be introduced as part of a separate session a day or two later.

▶ *Previously I have thought of training as a matter of information transfer. Here I am very interested to experience it as a 'people-process' and to be repeatedly challenged about what I am going to do differently in future.*

▶ *First of all I should change myself; only then can I help others to change. If I want to do differently, or improve, I should reflect on my experience and analyse critically, otherwise I remain the same.*

▶ *23rd April. Course participants showed clearly that participatory learning was a new concept to them. The common learning system is that of student and lecturer. A cloud of confusion hung over almost all of them as the three tutors went through the programme. One could see by the end of the day that doubt still hung on the faces of some.*

▶ *5th July. Now looking back to the beginning of the course, I said there was some cloud of confusion over the teaching methods. But now after eleven weeks I'm sure most of us would go back and try the participatory learning methods. I should however warn you here that we are going to experience the same doubt that we found ourselves in. We should learn to tolerate that as much as our tutors did.*

The Course Diary

▶ *... I volunteered to write the first page of this diary. It seemed a good idea at the time ...*

▶ *I'm always moved by things my fellow course-members come up with in this book ...*

▶ *I find that on days when I write the diary I benefit more from the day's work than on other days — because I am more alert to the significant moments of the day and spend longer reflecting on the day's content ...*

▶ *... our dear diary is a very valuable document. It has our personalities, style, humour and more. It is the pulse of the group ...*

▶ *Well, valuable as it is, writing it is another matter.*

▶ *After the diary reading a moment of silence again. Followed by the question who takes the diary? Response is not immediate, all heads bent down reading the answer from the floor ... I stretch my hand, a sign of accepting ... This ends the silence, and brings life to the group, heads high up again ready for the day's work.*

The course diary follows the day-by-day experience of a course as it unfolds. It is primarily a tool for reflection, and forms part of the approach to learning in the course.

Members take turns to write the diary for a day, so each contribution is individual. The writer is asked to write about whatever has been significant in his/her own experience of that day. As the course proceeds, other members add their contributions and so the diary becomes a continuing and shared journal of the course group.

The diary itself can be a sturdy exercise book of about 200 pages. The writing is done overnight, and the writer reads his/her contribution as the first event of the next morning. Fifteen minutes are set aside at the beginning of the course day for this work.

The method may be introduced on the first morning of a new course, after Introducing the Methodology (page 67).

Objectives

- to stimulate reflection on the previous day's experience and learning;
- to develop skills and confidence in observing, writing and speaking;
- to produce a continuing commentary by members on the unfolding of the course and the life of the course group;
- to provide an opportunity for members to explore issues which concern them;
- to bring the course members to a shared starting point each morning;
- to encourage the practice of regular reflection in professional work.

Writing the Diary

■ Introduce the idea and purposes of the diary, based on the above and the points which follow below. If any members already keep their own journals, you can draw out the similarities and differences.

- Each day the writing is an individual task, but the task is shared by all members of the group in turn. The diary can be thought of as a contribution to the process of the course which is made by the members.

- Members will be asked to volunteer in turn each day. Asking for a volunteer, rather than setting up a rota, allows individuals more choice over when they take their turn. After every member has written, the cycle begins again, though not necessarily in the same order.

- Whoever writes the diary reads it aloud to the group and trainers on the following day. This is the first event of the working day, and is followed by any discussion arising from the diary. The reading usually takes about five minutes, and the discussion another five or ten minutes.

- The purpose of the diary is learning not reporting; reflection not evaluation; and personal experience not formal minutes. Some members may find these are difficult distinctions at first.

■ Distribute the guidelines for writing the diary (pages 75—76). At such an early stage in the course, these may need further discussion and clarification. Finally ask: 'Who will write the diary for the first day?' There may be silence in the group at this point, but someone will volunteer sooner or later!

Discussing the Diary

For the first days of a course trainers should introduce the reading of the diary, and moderate the group's discussion of it. This demonstrates the role of moderator, which lies between the chairperson at a meeting and the facilitator of a case study.

Some aspects of the role are:
- starting the day's work by inviting the writer of the diary to read it to the group;
- appreciating the writer for his/her work;
- encouraging reflection and exploration in the discussion, but discouraging evaluation;
- questioning general statements such as 'everyone ...' 'people always ...';
- encouraging 'I' statements, and contributions which are based on personal experience;
- acknowledging and exploring expressions of feeling either in the diary or in the discussion;
- drawing attention to the dynamics of the discussion, especially participation and any language difficulties;

- noting issues and questions to be discussed later;
- watching the time, and judging when to end the discussion. 'Hot discussions' can be continued if possible, otherwise taken up again later;
- summing up, and calling for the next diary writer.

At the end of the first week, or during the second week, trainers should pass the task of moderating the diary discussion to the course members. A simple arrangement is for today's diary writer to moderate tomorrow's discussion. The task gives every member practice in a further leadership role in the whole course group.

From this point onwards, trainers should participate in diary discussions on the same basis as the members, and should put themselves under the authority of the moderator during those 15 minutes. Some trainers may find this difficult, and should guard against slipping back into their usual training or leadership role. They may confine their contributions to aspects of the process which are being overlooked.

The Diary as a Creative Opportunity

As members take turns to record the life and learning of a course, their skills in writing and reading improve, and their confidence with the diary increases. Skills and abilities, hitherto unseen and unsuspected, often appear. Imagination, creativity, humour, candour and conviction enliven the contributions.

Some develop their individual style of writing. Some try out literary innovations. Some use the opportunity to clarify their position on an issue and to challenge the opinions of others. Some express their feelings and share values and beliefs. Some use the diary to give, and to request, feedback. Some reflect deeply on their concerns.

In some DS courses the diary even acquired a whimsical character as an additional member and friend of the group, as some of the following extracts from different courses illustrate. On occasion the diary was ceremoniously presented with new clothes — an honour in many cultures — in the form of a bright and cheerful dust jacket or other decoration!

▶ *I shall be sad to lose a friend such as you, who never asks questions, who never loses patience, who never answers back ...*

▶ *Dear Diary: but why am I calling you 'Dear'? You don't speak Spanish and it is difficult to understand one another, because my English is not enough. When you come to my room we spend many hours looking in the dictionary ... It's hard work for me to invite you.*

▶ *Dear Diary, I hope you have not been a talkative visitor because I could see that people are beginning to be hesitant to invite you again to their rooms. This morning was particularly a bad day for you because you really walked from door to door but people were not willing to let you in ...*

▶ *To my black leather-bound lady, with dangerous red trimming. I have now picked you up for the third time, and I think that my wife is becoming suspicious. She is out at the moment, so we are safe.*

But what if she comes in suddenly upon us? What if she finds you hiding in my bag? Ah, my dear, I think this affair may have to end, if not today then next time will certainly be the last.

▶ *Dear Diary, Are you becoming marginalized? Do you feel desolate? Are you feeling powerless? Are you exhausted and devoid of resources? Do you know, we are Development workers? We are concerned with the marginalized, the destitutes, the powerless, the alienated ...*

▶ *As I opened the diary, I felt that it is a burden, another 'heaviness' added to this day. But suddenly I realised that I have not prayed in the evening. I have forgotten my 'evening prayer'. So I started my evening prayer by offering all that happened, especially the diary of the morning and the following discussion ... My whole attitude changed. The diary was not a burden for me, it was not heavy. I found a real pleasure in it, because it became part of my evening prayer.*

▶ *I think we should keep on writing diaries which enable us to be reflective and hard-thinking. I know it's not an easy task, but that is exactly what I'm in need of. Quite often I do something spontaneously and I seldom reflect on what I've done and why I did it, which is very dangerous for a development worker.*

▶ *... this is your last visit to my room and I think there would be no chance to meet again. I am sorry for not being able to understand you properly. Sometimes I thought you were an enemy. Sometimes I thought you are a friend. And sometimes I thought you can change your gender to help homesick people ... But actually you are an active member of this group, and I believe you gained much from the course. Dear Diary, you are now an effective development worker ...*

Guidelines: The Course Diary

The main purposes of the Course Diary are:

1. To think further about some aspects of each day's experiences and learning.
2. To provide an opportunity for issues and concerns within the group to be raised.
3. To provide a continuing commentary by course members on the life of the group.
4. To bring the group members to a shared starting point each morning.

Guidelines for writing the diary

Whoever writes the diary may use the opportunity in whatever way seems best to him or her. However, the following guidelines may be helpful:

1. Write it as an informal diary, not a report or 'minutes'.
2. Keep the emphasis on the life of the group, on the members of the group, and on the process of learning.

3. Avoid recording and repeating the factual content or subject matter of sessions.

4. Choose only a few points or events or moments to mention. Do not try to write about every moment of the day.

5. Choose points or events or moments which strike you, or which seem important to you, or which you feel strongly about.

6. Write from your own personal observations and experience of the group and the day.

7. Remember that the purpose is reflection, not evaluation.

8. Use your own style of writing and your own ways of expression.

9. Write only THREE or FOUR SIDES.

John Staley, *Enticing the Learning: Trainers in Development*, University of Birmingham, pages 75—76

Why Have We Come? Sharing Expectations

▶ *Thinking back upon this day, my expectations are still increasing not only of the course, but of myself as well.*

Clarifying expectations and checking that they are realistic and achievable is a prerequisite for success in both training and development work. Course members are invited to state their reasons for coming to the course, and to say what they expect to gain as learning and what they expect to contribute.

Members identify their expectations individually and then share them in small groups. The work in small groups is a further opportunity for members to practise communicating and co-operating with each other. The work also offers an opportunity for some first reflections on process. All this serves as further introduction to the nature and methodology of the course.

Members will recognize the importance of stating their expectations at the beginning of a course. It is equally important for the trainers to hear these. The trainers can then check that members have been accurately informed about the course and its features, and that the expectations are realistic. If there is misinformation, or if expectations are unrealistic, this needs to be dealt with as soon as possible.[1]

This is work for the first day, probably in the afternoon. Taking it early in the course also demonstrates how members contribute to the shape and flow of the course from the beginning. The session usually follows Introducing the Methodology (page 67), and comes before How Should We Behave? Norms for the Group (page 82).

Tables for small groups, large sheets of paper and coloured marker pens will be required.

Objectives

- to identify members' expectations of the course, and to check that these are compatible with the practical possibilities of the course;
- to find out how far members have expectations and concerns in common, and how far their expectations diverge and differ;
- to provide an opportunity for members to work together, to communicate with each other, and to co-operate in order to complete a common task.

---

1. Occasionally individuals arrive without having received all the pre-course information. If this happens trainers should respond immediately. Any doubt about the suitability of a course for any member should be resolved before the life of the course group gains momentum.

Introducing the Task

■ Divide the course group into smaller groups of 5—7, sitting at tables. Put any colleagues, partners and compatriots in separate groups to expose them to the wider diversity of the group, and to increase the range of expectations in each small group.

Introduce the task with the points below.

- Members of the course have come together from many different places and situations. They have come with many different ideas, experiences and expectations.
- This session is an opportunity to share ideas and expectations, and to discover which are the common concerns and needs.
- The session allows the members and the trainers to check that they have similar and compatible expectations of the course.
- The work in the session will form part of the future planning of the course.

The first part of the work is done individually. Tell each member, on their own and without discussion, to jot down what they expect to receive from the course, and what they expect to contribute to the course. Ask them to think in terms of giving, as well as receiving; this emphasizes the principle that members learn from each other.

Invite them to think about their individual needs, as well as the needs of their job and organization. Members usually write items to do with course content, but some may include process items.

When members have recorded their expectations ask them to put these in order of importance, and make a list of their first five or six expectations of learning or receiving, and also two or three expectations of contributing.

This individual work may take 10 minutes.

After the individual work is done, tell the members to share in their small groups the expectations they have listed, clarifying and discussing them and discovering how many are common.

It is important that the work is first done individually. If the small groups move directly into discussion, the contributions of some may not be heard. If each member is asked to make his or her own list before any discussion begins, it demonstrates that each has a contribution to make, and that every member's expectations are to be given attention.

Trainers should not be surprised if the members of some small groups have difficulty in working together. This is not the first task of the course, but it may be the first where members feel that much is at stake. If it is an international course, then unfamiliar accents, differing practices in discussion, cultural preconceptions, holding on to back home roles, differing attitudes to seniority, even prejudice, may add to the difficulties.

■ After about 20 minutes of discussion, give the groups large sheets of paper and ask them to make a combined list, using the headings Giving and Receiving. If each group has pens of one colour, you can conveniently refer to them later as the Green Group, the Red Group, etc. This work may take another 20 minutes.

When the small group lists are ready, display them to the whole group, but ask members to remain in their small groups for the discussion. Ask each group to choose someone to read out their list and to answer questions. Allow questions for clarification only. After the whole group has considered the work of each small group, call for general comments. Ask the members, for example:

'How do the expectations seem as a whole?'
'Are the small groups' lists different or similar?'
'Is there common ground between the lists?'
'How do you feel, seeing all these items?'
'Is there a balance between receiving and giving?'
'How ambitious do you think this whole group is?'

Then go on to respond from your own perspective.

The Trainer's Response

Checking and clarifying expectations against opportunities and constraints is necessary for success in almost any venture, especially in training and learning. This session is the main opportunity for the course trainers to satisfy themselves that the expectations of the new group are compatible with the possibilities of the course.

■ In responding to the groups' lists, you should:
- appreciate the work the group has done;
- stress the importance of expectations in the learning process;
- say what you feel about the group's expectations in general, and whether you (and the other trainers) think such expectations are realistic and can be met;
- endorse those expectations which fit the possibilities and priorities of the course, but express caution about any which cannot be met in full or covered in depth;
- identify any expectations which are outside the scope of the course, and offer to discuss these with the members concerned.

Some expectations may be 'relevant,' but out of tune with the course. An example of this is: 'Learn how we can make other people accept our ideas.' Question such expectations, but do not make an issue of them at this stage.

Use the Levels of Development (page 122) to check that development at every level is represented among the expectations. If any levels are missing, point out their importance and suggest they should be included. If the International level is overlooked, stress its importance for development, especially its economic and environmental dimensions. If the Group and Individual levels are overlooked, point out the importance of issues such as leadership, communication, participation and decision-making.

■ You should also:

● notice whether the emphasis is on receiving from the course, or whether the members also expect to give to the course;

● notice whether the expectations refer to process as well as content. If not, you can at least refer to the process in terms such as getting to know each other, working together, having fun in the group, making friends, and so on;

● warn of the limited time available, suggest the need for additional reading and individual study, and mention the possibility of members forming their own groups to pursue special interests;

● show how the group's expectations will be incorporated into the objectives for the course, and will contribute to the planning and the evaluation.

Reflecting on the Process

This may be the first session in which members work together on a practical task. It gives an opportunity to look beyond the content and introduce some reflection on the process in the small groups.

■ Point out that the discussion so far has been about the task itself, the expectations, the lists, and so on. Suggest to the members that a lot has also happened between them in the small groups. For example, communication has taken place, sharing has been accomplished, decisions have been made, feelings have been aroused, action has been taken, and so on.

Ask the small groups to discuss some of the following questions:

'How did your small group set about its task?'
'Could you understand each other? Were there any language difficulties?'
'Did everyone participate? How did you manage the participation?'
'How did you deal with members whose expectations were not shared by anyone else?'
'How did you decide who would write out the combined list for the group?'
'How did you decide who would read your list in the whole group?'
'Were you aware of any gender or seniority issues in the group?'
'What can you say about leadership in the group?'

After they have discussed such questions for a few minutes, ask each group to share any insights or issues. It often emerges that the experience, the procedures and the decision-making in each group has been different. If so, point that out; it is valuable learning for those who assume that there is only one path.

Often the discussion about decision-making and leadership identifies small factors which are significant. For example someone who is fluent in English, or has skill in writing on large sheets, or who happens to pick up the group's pen or paper, or happens to be of a certain sex or a certain age, may acquire a particular role as a result.

You can then suggest a link between this experience and what happens in development work. From such small factors and small 'advantages' great consequences may flow, such as the

■ roles people come to play, the influence they gain in the community, and perhaps their emergence as leaders and their exercise of power.

If members are unused to reflecting on process, any who are named may feel embarrassed, and become apologetic or defensive. So handle the discussion in a humourous, light-hearted and accepting manner at this stage, and do not take it too far. Nonetheless you can help the members to see how, even when they are working in a small group on a straightforward task, many development issues are already present.

▶ *The afternoon session was an interesting dialogue on what we hope to receive, and give as well, during this course ... This exercise gave most of us relief for having similarities in our expectations.*

▶ *... we identified our expectations to receive from the course. The converse question of what we expected to give to the course was a bit more tricky for some. Or more truthfully, for me. The simple answer is that we are here to give of ourselves, to the learning process, in whatever way we are able.*

▶ *Giving — Put simply:*
> *on-going experiences in life and development*
> *listening ears*
> *a willingness to share*
> *a desire to learn*
> *personality*

▶ *... when it comes to what participants expected to receive and what they thought they would give ... perhaps we can only learn as much as we are prepared to give. The course promises, or perhaps threatens, to be a very busy one.*

3.6 How Should We Behave? Norms for the Group

▶ ... *it seems that the outcome of the course will depend on our ability to keep an open atmosphere, allowing everybody to contribute and share ...*

▶ *We come from different backgrounds with cultural differences of what is polite or not, what is acceptable or not and so on, but after a while we will form our own culture in this group.*

This session gives members the opportunity to think about the kinds of contribution and behaviour they want from themselves and from others during the course. Members are invited to share their hopes and fears, and to propose norms for interacting and working together. The outcome is a set of expectations of each other, or 'guidelines for conduct', which can be adopted as a common standard for the life of the group.

It is a useful task at the beginning of a course because it draws attention to process. Members at least recognize that their own comfort is at stake. The discussion also reveals cultural differences which may need to be addressed. For example, there may be varying attitudes towards confidentiality and punctuality, and towards behaviour such as interrupting others and confronting them. Bringing such differences to the attention of the group early in the course helps to increase sensitivity in some members and relieve anxiety in others. All this helps to create a stake in working effectively together. If it becomes necessary later, the course members or trainers can refer back to the norms which have been agreed.

The topic follows Why Have We Come? Sharing Expectations (page 77) and leads on to Cosy or Challenging? The Climate in the Group (page 86). It fits well at the beginning of the second day of a course. The work requires at least one session. If more than one session is needed, part of the following session can be used to complete the work, then followed by Cosy or Challenging?

Tables for small groups, large sheets of paper and coloured marker pens will be required.

Objectives

- to raise awareness of individual behaviour and its effects on others and on the functioning of the course group as a whole;
- to allow members to explore cultural and other differences relevant to working with each other, and to become sensitive to the differences;
- to arrive at guidelines for how members are generally expected to behave towards each other during the course;
- to encourage a culture and climate in the group that will promote learning;
- to encourage members to give attention to process issues, and to their own responsibility for the effective functioning of the course group.

Introducing the Topic

■ Give a short introduction, drawing on the paragraphs above and those which follow. The introduction takes 5—10 minutes.

- In Sharing Expectations (page 77) we dealt mainly with content, with what we want to learn. Now we are going to share some expectations related to process, of how we want to work with each other. Both content and process will receive attention during the course. Norms are a part of the process.

- A norm means what is normal, or what is normally done, in a particular community, social class or culture. Norms are commonly-held beliefs about appropriate ways to behave. They tell us what is acceptable, and what may be less acceptable. Organizations, groups — and even families — also have their own norms within the wider community, class or culture.

- Usually norms are informal and unstated. We grow up with them in our own situation; we adopt others when we join a new group or a new organization; and we adapt, more or less, to the local norms when we visit a different culture. Usually we take our own norms for granted, but if we examine them we may find that, while many are helpful to us, some are a hindrance.

- In this course we are a new and mixed group. Each of us brings our own norms from our back home situation. If we are going to work effectively as a group, and help each other to learn, we need to be aware of norms, and we need to identify norms we can all accept and feel comfortable with. That is the task for this session.

Introducing the Task

■ After the introduction, allocate the members to groups of five or six. The groups should include men and women and be mixed geographically and culturally. Each group needs a table, one or two poster-sized sheets of paper and a marker pen of a particular colour. The small groups can be referred to by the colour of their pen.

Tell the members to start by working individually. They are to think about the kinds of behaviour which may occur in a course group such as this, and write a short list of what they want to happen and what they don't want. They should use the headings: 'What I Want' and 'What I Don't Want', and list up to six items of behaviour under each heading.[1] If the task is not clear, you could give examples of issues, such as interruptions and disagreement. The individual work may take 10—15 minutes.

When everyone in the small group is ready, tell the members to share their lists in the small groups, to explain their choices to each other, and to see how many of the items are common. In most small groups many items will be common, regardless of culture.

---

1. Adapted from *Training for Women Project Managers*, Module 1, FIT Canada, pages 5—6.

■ Many will also be personal — likes and dislikes, vulnerabilities, personal tendencies and so on. Sharing and clarifying these in the small groups will help in confidence and team-building, so this discussion should not be hurried.

When the sharing is complete, ask the small groups to see if they can arrive at a consensus and produce a common list. They should present this on a large sheet of paper in their small group's colour, using the headings: What We Want and What We Don't Want. Not more than ten items should be listed under each heading. This may take 30—45 minutes altogether.

Completing the Task

After all the groups have finished their lists, you should pass each list to the next group, circulating them in the same direction.[2] Each group is to read through the list they are given and respond to each point with their own colour. If they agree with the item, they should tick it. If they disagree they should put a cross. If they are not certain or need clarification, they should put a question mark. This may take ten minutes.

Then pass the lists on again, to the next group, and ask members to repeat the procedure, and so on until each small group has seen and marked each list. Each group should stick to its own colour, so that marks on the lists can be identified quickly. The later moves may take five minutes each.

When each list has been to each small group, display all the lists on the wall, and facilitate the reading and clarification of each in turn. Ticks indicate common ground and will be frequent, but there may be crosses and question marks that need explanation and clarification. Start by asking the group which put a cross or question mark, why they did so. Then ask the original group why they wrote what they did, or what they meant. The explanations often lead to further agreement and more common ground. Occasionally more difficult issues such as handling disagreement and challenge may be raised, and may need discussion.

Much of the clarification can be done quickly, but ensure that each group takes responsibility for whatever it has written, and especially for its marks on the lists of the other groups. If necessary, challenge facetious remarks:

'Why do you say that?'
'What do you mean by that?'
'Are you serious?'

Despite the diversity of cultures, manners, and personal styles which may be present in a heterogeneous course group, there is usually a consensus around the norms that the members want — and around those that they don't want.

Displaying the lists and clarifying them may take 30 minutes.

Leave the lists on the wall as guidelines, to be referred to later if necessary.[3]

---

2. If two groups happen to finish early do not invite them to exchange their lists while waiting, or the circulation later will not work!

3. If the course later includes interim evaluations (see page 243), members can then be asked how well they think the norms are being followed.

▶ *This morning we continued exploring our expectations, not only of the course, but of each other. We are beginning to see that the most valuable resource in our learning process is one another ... What might we expect from one another? What can we look forward to in our relationships during the next 11 weeks? Also, what do we fear about such close dependency? What do we want to avoid? We looked at these questions in some depth in three groups, an exercise which in itself enabled us to get to know and appreciate each other.*

▶ *Openness and honesty, good listening, mutual respect, and encouragement were unanimously agreed as being highly desirable. We also wanted a good dose of humour. We expressed our fears of possible prejudice and discrimination, domineering attitudes, and any attitudes of aloofness. And we agreed: there are no silly questions ... Perhaps the biggest mistake we can make is to fear to make a mistake.*

▶ *Some common Wants were sharing, participation, tolerance, respect, gender sensitivity, good listening, involvement, open and frank discussion, sensitivity towards others' feelings, tidiness and punctuality. And some of the Don't Wants were late-coming, superiority complex, dominating in discussions, avoiding issues, rude interruptions and insensitivity towards diversity among participants. Relating all this to development work, it read like a charge sheet against us when out in the field ...*

Later in the course:

▶ *Punctuality which was among the guidelines set during the begining of the course, seems to be neglected as some course members come very late... May I ask everybody to review the guidelines we set and agreed upon?*

▶ *Some course members (us) have forgot the guidelines and rules set up and agreed upon in the beginning of the course ... Am particularly concerned of the frequent interruption of others while talking.*

Cosy or Challenging?
The Climate in the Group

▶ *We are perhaps starting to become a team but we still have to learn how to argue and stay friends.*

▶ *I think it was good for the group that a few people started to disagree with each other ...*

Most of us recognize that we feel more comfortable when we are with certain groups of people, and less comfortable with others. Some groups feel supportive or welcoming, others tense or hostile. Some feel energetic and others lifeless.

The 'climate' which prevails in a group has an effect on what the members of the group learn, and how much they learn. One of the factors which influences the climate is the level of support which members experience from others. A second is the level of challenge which prevails between the members. Many other factors contribute too, but these two factors, and their combined effect on the learning, can be considered in a simple model or diagram.[1]

The model can be introduced at the beginning of a course. It follows naturally after How Should We Behave? Norms for the Group (page 82), or it can come before Respecting the Other (page 96).

Half a session is required to present the model.

Objectives

- to introduce the concept of climate in a group, together with two of the principal factors which contribute to climate;
- to raise awareness of climate and its effect on the process and learning in the course;
- to alert course members to the importance of challenge as a way to stimulate learning.

Introducing the Topic

 Start by asking course members to work in pairs, to think of an occasion when they were in a group that felt friendly and comfortable, and to share that experience with their partner. Then they should think of an occasion when they were in a group that felt uncomfortable, even hostile, and share with their partner the effect that this has for them. Invite a few reflections which can be shared in the whole group.

---

1 After Francesca Inskipp, *Counselling: The Trainer's Handbook*, National Extension College, Cambridge, page 14.

■ Introduce the idea of 'climate' or 'atmosphere' in groups, drawing on the points above and members' reflections. Point out that there are parallels with physical climate: a climate may be favourable or unfavourable towards the growth of plants. So it is with people. Mention the differences in climate between groups, and also changes in climate within the same group.

Then introduce the model shown below, stressing that it is two-dimensional only and a simplification.

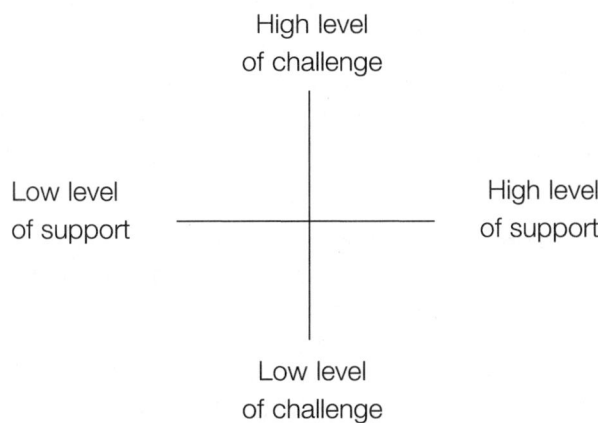

Support can be defined as being friendly, encouraging, helpful, accepting and sustaining towards all the members in the group.

Challenge can be defined as calling something or someone into question, perhaps asking the other person to justify what he/she has said, or asking him/her to give an example. It may mean presenting another point of view, or a different understanding, or even disagreeing and arguing. In such ways a challenge can stimulate further thinking and deeper analysis.

The Climate Model

Build the model up on the board. As each quadrant appears, ask the course members to describe how they imagine it. Start with high support and low challenge, as the 'safest'. Move round the diagram in a clockwise direction, building up the characteristics of the four quadrants with the contributions of the members, and with some of your own if necessary. If the work on Norms for the Group has already been done, bring in some of those norms.

When the diagram is complete, ask the members:
  'Which of the quadrants will favour the most learning?'
  'How do you feel about moving into the high-support and high-challenge
  quadrant as the course progresses?'
  'Is there a risk that a group of development workers may slip into the
  comfortable and cosy quadrant?'

■ Invite members to talk over with their partners any cultural expectations or difficulties, especially over high levels of challenge. Such cultural preferences must be kept in mind as the course progresses.

Then ask the members how they assess the climate in the course group at this very moment.

Some further questions are:

'Has the climate changed since the first session of the course?'

'How does the climate today differ from that of the first day?'

'Does the climate, as you experience it now, seem satisfactory for this stage of a new course, and in the life of a new group?'

If they assess it as satisfactory, ask if they want it to remain at that same level all through the course? If they reply 'yes', it would imply a failure to deepen their experience during the course, and you should challenge them. That in itself can serve as an example of the usefulness of challenge.

Finally, suggest that it is useful for any group to consider its levels of support and challenge from time to time, to assess whether these are helping or hindering the learning in the group, and to decide whether they need to be adjusted. Such questions can be discussed from time to time and during any evaluation.

The climate in the group will be greatly influenced by the way the trainers play their roles. They too should be working towards the levels of support and challenge that will maximize learning. They should remember that they themselves may feel more comfortable working in a climate of high support, and that there needs to be an appropriate level of challenge between trainers and members, as well as among the members.

▶ *We are still all being careful in what we say, and how we say it, being sure not to tread on anyone's toes. For the time being I would rather err on this side of the support/challenge graph. However, we have all agreed that we need challenges to grow and learn — and if we are to learn from each other, then we should expect that this is where the challenge will come from. If we stick to our objectives of being open, honest and supportive then we have nothing to fear.*

▶ *It seemed to me we have yet to go through a time of testing — we are still in the honeymoon period to be too sure of ourselves, but we have a lot to be pleased about.*

▶ *I think that it is a good sign that we are now not only listening to each other, but we have begun stating when we don't agree with each other, and challenge each other more.*

▶ *I liked very much the expression, 'I am glad now that the honeymoon is over.' That meant that we are digging deep down in the different issues and the debate has started. We will not be smiling nicely at each other accepting some opinion because we don't want to hurt the other party.*

▶ *... today's diary produced an emotional interaction in the group, on uses of language, right of expression, demand to recognition of ideas, etc. And suggestions were made to take a risk of conflict in the group, and also take care, and forgive if one's heart is hurt.*

CHAPTER 4

Getting To Know Each Other

Me and My Work

▶ *Me and My Work presentations started with Bolivia, to Ethiopia, Pakistan, Afghanistan, China, to India, Zimbabwe, South Africa and Britain. I must say I enjoyed presenting mine.*

▶ *... the posters of 'Me and My Work', giving the rest of the group an idea of who the others were, but also giving each of us the opportunity to address the group and speak about something in 'public' that we felt comfortable with ...*

Many members come to a course direct from their daily work back home, with all its complexity and detail fresh in their minds. One of their immediate needs is to tell others on the course about that work, and to have their experience acknowledged as part of what they bring to the new group.

Yet if all members speak at will about their work, many sessions may be required. Moreover the amount of information which others can absorb, especially within a heterogeneous group and so early in a course, is limited.[1] A balance has to be found between the need and expectations of members that they should speak, the usefulness to others of their doing so, and other claims on course time.

So each member is asked to prepare a poster or chart which illustrates their work and role/s. Posters impose limits on the amount of information that can be conveyed, so members are forced to choose the aspects they will present. Making some of their material visual, and having to think about this as a communication task, also helps members to find a level that is helpful to the rest of the group.

The task is begun in small groups for mutual support and clarification, and is completed in the individual's own time.

In later sessions members take turns to introduce their work and roles, speaking for a limited time, and using their poster as a visual aid.

For some members, to speak to a largely unknown group, and perhaps in a foreign language, can be an ordeal. But at least the task concerns information which is familiar to members and can hardly be disputed by others; and the method allows a minimum of speaking.

The task is normally given on the second day of a course, and the posters should be ready for use by the third day.

Tables will be needed for small groups, with large sheets of paper and two or three coloured marker pens for each member.

---

1. Members fresh from the field may be out of practice at listening in a training situation. In an international group there may be difficulties of accent, vocabulary and technical language. In addition, there will be a lack of familiarity with the physical, social, cultural and organizational settings in which other members are working.

Objectives

- to continue the process of working together in the course group, communicating, sharing experience and listening to each other;
- to make known the professional roles and work situations of members of the course;
- to make known the experience, skills and other resources available within the course group;
- to assist members to make the transition from their work and organization back home to their work within the course group;
- to consider and practise the skills and discipline required to describe one's work effectively to an audience.

Introducing the Task

■ Acknowledge members' wish to speak about their work at length, but explain that this is not practicable — nor useful to other members — so early in the course. Only limited information can be shared at this time.

Introduce the task briefly and distribute the guidelines on pages 94—95. Explain that most of the work is to be done in members' own time, and tell them when the posters should be ready. Emphasize that it is an individual task, and that you want individuals to include themselves, as persons, in the posters as well as their organization and work.

Divide the course into small groups of three or four for the remainder of the session. Allocate members from different regions, different cultures and different kinds of organization to the same group.

Ask members to start thinking — and sharing with each other — how they might draw up their own poster. Explain that the purpose of the small groups is to help each other get started. Some members may be daunted or puzzled by the task. It may help if you point out the variety of methods possible, and emphasize that artistic or design skills are not required.

Suggest that members discuss the sort of thing they want to know about each other's work, and what kind of poster will be useful.

Members can sketch a first draft of their poster and see how it is understood in their small group.

In the early days of a new course some members may hesitate to express difficulties. Visit the small groups and check that members have understood the task and have at least some ideas about how to proceed with their poster.

At the end of the session distribute the paper and pens.

Looking at the Posters

■ This work can be started a day or two later, and may require two or three sessions. Even if the time limit of ten minutes for each individual is strictly observed, only eight posters can be presented in a single session.

Put the posters up around the walls of the course room, arranging them in whatever groups or categories seem appropriate — the same country, the same region or continent, similar organizations, or similar work and roles.[2]

Take on the roles of chairperson and time-keeper. Direct attention to a group of posters, and invite each of the members concerned to speak for five minutes, and then to be ready to answer questions for a further five minutes.

A course member explains her poster

As each group of posters is considered, the group's attention shifts around the walls of the room. The members then change position and move their chairs. This movement helps to renew energy and attention.

Give praise for the work which members have done on their posters. Such encouragement is important during the early days of a course. The effectiveness and quality of the posters may vary widely — and some members will learn a lot from the way that others have prepared theirs — but you should discourage evaluative comparisons. Affirmation is more important at this stage.

Notice whether the questions asked are about matters such as role, organization and funding, or whether they relate to the person and those with whom he/she is working. This may indicate some of the group's preoccupations.

---

2. If the posters can be left on display in the course room they will serve as reminders about the work of members.

Reflecting on the Posters

■ A day or two later, perhaps at the end of the first week, return to the posters and invite some reflection. This may take up to half a session. Tell members to sit in groups of five or six and consider the question:

'What common elements do you see in the work of members of this course?'

Ask the groups to list the common elements they see, and then display the lists briefly in the whole group. The question requires members to look again at the posters, to reconsider each others' work, and to think about what they have in common rather than what divides them. The discussion helps to establish shared ground within the group, and contributes to group solidarity.

Then ask the small groups to consider a second question and again make lists:

'How would you describe the members of the course in relation to their work?'

Again, display the lists briefly in the whole group. Responses to this question are usually supportive and affirming, which is helpful to individuals and to the group at the beginning of a course. If some responses to the question seem over-idealistic ask the group concerned what evidence there is to support it.

A third question, which might be raised now or later, is:

'An idea from Me and My Work which I can apply back home is ...'

Later in the course, after the group has begun to separate reflection from evaluation, it may be useful to return to the posters for a brief discussion on visual communication. Members can be asked to look again at the posters and identify what makes a poster more effective. They can be asked whether they would prepare their own poster in the same way again, or differently, and how and why.

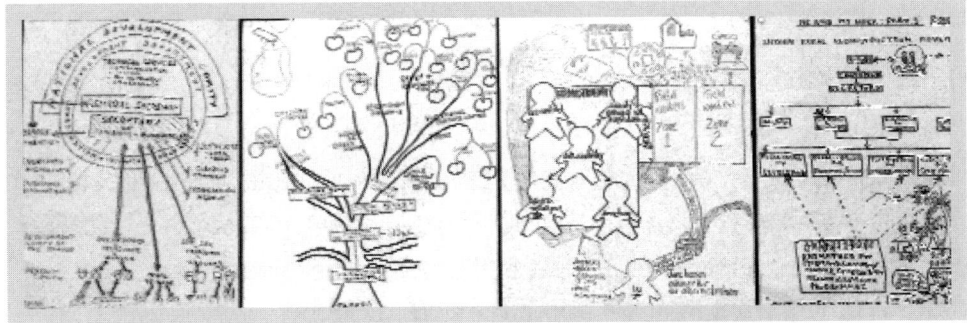

Posters on display

▶ *The room was adorned with sheets of paper showing boxes, circles, webs, pictures, photos, arrows and words of explanation — all in multi colours. Our mental travels were across the world and across a range of activities ... this was a quick look into 'books' which will be studied further during the course.*

▶ *People at the course are getting clearer and clearer as each poster is presented. They are not only a name, which I learnt already after the first day. I realise more and more that there is an enormous amount of experience gathered together here.*

93

▶ *'Me and My Work' then took on some fascinating self-styled presentations. O called his 'Fishbone of my Life'; P had the 'Railway of his Life'; S, a coral island; F had photos; J a baobab tree; T's clearly labelled boxes; and H's large horseshoe-shaped tables. What a wealth of experience and responsibilities could be picked up about these colleagues ...*

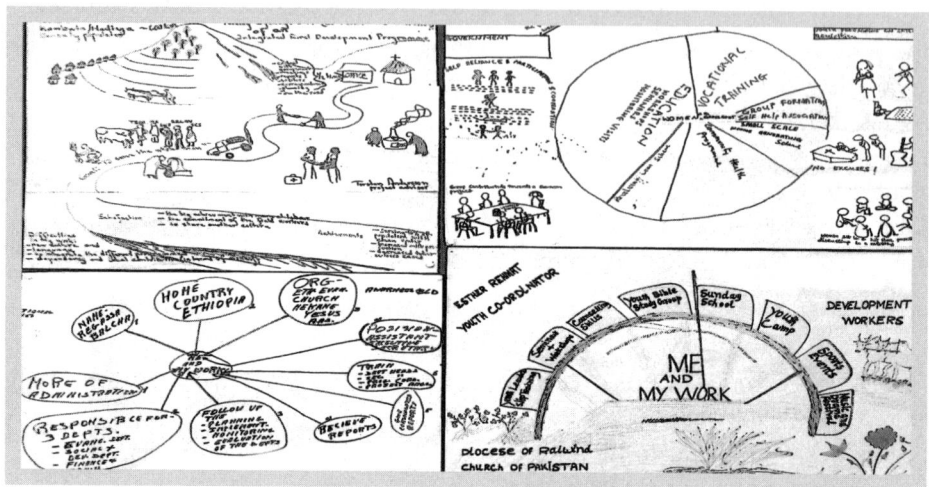

Four more posters

Guidelines: Me and My Work

Your task is to prepare a 'poster' or 'chart' which will convey to other members of the course some aspects of yourself and your work.

When it is finished, other people should be able to understand your poster simply by looking at it, and without any additional explanation from you.

In choosing which aspects to include in the poster, ask yourself:
- what will others want to know about me and my work?

- what do I want others to know about me and my work?

- what will be helpful to the learning in the group at this stage of the course?

- what is essential, and what can be left out?

Some of the aspects which you might consider are:
- your job title or designation;

- your main roles and responsibilities;

- the organization you work for, its nature and purpose;

- important relationships in your work;

- what gives you most satisfaction;

- what causes you most difficulty?

Remember that we want *you* to be included in the poster as well as your work.

Remember also that this is a communication task. How are you going to present the aspects of your work and yourself which you have chosen? Some methods which you might consider are:

- a sequence of pictures;

- an arrangement of words and/or pictures;

- a timetable (or pictures) of a typical day in your work;

- a diagram with notes;

- a list of points in sequence;

- a web chart.

Creativity in method is welcome, but remember that the most successful posters are often the simplest. In the past, pictures and web charts have communicated well. If you use words, you should not use more than 100.

During this current session you will be asked to start on the task by working in groups of three or four. Allow time for each member in turn to talk about his or her work, and to begin to draft the poster on a small sheet of paper.

The task of the other members is to listen; to ask questions; to clarify what is said, drawn or written; and to make suggestions.

At the end of this session, you will be asked to continue the task in your own time and to prepare your poster on a large sheet of paper with marker pens so that it can be clearly seen from across a room. We shall be able to spend only 5—10 minutes looking at each poster, so please do remember that they should be brief, simple and clear.

John Staley, *Enticing the Learning: Trainers in Development*, University of Birmingham, pages 94—95

▶ *The ideal relationship should be one of respect, that is respect them as people, for they also have the same authority to live and show their values.*

An attitude of respect towards other people is essential for development work.[1] Unless we have this attitude we cannot do the work responsibly, or effectively. Without it, we have no basis — and no moral right — to intervene in the lives of others, and even less right to expect them to change their lives.

Yet the attitude of respect is not always strong among development workers. Some workers behave in ways that contribute to the very situation which they seek to change. For example, excessive regard for those who have power, together with contempt for those without power, tends to reinforce the disparities. Occasionally workers are influenced by attitudes that are actually opposed to development. Examples are paternalism and an attitude of 'uplifting' others, unquestioning acceptance of convention, an unacknowledged need to control others, and prejudices.

At the beginning of a new course the trainers will have to decide whether to include work on respect. Some groups may not need this. But if the early interactions suggest a lack of respect towards other people — or any of the difficulties mentioned above — either in the work back home or within the course group itself, then the topic should be included. As a topic it follows naturally after How Should We Behave? Norms for the Group (page 82).

Guidelines about an attitude of respect are included (pages 97—98), together with a concepts check (pages 99—100). If the guidelines are to be read and discussed during course time, and the other work is to be completed then too, a whole session will be required.

Alternatively, the topic can be introduced at the end of a session, perhaps after Cosy Or Challenging? The Climate in the Group (page 86), and the guidelines can be given for reading overnight. The other work — the concepts check, the additional exercise, and final reflections — can then be taken up on the following day.

Objectives

- to recognize and explore different concepts of respect;
- to help members to consider and adopt an attitude of respect towards other people which is appropriate for professional development work;
- to raise levels of mutual respect, and enhance the learning, within the course group.

---

1. The same is true for training, and trainers should review their own attitudes.

Introducing the Task

■ Ask members what they understand by respect. Draw out briefly some concepts of respect found in different traditions, among different age groups, in different periods, and in the cultures represented in the group. This may show that there are varying concepts of respect. Ask which concepts help or hinder development work.

Suggest that development work is based on the significance, worth, and potential of every human being. Explain this concept of respect, drawing on paragraphs 3—5 and 8—9 in the guidelines.

Development workers need such an attitude of respect towards those they work with. This is especially the case when those people are poor, uneducated, dependent, powerless, and have low self-esteem.

Distribute the guidelines and ask members to read them carefully, whether in the session or overnight. After members have read the guidelines then distribute the concepts check. This helps to clarify the concept of respect which is being encouraged. Ask members to complete the check and then to share their responses in groups of three.

Additional Exercise: Individual Reflection

This can be used if the group has been generally responsive to the issue. Tell the members to work individually, and in silence. Tell them the think about every other member of the course group in turn, and to ask themselves,

'Do I have an attitude of respect towards this person?'
'If not, what is the obstacle within myself which is preventing that?'
Finish with the members' conclusions and final reflections.

Guidelines: An Attitude of Respect

1. Anyone who works in support of development or learning — whether in a community or in a training course — needs an attitude of respect towards others.

2. We shall need this attitude if we are to establish relationships of confidence and trust, and succeed in promoting change. Without it we shall not be able to work effectively towards development or learning.

3. Such respect is based on a sense of the significance, worth and potential of every human being. It implies seeing and responding to others as the people they are, rather than labelling them as 'villagers' or 'the poor' or 'students' and then treating them merely as a category, or as a stereotype, or even as objects.

4. If you have an attitude of respect towards people as individuals, it means that you will have confidence in their ability and potential to learn and to make changes in their own lives.

5. If you have an attitude of respect towards people collectively, in the context of development work, it means that you will have confidence in the potential of communities or other groups to take control of their own lives, to identify and solve their problems for themselves, and to work for development and change in their own situation.

6. By showing respect to other people, you help them to respect themselves and to have confidence in themselves. For communities which are oppressed or in despair, this is important. Their present attitude towards themselves may be one of disrespect or hopelessness. We often hear poor people saying things like:

'We are poor unfortunate people.'

'We are uneducated and unimportant.'

'We can't do anything.'

'We are helpless and useless.'

Statements such as these suggest that people do not have confidence or respect in themselves. If you show respect towards them, you will be helping them to respect themselves and each other, and helping to change those attitudes of helplessness and worthlessness. You will be helping them to recover their self-esteem and regain their dignity as human beings.

7. Respect for others is based ultimately on respect for oneself. Unless you respect yourself, you will not be able to respect others as equal human beings. We often find in development work that there is a parallel between our attitudes and behaviour towards ourselves and our attitudes and behaviour towards others.

8. You will be showing respect towards others if you give time and attention to them, listen to them, take them seriously, understand them, express warmth towards them, and allow them to make decisions for themselves.

9. This does not mean that you have to agree with them, or accept whatever they say. In a relationship of mutual respect, disagreement — and also challenge — are necessary parts of the relationship.

10. This understanding of respect may be different from the one that you are used to, or which you experience among your friends, colleagues and co-workers.

11. It rests on the fundamental value of equality, the belief that every individual person is ultimately of great and equal value.

Based on: John Staley and Chris Sugden, *Poverty and Development: A Programmed Course,* SEARCH and TAFTEE, Bangalore, pages 18—20

The questions below are to help you check your understanding of the guidelines. Indicate which you think are the correct answers, and which are incorrect.

1. According to the paper, respect is:

( ) a. having confidence in people's ability to manage their own lives

( ) b. advising people who are less fortunate about what they should do

( ) c. agreeing with the opinions of more important people than oneself

2. Respect is based upon:

( ) a. recognizing the worth of every human being

( ) b. giving honour to one who is superior in status

( ) c. giving value to every person, including oneself

3. Why is it helpful to give respect to those who are poor or powerless?

( ) a. it helps them to respect themselves and increases their self-confidence

( ) b. it gives them an exaggerated idea of their own importance

( ) c. it helps them to change their attitude of helplessness

( ) d. it helps them accept poverty and oppression as their fate

4. Why is respect for other people important in development work?

( ) a. it shows confidence in their ability to solve their own problems

( ) b. it increases their self-respect

( ) c. it makes them more willing to do what they are told

( ) d. it helps them regain their dignity

5. How do you show respect for others?

( ) a. by giving time to them

( ) b. by making decisions for them

( ) c. by listening to them and understanding them

( ) d. by allowing them to make decisions for themselves

( ) e. by agreeing with whatever they say

( ) f. by expressing warmth towards them and interest in them

6. How does the understanding of respect in the paper seem to you?

( ) a. it is different from the usual understanding of respect in my culture

( ) b. it seems idealistic and impractical

( ) c. it seems familiar and agreeable

( ) d. I try to show such an attitude of respect for all the people I work with

( ) e. the paper has given me some new ideas to think about

( ) f. my organization already gives enough attention to such matters

When you have answered the questions, sit with one or two other members you have not previously worked with much. Share and compare your answers.

John Staley, *Enticing the Learning: Trainers in Development*, University of Birmingham, pages 99—100

Photolanguage: Talking through Pictures

▶ *What struck us most was how two individuals looking at the same photograph could give two entirely different interpretations.*

Photolanguage is a flexible exercise with varied uses.[1] During the first days of a course it can be used to help members begin to share their individual experiences, reactions and perspectives.

The exercise is helpful because it allows members to speak to one another 'indirectly', through the medium of photographs or pictures. While members are still strangers to one another, this may feel safer than sharing experience or opinions directly. Those with hesitations over language may find that the exercise helps them to talk more freely than they would in face-to-face discussion. It can also help a group make a distinction between content and process.

When used as an introductory exercise it takes up to one hour. If it is used in the same session as Merry-Go-Round (see page 104), then Photolanguage should come first.

Objectives

- to provide opportunities for individual members to communicate with each other at a personal level but in an indirect and unthreatening way;
- to encourage a process of sharing and listening, self-disclosure and acceptance;
- to contribute towards a supportive group climate;
- to demonstrate that members' perceptions and interpretations are formed by their previous experience.

Materials

The exercise requires a set of photographs which are appropriate for the group concerned. Generally the photos illustrate 'human realities', and should be intriguing rather than obvious. For an international group they may come from all parts of the world and all walks of life.

The photos should be evocative and symbolic, with a quality that raises the curiosity and supports the imagination. They may suggest issues in life or society, or contain contrasts which encourage a response, but they should not show solutions. Instead they can be ambiguous and uncertain, and offer alternative perceptions and interpretations. Photos which are easily identified as being of specific or familiar subjects — whether people, places, events or activities — or which illustrate a limited subject, are less useful.

---

1. The term Photolanguage was coined by Pierre Babin and Claire Belisle, who drew on the awareness-raising methodology of Paulo Friere, and used photographs to assist the members of communities to reflect on their realities and experience.

The size of the photographs is approximately 10in x 6in (25cm x 15cm), and they may be in colour or black-and-white. There should be two or three times as many photos as there are members in the group.

Using the Exercise

■ Tell the members that they are going to work with photographs. Lay the photos separately, face up, on the floor in the centre of the group. Then invite the members to stand and walk slowly round all the photos, looking at them. Any available trainers should participate, especially when the exercise forms part of the introductions to the course.

As they look at the photos, ask the members to make a choice in their own minds of a photo which 'strikes you especially'. Perhaps it 'reminds you of something' or 'seems familiar' or 'seems strange'. After another minute or two, ask them to pick up that photo, find a partner and sit down together. If two members happen to choose the same photo they can still discuss it: they are likely to have chosen it for different reasons.

Tell them that the task for each member is to tell their partner about their photo — what they think it is, why it struck them, what it reminds them of, how it connects with their own life or work, how they react to it, and so on. It may take ten minutes for both partners to share.

Ask them to return the photos, to circulate again, view all the photos, and then again choose one. The task this time can be to choose a photo which in some way 'speaks to you', or links with 'how you feel at the moment'. Ask members to sit with a different partner this time, perhaps someone they have not yet worked with.

When they have finished, ask members to return the photographs, and then to sit again in the whole group circle.[2]

Reflecting on the Exercise

Invite the members to reflect on the experience they have just had. If this is one of the first 'reflections' of the course, it may be helpful to refer to the Action-Reflection Learning Model (page 69).

Remind members that this reflection is about their experience, rather than the subjects in the photographs.

During the discussion keep the focus on what the members have experienced and the process they have been though. Members who are not used to the method may tend to

---

2. Twice is usually enough, but if time permits and the members are enjoying the interaction, you can give them new criteria and ask them to choose for a third time.

■ focus mainly on content, and on the photographs themselves. They may assume that the task is to 'report' on the earlier discussion about particular photographs to the whole group.

Some possible questions are:

'Was it easy or difficult to choose a picture?'
'Did you make a quick choice or a slow thoughtful one?'
'How did you decide which picture to pick up?'
'Was it a picture of something familiar or something strange?'

'When you explained your picture, did your partner look at it in the same way? Or did you have different ideas about the same picture?'
'Did you understand what your partner told you about his/her picture?'

'Did the picture help you or hinder you in talking to your partner?'
'While you were talking about your picture, did you also talk about yourself and your own experience?'

'Were you aware of any feelings during the exercise? Did you feel comfortable? Were there any difficulties?'
'What strikes you about the exercise? What have you gained from it?'

Some conclusions which may emerge from the discussion are:

- It may seem safer to speak and share 'through' a picture than to speak to a partner directly. Attention is focussed on the picture instead of on the person.

- When we talk about our pictures we are often talking about ourselves, but indirectly and 'at a distance'. Such a discussion may seem less personal, easier to control, and less risky.

- We often respond out of our previous experience to what we are seeing in the present. Our experience influences the way we perceive things. Individuals with different experience may look at the same picture, yet interpret it and respond to it differently. This has implications for working together.

▶ *The exercises of picking pictures and discussing them in pairs made a tremendous impact. It generated much action and liveliness in all the members. I found that every member was able to share ideas freely and intimately with the other person. This struck me as further removing barriers in our communication with one another and creating an atmosphere for greater dialogue among us.*

▶ *It was hard to choose from so many fascinating pictures — but soon we had chosen and were talking eagerly in pairs. Within minutes ideas were spilling out, often far off the original subject. As new pictures and partners were chosen, I found my conversations moving from safe theoretical topics to more personal reflections.*

▶ *I picked up a picture of a little girl who reminded me about children in slum districts in Ecuador. I wanted to help that little girl so much, take her into my arms, give her clean clothes, food and love. It was also emotionally strong to listen to my partners who told me about their work in their countries. They all wanted to help people to a better life.*

4.4 Merry-Go-Round

▶ *The next event was not so 'safe' ... even the arrangement of the chairs — facing directly one in front of the other — required direct eye contact.*

▶ *The merry-go-round enabled us to come closer as individuals and as a group.*

This is an exercise in which individuals talk about themselves and their lives to a succession of partners.[1] It helps members to encounter each other as persons rather than as representatives or stereotypes. It is useful as an introductory tool in a heterogeneous group.

When used in this way the main learning is that — however different our national, ethnic or social backgrounds, however varied our cultures and languages, and however widespread our organizational roles — we all share the common experiences of human life, and we all have individual and personal responses to that life.

The exercise also gives useful practice in speaking and listening to others, especially in the early stages of a course when accents and vocabularies may be unfamiliar, and there may be hesitation to speak in larger groups.

Merry-Go-Round can also be used for one-to-one sharing later in a course. It is useful, for example, during work on feelings, self-disclosure and conflict.

It is described here as an introductory exercise. It can be used in this way during the first or second week of a course. Additional trainers should participate to make up the numbers as necessary, and to make themselves known as persons.

If Photolanguage (page 101) and Merry-Go-Round are used together, Merry-Go-Round should come second. It takes about 45 minutes.

Objectives

- to provide opportunities for members to communicate in successive pairs, face-to-face, at a personal level;

- to encourage a process between individuals of sharing and self-disclosure, listening and acceptance;

- to help the members of a newly-formed group to meet each other and get to know each other as persons;

- to encourage an open and supportive group climate.

---

1. Adapted from *Serendipity*, AICUF, Madras, pages 9—10.

Preparation

■ If possible, arrange the chairs before the group members enter the room. Place chairs for half of the members in a circle at the centre of the room, facing outwards. If the size of the room permits, place the chairs up to one metre (3 ft) apart.

Place chairs for the other half of the members in an outer circle, each one opposite a chair of the inner circle, facing inwards and at a suitable distance for comfortable communication. Care in arranging the chairs will assist the members to participate in the exercise.

Introducing the Exercise

When the members enter the room ask them to sit on the chairs without moving them. When all are seated tell them that they are going to work in pairs, starting with the partner seated opposite, but that the pairs will keep changing.

Those in the outer circle will be moving clockwise at each stage in the exercise: hence the name of Merry-Go-Round or Roundabout.

Tell them that at each stage you will give them a topic. One member in each pair is invited to speak to his/her partner on that topic for about two minutes. Then the partner speaks on the same topic for another two minutes.

Then you will give the signal for those in the outer circle to move to the next chair on their left, where they will meet a new partner and be given a new topic. Those in the inner circle are to remain where they are.

Warn members that the time for each topic is limited, and that they may get cut off by a change of partner.

The Topics

The topics and questions for the exercise follow below. Use at least six of them, but not more than nine. They are given in a deliberate sequence, so follow the same order.

Start with one or two of these more general topics:
   'My favourite time of year...'
   'My favourite food...'
   'My favourite kind of music...'

These are 'safe', and allow the members to adjust to the structure of the exercise. Allow a couple of minutes for each partner to speak and give clarifications, but not enough time for the sharing to develop into discussions or arguments. So after four minutes for each topic tell the outer circle to move round .

■ Continue with two or three increasingly personal topics, such as:
  'My friends at home...'
  'When I was a child, something that I liked to do...'
  'My mother...'[2]

Notice how the mood and noise level in the group changes with these topics. Allow a little more time for these topics, perhaps five or six minutes for both partners to share. Continue with two questions about feelings:
  'Something that makes me laugh...'
  'Something that makes me angry...'

Again notice the changes in mood. Allow four or five minutes for both partners to share.

Conclude with an affirming question:
  'Something that I am really good at doing...' (Not something good that I do!)

If time permits the final question can be:
  'What I feel about this exercise...'

Tell the group which is to be the final question as you give it to them. The exercise itself may take about 30 minutes.

Reflecting on the Exercise

As they finish the exercise, ask the members to move their chairs back into the large circle, and then invite some reflection. Keep the focus on the experience, and avoid any repetition or evaluation of what has been shared. The reflection may take 15 minutes.

Some questions which may be useful are:
  'Do you have any thoughts or feelings about this experience generally?'
  'Was it tiring? Or has it given you more energy? Why?'
  'Were you aware of different levels of involvement with different topics?'
  'Did the levels of noise in the group change? When and why?'
  'Were some topics easier to talk about? Why?'
  'Were you aware of any feelings about some of the topics? Anxiety? Irritation? Happiness? Enthusiasm?'
  'Did you find it easier to talk or to listen?'

Point out that, despite our diversity, we all have the same kinds of human experiences. We all have favourite food or music. We all have friends or relatives. We all have feelings. We have all been children and done the things that children do.

If Mery-Go-Round comes after Expressing Our Anxieties and/or Photolanguage, ask the members how they compare their experience of the different structures for one-to-one sharing. Conclude with any final thoughts about the exercise.

---

2. Use your discretion with this topic. In most groups it is well received and generates warmth and acceptance between partners. However, if there have been family tragedies within the group, or if some members' families have suffered from armed conflict, there may be some expressions of grief.

▶ *The rotation of members in an outer circle from chair to chair to share with partners ... created fun but I realized that they led us to communicate what we are to one another.*

▶ *... we went around merrily talking about things like music, books, friends, childhood, and even boasting about what we were really good at ... I wonder now if it was a class or a game! In any case it helps a lot to develop better human relationships.*

▶ *This game has taught me that I not only want to be sensitive to my own feelings, but more sensitive to the feelings of others also.*

This is a versatile method which can be used to demonstrate and explore differences among the members of a group. An invisible line across the room is imagined to represent the range of opinions or attitudes on a particular matter. The line is imagined as an unbroken sequence, or continuum, with the ends representing opposite extremes. Members are invited to stand on this line, to 'take a position', which indicates their opinion or attitude on the matter.

The method can be introduced early in a course as a light-hearted way of helping members get to know each other. For example, they might be asked to position themselves on a line between tidy and untidy, or between punctual and unpunctual, or between talkative and silent.

Later, as new topics are introduced, the method can be used to open up discussion and to demonstrate that members already have varying opinions or attitudes on each topic. Later still, after the group has gained trust, the method can be used to explore differences which are more hidden, and which may be more contentious, such as values and beliefs.

The method requires individuals to take responsibility for where they put themselves on the line, and so it encourages self-assertion and clarity. The principle is that individuals place themselves according to their own perception. It is then for the trainer to decide whether to encourage members to question each other and to challenge the positions that others have taken.

Objectives

- to help course members and trainers see where the course group stands, and where individuals stand;
- to demonstrate in a visual way the range of difference within the course group in relation to a specified issue, characteristic or value;
- to gain a more accurate awareness of the 'positions' of other group members, and to explore these;
- to encourage self-assertion, together with clarity of opinion and self-perception.

Using the Method

■ Use the method after introducing the issue or aspect or topic to be considered. Indicate an imaginary line or continuum from one corner of the room to the opposite corner. Express the issue in an everyday form, and designate the ends of the line to represent opposing views or responses.

■ For example, if the topic being introduced is conflict, a continuum might run from 'enjoy argument' to 'avoid argument.' If the topic is to be individual decision-making, a continuum might run from 'guided by the head' to 'guided by the heart'.

Invite the members to leave their chairs and walk to the point on the line where they see themselves, and to stand there. Most people occupy intermediate positions, rather than the polarized extremes.

When all the members have placed themselves, ask them to talk about their position with those standing near them and to compare notes. Invite them to adjust positions in relation to each other if that now seems appropriate.

Ask questions to the group and to individuals:
    'How do you react to the way the group has arranged itself?'
    'Is this how you see the group?'
    'Are you surprised by the position you see anyone else standing in?'
    'If so, who? And why?'
    'Are you happy with where you stand yourself? If so, why? If not, why not?'
    'Would you prefer to be in another position? If so, why?'

Invite those who would like to make a change to move to where they would like to be on the continuum. Ask those who move to explain the difference, and to say what they think is holding them back.

Once a group is familiar with the method, it can be used as a quick alternative to asking individuals around the circle to share their views.

The method can also be used to form small groups of those who take up similar positions or 'levels' in relation to the matter being considered.

Continuum gives us a representation, or 'snapshot', of individual positions at a particular time. Unless it is part of a process of learning and change, it can become repetitive and superficial, and so it should not be over-used.

▶ *Frankly speaking I thought it was a game, but when we analysed it, it meant a lot. The group learned more as a result of my mistakes. If it were to be like that in the field, it would have caused some difficulties.*

This is a well-known exercise which provides immediate experience of the dynamics of co-operation within a small group.[1] It is fun to play, and generates a lot of useful learning together with some strong, if temporary, feelings.

The exercise requires members to engage with one another in small groups with a shared task, and the learning flows clearly from the experience.

It is a good example of a structured exercise, and also helps to illustrate action and reflection. It can be used within the first few days of a course.

Altogether, with discussion afterwards, the exercise takes 1—1½ hours.

Objectives

- to introduce the method of structured exercises for learning;
- to analyse some aspects and dynamics of co-operation within a small group or team;
- to raise members' awareness of their own behaviour when working at a task with others.

Materials

A table and a set of five squares will be required for each small group. The squares are shown in the following diagram, and can be easily prepared beforehand.

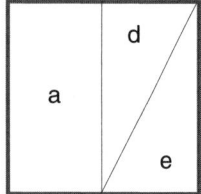 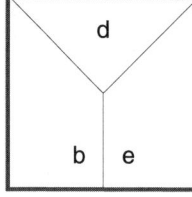 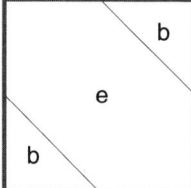 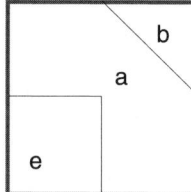 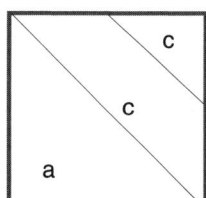

1. The exercise is well known in training circles. It has been published many times, sometimes under other names such as Broken Squares and Getting It Together. The original source seems to be J. William Pfieffer and John E. Jones, *A Handbook of Structured Experiences for Human Relations Training*, Volume 1, University Associates Press, Iowa, pages 24—30.

Cut each square from thin plain cardboard to measure 6 x 6 inches or 15 cm x 15 cm. Then cut the squares into three or more smaller shapes as shown, measuring from the mid-points of the sides. Cut the pieces exactly, with clean straight lines, so that they will fit together in different combinations.

Mark the pieces with small letters as shown. Mark five envelopes a — e, and put the pieces into the appropriate envelopes. Envelope a should have three pieces; b four pieces; c two pieces; d two pieces; and e four pieces.

 ## Introducing the Exercise

■ Ask members to sit at tables in groups of five. The tables should be far enough apart that members cannot easily see another group's work. Check whether any members are already familiar with the exercise.[2] If there are surplus members ask them to observe the working of the groups and to ensure that the rules are followed.

Start by saying that this is a simple exercise about working together in a group, and that you hope it will be fun. Remind the members that, with this kind of method, they will have the experience first, and will discuss it afterwards to see what they can learn from it.

Distribute the envelopes with the pieces of card to the five members in each group, but tell them not to open the envelopes yet.

Inform them that the envelope in front of each of them contains some pieces of card. The pieces of card can be fitted together to make shapes, such as squares, rectangles and triangles. The task is to complete five squares from the pieces of card. Each of the five squares must be the same size as the other four.

The task will be finished when five squares have been made, and each member has one of the squares on the table in front of him/her.

Tell the members that they must obey the following rules.

● You must not speak to one another. The exercise is done in silence. You must not use gestures or any other signals.

● You must not touch or take any piece of card from in front of any other member. However much you want a particular piece, you must not give any sign of wanting it.

● There must be no talking, no asking, no signals, and no taking.

● However, if you wish, you may give away your pieces of card to other members. If you decide to give a piece away, you must pass it directly to another member. Do not push it into the middle of the table and leave it there.

● If you feel you have completed your work, you may fold your arms and sit back.

2. The success of the exercise as a tool for learning depends on a majority of members coming to it new. If two or more members in a small group already know the exercise, it may not have such impact. If there are members who know it, make sure they are in different groups and ask them to 'play the game'. Or, if the numbers fit, invite them to be observers.

■ Ask if there are any questions or clarifications, and then announce that members may open their envelopes and begin. While members are working on the task, observe the process in different groups and prevent any major infringements of the rules.

Most groups take 15—25 minutes to complete their five squares. If any group happens to finish much sooner, ask them to cover the squares, and to observe the other groups silently. If one group is left struggling at the end without the likelihood of finishing, you can suspend the rule about not talking within that group.

Reflecting on the Exercise

This may be one of the course group's first experiences of reflecting on an exercise, so enough time should be allotted. Trainers must expect that the discussion in an unpractised group may seem disjointed and unfocussed at times.

In this exercise, as in any situation in life, some individual behaviour helps the group to achieve its objectives, while some hinders the group.[3] This may emerge during the discussion, and is rich material for private reflection.

But in a newly-formed group, trainers should not allow the behaviour of individuals to be criticized. If members feel that their performance in exercises is being evaluated they will neither accept the methodology nor learn from it. The cohesion and climate of the group may suffer as well.

■ When the game ends, ask the members to remain sitting in their small groups. After working in silence, members may have things to say to each other. Allow a few minutes for this, and for 'letting off steam' within the groups.

Then invite the whole group to discuss the experience. The exercise usually ends with relief and laughter, and it will help if the discussion is light-hearted as well.

Keep turning the discussion back to what actually happened, and how the members felt. Discourage members from giving blame or praise to the behaviour of particular individuals.

Do not let the discussion lead too far into what happened in one small group, or you may lose the attention of the other groups. It is better to use questions to focus on one aspect of the exercise, or on an issue, and to move that focus from one small group to another.

Use some, but not all, of the following questions to help individuals and groups explore the experience.

The task and the group:

'What happened in your group?'
'What was the mood in the group during the exercise? Did it change?'

---

3. For example, some members may have shared their original pieces, while others may have kept all of theirs. Some members may have recognized the needs of others quickly. Some may have received pieces from others, but neither made use of them nor passed them on. One or two may have completed a small square, reserved it for themselves and then withdrawn.

■ 'What were the difficulties in the group?'
'Were you aware of feelings? Was anyone frustrated? Why? Other feelings?'

Giving pieces away:

'Did anyone give away any of their pieces? If so, why?'
'Was anyone unwilling to give away their pieces? If so, why?'
'If someone gave you a piece, how did you feel? Did you think they gave you that piece because you needed it? Or because they wanted to get rid of it?'

Using the pieces:

'Did anyone make their square and then sit back and withdraw? Why?'
'Did anyone collect a lot of pieces and struggle with all of them?'
'How did other people feel at that time?'
'How did it feel when you could see what had to be done, but could not do anything about it?'
'Did anyone make their own square and then break it up? If so, why? How did that feel?'

Co-operation:

'Did you see it as a task for yourself or a task for the group?'
'Did you start by thinking about your own square?'
'When did you start to think about the group?'
'At what stage did co-operation start? How did it start?'
'How much were you aware of the needs of others in the group?'

Other questions:

'Did anyone break any of the rules? If so, why?'
'Did anyone make a square and give it, already completed, to another member? If so, how did that feel to the giver? How did that feel to the receiver?'
'When your group finished the task, how did you feel?'
'Were you aware of the other small groups? Did they have any effect on you?'
'When another group finished, what effect did this have on your group?'
'Did you feel there was a competition? If so, why?'

Relate the experience to real life:

'Do we see the same things happening in groups back home?'
'Do we have the same feelings in real life?'
'What do you think this exercise was about?'
'What can we learn about co-operation from this experience?'

If there are observers invite them to make contributions as the discussion proceeds. Encourage them to describe what they saw, but not to evaluate it.

By the end of the reflection, many of the following points will have emerged, although they may have been scattered in the discussion:

● the members of a group are mutually interdependent, and need the contribution and co-operation of every other member. Individual self-reliance cannot achieve the task;

- everyone has to understand the whole task;
- everyone has to know how to play his/her own part;
- we have to understand the needs of others, and the potential contribution of others;
- we have to recognize the problems of others, and be able to help without taking over;
- we may have to surrender our personal achievement and give up our own security;
- groups which give attention to co-operating together are more effective in achieving their task.

■ It will help to consolidate the learning if you summarize the conclusions which have been made.

Finally invite members to reflect in their own time on the questions:
'What was your own role in your group?
'What did you do?'
'In what ways do you think you helped or hindered the group?'
'What have you learned about yourself and co-operation?'

▶ *We were then invited to play a game! Is this what development studies is about? Games!
... No speaking, no talking; only giving our little pieces of cardboard to each other ... We have discovered that it is sometimes hard to give something to a person ... that if someone does not want help it is very difficult to give. Also that when we give, we have to let go of our gift. We can now see clearly that there are many reasons for wanting to give something.*

There were also other lessons:
  we all have things to share
  ultimately we all depend on one another ...
We were asked to think about our own attitudes and tendencies during the game and to be aware of how we felt. I wonder how many of us managed to do that?

▶ *... an exercise of working with others ... Observations made afterwards were:*
  1. Some did it quicker than others — then sat and watched.
  2. Some struggled on their own and did not look around for help.
  3. Some sat aside and not involved, watching others struggle.
  4. Some struggled and got the result without help.
  5. Someone was not given a chance to attempt it, as someone else did it for him.
  6. Some were frustrated as they were prevented from helping others.
  7. Some broke rules to help others.
  8. Some broke rules because of pressure of competition and pressure of time.
  9. Some made mistakes, and others learnt from them ...

▶ *The game has been quite an experience, at least for some of us. After a short time I had received the missing pieces for my square. Several others had also finished but it seemed impossible to complete all the squares. Everybody in my group looked hard for a solution except me, and I felt that they didn't like it. But I was quite confused and didn't see how I could help them ... It has been important for me to exchange the feelings we have had. It is interesting that so much frustration is possible during a harmless game.*

4.7 The Reception at The International Academy

▶ *Wha! this is what we really need on a Friday afternoon — said I ... Those who played the role were strictly instructed and I tell you, they were fantastic. Great process to end the week with. We went home with a big smile.*

Cultural differences between members are likely to be an issue in the early life of an international course group. This is a short and informal exercise that can help groups consider cultural diversity in a light-hearted way. Individuals take on roles and follow the rules of 'their culture' according to the briefs they are given.[1] They then interact with each other in their roles.

The exercise provides members with an opportunity to acknowledge and confront the differences in an indirect and non-threatening way. It is an opportunity to fool around together and have fun, and so contributes to group formation. It allows members to behave in ways they might not normally, and in that sense can be 'freeing'. It also provides practice in entering into a given role and in using the imagination. All this is useful preparation for later work with simulations and role play.

The exercise is appropriate for the early days of a course, perhaps in an afternoon at the end of the first week or beginning of the second week. It can provide welcome relief after a weighty subject or a tense issue. The exercise may take up to an hour. An extra room will be needed.

Objectives

- to help course members to acknowledge the difficulties of communication in a training group with diverse cultures;
- to encourage members to use their imagination, to try out new roles and new behaviour, and to have fun together;
- to contribute towards group formation and cohesion;
- to allow members to practise reflecting together on shared experience.

Introducing the Exercise

 Tell the members that the exercise is intended to be fun, and should not be taken too seriously. Ask a quarter or a third of the members to remain in the course room, and ask an even number of the remaining members to move to another room. Additional trainers should also participate.

1. Based on "Ambassadors' Role Play; a Cross-Cultural Communications Activity", *Basics and Tools: Adult Education*, CUSO, Ottawa, pages 1—3

■ Tell the members left in the course room that they are about to become the staff of The International Academy, which is a training institute in an imaginary country called Asica.

Give each of them a copy of the role outline, Staff of International Academy (pages 117—118). Ask them to read and then discuss it briefly among themselves, and get ready to receive their new students in a few minutes.

Divide the members who are in the other room into pairs. If you think that certain members may enter a given role more easily, pair them with those who may find this more difficult. Then the former can assist and support the latter.

There are different role outlines for up to six pairs of students (pages 118—120). Each pair comes from one of the following imaginary countries:

The Peoples' Democracy of Rabaria
Zhapuria
The Republic of Laaghistan
Lattifaria
Besinia
The Great Islands

If there are less than six pairs, omit Besinia and/or The Great Islands. If there are enough members for more than six pairs, divide them into groups of three.

Tell these members that they are about to become students on a training course at The International Academy in a country called Asica. They have just arrived and are about to have their first meeting with the staff of the Academy, and with their fellow students.

Explain that each pair represents students who have come from a particular country and culture.

Give each pair copies of the role outline for 'their' country. Ask members to read it and to practise their new culture with each other for a few minutes.

When the pairs have absorbed their roles, and when 'the staff' are ready, invite 'the students' to enter the course room which now represents The International Academy.

If members feel comfortable with this exercise and enter into the roles, there may be a lot of noise and hilarity as the students meet the staff, and the different cultures try to communicate with each other.

Allow the interactions to proceed for about 15 minutes, and then ask 'the staff' to announce that the reception is coming to an end. Encourage 'the students' to leave the International Academy reception while still in their roles, to come out of their roles in their pairs in the other room, and then to return to the course room as themselves.

Reflecting on the Exercise

If this is the first exercise or role play of a new course, the discussion of it may seem unfocussed and erratic. Groups have to learn the skills of reflecting on a shared experience and of learning from it. This exercise — in which the task is nonsensical, yet the experience is sharp — may provide a useful opportunity for the group to practise sharing and reflecting together.

■ Keep the discussion focussed on what members felt, what they experienced, and how they understood the behaviour of others. Discourage the passing of judgements, blame and criticism. If it is helpful invite a member from each culture to read out the second paragraph of their role brief.

When members are ready to move on from the experience itself, encourage them to identify issues, reach conclusions and identify learning. Ask the group what implications the exercise has for the real course.

Although a light-hearted discussion is appropriate, the exercise can raise awareness and sensitivity, generate useful learning, and be valuable preparation for further creative work together.

▶ *It was short but impressing as different members acted out the roles they had been given. A's loud voice disturbed quite a few of us. F and V's way of avoiding eye contact when talking to people made us feel a bit embarrassed when we started a conversation with them. S's standing close shocked people who greeted him. First laughing, then digesting, we've learnt a lot.*

Role Outlines: The Reception at The International Academy

You are a staff member of the International Academy for Training

The Academy is located in the capital city of an imaginary country called Asica. Some of the staff of the Academy are from Asica, but most are from other countries.

The Academy runs many short courses related to Development Work. These courses are very well known, and people from all over the world come to attend them.

The courses are for anyone involved in Development Work, including government officials, politicians, voluntary agency staff, academics, college students, environmentalists, and specialists in particular subjects.

It is the first day of a new course, and a group of students has just arrived at the Academy. They are from some or all of the following countries: The Republic of Laaghistan; Lattifaria; The People's Democracy of Rabaria; Zhapuria; Besinia; and The Great Islands.

You have invited the new students to an informal reception, which will start in this room at the Academy in a few minutes. You want to welcome the students to Asica and to the Academy, to tell them about the course, to learn something about them, and to make them feel relaxed and comfortable. You also want to introduce them to each other as fellow students. You may, or you may not, already be familiar with the different cultures of the countries which are represented.

The reception will be quite brief. You may be asked to bring it to a close after about 15 minutes.

You are a citizen of the People's Democracy of Rabaria

You were born and brought up there, and naturally you behave according to the culture of Rabaria. Please follow the rules of this culture.

In the culture of Rabaria it is normal for people to stand very close to each other whenever they speak to each other.

In any polite conversation with another person you should move forward as close to them as you can, without touching them, before you begin to speak. The closer you stand close to them, the more you are expressing warm and friendly feelings towards them.

People who are meeting each other for the *first* time often express their pleasure by quickly moving towards each other.

To stand back from another person while speaking to them is considered rude and insulting. To touch them is not an insult, but it is considered careless.

You have just arrived at the Academy from Rabaria. When you meet the staff and other students there you want to be especially friendly and polite towards them.

You are a citizen of Zhapuria

You were born and brought up there, and naturally you behave according to the culture of Zhapuria. Please follow the rules of this culture.

In the culture of Zhapuria it is normal for people to stand some paces apart whenever they are speaking to each other.

In any polite conversation you are expected to keep your distance from the other person, and to give that person plenty of space before you begin to speak. The more you stand clear of them the more you are expressing respectful and friendly feelings towards them.

People who are meeting each other for the *first* time often express their pleasure by stepping backwards from each other.

To stand close to another person is considered rude and insulting. If two people happen to touch each other in public, it is thought to be very embarrassing.

You have just arrived at the Academy from Zhapuria. When you meet the staff and other students there you want to be especially friendly and polite towards them.

You are a citizen of the Republic of Laaghistan

You were born and brought up there, and naturally you behave according to the culture of Laaghistan. Please follow the rules of this culture.

In the culture of Laaghistan people who want to be friendly speak very loudly and use a lot of wide gestures with their hands and arms.

It is also considered polite in Laaghistan to begin speaking before the other person has finished their sentence. This shows you are attending to what the other person is saying so well that you do not need to hear the rest of their sentence.

When you meet someone for the first time it is normal to express pleasure by being the first and loudest to speak.

To listen until the end, or to speak softly without gestures, is considered rude and insulting.

You have just arrived at the Academy from Laaghistan. When you meet the staff and other students there you want to be especially friendly and polite towards them.

You are a citizen of Lattifaria

You were born and brought up there, and naturally you behave according to the culture of Lattifaria. Please follow the rules of this culture.

In the culture of Lattifaria people give a lot of importance to touching each other.

In any polite conversation it is normal to keep touching the other person — on the shoulder, on the arm, or on the hand — in order to emphasize what is being said, and to maintain a good relationship.

People who are meeting for the *first* time often hold hands firmly for half a minute to express their pleasure at the meeting and to demonstrate friendliness.

Not to touch the other person, and not to hold hands with them, is considered rude and insulting.

You have just arrived at the Academy from Lattifaria. When you meet the staff and other students there you want to be especially friendly and polite towards them.

You are a citizen of Besinia

You were born and brought up there, and naturally you behave according to the culture of Besinia. Please follow the rules of this culture.

In the culture of Besinia you can talk to everyone freely, but you must avoid looking directly at the face of any person of the opposite sex.

In any polite conversation with members of the opposite sex you must keep your eyes away from that person's face. You can listen and speak, but you must be looking down at the floor, or up at the ceiling, or to the side. To express friendliness, and show you are listening, keep your eyes moving from ceiling to floor and from side to side, but do not look directly at the person you are speaking to.

People of different sex who are meeting each other for the *first* time often express their pleasure by gazing out of the window.

You may look at people of the same sex, but if you allow your eyes to rest on a person of the other sex it is considered rude and insulting.

You are a citizen of The Great Islands

You were born and brought up there, and naturally you behave according to the culture of the Islands. Please follow the rules of this culture.

In the culture of the Islands, people look at each other and think carefully for some moments about what the other person has said before they make any reply.

In polite conversation you are expected to watch the other person's face and consider their words for at least ten seconds before you speak yourself. To express friendliness, and to show that you are taking the other person seriously, you may look and wait even longer before replying.

People who are meeting each other for the *first* time often express their pleasure by looking at each other in silence for as much as 20 seconds.

To reply immediately to any other person is always considered rude and insulting.

You have just arrived at the Academy from The Great Islands. When you meet the staff and other students there you want to be especially friendly and polite towards them.

CHAPTER 5

Working In The Group

5.1   More about the Methodology

▶ *The course demands unlearning as well as learning. We have to abandon any easy incremental concept of education.*

▶ *At first I found the course strange ... Now I realise that this is a very good process, parallel to the development process in real life.*

This is a continuation of Introducing the Methodology (page 67) and should follow it within a day or two. It explains how the methodology, together with the understanding of development, give certain characteristics to the course and the learning. Introducing these to the members helps them to a stronger understanding and commitment towards the course.

The topic of methodology can be followed up later in the course with Approaches to Training (page 156).

Levels for Development

 Explain to the members how this work continues from the earlier session on methodology. Tell them that you will explain certain features of the course which may seem surprising at first.

The first is the 'levels' which we have to consider when we think about the process of development. Make use of the following points.

- We can think of a continuum from the level of the individual up to the world as a whole. Where development is concerned, there will be at least six levels:

  Individual ↔ Group ↔ Organization ↔ Community ↔ Society ↔ World

  Individual: ideas or examples at this level are the individual course member; each member in his/her work roles back home; the development worker; each one of us; the individual person; the unique personality; and so on.

  Group: examples at this level are a course group (such as the present one); a committee; a work team in the organization back home; a group of colleagues; a group of friends; members' own families; and so on.

  Organization: examples are NGOs and voluntary agencies; members' own organizations back home; donor agencies; commercial companies; the United Nations agencies.

  Community: the village; the tribe; the neighbourhood, the locality; people who live together in the same place.

  Society: the national level; the country, the nation.

World: this refers to the international level; the global; the planet; the universal; all humanity; and so on.

- None of these levels should be considered in isolation. For example, what happens in society influences me as an individual. What happens within and to me affects my family and the other groups I belong to. What happens in my family affects my community. What happens at the global level influences my nation. Each level interacts with the others and affects them.

- Each level is capable of development. Development — or its absence — at any level affects the prospects of all the other levels. Therefore every level is important in the study of development.

- Each training event in a course about development is focussed on one or more levels, but not always in the order shown in the diagram. A session at the individual level may be followed by one at the community level. The focus of the following session may move to the national level, then back to the group level, and so on. During the early weeks of a course the focus may be more upon the individual and group, or 'micro-level'. Later the focus shifts towards the wider or 'macro-level'. But there should be continuing movement up and down the continuum, and members should give attention to every level.[1]

Linking the individual to the world level may be a new idea for some members. They may not have thought of themselves as having a role in relation to humanity as a whole, or a part to play in the world. Recognizing such possibilities can be empowering.

Persons and Personalities in Development Work

One reason why experience-based training is appropriate for people who work professionally with other people, such as development workers, is that it recognizes the individual as a person and a personality. Course members who are new to the approach may be surprised by this. They may not expect attention to be given to individuals beyond their professional roles or job descriptions.

■ Explain to the members why the person in the job is important, as well as the job. Draw on the following points.

- Part of the work in any job is routine, regular, and predictable. For work of this kind we follow rules, observe procedures, and do whatever we have been taught or told to do. When considering this part of the job it is usually enough to think only about the work to be done. There is little need to think about the particular person who is doing the work, because every person does the work in more or less the same way. Many jobs are like this for at least part of the time.

---

1. This is another application of Alternation. See Action-Reflection (page 160).

- Some jobs are like it all of the time. Ask members for examples, such as assembly work in factories, packing, clerical work, record-keeping, maintenance and cleaning. In jobs of this kind the person doing the work does not affect the outcome much.

- Discuss with members whether development work is like that. Much of development work is uncertain and unpredictable, especially at senior levels. There may be general principles, but there are few rules in development work. There may be agreement on objectives, but there is disagreement on how to achieve them.

- Instead, there are the pros and cons, the advantages and disadvantages, conflicting priorities, conflicting needs, a range of possible answers, and so on.

- Development workers have to make choices, balancing priorities and making up their own minds, often with limited information. They have to rely on themselves, drawing on their own experience and understanding, and on their own ideas, values, preferences and skills. Work of this kind relies much more on the person who is doing the work. It is no longer enough to think only of the work. We have to give attention to the person, and to the personal resources that he or she brings to the job.

Content and Process

The parallels between the development process and the learning process in the course have already been referred to. The best way to understand process is to work with it; but a short explanation may be helpful to members.

■ Give a short explanation based on the following points.

- What is process? In any interaction between people we can say there are two levels. One level is *what* is being done, or what is being discussed. This is the content, the task, or the subject. The other level is *how* things are being done, or how things are being discussed, or decided upon, or led, or communicated. This is the process.

- If we want to be competent with the central issues of development work — such as participation, decision-making, communication, co-operation, gender relations, leadership — we need an awareness of 'process' and skill in dealing with it.

- We can use the process of the course itself to help us increase our awareness and improve our skills. We are all part of this process already through our participation in the course and its events.

- Many of us have difficulty in identifying the process and distinguishing it from the content. In life generally, and especially in formal education, most of our attention is given to the content. It is said that usually we attend to the process only when it goes wrong, for example if a necessary task is not getting done, or when there are difficulties between people.

- In our own work we know that sometimes things go better than at other times. Sometimes everything seems harmonious, everyone seems committed, and all are working to complete the task. The process is favourable, and the task gets done.

- We also know that at other times there are difficulties. For example, someone is preoccupied, or there is a lack of trust, or people disagree with each other. Then the process does not go smoothly, and less of the task gets done. If the process goes badly wrong there may be conflict, and people may be upset and angry.

- We see such happenings, whether favourable or difficult, in every group, organization, community, and development programme, and even in our own families. Process is always part of human interaction and we are already familiar with it, although we may not have thought of it, as such.

- We can also think of the process in terms of energy. When people come together to take up some task, they contribute energy. If the process of working together is appropriate and acceptable, most of the energy can be directed to the task, and the task gets done. But if there are difficulties in the process, peoples' energy gets used up in that, and less energy is available for the task. Getting the task done is then more difficult.

- One of the tasks of the development worker is to ensure that the process — whether in the group, or in the community, or at any other level — is developmental.

■ Use every opportunity in the whole group and in small groups to focus members' attention on the process as well as the content. Discussion of the process, clearly separated from discussion of the content, will soon make the distinction clear.[2]

The Practice of Reflection

When you invite course members to reflect on an event in the course, or on some past action back home, they may respond by evaluating it instead. You should help them to clearly distinguish between the two processes.

Distinguishing Reflection from Evaluation

The purpose of evaluation is to test whether actions and consequences measure up to some predetermined expectation. Evaluation asks predetermined questions and produces positive and negative judgements about the answers. It tends to discover what it is designed to discover, but only that. It assesses performance and outcomes. It is a form of examination.

2. See also The Task and The Process (page 128) and Working Away: A Course Excursion (page 139).

Reflection has a more open, unassuming and enquiring character. It asks questions in order to explore and identify and reach conclusions, but with judgement suspended. The focus is on what happened, rather than on what should have happened; on what is, rather than on what ought to be. The kind of enquiry it generates is wider, more accepting, more creative and more challenging. It is to do with learning and understanding rather than performance.

Members may have to practise the discipline of reflection before they recognize and appreciate the difference. Trainers should not be surprised if many of their early observations are evaluative.

Review and Reflection

■ Introduce the idea of review and reflection during this session if you think that members are ready for it. If not, wait until a later occasion, after members have gained experience of reflection from events in the course. Draw on the following points.

- In academic systems, where formal teaching methods are used, the students are 'examined' to find out how much they have learned. The teachers take responsibility for this. They ask the questions, assess the answers, and tell the students whether they have passed or failed. Such examinations assess levels of information and theory, but they do not assess other kinds of learning.

- When an experience-based approach is used, course members take more responsibility for themselves. They not only manage their own participation and role during a course, but they also monitor and assess their own learning. As well as information and theory, their learning may be in changed attitudes, increased self-understanding, new insights and commitments, improved skills and greater professional effectiveness. This kind of learning can be evaluated best after members have returned to their work.

- Meanwhile this learning needs to be fostered and encouraged. Experience-based learning does not simply result from having experiences. We must reflect upon action and experience if we want to learn from it. It is through reflection that we build up a 'body of experience'.

- Experience-based methods include reflection after each event. But we can extend and strengthen the learning by looking back, perhaps over the day as it ends, or over a week in the course, or after we have been pre-occupied by action. The focus is ourselves. As we look back, what do we see ourselves doing? How did we participate and behave, and why?

- To 're-view' means to see again. Can we 'see ourselves again' in the situations we have been in? Can I see myself as I was in the small group this morning? Can I see myself in the large group discussion yesterday? During the tea break this afternoon? Can I picture myself in the simulation? How did I behave during the case studies? How much did I say? How much did I keep to myself? What have I been thinking?

What have I been feeling? How am I affecting others? How do they affect me? How am I helping the group? How am I hindering? What roles do I see myself playing in the group? And so on.

- Some say that such review is like playing back an imaginary film of whatever has happened, and looking at our own part in it. The focus is on the process, and the key is being able to 'see ourselves in the process'. Reflection is thinking about this reviewed material, analyzing and understanding it, recognizing our general tendencies, seeing alternatives, identifying moments when we might have done or said something differently.

- In our everyday lives we have our habitual thoughts and we reach our usual conclusions; but review and reflection may lead us to new thoughts and conclusions. It is an opportunity to question our usual perceptions and assumptions, and to renew our understanding. We cannot expect to be able to renew a community or society unless we can renew ourselves.

- Review and reflection, when focussed on our behaviour and role, and combined with feedback from others (Feedback, page 330), is one of the routes to individual change and growth. We should not expect others to change their lives and behaviour unless we are willing to change our own.

- Each of us has to find the way of review and reflection that suits us best. For some of us it is mainly an active thinking process. For others it is more intuitive. Some like to take time for themselves and reflect on their own. Some like to talk things over with other people. Some like to go for a walk. Some like to 'sleep on it'. Some like to write a diary.

- If we can make review and reflection part of our daily work routine, and of our lives generally, it becomes a source of life-long learning.

▶ *I wonder who do we learn more from — the course, or each other?*

▶ <u>*Reflection*</u>*: I am finding that this 'idea' is very important and how much we need to do it in our development situations.*

▶ *It's not that I don't like the diary sessions — I do ... It's just that ... I find this reflection difficult to do. I find the whole idea of sitting down and thinking through the day's events and chewing over what happened, and why, and what it all means, very tricky. Also the thoughts we give are our own, which we take responsibility for — much of what I'm used to is simply repeating or evaluating other people's views or actions. The diary is exposing and personal. However if there's one thing that I've learnt at Selly Oak, it's the value of spending time remembering and considering things — work, relationships, problems, whatever — i.e. learning from reflection.*

▶ *The participatory involvement of course members I should mention proved one point: that people when involved do not go to sleep during sessions. This is a problem which is otherwise rampant after lunch.*

The Task and the Process

▶ *We used a method called the 'fish bowl'. One group worked in the middle ... The others in an outer circle, just listening ... the group outside had a heavy task. Just to be a good listener is a hard work.*

This exercise is a useful introduction to the concepts of task (or content) and process, and quickly raises awareness of the difference between them.

Members work at a given task in three or four small groups to start with. Then the whole group reassembles, and two members from each of the small groups join to form an inner circle. This inner circle again works at the task, while the remaining members form an outer circle to observe the process and the dynamics of the inner circle.

The work requires a whole session. During the first 30 minutes each small group requires a separate room or working space.

The exercise is suitable for the second week of a course, when members are adjusting to the methodology and beginning to work with each other. The learning from it may improve their work together.

It can used to illustrate Content and Process (page 124), and is useful preparation for Working Away: A Course Excursion (page 139).

Objectives

- to illustrate the difference between content and process, and to help members understand how the process may help or hinder achievement of a task;
- to raise awareness of interpersonal and small group process and to increase skills in working with these;
- to demonstrate how our previous experience affects our present position;
- to improve the quality of co-operative work within the course group.

◼ Divide the course group into three or four smaller groups. There should be from four to eight members in each small group.

Distribute copies of the handout (page 132) with the statements about an effective development worker.[1] Tell the members that their task in the small groups is to rank the eight statements in order of importance. Tell them to move to their separate rooms and to finish the task in 20 minutes.

Visit the groups in their rooms and check that they have understood the task. If necessary extend the time by five minutes. At the end of the 20 or 25 minutes, while members are

---

1. The focus of the exercise is not the statements themselves, but the process of the discussions. Other statements could be used, but if the statements relate to the course content members find it easier to enter into the exercise.

■ still in the small groups, tell them to choose two people from their group. Say that you will give the two people further instructions shortly. Do not say that the two are to represent their group. Tell the small groups to return to the course room after they have chosen two people.

Discussion in a 'Fishbowl'

When all the small groups have returned, arrange a circle of chairs in the middle of the room, providing two chairs for each small group. Invite the chosen people to sit in those chairs, and tell the remaining members to form an outer circle around them. This should be a separate circle, but close enough to hear the discussion in the inner circle.

Explain to the whole group that this arrangement is usually known as a 'fishbowl'. Those in the inner circle are the 'fish in a glass bowl', and those outside are looking in at them. While the fishbowl is functioning the members of the inner circle may talk and interact; but those in the outer circle must remain silent, listen and observe.

Tell the inner circle that they are a group, and that their task is to rank the eight statements in order of importance. If anyone asks if they are to represent their former small group reply that you do not know.[2] Remind them that the outer circle is to remain silent and to listen and observe. Tell the inner group that you will stop the discussion after some time, and will invite those in the outer circle to make observations and give feedback.

Tell the outer group that their task is to give attention to the process of the inner circle's discussion, rather than to the statements themselves. What attitudes, behaviour, or feelings do they observe in the inner group? What are the effects of these? Warn them that they will be invited to make observations, and that these should be descriptive and informative only. Criticism and evaluation of the inner circle will not be permitted. Remind them to remain silent meanwhile.

Allow the discussion in the inner group to continue for 10—20 minutes, until there has been enough interaction for the process to be worth discussing. Then stop the inner group, ask them to remain silent, and invite observations from the outer group.

Some members of the outer group may want to continue with the content of the inner group's discussion. They may want to share their views on the ranking and continue the argument for and against particular statements. If this happens, gently point it out, and use it to illustrate the difference between content and process.

Other contributions may be evaluative and may criticize or judge individuals in the inner group. Again point out what is happening, and remind the outer group that their task is observation, but not evaluation. This can be another useful illustration of the differences.

2. This is for the individual members to decide. What each of them decides will affect the process. These effects should emerge in the discussion later.

■ Some members may make generalized statements or contribute conclusions rather than observations. Counteract this by asking for the evidence:

'What makes you say that?'
'Why do you think that?'
'What did you see?'
'What did you hear?'
'What is your evidence?'

If the outer group get stuck help them by asking questions, such as:

'How did the inner group start their discussion?'
'Who spoke more at the beginning? Had everyone spoken by the end?'
'Was the energy level high or low? Did it change? What affected it?'

'Was it an easy discussion or were there difficulties? What is the evidence for that?'
'What made it easy or difficult?'
'What was the mood of the discussion? Tense or relaxed? Co-operative or competitive?'
'Did you detect any feelings? What is the evidence?'

A 'fishbowl': discussion in the inner circle

Some other useful questions are:

'Was it clear whether individuals were speaking for themselves, or representing their former small groups? What effect did that have?'
'Did anyone take on any leadership role?'

'What effect do you think your outer group was having on the inner group? What is the evidence?'
'Did the inner group give explicit attention to the process of their discussion?'

■ After hearing from the outer group, add any observations you want to make yourself. Then invite the inner group to continue their discussion while the outer group again listens and observes. Allow the discussion to continue for another 10 or 15 minutes. Again invite observations from the outer group.

Use any of the above questions again, and also:
'Was the process similar in the two discussions, or different?'
'What were the differences, if any?'
'What do you think are the reasons?'

Invite the members of the inner group to report on their experience and respond to what they have heard. Raise questions such as:
'What helped your discussions? What made them more difficult?'
'Did the original discussions in small groups help or hinder your discussion in this new group?'
'Did anyone in this group change their mind about the ranking? If so, why?'
'Were you really convinced, or did you change your position for some other reason?'
'What was the effect on the group when you changed your mind?'
'What was it like to have the outer group observing and listening?'
'Did the outer group's observations affect the way you carried on with the second part of your discussion?'

Conclude with any insights from the members into content (or task) and process.

▶ *...six are flung into the fishbowl to go through the same excruciating process again, this time with everyone watching...*

▶ *When we gathered for the plenary session we were put through it once again, but this time with two-thirds of the group as observers. They were to watch and study the process going on in the group, and this gave some interesting results. When you are in the group, you are too busy with what is being discussed to be able to catch all the ways we are influencing one another... I think it is important to be made aware... even though it can sometimes be difficult or maybe even painful.*

▶ *When two people from each of the groups were chosen to sit together they initially assumed group representative role. They later gave it up, realising it was a hindrance to progressive and productive discussion... A lot went on here, and it was worth noting how the discussions went.*

Rank the following statements in order of importance from 1 to 8:

An effective development worker...

_____ is a good communicator

_____ has intimate knowledge of the people in the community

_____ is a visionary

_____ can influence and motivate people in the community

_____ is sincere and honest

_____ is hardworking

_____ does not easily get discouraged

_____ has informal social relationships with the community.

5.3 Do We Listen?

This work underlines the importance of effective listening in any work with other people. A simple questionnaire is used to introduce the topic in a non-threatening way.

The questionnaire deals with listening at a conceptual level, but this is useful as a starting point in a group which needs more awareness of listening, or where the quality of listening is low.

The questionnaire turns members' attention towards what is said, but also points to the attitude of respect, and sensitivity to feelings, which are necessary. In other words it points to the process as well as the content.

It can be used in the early days of the course group's life, and requires most of a session.

It should be followed by listening exercises such as How Do We Listen? (page 136) for members to assess and improve their skills.

Objectives

- to raise awareness of the importance of listening in all work with other people;
- to introduce some aspects and issues related to effective listening;
- to draw attention to content and process in listening.

Using the Questionnaire

 Introduce the topic briefly and distribute the questionnaire which follows for members to complete individually. This may take 20—30 minutes.

Then ask them to sit in small groups of four and to share their responses and comments, explaining to each other how they have understood the statements. Make it clear that the groups are not being asked to reach a consensus. This may take a further 30 minutes.

Bring the small groups back into the larger group. Start by asking them how they assess the quality of listening they have just experienced in their small groups.

Move on to take up any of the statements that you want to emphasize, or which members want to discuss further.

Remember that the purpose is to stimulate thinking rather than to arrive at correct answers, although there will probably be general agreement.

Avoid repeating the discussions which have already taken place in the small groups.

Reflect on the following statements and indicate in one of the two boxes whether you agree or disagree with them.

Statements	Agree	Disagree
1. Listening is like breathing. We do it anyway; we do not need to think about it	☐	☐
2. In effective communication, speaking is more important than listening	☐	☐
3. Listening is an automatic process; it doesn't need our attention or any special effort	☐	☐
4. It is important that we give other people a chance to speak; it doesn't matter whether we understand them	☐	☐
5. Understanding the other person means agreeing with him or her	☐	☐
6. The person who listens with understanding runs a risk of being changed himself/herself	☐	☐
7. We can understand another person well, even if we don't understand his or her feelings	☐	☐
8. If I am aware of my own feelings it will help my communication with others	☐	☐
9. Our natural tendency to evaluate helps us to listen more effectively	☐	☐
10. It is more difficult to listen when the subject is unfamiliar	☐	☐

11. We tend to hear things which support our own opinions, and not to hear things which contradict them ☐ ☐

12. It is more difficult to listen to people whose values are opposed to our own ☐ ☐

13. It is easier to listen to those in authority over us than to listen to those who are 'subordinates' ☐ ☐

14. Understanding *about* another person is more important for effective communication than any understanding *with* that person ☐ ☐

15. I can listen better to the people I work with if we have shared our expectations of each other ☐ ☐

16. An effective listener pays attention to what a person is saying and to what he or she is not saying ☐ ☐

17. Effective listening includes 'listening' with the eyes ☐ ☐

18. Some things can only be said with the help of the listener ☐ ☐

19. The best way to show that you are listening to another person is to keep interrupting ☐ ☐

20. Silence does not communicate ☐ ☐

Adapted from E.H. McGrath, *Basic Leadership Skills*, XLRI, Jamshedpur, pages 45—47

How Do We Listen?

▶ *Is listening easy? It is difficult... The participants were divided into seven groups of three to experiment on listening. They did it successfully.*

It goes without saying that listening is an essential skill for any kind of face-to-face communication with other people. Being able to understand the experience of others, appreciate their opinions and recognize their feelings, are essential requirements for every development worker. Whether our current work is in the community or in the organization, in large groups or small, in situations of co-operation or contention, it will require active and effective listening at every level. Furthermore, listening is one of the best ways of preventing conflict from arising, and of dealing with it if it does arise.

Skills in listening, together with the attitude of respect which is also needed, can be strengthened. The exercise below is intended to raise awareness and improve skills. The work follows Do We Listen? (page 133) and links with Respecting the Other (page 96). It is useful preparation during the early part of a course before the members work together in simulations, role plays and other experience-based events.

If the exercise is to be concluded in the whole course group, one hour will be required.

Objectives

- to provide an opportunity for course members to assess their listening and speaking skills;
- to identify some factors which help and hinder effective communication;
- to improve the skills and quality of listening within the course group and among the members.

Conducting the Exercise

■ Introduce the topic briefly, and ask the members to sit in threes.[1] If members have already been working together for two weeks or more, you may suggest that they sit with people whom they have difficulty in listening to and understanding.

Tell them to designate themselves A, B and C. A will start by speaking for two minutes about a current problem of his/her own choice. B will listen to A, and then respond.

---

1. You should use this exercise with caution if any course member is deaf or hard of hearing. Also bear in mind that the exercise may draw attention to other difficulties in communication, such as an incomprehensible accent, or a tendency to talk too much, or mumbling. If the member involved has not previously been aware of such a difficulty the new knowledge can be disturbing.

■ C will observe the process between A and B, but will make his/her observations only after B has responded.

Alternatively you can ask the As to speak on a given topic, such as:

something I would like to do better;

people who irritate me;

capital punishment;

the arms trade;

abortion;

inter-religious marriage;

'religion is the opium of the people'.

While A is speaking, B may ask questions, but only to clarify anything which is not clear to him/her. After the two minutes, B is to 'feed back' to A the sense and feeling of what he/she has heard. B's task is not to repeat what A has said word for word, but to convey the meaning and feelings in what A said. A then comments on B's feedback, and reports on how well he/she feels understood by A.

C then makes his/her observations of the process from the beginning. Make it clear that C's role is that of observer, not evaluator or adjudicator! By the time C has finished about ten minutes will have passed. Ask members to continue in the same groups, but to exchange the roles and repeat the procedure. And then, similarly, for a third time.

Use the exercise in a light-hearted way, without formality. The test of good listening is how well the As feel understood by the Bs; but take care not to categorize some members as good listeners, or blame others for not listening so effectively. The purpose of the exercise is to raise awareness of listening throughout the group.

Effective listening is mainly to do with awareness, attitudes and skill. You can finish the exercise at this point by returning to the whole group and inviting any comments and conclusions the members want to make.

Alternative Ending

Alternatively, if you want to encourage more discussion and analysis, ask the members what seemed to help their communication and listening, and what made it more difficult. Collect their responses on the board.

Issues that may be mentioned include: complicated and technical words; the length of sentences; the listener's interest in the subject; the arousal of feelings; thinking about responses; the listener's preconceptions; eye contact; nodding and the use of gestures.

Further questions which may be useful are:

'While you were speaking, were you thinking about the content (what you wanted to say), or about the process (how you were communicating)?'
'Which helped the As to feel understood — when the Bs reported the facts correctly, or the feelings correctly?'

■ 'How do we know when someone is listening to us effectively?'

'We should also listen for what is *not* said. What does this mean?'

'Do you notice any repeated tendency or pattern or problem in your own listening?'

'Were you aware of your own "body language" during the exercise? Did it change with the different roles, A, B and C?'

'How is the listening in your work situation back home?'

▶ *And behind all this learning, understanding and self-awareness I hear, ever stronger, 'Listen', 'Take time to listen', 'Learn how to listen', 'Find the opportunity to listen', 'Create the environment to listen'.*

▶ *...I would say that all of us won't develop our people or community unless we develop the habit of deep, respectful listening to one another.*

Working Away: A Course Excursion

▶ *The visit to Ludlow was another important step in developing our relations, respect, and appreciation for each other — a necessary requirement for carrying out the various stages of the course still to come.*

▶ *Oh! Nice! Ludlow! Ludlow! Ludlow!*

▶ *Are we outside or inside course time? It appears that group A has occupied the kitchen. Onions are being cut up ...*

▶ *J and V surprised me by the sort of questions they asked us... I thought our visit to Ludlow was for relaxation.*

Many training courses benefit from a short period, perhaps two days and a night, when the group and trainers make an excursion away from the usual course venue. If the whole course group stays overnight, preferably in a self-catering institution, this provides opportunities for working together and for learning about personal and group processes.

The course members can be asked to work in small groups at tasks which contribute directly to the well-being of the whole party. Reflection on such work usually covers the functioning of the group, communication and participation, the roles of individuals, leadership and decision-making — all central issues of development and community work. If the excursion is made in the second or third week, such reflection upon 'real action' can deepen members' understanding of the course methodology.

An excursion can strengthen the growth and cohesion of the course group as a whole. The members not only study together: they also travel, explore, reside, eat and socialize together. All this provides additional opportunities for getting to know one another. It can also increase the level of challenge in the course at a stage when this is helpful.

An excursion is an important event in a course. For the members themselves it is usually a 'highlight,' much enjoyed at the time, and warmly remembered long afterwards.[1]

Objectives

- to provide time away from the training venue for members to enjoy together and to get to know each other better;

- to increase the cohesion of the training group as a result of working together at shared and necessary tasks;

---

1. The DSC made an excursion for two days and a night to a small conference centre in Ludlow, 40 miles west of Birmingham. Ludlow is a traditional market town, with a fine mediaeval parish church and castle. There were opportunities for course members to wander in the town, attend a cattle auction, see the ancient buildings, visit shops and public houses and meet local people. Members also enjoyed the hospitality of Ernest and Muriel Taylor.

- to demonstrate that many of the central issues of development and management are present in any situation where people work together with others;
- to raise awareness of issues such as leadership, participation, decision-making, co-operation and conflict;
- to demonstrate how reflecting together on shared activity and small group process leads to increased understanding and learning about such issues;
- to raise awareness of the skills and resources available within the course group.

The Training Perspective

An excursion takes a course group away from its familiar place, structures and time-table. Members are freed from some of their usual patterns and pressures, which allows them to give more attention to each other.

There may be a sense of time out, or time away, or even time off. Being in a new place together can generate a sense of excitement and exploration. As members explore the place they also explore each other. Personal defences may soften as people engage more closely with each other. Later, when they work together in small groups on shared tasks, they recognize each others' contribution, enjoy each others' company and gain respect for each other. All this contributes to cohesion within the group.

The tasks for the small groups should be practical as well as meaningful. The more necessary they are, the better. An ideal task is preparing a meal for the whole party. Our next meal has a compulsively 'real' quality for every one of us! All members — whether they cook or eat — will agree that something important is at stake. This is more than a classroom exercise.

The 'real life' quality of such a task gives it meaning, and deepens commitment and involvement. The discussion of such a task afterwards often clearly demonstrates to members how learning flows from analysing the process and reflecting upon the experience. One result is increased understanding and acceptance of the approach to training and the methodology. Another result is a recognition that other members have hitherto unseen human resources and skills to contribute to the course.

The trainers who accompany the group have several and changing roles or sub-roles. They organize the visit, arrange the programme and the timetable, introduce the course members to the new venue and its facilities, set the tasks for the small groups and perhaps agree timings and boundaries.

They then withdraw from involvement with the course members, refrain from giving advice or further information, and leave the small groups to set about their tasks. If members do seek assistance — 'Should we do this? How do you think we ought to do that?' — trainers will have to decide whether a response is needed, or whether the matter can be referred back to the group.

Later — for example, if a meal has been prepared — the trainers become participants in the life of the group. They eat and enjoy the meal with the members, express their personal appreciation, and join in the life of the group at that time.

As the tasks are completed, the trainers' role changes again to assisting members, in their small groups, to reflect on their experience of working together. The tasks are challenging, and the process in the small groups is lengthy and often rich. There is much to unravel and learn from.

 ## The Tasks

■ The task of preparing a meal for a whole course group is suitable for a small group of four to six members.

Ask each small group to prepare one meal, but give the task a special emphasis each time. This encourages the groups to think about the meaning and significance of their particular task, and diverts them from competing with each other.

The life of a course group of international development workers offers many aspects which can be emphasized. For example:

- the members coming together, and achieving solidarity in the group;
- diversity within the unity, different food and cooking cultures;
- hospitality, procedures for eating together, ritual, ceremony;
- what is 'appropriate' for development workers, 'available resources';2
- encouraging creativity, imagination, innovation, experimentation;
- celebration, fun, laughter.

Examples of tasks with a special emphasis are:

- to prepare an evening meal 'that symbolizes our joining together as an international group';
- to prepare a lunch 'that combines simplicity with ceremony';
- to prepare a meal 'suitable for development workers'.

Decide on the sizes of the small groups, and announce the tasks, a few days before the excursion. As far as possible allow members to choose the task and group they prefer to work with. If the tasks are set, and the small groups are formed a few days before the excursion, then members can choose whether or not to do any preliminary planning.

Give each small group an appropriate budget, or ask them to draft a budget and then negotiate it with them. Take care not to influence the way they interpret the task.

---

2. There may be 'left-overs' from earlier meals to be incorporated.

■ Simply advance the cash agreed upon, so that they can buy the food or supplies they calculate they need, and ask them to account for the money afterwards.[3] Remember that the task is theirs. They should decide how the task is to be understood, and how it is to be done.

Cooking a meal may occupy a small group for several hours, what with planning, budgeting, shopping, keeping accounts, preparing ingredients, cooking, and deciding on the serving and dining arrangements.[4]

If the excursion is too short for all members to take a turn in preparing a meal, there are other tasks small groups can be asked to undertake. Indeed members who prefer not to cook may welcome a different task. For example, referring back to the aspects above, a small group can be asked 'to prepare a 45-minute programme for the whole course which combines solidarity with celebration'. As with the cooking, other people will be affected by the performance of this task, so something 'real' is again at stake.[5]

Reflecting on the Process

If practicable, the reflection should be arranged during the excursion itself, while the process and details are fresh in members' minds. One small group may be sitting with a trainer and reflecting, while another group is working on its task. Allow one session for each small group's reflection.

Start by expressing appreciation to the members of the small group for their efforts.

Then encourage members of the group to review the whole of the experience they have had together, from the formation of their small group until the completion of their task. Make it clear that the discussion will not be evaluative; the intention is to reflect upon individual and group experience without passing judgement. Members may be used to evaluating any work that has been completed, and you may have to discourage this.

Ask simple questions: Who? How? When? Where? What? Why?

Take the members through the stages of their interaction and work together, starting with their individual reasons for joining the group, and ending with the completion of the group's task and their feelings about that.

Some examples of early questions are:
  'Why did you choose this task?'
  'When did your small group first meet?'

---

3. This raises the question of which member receives the cash? How is that decided? The person who holds the cash in any group often has a controlling role. This can be explored during the reflection.
4. Groups which have cooked may be spared cleaning up afterwards, but trainers — who have not cooked — should consider helping to clean up! This may help to reduce the 'distance' between trainers and members.
5. When setting this task avoid using words such as 'entertainment'. It is for the small group to decide whether they understand the task as that or as something else. However it is understood, this task is as challenging as cooking a meal. The interpersonal and small group issues are as rich and complex. Who can do what? What will be suitable? Skills in music, song, drama, games and dance may be offered. How does the group decide which will be appropriate? If individuals are to 'perform', should it be members of that small group only? Or should members of the other groups — or the trainers — be invited? There are cultural issues around humour, not least 'laughing at' or 'laughing with'. There will also be the uncertainties of timing and 'staging'.

■ 'How did you proceed?'
'What was the mood of that meeting?'
'Who received the money?'
'How did that happen?'
'When did you meet again?'
'Who was there?'
'What did you discuss?'
'How did you decide what to do?'
'How did the group function at that meeting?'
'Who was giving leadership?'
'How did you feel during the meeting?'

Similar questions will help members to reflect on the rest of the process.

Such a review, uncovering and examining the process of a 'real' task, may be a new experience for members. Unravelling the sequence of events, describing who did what and when, looking back at what the difficulties were and how decisions were made, discussing leadership, formal and informal, and inviting individuals to share feelings and reactions from various stages may be as much as you can achieve. With an unpractised group it may not be feasible to go into depth. Even so members are often astonished to realize how rich and complex the group process has been, and to see how much members have contributed to the interaction and communication.

Point out that usually we take the process for granted. We do not examine it — at least until something goes wrong. Yet success or failure in performing any task depends, to a large extent, on a successful and appropriate process. This is true for a daily task such as cooking a meal; it is equally true for the process of development in a community.

Some of the issues which are likely to emerge during the reflection are: communication; feelings; participation; influence; cultural differences; leadership; decision-making; co-ordination; the functioning of the group; the roles individuals played; and perhaps relations with the other small groups.[6] Encourage members to recognize the parallels with their work and roles back home.

Group A: *to prepare an evening meal that symbolizes our joining together as an international group*

▶ *...discussion about our trip to Ludlow continued intensively, specially about what type of food to cook and who will do the cooking. For me personally, being an African man, going to the kitchen for cooking is not a simple task, as it is against my culture. But as D continued challenging me to go against my tradition, I finally accepted the cooking task willingly. Generally the participation during discussion was very good.*

▶ *Finally we met to decide on the meal we planned to prepare — this showed development at its worst — no one wanted to stop and talk, everyone was busy. Those with the biggest voice got through what they wanted, and the level of participation was minimal.*

---

6. Avoid using management categories, such as planning and implementation, as a structure for the discussion. Such categories are limiting and tend towards evaluation. Reflection should go beyond 'management' to what was actually happening and why.

▶ *Now I'll tell you a little from our work in Group A: eight persons from seven different countries. We went to the supermarket, laughing enthusiastically. We filled the bag with different kinds of food; and we all agreed until we found that the beef was more expensive... We bought the beef...*

▶ *As soon as we entered the Centre, our noses informed us that Group A had succeeded in producing an international meal. There was universal acclaim for their efforts.*

▶ *After the diary, Group A was joined by J and N to talk about how we prepared the dinner for last evening. J said it was not necessary to evaluate the work we had done. Since everyone appreciated and enjoyed the meal at the table that was enough. But it was necessary to have some reflections about it. We discussed about each one's participation in the whole process... we discussed about formal and informal leadership in our group... I liked that there was the possibility to share our cultural background...*

▶ *Through Ludlow cooking experience each one of us started thinking of our role in terms of our work. It's really surprising how a simple cooking experience leads to thinking and learning related to our work.*

A group prepares a meal

Group B: to prepare a 45-minute programme that combines solidarity with celebration

▶ *Now we come to the excellent programme of Group B. First Ss led a song with her beautiful voice, and A played his guitar so well. Then Sn organised an exciting game, asking people to form two groups and shout at each other like lions. It was very funny to see people trying their best to frighten their opponents, but the funniest thing was to see a group of ladies and gentlemen roar loudly and do dreadful gestures... Following that, we had another exciting game about 'Cats and Rats' organised by Ss. Everybody got nervous because nobody wanted to be the rats. Then came Ni's story about a small village in the forest and people sat around with lovely candles in their hands, which gave a romantic*

144

sense to our party. Then we had a genuine African dancer who performed an exciting dance with the sound of the drum. Mu had his national gown on, and we saw Ss, Nk, F and Mo in their beautiful national dresses. Finally, we sang a song together, hand in hand in the light of candles, and I was moved quite a lot.

Group C: to prepare a lunch that combines simplicity with ceremony

▶ *Group C was a little excited at the start, maybe due to the fantastic meal we had on the previous evening. However things began to cool down, and off we went on shopping and other preparation. Now experts from different parts of the world are on the show ... As we were drawing towards meal hour, we found that we were much closer and knew each other much better.*

▶ *At 12.45 we were all invited to lunch ... The way the meal was served reminds us of the existing situations in our project areas. The 'donors' were invited to a well-decorated table, and the 'others' to sit and eat on the floor. Food was good ...*

▶ *Our group had a short meeting about 'ceremony', and we decided to act as a small family, sisters and brothers. We would wash the hands of the guests, and also we would eat after the guests, according to the custom of some of our countries ...*

▶ *Every effort was made to utilise the 'available local resources' in the kitchen (leftovers), fully conscious about the lunch to be fitting to development workers ... Then the group was subjected to a cut and dissect operation ... everything was stretched apart to the maximum, but it was a good opportunity to think and reflect on similarities between present and back-home roles. I could in fact find a lot of similarities and that indeed made me happy.*

▶ *Sharing of perceptions and reflection: mixed feelings. For me the exercise was a practical and powerful lesson in group dynamics. Most of all it demonstrated that participation has to be deliberate. It does not happen by chance: it has to be activated ....*

▶ *At breakfast a rather starchy Professor on sabbatical leave asks me to explain what we did at Ludlow. I try to explain and he says: 'Sounds like a primary school outing to me.' I try to explain how complicated and interesting it all was and he says: 'I can plan a supper for ten people by myself, no problem.' I think he has missed the point. I give up trying to persuade him, and eat my breakfast. I have increasingly the feeling that Development Studies Course members live at a more intense pace, or at a different level...*

Where Am I in the Group?

▶ *Why did I rush forward to put my initials quite close to the centre of the circle which represented the group, and why did some others hold back?*

This is a simple exercise to raise awareness about the roles that members are playing in the whole course group. It is a useful way of encouraging members to reflect on their own participation, and helps to sensitize them to each other's experience in the group.

It can be used from time to time as a check on perceptions and roles, and may demonstrate how these can change as the course progresses.

There should be ample time for reflection, and for the discussion of any group issues. Allow an hour altogether with an unpractised group, and 45 minutes with a more experienced group.

The exercise can be linked with Making Ourselves Known: Self-Disclosure (page 325) and The Use and Usefulness of Feedback (page 330).

Objectives

- to encourage self-disclosure and feedback among members;
- to raise the awareness of members about the roles that they and others are playing in the group;
- to share perceptions of the internal dynamics of the course group and possible changes in these over time.

Materials

A portable chalk-board or equivalent, approximately 5ft x 3ft 6in (1.5m x 1m), is needed, together with some pieces of chalk.

Introducing the Exercise

■ Lay the portable chalk-board on the floor in the centre of the room, and ask the group to sit round it. Draw a large circle on the board.

Tell members that the space inside the circle represents the group, with its life and work. The chalk line represents the outer boundary of group activity. Outside the line is beyond the group.

Ask the members to reflect on where they see themselves in the course group. Ask them to indicate their 'position' by writing their initial within the circle. Tell them to take as much

■ time as they need to think, but to do this in silence. Tell them to observe where other members place themselves. If they wish they can subsequently change their own position, but no one may change another's position, however 'wrong' they may think it is.

Some members find this a difficult task, and will need time. Others may respond immediately. If the group is large, provide several pieces of chalk so that two or three members can write at the same time. When the task is nearly completed, the trainers should indicate their own positions in the circle, as they perceive them.

Reflecting on the Exercise

After everyone has indicated where they see themselves, invite comments and discussion. Confine the discussion to description, observation, analysis, questions, and reflections. Encourage members to share their perceptions of others' positions, and to explore any differences in perception, but not to evaluate the performance of other members.

Some useful questions may be:
    'How did you feel while you were doing that?'
    'How do you react to the way it has come out?'

    'Why did you put your mark in the circle where you did?'
    'Are you happy with where you see yourself?'
    'Where would you like to be?'

    'Did anyone change their position? Why?'
    'Are you surprised by the position where anyone else has put him/herself?'
    'Do you want to change anyone else's position? Whose and why?'

    'What does this 'diagram' suggest to you about the group at present?'

The exercise may provide an opportunity for members to raise any difficulties they have in the working of the group or in the role of other members. It is not always a 'tidy' exercise to finish off the day or the week.

▶ *The final exercise for the day was to place ourselves in a drawn circle which represented the group. I was happy to see that there is a great sense of belonging among us, with nobody apart.*

▶ *...all the group members had to decide where they saw themselves in relation to the group, represented by a circle on the blackboard lying on the floor. People were obviously thinking very hard at this stage, and many people's judgement of themselves surprised us.*

▶ *We all tried to mark where we think our place is among the group ... all are floating around the Centre, which is marked by S. The Centre is popular, but is it the best place? Would all of us want to be in the Centre? A's selection of his position was not satisfactory, commented some of the group.*

The Individual in the Group

As a course unfolds individual course members often become increasingly aware of the roles they are playing within the course group. This section introduces a simple model which can help individuals to think about their roles (and sub-roles) and about how they are behaving.[1] The model is applicable in informal groups, such as training groups.[2] It may not be so relevant in more structured groups.

The model is intended as an aid to self-observation. It can be used for self-evaluation, but it should not be used to evaluate the performance of others.

It may be introduced during the early weeks of a course: half a session may be enough for this. The model can then be referred to during reflection upon course events.

Objectives

- to provide course members with a simple model of individual functioning in a group, within which they can identify their own behaviour and role or sub-role;
- to help members to observe how their own role or sub-role in the group may change from time to time, and to reflect on the reasons for that;
- to encourage members to try to change the role or sub-role they are playing if they wish to do so.

 ## Introducing the Model

■ Introduce the idea of the roles we play in groups and other settings. Point out to members that while on the course they are all in the role of course member, but that the way each of them plays that role varies from one individual to another. Furthermore the same individual may play that role in different ways at different times.

Distribute the handout, and refer to the five 'levels'. Each level can be thought of as a sub-role within the role of course member. Point out how each of us tends to have a sub-role we are comfortable with, and to function in a group at that level. Point out also that sometimes we switch from one level to another. For example, any of us may become a detractor if we feel hurt or offended, or if our needs are not being recognized.

If we want to develop leadership in ourselves, we can aim to function at progressively higher levels, although it may be unrealistic to attempt to move too far or too fast.

---

1. After a model contributed by J.M. Fuster.
2. See Functional Leadership page 418.

■ Making lasting changes in our behaviour, even to move from one sub-role to the next, is not easy!

Explain that the model is offered as a way for members to think about their own sub-role and behaviour. It is not intended to be a tool for evaluating the behaviour of others.

Ask members to identify their own usual sub-role or level, and to think of specific examples and occasions during the course which have demonstrated this. Then ask them to share their thoughts in groups of three or four, and to consider the questions in the handout.

Refer back to the model whenever it may be useful in later discussions about roles and sub-roles in groups.

Guidelines: The Individual in the Group

Below are five ways in which individual members may behave in the group. These can also be understood as sub-roles or 'levels' of functioning.

Leader (this literally means to go in front and show the way ahead)

- attends and responds to others, and is involved
- seeks clarification of what is not clear
- contributes his/her own learning, insights, concerns, feelings, etc
- draws attention to the group's concerns, problems and needs
- takes initiatives to help the group to solve its problems and meet its needs.

Contributor (this literally means to put in, or give for a shared purpose)

- attends to what is happening in the group, and is involved
- seeks clarification of what is not clear
- contributes his/her own learning, insights, concerns, feelings, etc.
- draws attention to concerns of the group, and voices its problems and needs

Participant (this literally means to take a part in, or to have a share in)

- attends to, and takes part in, whatever is happening in the group, but does not take any initiatives
- responds to others and reacts to the issues, but only when he/she is asked or invited to do so
- does not contribute to the group on his/her own account

On-looker (this literally means to watch what is happening, to be a spectator)

- attends to what is happening, but is not actively involved
- often makes postive comments, but makes them aside to his/her neighbour, so that the group as a whole does not benefit from them

Detractor (this literally means to take out, or take away from)

- often does not attend to what is happening in the group or to what others are saying
- makes complaints, and sometimes destructive criticisms, but does this outside the group, so that the group as a whole is not aware of them

Which of these sub-roles do you think you play most of the time? Think of occasions in the course which demonstrate the sub-role you usually play.

Which sub-roles do you also play occasionally? What causes the change? Why do you sometimes switch 'levels'?

After reflecting on your own, discuss your thoughts in small groups of three or four. Check with the other members whether they perceive your sub-role in the same way.

Ask yourself whether you play similar sub-roles in other groups, and in your work back home? Are you satisfied with your usual sub-role?

John Staley, *Enticing the Learning: Trainers in Development*, University of Birmingham, pages 149—150 (After J.M. Fuster)

Fruit:
An Exercise for the Senses and Imagination

▶ *At the end of the day I forgot the film and the world system. I was so busy studying. What I study? My apple. My very special apple, with a big red spot and a yellow line on one of the sides. It looked special, and it tasted special.*

This is an exercise in sensory awareness and observation.[1] It can be used to engage with wider issues, such as appreciation of the natural world and attention to detail in the environment.

It calls for the use of the imagination, and is best introduced after some weeks, when the course members have become used to working with one another.

The exercise follows well at the end of a demanding day when the need is for light-hearted activity and relaxation. It's a lot of fun. Allow up to one hour.

Objectives

- to raise sensory awareness and increase sensory skills;
- to encourage appreciation of the natural world and its fruits;
- to practice attending to detail and using the imagination;
- to link the small-scale and everyday with awareness of the wider environment;
- to contribute to the imaginative and creative life of the course group.

Materials

The exercise requires one fruit of the same variety per member. Apples are a suitable fruit, and Cox or Gala are suitable varieties. If apples are not available, another kind of fruit can be used, such as guavas, mangoes or pears. Each piece of fruit should be similar though not identical, firm enough to be handled without damage, ripe, appealing — and edible!

Conducting the Exercise

■ Ask the members of the whole group to sit in a circle on the floor. Distribute one apple to each member. Explain that all apples of the same variety may seem the same, but in fact each one is different. Each member is to get to know his/her own apple. Ask them

1. After J. William Pfeiffer and John E. Jones, *A Handbook of Structured Exercises for Human Relations Training*, Volume III, University Associates Press, Iowa, pages 102—103.

■ to take four or five minutes to look closely at their own apples and observe the shape, colour, shading, texture, markings, blemishes, stalk, etc. Invite the members to close their eyes and take a few more minutes to feel their apple — and to smell it. Some may feel uncomfortable to work with their eyes closed, so do not insist.

Suggest that they can go further in getting to know their apples. Invite them to relax, to slow down, to take a deep breath. Invite them to think about where the apple may have grown, who picked it, and how they imagine it was brought from its tree, and by whom:

'What has been your apple's experience?'
'Did it have an easy or a difficult journey?'
'How is the life of your apple going?'

If members seem comfortable, take this a stage further:

'Put your apple to your ear and listen to it. Can you imagine what your apple might say to you if it could speak?'
'Talk to it, and tell it what you are thinking and feeling about it.'

Some may find this difficult, but others will enter into it.

Then ask members to sit in pairs and 'introduce' their apple to each other. They should show their partner the apple's particular characteristics and relate something of its possible history. Tell them to exchange apples, feel the differences, and become acquainted with their partner's apple.

Tell the pairs to join with other pairs in groups of four or six. The members of each small group should place their apples together in the centre of the group and mix them up. Then, with their eyes closed, they should feel among the apples until they find their own.

Tell all members to sit in a large circle again. Collect all the apples, and redistribute them at random, one to each member. Tell them to close their eyes and to pass the apples from left to right, handling each one and keeping their eyes closed, until they identify their own. When a member identifies his/her own apple, he/she should keep it, but continue to pass the other apples until all have been claimed.

In most groups all members correctly identify their apples. Occasionally one or two members may be uncertain, but this does not detract from the group's overall surprise and satisfaction with the result.

Finally you should lead a discussion of the experience, drawing out the members' reactions and insights, and making links between the experience and wider issues.

To conclude the exercise, you can suggest to members that they ask for the forgiveness of their apples before they eat them.[2]

▶ *Then we found ourselves sitting on the floor in a circle. N distributed one apple each. J advised us to observe our apple carefully, feel it, smell it, and listen to it. Most of us heard our apple saying 'eat me'. But after the exercise, and after searching for and finding our own apples with closed eyes, we felt in love with our apples and kept them with us safely — but of course there were some exceptions...*

2. Occasionally a member objects to this for theological reasons.

▶ *L: Hello, my dear apple ...*

A: Hi L ... what was that joyful noise?

L: We were laughing at our apple stories ... You know, I was so happy to recognize you with closed eyes among 20 other apples.

A: We haven't known each other for many hours, but I have got the feeling you enjoyed your day today. Am I right?

L: Yes, you are. This has been very different from yesterday when I was in tears after the frustrating group exercise ...

A: ... I liked it so much when I was rolled from hand to hand with all those gentle touches on my skin ...

L: I almost feel guilty to bite you. You are the closest apple I have ever had. But I'm going to be realistic and remember who we really are.

CHAPTER 6

Learning Together

Approaches to Training

▶ *In ten years time I may have forgotten the content but I will remember the approach.*

This section is directed mainly towards trainers. The section sets out four approaches to training and learning, with their characteristics and their advantages and disadvantages. The purpose is to provide an overall perspective for people who have training responsibilities, and a rationale for the experience-based approach of this manual.

Course trainers may want to offer the material to course members also. If members become familiar with the approaches and their characteristics it will add perspective to their experience of their own course, and will increase their understanding of its methodology.

■ If the topic is offered to course members, it is best dealt with after three or four weeks, by which time members will be able to relate it to their own experience of the course. The information and ideas can be conveyed through a short presentation: do not give a continuous lecture (see page 158).

The short questionnaire Our Ideas about Training (page 163) can be used to open up the topic beforehand. The questionnaire is light-hearted in style, but it will help members to clarify and question some of their assumptions about training and the role of the trainer.

When we consider the education and training of adults as development workers, we can identify four different approaches, each with advantages and disadvantages. The four approaches can be illustrated with a simple diagram which has two axes.[1]

The first axis has Theory as one extreme and Practice as the other. The second axis has Content as one extreme and Process as the other.[2] The two axes produce four quadrants each representing an approach to training. Please refer to the diagram on the next page.

Academic

In the first quadrant which lies between Content and Theory, the approach can be described as 'academic'. The main tool here is 'teaching'. The purpose of academic teaching is to convey information and to pass on theoretical understanding. The characteristic method is the lecture, supported by individual reading and the writing of

---

1. After Rolf P. Lynton and Udai Pareek, *Training for Development*, Taraporevala, Bombay, page 40 ff.
2. In training 'the content' refers to the substance, the task, the topic or the subject. When we observe what a group is working at, or listen to what a group is discussing, we are focussing on the content. When we observe how the group is working or discussing, we are focussing on 'the process'.

essays. The goals are contained in a syllabus or curriculum. Appraisal is by means of examinations, usually written and competitive. The principal roles are lecturer or teacher, and student or pupil.

The approach assumes that education is an intellectual process of acquiring knowledge. Knowledge is to be passed from those who 'know' (the teachers) to those who don't (the students), who are 'ignorant'. A further assumption is that when students acquire knowledge they are then able to transform it into effective action in the 'real world'.

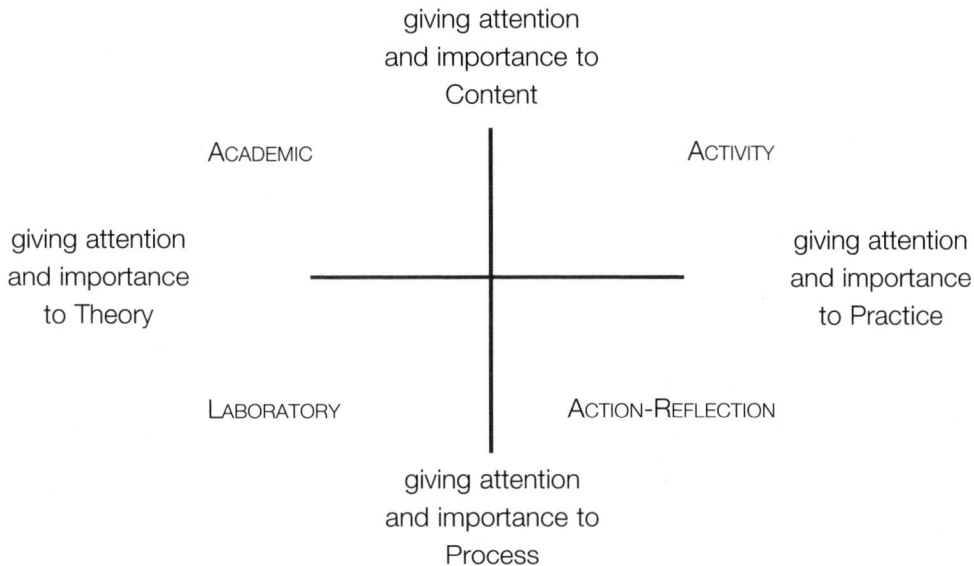

The formal education systems, with their schools and universities, fall in this quadrant. These systems are usually individualistic and competitive. Authority and responsibility for the learning process and for appraisal lies mainly with the teachers and lecturers. The approach is attractive to teachers and lecturers because it ensures they have higher status.[3] Furthermore, the process of teaching is predictable, and normally remains within the teachers' control.

The approach is useful for disseminating information and strengthening theoretical thinking. But on its own it may not lead to better professional practice or more effective development work. Too many practising workers attend academic courses, listen to lectures, acquire a lot of information, pass exams, and gain qualifications — and then carry on working as before, without any improvement in effectiveness or in the quality of their work. The links between academic learning and practice are weak. Practitioners need an approach to training which emphasizes change in practice.

---

3. There are parallels in development work: the worker who 'knows', the 'villagers' who do not know, and the top-down one-way communication.

The principal academic method, the lecture, is also inefficient. If a lecture goes on, without a break, for more than 20 minutes (as most do) it is said that students carry away only 40% of what they have heard and half of that has been forgotten one week later. Confucius is supposed to have said, 'What we hear, we forget.'

Activity

The second quadrant lies between Content and Practice. This approach can be called 'activity'. Its purpose is to teach and improve practical skills. This is the kind of learning often found in traditional societies.

Those who have acquired skills from their elders in a previous generation 'pass them down' to the next generation. An obvious example is children who learn adult roles and skills from their parents and grandparents. Another is the young person learning a skill or craft from an older practitioner who has the required expertise and experience. Typical learning roles are the apprentice, the novice, the intern, and the disciple. Teaching roles are the 'master', the demonstrator, the instructor, and the expert. The methods include observation, instruction, copying, and practice under supervision. Training-on-the-job, field placements, coaching, secondment and counterparts are refinements of such methods.

Confucius is supposed to have said, 'What we see, we remember.' The approach leads to the learning of whatever skills, procedures and expertise have been expounded or demonstrated, but it may not go further. It assumes that whatever apprentices have seen or been told will enable them to deal, not only with the regular demands of the job, but also with unfamiliar and unexpected challenges. But those who follow and rely on regular and routine procedures may find they lack the theoretical understanding or the insight to deal with situations outside their previous experience. And many of the situations we encounter in development work will be outside our previous experience. It has been said that practice without theory is blind.

Despite its limitations 'activity' is long established and widely recognized as the simplest way to train the staff of organizations. Much of the training conducted by voluntary development agencies and NGOs follows this approach. One advantage is that it is cheap. Another is that it does not require any specialized training facilities or staff.

Many development workers have been inducted into their work through 'reading the files', or 'sitting with colleague X', or 'going on visits with Y', or 'seeing how Z does the work'. Such induction may allow the newcomer to 'get the feel' of the job and get started; but later he or she will be faced by new and greater demands, and may end up by resorting to trial and error methods and repeating the past mistakes of others. Some training courses combine the academic with activity, so that the two approaches then complement and inform each other.

The third approach emphasizes Process and Theory, and is known as 'laboratory' training. This is represented in the third quadrant of the diagram.

Laboratory

The name laboratory is used because there are parallels with the working of a scientific laboratory. One parallel is the experimental nature of what takes place. Individuals or groups try things out and observe what happens. For example, they may take new risks, express hidden feelings, practise new roles, experiment with new behaviour, and explore how they are relating to others and how others perceive them. Another parallel with a laboratory is the separation of the work from the rest of the world. Attention can then be concentrated on the task or process under study, and what is not relevant can be left 'outside'. This makes it easier to focus on particular factors, trace their effects, and draw conclusions.

Another name which is sometimes used is 'unstructured'.

The approach is essentially person-centred and group-based. The task of the group is to observe and study the way the group is functioning while this is actually happening. The task of the individual is to examine his or her own behaviour and personal role within the group, and the impact that he/she is having on others, again while actually engaged with the group. Attention is therefore on the present moment. This is often referred to as 'working in the here and now'.

The reference points, and the data for study, come from within the group itself. Outside forces, back home situations, and formal designations are all left 'outside' the 'laboratory'. There is little or no external accountability. The learning is the conceptual understanding and insight which comes from this experience, together with increased self-awareness, improved sensitivity, and enhanced skills in relating to others.

The role of the trainer, typically called a facilitator here, is to help members to focus on the way the group is working, and on the issues facing the group. He/she also helps individuals and the group to examine and understand experiences within the group. The 'methods' include group dynamics, sensitivity training, personal growth laboratory, T-groups, community change laboratory, and group relations conferences.

If the focus is mainly on the working of the group, rather than on individuals, then the dynamics of participation, decision-making, leadership, power, authority and conflict are all likely to be examined, along with other dimensions. These are all central issues in any organizational or community setting, and development workers need, not only to recognize them, but be able to work with them.

If the focus is mainly on individuals within the group then the members become more aware of themselves and how they are perceived by others, understand more about how they themselves function and relate to others, and how they can improve their 'people skills' and become more effective in their work roles. Such understanding is also central in development work.

The approach assumes that a person's inner psychological realities are relevant to learning and to their work in the outer world. It makes more explicit the link between the assumptions, aspirations, values, etc of the inner world, and the roles, decision-making, leadership, and action of the outer world. It also assumes that people can translate their experience and learning in the 'laboratory' into new ways of working when they return home.

The learning has a deep and lasting quality, which is often personal to the learner. The individual who joins such a training group may be expected to disclose more of him/herself, and to receive more feedback, than in other approaches. Feelings are often exposed. The experience can be exciting and challenging; it may also have disturbing and even painful moments. Some people say that if learning is to be effective it should disturb us!

Such training can be difficult to handle effectively, and requires trained facilitators. Teachers and trainers who are used to a more conventional academic approach may find this approach open-ended, unpredictable and complex.

This kind of training is usually offered to those who want to increase their own awareness and improve their own skills. It is particularly helpful in situations and professions where there are systemic disparities in power, such as community and development work, social and youth work, prison and probation services, and management. Many development workers who have experienced such training have gained important insights and have greatly improved the quality of their work with others. It is especially useful for those with responsibility for training.

Action-Reflection

Finally there is the quadrant which lies between Process and Action. Training here consists mainly of providing course members with alternating opportunities for 'action and reflection'. They experience an action, and then they reflect on it. They work at a task which is related to some aspect of development work, and then they think about the process. What happened? How did it happen? Why did it happen? How is it relevant?

The approach is also referred to as experience-based or experiential. Learning arises from the direct experience of the course member, but that experience has to be analyzed. Simply doing something is not enough. We need to look at ourselves in the process of doing it. Experience that is not analyzed and reflected upon is like food we eat but which passes through our system undigested — it does us no good.

The basic tool for the approach is alternations which reinforce learning. Action is followed by reflection, group events alternate with individual work, personal involvement alternates with impersonal analysis and input. We move between the specific and the general. We do something and then talk about it, and vice versa. We generalize from practice to build up theory, and understand theory by putting it into practice.

In methods such as simulation, role play and case studies, members encounter problems which are similar to those they encounter back home. They work on these in collaboration with the other members, whose perspectives are more, or less, similar.

> ...they analyze, elucidate, and understand the factors that underlie the experiences they have just had and the points of view with which they approached them.[4]

Trainers take up supporting and interactive roles as much as leading roles. They become organizers of learning opportunities, facilitators, resource people, observers and participants. Trainees and course members take much of the responsibility for their own learning. This approach encourages members to mobilize their own experience and resources, and they learn much from each other. The emphasis is on sharing perceptions and insights. The learning process is co-operative.

The approach assumes that training and learning embrace many aspects of the person — attitudes, assumptions, feelings, values, motivation, behaviour, creativity — as well as knowledge and skills. Learning is more than intellectual, it is wholistic. 'Education is not for knowing more, but for behaving differently.'[5]

A climate in the group which encourages exploration, and supports divergent thinking, is more important than a consensus around 'right answers'. 'Right answers' in development work are often dangerous.

> This strategy does not lead to improvements limited to a specific job or situation but to widening and deepening the participants' competence to understand and deal with many situations. What to think is taken to be a less potent learning than how to think.[6]

The learning from this approach is often deep. Confucius is supposed to have said, 'What we do, we know.' Research suggests that we remember 80—90% of what we discover and do for ourselves.

> The outcomes of such training, when successful, include greater effectiveness in communicating and working with others; greater awareness of process; greater understanding of individual, group and organisational roles and relationships; greater sensitivity to the needs of others; greater self-confidence; more listening and less 'telling'; a greater understanding of power, conflict, and change; a clearer insight into the dynamics of autonomy and participation; and an increased commitment to participation. Such outcomes are democratic, developmental, and — to some — subversive.[7]

---

4. Lynton and Pareek, page 45.
5. Attributed to John Ruskin, British educationist and writer.
6. Lynton and Pareek, page 45.
7. John Staley, 'Participation in Training or Training in Participation?' *The Rural Extension Bulletin*, Number 6, pages 13—15.

In conclusion, and perhaps needless to add, approaches to training cannot be separated into quadrants as neatly as the diagram suggests. Most courses include elements from more than one approach. The DSC itself was a combination of the academic with action-reflection.

It is the events and methods which contributed to the action-reflection approach that are included in this manual.

▶ ...*the action and reflection method has emphasised our own feelings, beliefs, opinions, strengths and weaknesses. This method increases creativity and self-confidence. It addresses the whole human being...*

▶ *Not a day has passed without some exercise, simulation, role play, case study or visit, followed of course by reflection and sharing. Yes, by now we all reflect in our sleep. J expressed his preference for this type of training. I too think it is an excellent method. But I have done these activities in other courses with little or no success. I realise the importance of preparation, and I would say that the reason this process has been such a success is that our tutors have prepared and developed the course...*

▶ ...*we've been challenged and questioned, sculpted and directed, we've planned and presented, talked and persuaded...*

▶ ...*the varied training methods make each day different and interesting.*

▶ ...*the day has been a real cocktail.*

▶ *Some days it is just too much, with all this group work.*

Indicate which statement in each pair (a or b) fits better with your own ideas about training.

a (   ) The main focus of training should be the job which has to be done.
b (   ) The main focus of training should be the person who has to do the job.

a (   ) It is most important that a trainer should understand the subject and its applications.
b (   ) It is most important that a trainer should understand the course members and their situations.

a (   ) One of the trainer's tasks is to 'cover' the topics and issues which are to be studied.
b (   ) One of the trainer's tasks is to 'uncover' the course members' experience of the topics and issues which are to be studied.

a (   ) One of the trainer's tasks is to provide answers which course members can apply to their own situations.
b (   ) One of the trainer's tasks is to raise questions which course members can apply to their own situations.

a (   ) An outcome of training should be that course members do more things right
b (   ) An outcome of training should be that course members do more right things.

Discuss your choices in groups of three or four.

Adapted in part from 'Approaches to Training' in *Management Self-Development: A Practical Guide for Managers and Trainers*, MSC, pages 314—316

Puzzling It Out: Using Case Studies

▶ *The next session was a case study. Participants were divided into two groups and went into different rooms for a critical study of the document... My group of people were really interacting and they analysed every aspect ...*

▶ *One gets the feeling that most of the people find themselves somewhere in the case studies ...*

A case study is 'a slice of real life' from the experience of an actual person in a role similar to the one that we ourselves are in. Through the case that person offers his or her experience as material for us to work with. As we respond to it, in discussion with others, we find that we are also working with our own experience, perhaps at several levels.

> The teaching of cases is one of many attempts to get more of real life into classrooms and training programmes. Ideally, cases confront the member of the discussion group with situations which faced someone like himself somewhere, sometime. They present a chunk of somebody's real life, but not of the member's own life. As pieces of real life they are full of people, not of abstractions, and too complex to be fitted into neat categories, generalizations, and other intellectual equipment.
>
> As somebody else's experience, a case can help the member explore his own attitudes and behaviour as if by personal analogy, at moments when direct attention to his own experiences would provoke only fear and defence, not learning. Doing it by analogy instead of for himself in the commitments of real life increases his freedom to explore more of the ins and outs of a problem which he might otherwise ignore, and to go beyond his habitual response into an exploration of second and third thoughts instead of settling for the first.[1]

Some training programmes use the term 'case study' more loosely. They apply it to examples of organizational practice or to models of 'how to do' something. Some use it to illustrate issues and principles. When used like this, the material is no longer drawn from the real world of individual experience; but becomes the means of teaching a lesson. The more didactic the material, the less real it will seem. This is not to dismiss the usefulness of written 'teaching' materials as such, but to suggest that they belong to other methods, such as discussion papers (page 210). Throughout this manual, the method of case study is understood in a person-centred, 'real life', and exploratory sense.

The essence of the method is individual reading and reflection followed by discussion in groups of six to eight members, assisted by a trainer in the role of facilitator. The length of case varies, but short ones of a page or two are suitable to start with. It is

---

1. Harriet Lynton and Rolf P. Lynton, *Asican Cases*, Volume I, Aloka, Mysore, page 1.

usually possible to discuss two short cases in one session. The method is suitable for the afternoon because it is interactive (less likelihood of members sleeping), but also because there may be less pressure on time in the afternoon and so the discussion can be more considered and reflective. For members who are accustomed to constant activity, the method offers a change of pace which may be beneficial in itself.

It is a method that needs practice and continuation. Case studies should be introduced during the first week, and should then be included several times a week. Isolated cases once in a while will not be effective.

Objectives

- to improve members' skills:
  in the handling of information and assumptions;
  in the formulation and use of questions;
  in the analysis of situations and problems;
  in seeking resolutions and making decisions;
  in presenting an understanding and a point of view.

- to encourage members:
  to practise using their imagination;
  to seek alternative interpretations and to value differing 'points of view';
  to take more factors into account and to give importance to 'second thoughts';
  to work with alternative or conditional conclusions, as opposed to 'right answers';
  to 're-view' past experience and reconsider conclusions that they may have drawn.

- to increase members' sensitivity to, and understanding of, human behaviour, feelings, motives, and the dynamics of relationships;

- to improve members' effectiveness in communicating and working with others.

Introducing the Case Study Method

■ Before taking the first case study in a course you should introduce the method to the whole group briefly, drawing on the above and the following points. If any members have come across case studies previously make it clear to them that an exploratory — rather than didactic — approach will be followed.

- Case studies are narrative descriptions of individual experience in everyday life. They are usually told in the first person, and are concrete and specific, rather than abstract or general.

- They are about people. They are essentially an account of someone's experience with other people in some situation or sequence of events, and often lead to a difficulty or a dilemma, or even a conflict. All names are disguised, both to protect the originator of the case, and to avoid the possibility of 'inside information'.[2]

- The obvious task is to study the case, to look at the facts and information which are given, to uncover the assumptions being made, to analyse the forces and factors that may be at work, to recognize the ways in which the situation can be understood, and to identify the questions that need to be raised.

- The more subtle task is to 'enter into' the case in imagination, and apply sensitivity and insight to the feelings, motives and behaviour of the people involved. When the case study presents experience from a role which is similar to our own, then our identification with it may be deeper:
  'I had an experience like that ...'
  'That happened to me once ...'
  'I used to work with someone like that ...'

- This process of identification allows the member to bring more of his/her own experience to bear in the analysis and discussion. Without such identification, the case study may remain at a distance — interesting reading perhaps, but without engagement or challenge.

- The learning from case studies is individual. There may be a general consensus or broad agreement at the end of the discussion — or there may not. Agreed conclusions within the group are not required. Indeed an effective case study will generate differing perceptions and points of view, and lead to differing interpretations and alternative 'solutions'.

- Perhaps the most valuable learning from the method is that there is seldom a single conclusion or 'right answer' in any situation. Development itself is about generating alternatives and then making choices, rather than accepting the first or the simplest or the conventional answer. Case studies — like development work — are about recognizing the alternatives.

- Some members will be comfortable with the method from the beginning, but others may find it uncomfortable — inconclusive, or diffuse, or divergent. Make it clear that it is a method which repays practice. Once any initial hesitation had been overcome it became a favourite method with every DSC group.

- The role of the trainer is to encourage members to respond to the case and to each other, to encourage divergent views, and to help the group sort out its ideas. It is not the role of the trainer to 'chair' and control the discussion, nor to lead the group to 'correct' conclusions.

■ Distribute the case studies in advance for members to read. If it is a short case you may do this at the beginning of the session itself, and allow 10 or 15 minutes for reading

---

2. Even the broadest labels should be disguised. For example, if a case is labelled 'North African', any North Africans in the group may be assumed to have expert knowledge, while those from elsewhere may withdraw and say that they do not know that region.

■ and individual reflection before beginning the discussion. Every member then has the same opportunity for reading, and the material will be fresh in their minds. If two short cases are to be taken in one session you should give one at a time. This allows you to make a final choice of the second case after you see how the group responds to the first and how the time is going.

Alternatively, distribute the cases a day or two in advance. This helps any members who have difficulty with the language, gives time in advance for reflection, and allows the whole session to be devoted to the discussion. The disadvantage is that some members may fail to prepare in advance, and may be reading — or rereading and reminding themselves — while others are trying to start the discussion.

When a case study is to be distributed and read in the session itself, some members may like to take it in turn to read paragraphs aloud. Others prefer to read individually and silently. Ask the group if they have any preference, or try both procedures and discuss them.

As the method is exploratory and reflective allow the members ample time, not only for reading the material and thinking about it, but also for discussing it. It is better to work with one case in depth than to touch on two superficially.

Form the small groups at random. A group of seven or eight is ideal. Less than five members do not generate enough variation, while more than ten becomes unwieldy. Change the composition of the groups with each case study session.

Each small group will require a trainer to act as facilitator. It is important that trainers approach the role and the method with similar understandings.

Using Case Studies

The Trainer as Facilitator

One of the skills every trainer needs is to be able to change roles, and to adopt a role which is appropriate to the method being used. In the discussion of case studies the trainer's role is that of 'facilitator', which literally means someone who makes matters easier.

> The role of the facilitator is to assist the members in their discussion. The facilitator does this by asking questions, seeking clarifications, inviting interpretations and speculations, and pointing out contradictions. He/she helps members to identify, and bring out into the open, the values they demonstrate and the assumptions they are making; and helps them to distinguish conclusions for which there is evidence from those which are based on intuition or guess-work. When the group has exhausted its own insights, he/she may add to them with his own. The facilitator also maintains the links between the material in the case, the members' own personal experiences and

viewpoints, and their individual reactions to the case. In short, the facilitator helps the members to look at the data, to listen to each other, and to understand the experience that is being shared with them.[3]

This is clearly different from chairing a meeting or moderating a discussion, which may be more familiar roles. Compared with those roles, the facilitator of a case study is more attentive to the group and members themselves, and more responsive to their contributions, working with these and with the case material as the discussion emerges. The main tool for the role is questions directed to the group.

■ Before the work begins make it clear to the members of your small group that you will be adopting the role of facilitator.[4] To emphasize the switch in role, you may choose not to sit in a chair or position usually associated with leading or authority. It is enough for this role if you are able to see every person in the group.

After the members have had an opportunity to read and reflect on the first case study — either in the session or in advance — start by inviting them to react, to comment, or to interpret anything they have perceived or felt or understood:
　'What strikes you as you read this?'
　'Are there any difficult words you would like explained?'
　'Does it seem familiar or strange?'
　'Who is going to begin?'

Listen to any contributions in whatever order they are offered, and allow them to flow. Do not call the members to order, nor control who speaks, nor direct the discussion, nor confine it to a particular content or agenda, nor expound your own ideas.

In the first session or two the contributions may not flow freely. There can be many reasons. The course methodology as a whole may still be unfamiliar. In an international group the language or culture may be unfamiliar. The level of dependency in the group may be high, and the members may be expecting you, as trainer, to tell them how they should understand the case. There may be unresolved difficulties between the members of the group itself.

You should anticipate such constraints and be ready to accept silence from some or all of the group. Do not allow your own feelings of anxiety to be the reason for taking too much of a lead. In this situation some more broad questions may help:
　'Do you think you have understood the situation in the case?'
　'As you were reading it, how did you react?'
　'Can you imagine such a situation/conversation/thing happening ...?'
　'Where would anyone like to start?'

---

3. Adapted from John Staley, *The Watch: A Case*, SEARCH, Bangalore, page 1.
4. It is then important that you do adopt the role of facilitator and stick to it. Resist the habit or comfort of a more familiar role. The group members too may feel more comfortable if the trainer reverts to a familiar role, and their expectations can add to the pressure on a trainer if he/she is not clear about this.

■ If the group continues to have difficulty in getting to grips with the case — or with each other — some discussion may start which is not on the case but on some other external matter or preoccupation. If this continues for some minutes, draw attention to it, and perhaps ask why it is happening. Then bring attention back to the case:

'We seem to have moved our attention from the case. Is there a reason for that?'

'We seem to be far away from the situation in the case now.'

'Is there a difficulty in getting to grips with this case?'

'How do you feel about the discussion so far?'

If members complain that there is not enough information given, or that key facts are missing or that there is no conclusion to the narrative, remind them of some of the introductory points. You may also point out that in case studies — as in our work back home — we 'manage' with what is available. If the group continues to have difficulty in getting started, some more facilitating questions may help them:

'How familiar does this problem seem to anyone?'

'Does anyone recognize this kind of situation?'

'Has anyone had an experience of this kind?'

Sooner or later the discussion will start!

In the early sessions, before they have worked together much, members may tend to talk about whatever is suggested to their own minds by the case, and their contributions may seem scattered and unrelated to each other. Sometimes two or three topics prompted by the material come under discussion at the same time, each being pursued separately by one or more members, without reference to what others may be discussing. This does not matter, but if the discussion continues in this fashion you may draw attention to it, and invite the members to consider why it is happening:

'What does our discussion suggest to you about the way this group is working?'

'How many discussions are we having in the group at present?'

'How do you see the members of our group here relating to one another?'

'Does what is happening in our discussion reflect anything about the case itself?'

Disconnected and simultaneous contributions tend to be made in newly-formed groups, especially while members' attention remains on content and issues. Later, as the members work more together, and gain experience of each other, their contributions will tend to overlap and relate to what has gone before. Finally, as the group itself grows, they will be able to listen to each other and build on each others' contributions. Achieving this may take days, or weeks, but when it happens it gives satisfaction to members and to the facilitator.

Holding On to the Role

Members' previous experience of work in groups, large or small, may have accustomed them to speak to a person in authority — the chairperson or the supervisor — whereas the case study method is based on peer interaction. You may need to encourage members to make contributions into the group as a whole, and to speak directly to one another.

Beware of behaving like a chairperson — catching eyes, nodding, giving small signals of approval or disapproval — especially after you have already said that you are not in that role!

■ If members continue to address their contributions to you, even after several case studies, it may indicate dependence, and you can draw attention to it and discuss it.

If the members seem to be focussing only on issues — which is again more likely when the method is new — draw attention to the people in the case and encourage the members to consider the human dimension:

'Who are the people in this case study?'
'Are we focussing on the problem and overlooking the person?'
'What do we know about this development worker?'
'What do you imagine the community leader was feeling at that moment?'
'What is the mood of the writer of the case study?'
'We are a small group sitting here now: is that an issue among us too?'

After the initial contributions, and as the discussion proceeds, you may think that the members could probe more. Raise questions to help them look deeper, both at the situation and at the people in the case:

'Why has Mr A caused the difficulty? How do you imagine that?'
'How do you see Mr B's position in that situation?'
'How do you understand Mr C's behaviour?'

'What assumptions are you making?'
'Can you reconcile your view with what W said earlier?'
'Do the suggestions of X contradict those of Y?'
'Is there another possible view?'

Deepening the thinking and understanding will help to expose and dispel trite or easy answers.

Some members may be used to reaching decisions and judgements quickly, and may be less comfortable with an exploratory and — for them — discursive discussion. You should be alert for any tendency among members to pass rapid judgements on the people in the case, to criticize their actions in a dismissive way, to produce 'the obvious solution' or 'the correct answer', or to diminish a situation by over-simplification. If there are tendencies in the group to arrive at comfortable conclusions be ready to challenge them:

'That is one view of Mr D's conduct? Can there be other views of it?'
'What other options did the development worker have at that moment?'
'Can you say why you are so critical of the decision which Mrs E took?'
'You think that the problem is simply Mr F's incompetence: does that explain everything?'
'What would you have done yourself in Mrs G's situation?'
'Is it as simple as that?'
'Does anyone have any second thoughts now?'

Sometimes the discussion may lead to a certain view being taken at the beginning, but another view coming to prevail later on. There may even be a complete reversal of the perceptions of the group by the end of the discussion. If this happens it may be helpful to draw attention to it, especially if some members did rush to judgement in the early part of the discussion.

■ Help the members to sort out and clarify which of their contributions and opinions are based on previous experience, which are based on attitudes or preconceptions, which are based on imagination and guess-work, and which are based on facts and information given in the case. All may be acceptable and helpful during the discussion of a case, but it is important that members begin to make such distinctions and recognize them for what they are:

'What is the evidence for what you are saying?'
'Is there anything in the case itself to support that idea?'
'Can you say where your suggestion comes from?'
'Are you speaking now about some experience of your own?'
'Is that a guess?'
'What is your attitude towards someone who does that?'

If members make different or even contradictory contributions, encourage this but draw attention to the differences:

'It seems to me that T is seeing it like this... and Z is seeing it like that...'
'V likes the suggestion... Y accepts the suggestion, but would handle the matter differently... U distrusts the suggestion...'
'W and X have different opinions about what could be done — why is that?'

Indeed if differences of understanding and opinion do not emerge in the group after two or three cases, you may want to help the group to deal with their avoidance of each other:

'Are there other opinions?'
'Can we imagine how other managers might have done it?'
'We have had one view, but there are others? What are they?'
'How else could we understand Mr H's behaviour in the case study?'

The purpose is not to encourage disagreement or conflict for its own sake, but to work towards a climate in which individual members feel able to say what they think and feel, and are willing to disagree with one another.

When differences of interpretation are apparent, you should help the members to unravel the assumptions, perceptions, values, culture, experience, ideology and so on which may underlie the differences and contradictions.

You may be able to help members to discover that the group can contain its differences, and that members can 'disagree agreeably' without damaging relationships or each other.

The Process in the Group

At one or more points during the discussion, if you think that it will be helpful, invite the members to consider the process taking place within the discussion group:

'How do you feel about the discussion we are having on this case?'
'What did you think about the participation in our group here?'
'Is this group functioning differently from the group in the case study?'

■ 'Do you see any parallels between this group's functioning and the conflict which we have identified in the case?'

Some members will contribute more than others. Some will thrive on the method, some will have had more relevant experience, some are more articulate, some simply talk more freely. As the course progresses, some members may become aware that they have a tendency to dominate discussions, and will reduce their contributions accordingly. Other members may hold back only if they receive feedback that they are dominating.

On the other hand there may be members whose culture or personality makes it difficult for them to contribute to a discussion without a specific invitation. If you recognize this during the early days of a course, you may want to offer openings to such members:

'Would anyone who has not already spoken like to speak now?'
'Would *you* like to say anything?'
'Is there anything *you* would like to add?'
'Do *you* have any other view on this?'

It is important to present these openings as invitations. Do not to put silent members on the spot by confronting them over their silence, or expecting them to speak and demanding their opinion.

If the case is a familiar one, you may know already some of the possibilities it holds for discussion, but you should hold these in reserve. The purpose is not to keep something from the group, nor to remain aloof, but to make space for the members' contributions, to encourage and give attention to all their views, and to avoid the risk of your interpretation being assumed the correct one.

So only after the group has exhausted its own insights, should you share your own, perhaps as further possibilities or questions:

'Is there another possibility we have not considered...?'
'I would like you to think about another way we might understand this ...'
'You have all assumed that ...'
'We have had two interpretations of the manager's behaviour, but I think
there could be a third ...'
'In my own imagination this development worker ...'

The trainer's opinion will be more of an issue at the beginning of a course. Later you can expect that all views expressed in a case discussion will be heard and considered for what they are worth, irrespective of the contributor.

As the discussion proceeds, the material in the case may unravel so far that it seems impossible for the group to come to any agreed or clear conclusion. Some members will find this most uncomfortable. They may be committed to the idea of identifying a 'right answer' and then deciding how they would act on it. If they cannot identify the answer for themselves they may expect to be told what it is. When you, as the facilitator, fail to do this, or sum up by presenting a range of alternatives, such members may express frustration over a method that they find inconclusive and even disturbing.

■ It is important that you accept such feelings, explain the rationale, but adhere to the method. It is also important that any uncertainty about outcomes and conclusions is clearly identified, accepted and stated by you. If you handle uncertainty in an irresolute or vacillating way yourself, you may not help members to confront uncertainty for themselves.

Coming to an End

As discussion of a case comes towards an end, there may be suggestions about what could be done 'in a case like that'. Here again there may be differing opinions, and the group can be encouraged to identify all the possibilities. You should encourage members to 'test' their ideas and suggestions against real life experience. Some suggestions may need to be challenged:

'How would that work in practice...?'

'How will you explain your proposal to the local leaders...?'

'Has anyone any experience of action of that kind?'

'Can you really imagine saying that to the boss?'

'Would that suggestion be feasible in your own organization?'

'Would it work in that culture?'

This testing against reality helps the group to avoid the trap of 'classroom solutions'.

The discussion of some case studies may lead into simple role-play. At the end of a discussion of Mr Ebor (page 183), for example, you can invite two members to take the roles of Mr Ebor and Mr Vasar and try out different approaches.

Bringing the discussion of a case study to an end offers opportunities for three kinds of reflection. The first is on the content of the case study. Make a summary of the content of the discussion, and review the ground which has been covered. You can point to where the group's attention has been concentrated in the case, to the analysis and interpretations which have been offered, and to the contradictions, questions and speculations which have emerged. Invite the members to make any final comments on the case and to share their individual conclusions.

Secondly, turn attention to the process of the discussion. Invite members to make their observations, and make your own. It may be useful if members can relate their experience of working on the case to experiences in other groups and in communities back home. Levels of participation, the roles we play, the quality of listening, disagreements, silence, levels of energy and so on, are the phenomena of any group at work together.

Thirdly, invite the members to reflect individually on how they have responded to the case, on what feelings were triggered in them during the discussion, on what was motivating them when they contributed, and whether they have gained any insight into themselves.[5]

---

5. 'The subtle process of identifying with people and their feelings in a case is not only a means to elucidate the case material. It is also an opportunity for me to work on my own experience, but at one stage removed. In this process I become simultaneously observer and participant. If I am conscious of myself as this happens, I have a rich opportunity for learning about myself. I may realize that when I talk about a person in the case, I am saying something about myself. When I react in the discussion with feeling, I can ask myself, 'Why...?' Why do I find myself defending certain behaviour in the case? Or criticising other behaviour? What does this tell me about my own values and assumptions? When identification is strong, a case study becomes a clear and powerful mirror.' John Staley, unpublished MS.

■ Inevitably, the points above deal more with the possible pitfalls in discussing case studies. However many groups quickly become skilled at the method, and are then able to analyze cases and enter into them in an effective and fruitful way.

Listening to a group that has this skill and insight is an affirming experience for the trainer.

▶ *Our tutors are very clever. Now I understand why they always have group activity or case studies in the afternoon sessions. Do you know why, dear Diary? Because we are here to learn and study, not to have sleep during the sessions.*

▶ *We are not sure about the 'results' of cases... One friend said if we have 'the answers' to the cases we can compare them with our own conclusions. Another member said we had different ideas. L said case study is telling the story to a certain point and we don't know about the future of the case, so people share their feeling and judgement... To support this idea members said that:*

    1. Cases are open and tutors don't know the right answer

    2. Nobody can give us the right answer

    3. We are seeing case studies from different angles

and I am saying that if we have all information that is not a case...

▶ *...we discussed two case studies. Two observations:*

    1. We are still not challenging one another in such group discussions. Why?

    2. We are tearing the poor 'development actors' in the case studies apart. Why?

▶ *We shared freely, covering different points of view, neither threatened nor keen on converting any to our point of view. One case and then another. The point is I could have been that community worker, or the chairman, or Mrs D' Souza...*

▶ *We came to the conclusion that in case study method one has to explore a lot... and that there are a lot of ways of looking at the case...*

Case studies are written accounts of experience from real life, 'slices' of life. They are therefore 'personal', concerned with persons in situations or in relationship with others. They are often written in the first person, 'I'. The focus is on the person or people and on processes, not on abstractions or principles, and not on generalized problems and issues. What makes them relevant and meaningful to the learning process is not so much their content, but the recognition of a similarity of role and of individual experience.

They are most effective when taken from ordinary everyday experience. Extraordinary events may attract attention, and may remain in the memory, but that does not make them useful as case studies. Ordinary experience which may be otherwise unexamined, but which contains some tension or unresolved matter, may be suitable.

The experience is usually presented in a 'concrete' way. The case relates what happened, who said what, and how particular people behaved on a particular occasion, but is presented without interpretation or resolution. The form is narrative, like a story, and the ending may be left open. If direct speech can be included — quoting the very words spoken between people — it is helpful both to illustrate the case and to add reality.

Case studies may be short — one page is often enough — but they should have enough depth to offer stimulation and puzzlement, with potential for differing interpretations, fresh insights, and second (or third) thoughts. If they lead to over-simple solutions, comfortable generalizations or easy consensus they will not serve their purpose. A successful case study encourages divergence in thinking rather than convergence.

It is not easy to find case studies that meet such criteria. Many of the so-called case studies which are in circulation are too didactic to be useful for this method. The difficulty may seem greater when the course group is international or multi-cultural or has a wide range of experience. However what unites the members of such a group, and enables them to work together effectively, is their shared humanity and their common experience of human relationships, which is precisely the subject matter of effective case studies.

Some international training courses in development work have published collections of their own case studies. These are particularly relevant because the cases have been contributed by the trainees on the courses. Batten's *The Human Factor in Community Work*[1] and Lynton's *Asican Cases*[2] are examples. Both contain case studies which relate to common human experience in familiar roles at an everyday level, and where the focus is on the process as much as upon the content. Neither publication is recent, but this is not important: the nature of human and organizational relationships hardly changes, any more than human nature changes. The experience contained in these cases is as relevant as experience today, and goes to show how each generation of workers goes through a similar learning process.

From the Batten collection the cases He Meant Well, The Brick Factory, Mrs de Souza, and The Would-Be Benefactors have been used regularly in the DSC. Each of them describes the process and dynamics of human relationships, none are as simple as they first appear, and all are capable of differing interpretations and conclusions. These four case studies, in versions adapted to voluntary agencies and NGOs, are included in this section as handouts. (Other cases from the same collection which have been useful in the DSC are The Tamarind Tree Group, The Unused Library, The Sheikh and the Schoolmaster, and The Dissatisfied Volunteers).

From the Lynton collection, Mr Ebor has often been used. This case is full of possibilities, and can support other work on listening and feelings. (Autobiography of a Future Trainer and The Grass-Planting have also been useful, but these require more time). Mr Ebor is included among the handouts in this section.

Other useful collections include those of Wadhera[3] (Working with the Community's Help and Dealing with Difficult Trainees); Bacie[4] (The New Emperor and The Training Department); Nturibi[5] (Mr. Musoma); Taylor and Jenkins[6] (The Famous Director and The Puppet Show); and Visocchi.[7] (Forty Years). The above cases from these collections have been used frequently in the DSC, and are included in adapted versions among the handouts. Some of the other cases in these collections are focused more on issues and content.

Members and tutors of the DSC have themselves contributed case studies. Those which have often been used include The VDC's Garden, Art and Cho, Silence, A Soft Discussion, Whom are We Serving? Dr Joseph, The Counterpart and the Director, The Diocesan Community Worker, Committee Meetings, and Working for a Foreign Agency. These are included among the handouts.

How does the trainer choose which case study to use, in which order, and when? This depends on how he/she observes and understands the process within the course group, on where the members' attention is directed at that time in the course, and on

1. T. R. Batten, *The Human Factor in Community Work*, OUP, Oxford.
2. Harriet Lynton and Rolf P. Lynton, *Asican Cases*, Volume 1, Aloka, Mysore.
3. Kiron Wadhera, *Case Study: A Method of Training*, Vishwa Yuvak Kendra, New Delhi.
4. *Bacie Case Studies*, British Association for Commercial and Industrial Education, London.
5. D. Nturibi, *With Practice*, Commonwealth Youth Programme, London.
6. Laurence Taylor and Peter Jenkins, *Time to Listen: the Human Aspect in Development*, IT Publications, London.
7. A. M. Visocchi, *Non-Formal Education for Rural Development*, Manchester Monographs 9, Manchester.

what stage the trainer thinks their learning has reached. For example, He Meant Well may be suitable in the early days of a course, partly because it is straightforward, and partly because the case itself concerns new relationships. A few days later Mrs de Souza may become appropriate, perhaps at a point when the group is finding that human behaviour is neither simple nor easily discerned. Mr Ebor may be helpful when feelings and ambiguity become an issue in the group itself, even if the members are not yet conscious of that. Dr Joseph may be useful as differences are explored. Mr Musoma and The Diocesan Community Worker are appropriate as members begin to anticipate applying their new learning back home.

As the course progresses, and as the group members become skilled in teasing case studies apart, and as they become more effective at working together, they can be given increasingly challenging material. In choosing case studies, trainers should be guided principally by their understanding of the group, its needs and its learning.

Trainers may be concerned that, after hearing a case discussed several times, they will become over-familiar with it. However this should not happen so long as their focus remains on the current group and the interaction of its members. With alert and effective groups an appropriate case study, however familiar, continues to generate new insights, new possibilities and new interactions, even for experienced trainers.

▶ *The first case study our group looked at was with Mr Ebor and Mr Vasar. Reflecting on the process, we read aloud and understood, discussed what happened and then tried to discover the feelings and motivations of the people involved. Mr Vasar seemed an understanding person and was able to find out what happened, but did not ask about Ebor's feelings. I felt Ebor was initially angry and hurt by the chairman's scolding which led him, like a child to a father, to Mr Vasar with a cry for help and support...*

▶ *...we tried to discover the feelings and relationship among Ebor, Vasar and the Chairman...*
   1. *Did Vasar and the Chairman know the feelings of Ebor?...*
   2. *Was Ebor angry with the Chairman?*
   3. *Was he unhappy with Vasar when he left the office?*

▶ *...all of us felt sorry for the community worker who waited and waited...*

▶ *...we would have advised the writer to take the job...*

A few years ago I was working with some village development committees in relation to whatever projects they wished to undertake. I got on quite well until one day I found difficulties at a meeting of a newly-formed committee.

The Chairman and committee members greeted me very warmly, and I was feeling happy when we got down to business. However this feeling did not last, for I soon realised that I was in for a really bad meeting. The members of the committee were keen enough, but they had no idea how a meeting should be run — and their Chairman, Mr Wong, least of all. He did nothing to keep the members in order, and since most of them were pushing their own schemes and arguing against the schemes of others, you can imagine what it was like. There was hardly a moment when three or four people were not talking at once.

I stuck it as long as I could but then I felt I could bear it no longer. Luckily, I was sitting next to the Chairman, so I pointed out what was happening and suggested that they would get on much better if he called the members to order and asked them to address their remarks to him instead of arguing among themselves as most of them were doing.

Well, I suppose he did his best, but his best was not much good. He knocked on the table and told them what I had said, but within a minute or two things were just as bad as before. Of course, the real trouble was that he had no idea at all of how to chair a meeting, and in a meeting like that it was quite impossible to try to teach him. Meanwhile, time was getting on. I realised that I would soon have to go, but I wanted to do something, and it seemed to me that the best thing to do would be to offer to come again for their next meeting to show them how a meeting ought to be run.

So that is what I did. I put my suggestion as tactfully as I could. Everyone seemed to think that it was quite a good idea. They agreed to meet again in two weeks' time, and I came away quite happy. It was true that the meeting had been a very bad one and that it had ended without any project being decided on, but I felt that there was now a real chance that things would go better next time.

However a few days later I received the following letter:

> *Thank you very much for so kindly visiting our committee meeting. It was good of you to come since we all know how busy you are. Regarding our next meeting, we have talked it over and feel it would be better if you did not come until after we had had a few more*

meetings and got more experience, as we do not want to waste too much of your time. Of course we shall be very pleased to see you later on.

It was a polite letter, but its meaning was clear enough. Rather than have me back they would prefer to muddle through on their own. But why? All I had done was to try and help them!

Adapted from T. R. Batten, *The Human Factor in Community Work*, OUP, pages 99—100

Case Study: The Brick Factory

I am a community worker in a country which suffered much during a recent war. One day last year I was visited by a group of six men all of whom came from the same village. They explained that they wanted to start again what had been a successful little brick-making factory. It had been destroyed during the war, and had not been started again afterwards because no one had enough money to rebuild it. They said, however, that they had now formed a co-operative society into which they were putting their savings, and they were also hoping to get a grant towards the cost of the building and the necessary machinery. There were many unemployed men in the village and everyone wanted the factory for the employment it would give. Could I do anything to help?

I said that I would be very willing to help them prepare their application for a grant, and that I could probably help them in other ways too. But, I said, were they quite sure that they would be able to make a success of the project in view of all the changes that had taken place since the war? I thought an expert opinion was needed, and offered to get an economist to study the situation and report on whether the project was likely to succeed or not.

The men agreed that this might be a good idea. I found a suitable expert and after a short time he made his report. In this report he advised against the project, mainly because he thought the men would have great trouble in selling their bricks, since they would now have to compete with the products of several big, modern brick-making factories. The men were very disappointed, and so were the people of the village from which they had come. The people were now divided, some arguing that they should go ahead with the project in spite of the expert's discouraging report, while many others were now afraid to try. This caused much bad feeling and in the end the project was given up. I was glad it was given up, for I didn't think it had much chance of success, but the whole episode has certainly had a bad effect on the villagers' attitude to me. Many of them think that I was not a bit interested in trying to help them, and some of them even think that I caused the project to fail. Was this result inevitable, or could I have avoided it if I had acted differently?

Adapted from T. R. Batten, *The Human Factor in Community Work*, OUP, pages 14—15

Case Study: Mrs de Souza

I am a development worker employed by a voluntary agency which runs a hospital and community health programme. It is my job to support communities that want to undertake self-help projects. I've had a good many successes, but also some failures. It is one of these failures that I want to tell you about now.

The whole thing began when the Doctor in charge of the programme asked me if I thought the people of Aurora village would be interested to lay a pipe to bring clean water to their school. The school's existing supply was very dirty and had to be brought to the school from a long way off. Many of the children were getting ill as a result.

Well, I discussed the idea with people in the village, and then I raised it at a meeting of the village development committee. The members received it favourably on the whole, but some of them wanted the water brought right into the centre of the village so that everyone could have it. Unfortunately, however, the spring from which the water was to be piped was very small and could not possibly provide enough water for everyone. When I pointed this out, one of the committee members, a Mrs de Souza, said immediately that if the spring was too small to supply the whole village she saw no point in discussing the idea any further. She thought it would be much better to think about some other project that would suit everyone.

This was too much for the schoolmaster, Mr Lawson, who quickly defended the scheme. He pointed out that the school was a long way away from the village well, and he stressed his difficulties at the school where water was always running short, and most of all in the hot weather. 'It's a real problem at times', he said, 'and I think we ought to have enough public spirit in the community to get support for this project. Besides, it needn't be only for the school. If the project goes through I shall be quite willing to let people take water there after school hours.'

This helped to turn opinion in favour of the project, and when at last the Chairman suggested that the committee should declare in favour of it, even Mrs de Souza unwillingly agreed. I went home that night feeling that I had done a good day's work, and within the next three months the pipe was laid.

After some time I visited Aurora again. When I had met the committee and congratulated its members on the good work they had already done, I asked if they were thinking of another project, and if so was there anything I could do to help.

Several members of the committee at once said that they had been thinking about building a village hall and were wondering whether I could help them get a grant. They wanted a hall badly as they had nowhere to meet except at the school, and that was not always convenient. They also proposed that our hospital should hold a weekly clinic in the new hall; and the Doctor readily agreed to the suggestion. I promised to do my best to get them a grant and said that I could also help with the plans. I then inquired about the site and was told by the schoolmaster, Mr. Lawson, that he and the Chairman had found a good site near the school, and that the owner was willing to give it free.

That seemed hopeful enough. We then got down to discussing details of planning and in due course I was able to help them get a grant from an agency in Europe. Thanks to the energy of the Chairman, the schoolmaster, and most other members of the committee, the people supported the project, cleared the site, and put in the foundations. But all was not really well. Apparently, Mrs de Souza had neither forgotten nor forgiven her defeat over the previous project. She felt resentment against the schoolmaster, and was further upset because this second project was also near the school. She lived at the far end of the village and benefitted least of all. She hadn't felt strong enough to challenge the committee openly, but now she did everything in her power to stir up discontent among her friends. What was even worse, she got up a petition which she sent to the Doctor.

I knew nothing of all this until one day I found a note on my desk from the Doctor. It read as follows:

> *I have been sent a petition signed by 97 of the villagers of Aurora protesting that the site selected for their new Village Hall is too far from the centre of the village, and complaining that they were not properly consulted at the time it was chosen.*
> *As it is our policy not to encourage or support any village project*

unless it is supported by everyone concerned, I do not understand the situation that has now arisen. Kindly meet me at your earliest convenience to explain the matter.

Well, that was that. Having that Mrs de Souza on the committee was a piece of bad luck. She's stirred up real trouble in that village and I don't think there's much chance of that village hall getting finished for a long time to come. But what can you do when you come up against people like that? What would you have done?

Adapted from T. R. Batten, *The Human Factor in Community Work*, OUP, pages 93—94

Case Study: The Would-Be Benefactors

I am a development worker employed by a voluntary organization. My organization supports and encourages the development efforts of local villages in various ways. I myself am a specialist in agriculture and fruit-growing. Fruit-growing is a major source of food in our area. If any village needs expertise in agriculture or fruit-growing, I am usually asked to help.

Last year I was asked to go to the village of San Pedro. The people there wanted to improve the varieties of fruit which they were growing, and the development committee of the village had asked my organization for some technical assistance. The problem was that this village was far from any nursery where saplings were being raised. So the development committee of the village wanted to know if they could raise saplings themselves. When I visited the village we discussed this, and I told them that, from the technical point of view, it would be possible to establish a nursery provided they could find a suitable site for it.

A couple of weeks later the chairman of the village committee wrote to say that two members of the committee, a Mr Degas and a Mr Bart, had both generously offered to give a site and that the committee would like my advice about which one to choose. The committee was meeting again in three days' time, and he suggested that I might inspect the sites before the meeting began.

So I went to San Pedro, inspected the sites, and decided on the one I preferred. At the meeting I congratulated the members of the committee on their decision to establish a nursery of their own, and on having on their committee two such public-spirited gentlemen as Mr Degas and Mr Bart. I then said that I had carefully inspected the two sites and had decided in favour of the one offered by Mr Bart.

'It has just the kind of well-drained sandy loam that young saplings like,' I said, 'and it has a well that can supply water during the dry season. Mr Degas's site has a good soil too, but it's a bit heavier and down there by the stream there's always a danger of flooding.'

Then the trouble started, for Mr Degas at once began arguing against my choice. 'It's all very well,' he said, 'for this gentleman to look around today and say that this site is better than that, but we've lived here all our lives and I, for one, don't agree with him. I doubt very much whether that well of Mr. Bart's will be able to supply all the water the nursery will need in the hot weather. And as for his talk about the danger of my site being flooded, I've never had any flood water there since the channel was cleared.'

This started a heated argument between the two men. I did what I could to smooth things over, and in the end most of the committee members came round to my way of thinking and voted in favour of Bart's site. Then we got down to making arrangements for work to start and this went through smoothly enough. In fact, Mr Degas never said another word. But although I've been to this village many times since, the nursery has never really got going.

To be quite honest, it's a flop and I wish it had never been started. I can't prove it, of course, but I'm sure that Degas has been stirring up trouble. He's got a lot of friends in the village and I don't think he's ever forgiven me for choosing Bart's site rather than his. Yet after all I only gave my honest opinion, and if I'd said that Degas's site was better, then Bart would have made trouble. So what else could I have done?

Adapted from T. R. Batten, *The Human Factor in Community Work*, OUP, pages 120—121

Case Study: Mr Ebor

The main purpose of the National Youth Agency is to encourage and train young people to take part in social service programmes. The Agency has a small paid staff, but is mostly run by part-time volunteers and committee members. Mr Ebor was the volunteer leader in charge of the Agency's work in a district near the national capital.

One Monday morning Mr Ebor entered the office of the national headquarters of the Agency. He made straight for the director's office. The director, Mr Vasar, was in and beckoned him to sit in the chair by his desk. Mr Ebor sat down but did not say a word, nor did he smile.

Vasar:
How are you, Ebor? Are you off work today?

Ebor:
No sir, I'm not free today, but I obtained permission from my boss to be off for the rest of this morning. I want to say something to you, so I came here.

Vasar:
What has happened, Ebor? Let me hear about it.

Ebor:
I want to lay down my post from today.

Vasar:
Why, what did you do?

Ebor: (Pause)
Well, yesterday afternoon I was training my group. During the training a young fellow, Roic, had a quarrel with his friend. As you know, he has had several quarrels with his friend before. I always thought he was a trouble-maker in his group. After every quarrel so far, I have always talked with him quietly and offered him advice. He replied each time that he would never quarrel again. When he did quarrel again yesterday I scolded him very loudly in front of the group. I thought I had to try some other method. Just then the chairman of our group committee came in and he saw that. After the training he called me to his home and said:
    'You are not right to scold your boys so loudly in front of your group.'
I appreciate his point, but I think it good for that boy to scold him in front of his group rather than telling him when he is on his own.

Vasar:
What did the chairman say after that?

Ebor:
He said he knew that boy since he was a baby. He is a little violent but only just a little bit. He said:
    'I have four children, three boys and one girl. These boys are very violent every day. Don't you know that a boy is full of high spirits? It must be very good for our group if there are many boys with high spirits. Roic is a boy, isn't he? You don't know about the psychology of boys because you do not have any child of your own.'

Vasar:
What do you think about his idea?

Ebor:
(Pause) I have held the position of the district leader for five years. I have attended many leaders' training courses. I know what the psychology of the boy is. I know the character of every boy in my group. I think it was the right thing to do to scold Roic in front of the group — right for him. Maybe that boy will never again pick a quarrel with his friends after this. Do you not think so?

Vasar:
I see. I think this is a very difficult problem in our work. I have understood what happened. But you know, I have only heard your side. I want to hear your chairman's point of view also. I will call him to come here tomorrow morning and ask him about yesterday's incident. I hope you will think again about what you did yesterday to the boy.

Ebor:
All right, I will see you tomorrow again. Goodbye.

Vasar: (Smiling)
Ebor, do you know what our Agency's motto is?
   'Service is a kindness, Service is a pleasure, Service is courage!'

Ebor also smiled and then left.

Adapted from Harriet Lynton and Rolf P. Lynton, *Asican Cases*, Volume 1, Aloka, page 7

Case Study: Working with the Community's Help

The Community Welfare Association was running a youth and community centre in a city slum area. In the beginning the association was quite active. Apart from running a kindergarten and tailoring classes, it conducted sanitation and vaccination campaigns, distributed medicines to the poorest and organized sports for the children. They were doing all this mainly with the help of part-time workers.

After five years, a new part-time worker, named Shila, was engaged by the CWA. Shila was a very enthusiastic worker, and had high hopes of improving the situation of the community. In her first visit to the community Shila was pleasantly surprised to find a number of young girls in the centre. She had a long chat with them, asking their names, what they were doing and so on. She also replied to questions put to her quite openly and informally.

The next day the number of girls increased to 35. On the third day she started playing games with them. The girls appeared to be quite happy.

After a week the number of girls started declining. When asked, those present gave evasive replies as to why others were absent. In another week the attendance declined further. Shila discussed this with the Director of the Centre, Mrs D. Mrs D told Shila that the attendance of girls always went up with the arrival of a new worker, and declined after their initial curiosity about the new worker was over.

Due to their indifference, she said, the CWA was unable to run any regular activities for them.

'They are simply not interested. What can we do?' she said.

This did not convince Shila. The next day Shila took one of the girls from the community with her and started visiting the girls' homes. She found most of the girls either engaged in some domestic activity or just idling around. They were quite surprised but happy to see Shila. Shila told them that since they were not coming to the centre she had decided to visit them.

Her conversation with the girls and their mothers revealed that they did not have a very high opinion of the centre and its workers. They considered the workers to be 'posh' people who came to the centre because they were paid. They did not believe that the workers were really interested in people.

Another important discovery was a fear among mothers who had grown-up daughters that these posh people would 'spoil' the daughters. They were not sure how their daughters spent their time in the centre.

With a view to building up mutual trust with the mothers, Shila started visiting them regularly. She asked them how they would like the girls to spend their time in the centre; and also invited them to visit the centre whenever they felt like it. The mothers said their girls should develop some talents and learn 'good things'.

After a month Shila introduced craft classes for them, and also arranged cooking demonstration classes. At the same time she started teaching them songs and dances. She also maintained contact with the girls' families, who were quite happy with the new activities.

National Day was just a month ahead. Shila suggested that they should organize a celebration of the day, and the girls should present their dances and songs. The girls were thrilled at the idea, but feared opposition from their parents. Shila took upon herself the responsibility of getting their parents' consent.

To her surprise, when Shila went and asked the parents for permission to bring their daughters onto the stage, they did not protest much. The general demand was that the centre should ensure peace and that no outsiders should be invited.

Shila discussed the matter with her other colleagues in the centre. They were not very enthusiastic. They said that the community was full of delinquents and thugs who would create problems, and that the centre had stopped conducting any public programmes because of this. Shila took upon herself the responsibility of seeing that everything would go well. After considerable discussion the other members agreed. However, they warned her against trouble, and told her to make arrangements for the police to come.

Shila did not like the idea of having the police around. However, to be on the safe side, she went to the local police station and arranged for the police to come if required.

She then found out from her colleagues who were the trouble-makers. The next day she invited these 'trouble-makers' to a cup of tea at the centre. They were six young men, 20 to 25 years old, and quite tough and well built. Soon after they arrived, one of them remarked sarcastically,

'We hear you are going to conduct a public programme to celebrate National Day.'

'Yes,' Shila said.

'You'd better give up the idea,' another one remarked.

'Why?' Shila asked.

'Because so far, in the last six years, no worker has succeeded in doing so,' replied the third.

'But why?'

'Oh, because there are so many trouble-makers here. Normally there is a fight and disturbance at such celebrations.'

'But let us make it different this time,' Shila said, 'In fact, this is the reason why I have called you. I want your help in making this celebration a success,' she said.

The boys exchanged glances, and then after a pause, the first one asked,

'What kind of help do you want from us?'

'Well, I want you to protect the place and to ensure that nobody makes any trouble. You are young men and tough also. I want you to undertake the responsibility of maintaining order in this place. You should take up positions at different corners, and also get the help of other boys of the slum as volunteers to see that the celebration runs smoothly.'

The young men assured her that they would do this, and that she should not worry. They asked her to arrange for some activities for boys also. Shila said she would discuss the matter with the people at the centre.

The National Day celebration was a grand success without any problems. Shila later thanked the young men. She also persuaded CWA to engage a voluntary worker to work with boys at the centre, and that was done within a month.

The worker visited twice a week and organized sports for boys. The boys of the slum were very happy about this.

Adapted from Kiron Wadhera, *Case Study: A Method of Training*, VYK, pages 40—43

Case Study: Dealing with Difficult Trainees

The Alexandra College organized a ten-days rural leadership course for forty of its final year male students. The students belonged to rural areas themselves. The purpose of the course was to prepare the boys to go back to their villages after completing their education and to work for development there.

The course was organized in a remote village, and was conducted in the village high school. The principal of the school was a very helpful person, and did all that he could to support the course.

As the programme went on, it was noticed that three of the boys — Soha, Moane and Dina — were uninterested and were not participating much. The organizers made efforts to speak to them about this and to interest them. However their efforts did not yield results. It was clear that the three boys were not interested in the programme.

On the morning of the sixth day the organizers noticed some uneasiness among the students. When asked, Soha said that they had been insulted by one of the teachers of the school the previous night. The students had been sitting and chatting together when the teacher (who lived in the school premises) came over and started shouting at them. The organizers said they were extremely sorry about this, and that they would discuss the matter with the principal of the school, who was their host.

This did not satisfy the boys. Moane said they would not stay in such a place any more. Dina started complaining about the poor facilities provided to the group. He said that the village people made fun of them because they were 'townees' and jeered at them when they walked outside. For this reason too they did not want to stay any longer. The organizers said that such behaviour by villagers, though not very pleasant, was understandable and should be tolerated. They suggested that the boys should make efforts to be friendly with the villagers, so that they would accept them. The organizers then asked the other members of the group if they also agreed that they should not stay any longer. The group gave no specific answer.

The organizers then asked the group how the decision to continue or to leave the training course could be related to the behaviour of one teacher who was not even concerned with the course. They pointed out to the group that they had all come to attend the training, and that they could not call it off for such a trivial reason.

They also told them that such situations frequently arise in life.

'In fact even worse things happen', they said, 'and if we react like this on such petty issues we will never progress, and we will never be able to fight the negative forces in our society. Moreover the principal, who is our real host, had been very nice to all of us.'

They again promised the trainees to speak to the principal about the issue. After this the organizers asked the group to discuss the matter among themselves for the next 15 minutes and inform them of their decision. Then they left the session, and went to speak to the principal.

The organizers related the incident to the principal, who was very upset. He apologized to the organizers on behalf of the teacher. The organizers said that they were not complaining, but only informing him of the incident. On their return to the session they told the students of their discussion with the principal. They also asked them what they had decided. Moane said they wanted the training programme to continue alright, but they wanted the venue to be changed immediately to a town about 70 km away.

This surprized the organizers. However, without showing much irritation, they told the group that they found their proposal unrealistic and impracticable. They told them that if the programme was to continue, it would be in the same premises, otherwise they would have to cancel it. Those who wanted to go were free to do so, because there was no point in forcing training upon tense and unwilling people. They said they would be content to complete the programme with those few who were really interested and who could take such petty matters gracefully.

They then asked who wanted to leave the course. Moane, Soha, Dina and Asho raised their hands. They were asked when they would leave, and they said it would be that same afternoon. The organizers told them that they were free to do so. They also explained that they would not be able to give them the return fare afterwards (as they were doing for others), and that they would have to reimburse to the college the fare for coming also. Since they were not attending the full programme they could not be given their fares. They would also not be given any certificate of participation. Dina said that the certificate part of it was alright, but they should be given the fare. The organizers expressed their helplessness as that was against the rules. Moreover, the participants had earlier agreed to come to the programme voluntarily, and the college was not responsible for the reversal of their decision.

After getting the agreement of the other participants, the organizers then started the day's work. As they had to set up some committees, they started asking for volunteers. Asho, one of the four who wanted to leave, gave his name for a committee. The organizer who was noting down the names smiled and asked:

'So you are not going?'

'No,' Asho said shyly.

The work proceeded normally thereafter. However Moane, Soha and Dina wore an angry look throughout the session. After the session the organizers asked them if they would like their meals prepared, or were they leaving? They said they would stay on.

Next day Dina started participating in the programme. Moane and Soha however remained indifferent till the end.

Adapted from Kiron Wadhera, *Case Study: A Method of Training*, VYK, pages 20—22

Case Study: The New Emperor

Mr Lee was the manager of one of the departments in a large voluntary organization. He was very much liked by his staff, with whom he was on friendly terms. Eventually Mr Lee left the organization on account of ill health, and Mr Chow took over as manager. Mr Chow soon discovered that the department was poorly organized and inefficient.

Mr Chow tried to make changes with care, but he always met with resistance from the staff of the department. They often made remarks like,

'Mr Lee wouldn't have liked this,' and 'Mr Lee wouldn't have done it that way.'

Eventually Mr Chow called all the staff of the department together and said, in effect, that he would no longer tolerate the lack of co-operation. While he was speaking, he used a traditional saying,

'The old emperor is dead. Long live the new emperor.'

The following morning some members of the staff of the department were absent: and others who were present requested a transfer.

If you are the Director of the organization, what will you do when you hear what has happened?

Adapted from *Bacie Case Studies* (*No. 60*), British Association for Commercial and Industrial Education, London

Case Study: The Training Department

A large voluntary agency which had several development programmes and a growing staff, decided to set up a training department. The person appointed as head of training was Mr James, aged 55, who had been a personnel officer for a large company. James was asked to arrange a series of short training courses for field and extension staff. Tutors for the training courses were to be volunteers from the various specialist departments within the agency.

One of the volunteer tutors was Mr Tony, a professionally qualified agriculturalist of 35. Tony was made temporarily responsible to James for the period of the training courses. This arrangement had not been made clear at the time that staff members were invited to volunteer as tutors for the courses.

After the first course Tony was congratulated by his own boss, Mr Victor, who was head of the agriculture department. Victor praised him for the contribution he had made and the clarity of his teaching. Victor intended to send Tony out on a tour of some villages between the training courses. Victor informed James of his intention.

James then wrote a letter to Tony scolding him and saying,
You have confused what you like doing with what needs to be done.

James also drew up an organization chart for the training department in which Tony was ranked with junior staff who were contributing to the training courses. Tony thought this was an insult, considering his age and his qualifications.

Tony ignored a visit to the training department by representatives of the donor agency, and kept a long-standing family engagement.

1a. How do you understand the behaviour of James and of Tony?

1b. If you are Victor will you take any action?

2a. Draw organizational diagrams to show what happened.

2b. What comments do you have on setting up a training department in this way?

Adapted from *Bacie Case Studies (No 86)*, British Association for Commercial and Industrial Education, London

Case Study: Mr Musoma

Mr Musoma is a trainer in adult education. He is aged 28. After completing his education in his own country he went abroad for training as a teacher. While undergoing training he was exposed to participatory learning methods. He attended a number of sessions where an experience-based approach was used. He was fascinated by the excitement he noticed among the trainees, and was convinced that this was a viable training approach to use.

Since returning to his own country Mr Musoma has been employed to teach agricultural extension workers at a College of Agriculture. Most of his students are pursuing diploma courses after doing their secondary school studies. Occasionally he also conducts in-service courses for serving extension workers, and short courses for practising farmers. His colleagues in the College received their training locally, and they use formal lecture methods, as they themselves were taught.

Mr Musoma, on the other hand, believes in involving learners in active participation. He seeks their views on their learning needs, organizes them to work in groups and to share their experiences, and often gives them individual and group exercises to do during class time and in their free time. The students are encouraged to make their own notes, or to jointly compile notes from group discussions.

Time and again Mr Musoma has faced students' dissatisfaction. They complain that they do not learn anything new through his methods: all they do is discuss their views or experiences. They say that Mr Musoma does not teach them, or tell them what he knows, which is what the other lecturers do. Furthermore his methods use a lot of time. His fellow teachers also criticise his methods as foreign and inappropriate.

Adapted from D. Nturibi, *With Practice*, CYP, page 231

In his young days, John Sitholl had become famous as a political activist working to free his nation from outside domination. During the struggle for liberation he had achieved great fame for his dynamic leadership, but after his nation achieved independence he failed to achieve high political office. In fact he transferred his energies from the struggle for independence to the struggle for justice amongst the poor communities of his country. He became active in social change organizations, and was a pioneer in the voluntary development movement.

After spending many years in both rural and urban programmes, he was appointed Regional Officer and later National Director for the well-known international aid agency, Justice International (JI). JI was providing financial support to a large number of development programmes in the country, and was very pleased to have a man of such a calibre to administer its programme.

John Sitholl's success was considerable, JI's programme grew, and the number of its staff increased. Before long Mr Sitholl was supported by two Assistant Directors, three Regional Officers, an office manager, an accountant and clerical staff.

Mr Sitholl became quite famous, both nationally and internationally, and many people came to seek his advice. I myself went to him for advice.

'I'd like to see Mr Sitholl,' I said to one of his colleagues in the JI office.
'I'm afraid Mr Sitholl is busy,' he replied, 'Can I help you?'
'No, thank you,' I said. 'I think I had better wait for Mr Sitholl. I want some advice from him personally. It's about an important decision.'

Later I was able to see Mr Sitholl.

'I'm glad you waited,' he said.
'I almost spoke about the matter with one of your assistants,' I said. 'But it is such an important decision.'
'Well, all decisions are referred to me anyway, for a final ruling, so it is always best to see me personally. I'm afraid my staff are not all that experienced, you know.'

I heard later that some of the younger staff had left Mr Sitholl, and wondered why they did not want to continue in such a prestigious job.

Adapted from Laurence Taylor and Peter Jenkins, *Time to Listen: the Human Aspect in Development*, IT Publications, page 25

A group of village animators were trying to get people to become aware of social problems within their society. They arranged a puppet show for the children of the village one evening, and several adults came to see what was happening.

The children laughed at the antics of the puppets, and when one of the puppet characters began behaving like a drunken man, the laughter increased. Then the drunken puppet began beating his wife with a stick, and the children fell silent. But one of the village women at the back of the crowd began to laugh sarcastically.

Suddenly her husband shouted at her,
    'Why are you laughing?'
She replied,
    'You know why,'
and a small ripple of laughter went through the group of adults watching the puppets.

Adapted from Laurence Taylor and Peter Jenkins, *Time to Listen: the Human Aspect in Development*, IT Publications, page 60

Reverend Joel has been a pastor for forty years, most of the time in rural areas. Revd. Joel's understanding of the people's needs has led him to conduct adult education programmes throughout this period. This education is intended mainly for leaders, either those whom he considers to be natural leaders, or those whom the community considers to be its leaders. Revd. Joel's philosophy is that people become leaders by experiencing leadership in others and encouraging leadership in others.

In the courses a series of talks are given on a variety of subjects. These include: public speaking; organizing clubs and groups; voting in elections; debating; political action; racial, social, class and political conflicts and resolving conflicts; child and adult education; the role of the individual and the community in social life; the role of work in society; the rights of workers; the State; the family; the church; trade unionism; trade; private and common good; the use and abuse of alcohol; distribution of wealth; rights and duties of ownership; capitalism and its problems.

After a talk, a question and answer period, or a discussion, generally follows. Revd. Joel encourages those who take the courses to reflect upon their own situation, and encourages them to make improvements. He also insists on people taking notes, otherwise the course is considered to be a waste of time. The courses also include training in practical skills.

At the beginning, some forty years ago, the organization of these courses was very informal. During a religious service it would be announced that there would be a series of talks in the village. The talks were then usually given in a chapel or a school, or even under a tree. In those days Revd. Joel would respond to any question that was asked, in an attempt to find out which subjects interested the people most of all.

However, over the years, the programme has become more structured, with the groups selecting what they want to discuss from a list of topics which is given. Nonetheless, the course remains essentially mobile, and for this reason Revd. Joel has never built special centres to house the course, but has continued to use whatever buildings are available.

The courses are usually given by Revd. Joel himself, with the help of someone else who has completed a course previously. He receives little encouragement from his fellow clergy, who are more interested in schools and the education of children.

The programme costs very little, and no money is requested or received from foreign funding agencies. What little money is needed is usually raised locally, and in many cases contributions from those attending the courses have been adequate.

During recent years, Revd. Joel has been giving courses every two or three months on request. The courses generally last two days, and are attended by 50 or 60 people. Note-taking is extensive, and the groups appear interested and ask a large number of questions. The groups attending the course have also been paying for Revd. Joel's transport to and from his home place.

Courses given many years ago are still remembered, and Revd. Joel is said to be the inspiration behind a large co-operative growers and marketing society, established more than twenty years ago, and still flourishing. Other attempts, such as a fish farm, have been less successful; nothing remains of that project, despite active Government support.

Adapted from A.M. Visocchi, *Non-Formal Education for Rural Development*, Manchester Monographs 9, pages 21—23

I am a village development worker. I work for a voluntary development agency. I live in a town around which there are many small villages. Every week I visit some of these villages.

Whenever I start to work in a village I like to build up strong relationships where there are no barriers. I want to be involved in the peoples' daily lives, good or bad: people accept that in our culture. People in these villages have been open with me, and I have been open with them.

They like me very much, and I like them too. They treat me like a brother. Some of the younger people call me 'Uncle'; although the older people say 'Mr ...'.

In each village I worked with the people to form a Village Development Committee (VDC). The members of the VDC were selected by the villagers, and it was agreed among themselves that any development worker who comes to their village has to work with the VDC.

One day the Chairman of one of these VDC's invited me to a meeting. This particular VDC had been active, always taking up whatever activities were possible. Already they had a drinking water project and a health and sanitation programme in the village. I went to the meeting and found all the members present, and many of the other villagers too, both men and women. Before they started to talk about the issues, the Chairman asked the people to open the meeting with a word of prayer. This is usually how they open their meetings.

After the opening prayer the Chairman started his introductory speech.

'Our village development committee met last week,' he said, 'and we
decided that we will have a well and garden project in our village.'

I could see that the people were happy to hear this.

'We decided that we ourselves are ready to provide the land, the sticks for
fencing the garden, and the labour for digging the well. But we would like
the development agency to help us by providing cement and iron bars, by
transporting sand and rock and by sending two trained well-diggers who
will show us how to do the job.'

This was the first I had heard of this proposal and I was so surprised I didn't know what to say. I saw it was a good idea in principle, but immediately I knew that it will not work in practice. This particular village has sandy soil, less than a metre deep, and below is solid rock. But the people of this village really have confidence in me that I will be able to help them, and I did not feel I could disappoint them, or risk the confidence they have in me. So I told them that I would think about what they had proposed, and then I left the meeting.

When I returned to my office I was wondering what I could say to them that would not spoil their confidence in me. Meanwhile the villagers sent a message to my office asking me for another meeting. I replied that I was thinking about their proposal, and that I would visit them again later. I told them they should not come to me in the office.

Contributed by a Development Studies Course member

Case Study: Art and Cho

An international course for development workers was held between the beginning of October and the middle of December. There were 20 course members from 11 countries and three tutors.

Each day the course members took it in turns by volunteering to write a diary of the day. This was read back to the group at the beginning of the following morning.

On 23rd October Art read the diary. He started as follows:

Somehow I knew it would be my turn to write the diary. I knew I could not put it off much longer. Twenty course members equals four weeks, therefore there are now only two more people who have not 'volunteered to write' the diary. Or maybe 'expected to write' is more appropriate by this stage. I do wonder if the last two really feel able to do it? Maybe as a group we are asking them to do something they feel unable to do, or don't want to do...

Art then proceeded to read his other reflections on the previous day. In the discussion which followed no reference was made to his opening remarks.

After the discussion the chairperson called for another volunteer, and Cho put his hand up.

The following morning Cho, who was one of the two persons referred to by Art, read the diary.

Cho started with the following sentences:

Art, a clever fellow, did not disappoint me. He mentioned that there is somebody who did not write the diary, surely thinking of a poor fellow from my country.

Anyway I had to confess I was the very man that never wrote the diary. Art, I am sure, felt victorious secretly in his heart.

In the discussion which followed, no reference was made to these remarks of Cho.

Contributed by a Development Studies Course tutor

Case Study: Silence

An international course for development workers was held between the beginning of May and the middle of July. There were 16 course members from 10 countries and three tutors.

Each day the course members took it in turns to write a diary of the day, which was read back to the group at the beginning of the following morning.

After the course one of the tutors made the following extracts from the diary.

8th May

During the reading of the diary, most members of the group seemed to be in a different world with their thoughts, and reactions came very slowly. Looking back to the past week, I must say that this group can be compared with a diesel engine: unless you warm it up, it is difficult to start.

10th May

The members of the group reported on time for the morning session....a request was made for a volunteer to keep the diary. Immediate response was not made, and there was a bit of silence which I couldn't understand. I hesitated before I raised my hand.

13th May

The session began lethargically with few contributions from the group...

14th May

R read the diary of 13th May which raised a few issues like silence by the course participants...

22nd May

There was not much participation by the members including myself.

5th June

...the question of the group being cautious and requiring motivation came up —

it was to reappear later in the morning. However, the group did not seem in the mood to discuss this, or any other matter, at length.

6th June

There was a little silence. I thought this would be pursued a bit but it ended there.

On the morning of 13th June the course members were invited by one of the tutors to conduct a structured analysis of their experience of the course. For the purpose they were divided into three small groups.

When they came to consider difficulties in the course, two of these groups listed 'silence' among other matters.

Contributed by a Development Studies Course tutor

Case Study: A Soft Discussion

One of the most important words I have learnt from this course is the word 'Participation'. If I have to summarize the meaning of development I will say that development for me is: 'People's full participation in decisions about their own destiny'.

During these few weeks we have had the opportunity to live with the experience of the participatory learning method. I feel fully responsible for my own learning. When, how and what I learn depends fully upon my personal decision and effort. I could not blame anybody else for the result I have. I wonder how much the other course members appreciate this experience and this method of learning: for me it has been a wonderful experience in my life.

But like all things in this world, the method has its difficulties too, and here I feel a little bit guilty. How far am I responsible for the learning of others? Doesn't my participation affect the learning of the other members? Sometimes my own carelessness has detracted from this participatory learning method.

Let me give you one example to explain my feeling. If I always come late to the session all the course members have to wait for me before they can begin the work. In a formal teaching situation 'teachers' have the responsibility to correct my carelessness; but when participatory methods are used, this responsibility passes to all the course members. In our own course, one member had mentioned this carelessness in a very soft way. We had a soft discussion about it. Later on, the problem continued, and we left it unsolved.

In a course it may not be a big problem, because we are not here permanently, but if we have such a situation and such a problem in our work back home, how shall we manage it? How can we avoid such a situation? How far does the responsibility of the course members go in this method of learning?

Please do understand that the purpose of my questions is not to blame anybody here. The example I have taken is just a simple example among others. My purpose is to explore the process of participatory learning, in order to improve its result.

_____

Contributed by a Development Studies Course member

Case Study: Whom Are We Serving?

I had been working for a church development programme for nearly three years. The programme had been in operation for eight years and was successful in raising awareness among the people and in implementing health, agriculture and village technology projects. I was an expatriate responsible for the implementation of village technology and worked as part of a team of extension advisers; my colleagues were local people.

Each month we held a Development Meeting to share ideas and co-ordinate work in the field. The meetings were attended by the extension advisers for each specialized programme and the Senior Development Adviser, who was my superior. The meetings were chaired by the Bishop. At this time I was acting as the Secretary of these Development Meetings.

At one of these development meetings the Bishop gave us a talk on Development Theology, and I remember him stressing the need to serve the poor. This challenged me to consider my own work and ask the question: 'Whom are we serving?'

I followed this up by talking further with the Bishop and some of my colleagues. Then I wrote a paper, 'Serving the Poor', which I showed to the Senior Development Adviser. With some alterations it was decided to discuss the paper at the next Development Meeting. A copy of the paper was given to each extension adviser and the Bishop a few days before the meeting. This is the paper:

Serving the Poor

The rural development programme is a service 'to uplift the standards of living of the people in the Province'. Can we give examples of churches or groups where the standards of living have been improved due to the rural development programme? A more difficult question to answer is which people in the community have improved their standard of living?

It is easier, when approaching the people, to work with those who are receptive to ideas put forward by the development programme. Those who are receptive are usually educated, have an income and thus capital, and time to 'risk' in development projects. In developmental terms these people are already sensitized, more so than the less educated subsistence farmer.

We are uplifting standards of living, but we need to examine whom our development programme reaches.

Questions Raised:
1. *Whom are we serving? The whole community or a small section of the community who are already sensitized?*
2. *The target group of the rural development programme is the 'poor'. When we visit a church do we meet the 'poor'?*
3. *Could we list the real needs of the 'poor'?*
4. *How can the programme be designed to reach the whole community?*
5. *Which projects would best serve the needs of the whole community?*

The meeting was well attended and started at 11.00 a.m. The items included a long discussion on expenses, which often came up. I had also raised some questions about how to improve co-ordination between departments, and we spent some time on that. So it was getting late, and had reached 12.30 p.m. before we got to the paper, which I had put as the last item on the agenda. I introduced the paper and explained that it was to provide a basis for discussion only.

The discussion was short, and although there was agreement that we should be serving the poor there was no real discussion on the questions. Some said that their work was reaching the poor. Some didn't say anything. I was rather disappointed, and it seemed to me that people felt threatened by the paper.

It was decided to discuss it again at the next meeting, but in the event that didn't happen. It was such an important issue, but now I am wondering if that was the best way for me to have tried to raise it.

Contributed by a Development Studies Course member

For some years I have been working as an expatriate in a Medical and Community Health Programme. I am a Community Health specialist.

Looking back, there is one situation which I feel especially sad about.

In the programme there were many expatriates, all in different leading positions. Three of them were doctors. Beside those three doctors we had one national, Doctor Joseph, who, due to his profession as a doctor, also had a leading position in the project He was the only national member of staff with such a position.

I myself did not live in the area where we had our base hospital. I stayed some miles away, running a Community Health Unit.

At the same time I also had some responsibilities for training the programme's community workers, which was done at the hospital. This meant that I had to spend three days a week at the main hospital.

Dr Joseph used to come to my unit once a week to see any patients who had been referred to a doctor.

All the expatriates and Dr Joseph used to take their tea-break in the Programme Director's office. When Dr Joseph was not among us, we all talked freely together in our own language, but when Dr Joseph joined us we started to speak English or the local language, although the conversation didn't go on as freely as before.

In the beginning Dr Joseph always joined us, but after some time he stopped coming to our tea-break. He also became very quiet and his face looked depressed. The expatriates became worried, and asked each other, 'What's wrong?' When I came to the hospital, I always got to know how the other expatriates were feeling about him.

I learned that Dr Joseph was going to have his tea together with the other national workers in the project. However, due to the culture, Dr Joseph thought that a man in his position should not mix with people in lower positions. Among the national staff, there were no other persons on Dr Joseph's level. He and his family didn't find friends in the local area.

When Dr Joseph came to my unit, we always had our tea together, and we came to know each other well.

One day I saw that he was very depressed and I asked, 'Joseph, what is wrong?'

Then he started to tell me about all his frustrations. Some of the frustrations were:

- the way the programme was being managed;
- what he felt was a lack of recognition of his own role;
- he didn't feel he was given any responsibility: he was just a doctor who was told to see some patients;
- he had been in need of borrowing some money, but the Programme Director didn't agree to advancing it;
- he felt that one of the other expatriates was actually ruling the whole project;
- he told me that he wanted to leave his job.

After listening to him I really wanted to make this known to the other expatriates, so that they could discuss it with him and find some solution together. I asked him if I could talk about it to the other expatriates or to the Programme Director, but he didn't allow me to do so, neither did he want to talk about it himself to the Programme Director.

After this we often talked together, and I tried to persuade him to stay in the Programme. However after some time he resigned from his job. He was a very well-qualified doctor and a capable person as well.

Could I/we have done something in another way, so that Dr Joseph would have become more included amongst us?

Contributed by a Development Studies Course member

Case Study: The Counterpart and the Director

Ours is a foreign operational agency. It supports community development projects in an area with 20 villages. Our office is based at the centre of the area. Two years ago I joined as a counterpart to the present Director, who is an expatriate. The field staff consists of three teams, each responsible for our work in a number of villages. They usually report to the office once or twice each fortnight.

Due to the increase in the administrative cost of the programme, the organization drew up a plan to replace the present Director, and offered the post to me. The period of handover was agreed to be nine months. After carefully considering the matter and discussion among the project staff I decided to accept the offer.

Since that I have started to think about the following aspects.

Although there are four levels in our organization — Director, Assistant Director, Team Leaders and Field Workers — there is not much difference made between the levels. In style it is a 'flat' organization, not hierarchical. The staff feel free, and all levels meet each other informally and openly.

This is different from our culture and from the style of other local development organizations. Many of the staff are not happy with the way the structure is used, or with this style of management, which they consider to be foreign and 'weak'. Those in the middle are sometimes uncomfortable when the Director talks with the field workers, and when meetings are held in an informal manner. They say that the Director should insist on the workers showing him more 'respect'. But other members of the staff, including myself, are happy with it because we believe it suits this kind of work.

Whenever there is a personnel problem, the Director takes a long time to come to a decision. He says, 'I am considering the cultural aspect, yours and mine.' Most of the staff think this is a weakness in management. Some of them would like to see firmer, faster action. They think that disciplinary measures are not being used sufficiently.

When he visits the villages he meets the field workers direct and informally. Sometimes they tell him false stories as excuses for not doing their job properly, bearing in mind he cannot communicate directly with the villagers and does not understand the local customs.

The present Director has little social contact within the area. He tends to spend a lot of time keeping himself busy in the office outside working hours. He thinks it is important, as a Director, that one should work hard. Some staff think he is a hard-worker, but still complain that he does not visit them at home except on occasions. Sometimes I also work with him in the evenings. But I have friends that I should meet and other social and family commitments that he does not have.

Last week I received a letter from the head office saying that the Director is going to leave sooner than expected because his expertise is needed somewhere else. The letter says that I have to assume responsibility as Director from the time I arrive home next month — that is, if I am still interested in taking over the job.

What are the main concerns and feelings of the writer?
If you were in the writer's situation, what would you do?

Contributed by a Development Studies Course member

After my training I was employed as a community worker for a Diocese in a large city. I was the only paid employee of the Social Responsibility Committee (SRC) of the Diocese. The committee was made up of representatives of the congregations of the Diocese.

My predecessors, up to that time, had all been social workers. As social workers they had been working for the disadvantaged people whom they had identified within the community. The focus of their work had been on the individual and family problems of such people, who were referred to as 'clients'. I quickly came to the conclusion that the diocese had been employing these social workers to 'deal with its problems' by 'doing good' for these problematic families and individuals.

Now it seemed that the SRC was hoping that, as a community worker, I would help the churches to start a programme of 'care in the community'. This would be a new approach, in which congregation members would volunteer to take responsibility, on behalf of the churches and the wider community, for the care of the 'clients' and the solution of their individual and family problems. I was expected to support the volunteers who were going to look after the clients.

I soon decided that the job had to be turned upside down. Instead of my taking on responsibility for the work of the volunteers, I thought that, as a community worker, I should be raising awareness about general community issues. I should be stimulating and challenging the churches and their congregations to think about their local situations and to take up projects appropriate to their situation and the community locally.

I found myself pushing the SRC to change its policy sharply, away from the focus on individuals and the relationships of dependency, towards awareness-raising and working with the community as a whole.

I persuaded the SRC that this was the right approach, and they reluctantly agreed to close down the remaining social work. I then began to make contacts with the churches of the Diocese to find ways in which to encourage them to adopt this new approach.

After some months, I began to discover that the SRC and the churches were dissatisfied with me. I heard that people were saying:

'What is this worker actually doing?.'
'We, the churches, are paying his salary, but what has he to show for it?'
'He's all thinking, but no action.'

I was told that the churches might stop funding the post.

At this point, which was after about 18 months, I decided to resign. No one on the SRC made much effort to persuade me to stay! Yet in some of the parishes community projects were already beginning to grow, and some of them are still going on years later.

Contributed by a Development Studies Course member

Case Study: Committee Meetings

I am an expatriate and have been working in the country for many years. I speak the local language fluently.

Along with three other expats, I am a member of several church committees in the locality where I work. The other 10—12 committee members are local people, mostly pastors and teachers. When we attend these meetings there is the usual agenda, which we work through, item by item, under the direction of the Chairman.

Yet I find in these meetings, although there is often a great deal of thorough discussion, we never seem to come to a clear decision. An example is the Building Committee. The agenda may include six or eight items such as repairing pastors' houses, maintenance work on the hospital, extending a school, repairing some church buildings, etc. Since the building budget is limited, some work can be taken up and some cannot: the Committee's task is therefore to decide on each item and to make priorities. There are also questions about the availability of materials, and whether it will be necessary to import materials for certain works. Each item is discussed in great depth and detail, and the meeting may go on for a whole morning or afternoon, yet there doesn't seem to be any clear decision one way or the other before the discussion moves on to the next item.

After these meetings I and the other expats are left puzzled, not knowing if anything has been decided or not. It is only when we receive the minutes of the meeting, several weeks later, that we come to know what decisions have been made.

Contributed by a Development Studies Course member

I work in my country for a foreign donor agency. One of the senior officials of the agency had to make a brief visit to the country to see community development projects with rural people in remote areas. It takes a long time to travel to these places through rough tracks across the desert. Food and accommodation are not readily available. Also the people have had very little contact with foreigners.

Therefore I travelled in advance through the route which we planned for the official and his colleagues to use on their visit, to arrange food and accommodation for them. It was not possible to send a letter. Anyway the people do not read. Nor was there any telephone.

I already knew the village leaders and elders very well. The first village to be visited was Gadal on October 19. I met Albe, the village leader, and other members of the village community, and discussed the possibility of arranging lunch for five people on October 29. I knew that the villagers were not used to such appointments, so I was careful to explain who was coming and why they wanted to meet the villagers. The village elders said they would be happy to see and talk to the officials and revealed enthusiasm. They estimated the cost of the lunch, and I provided the money required.

Usually people in the villages do not believe that visitors will come until they actually arrive. I knew this too, and that is why I stressed the date of the visit, and why I even paid the money in advance. When I left the village I was impressed with the elders, and envisaged no problems regarding food for the visitors.

I travelled further to Belur to arrange supper and accommodation for the delegation for the same day. Belur is bigger than Gadal, and there is a small hotel. So I didn't bother to involve the community leaders in arranging food and accommodation for the delegation. I visited the hotel manager and asked if it was possible to book supper and accommodation for five people for October 29. The manager said it would be no problem. I asked him the cost and paid him in advance accordingly to make sure that everything would be okay. I continued my travelling further north, arranging food and accommodation for the delegation in other places.

The officials arrived in the capital city where we met them at the airport. After spending a few days in the capital, and meeting different people in various places, the time to travel came. We left the capital city at 5 a.m. on the morning of 29th October. We were expecting to arrive at Gadal at 1 p.m. However, we lost the way in the desert and we arrived one hour late. We had not had breakfast because we left the capital early, and we had nothing on route. When we arrived I immediately realized from the faces of the villagers that no food had been prepared. They were not ready to receive us and their agitation was obvious. When I asked what had happened they said,

'We were not sure whether you were actually coming on time and we forgot the appointment.'

Albe, the leader, was restless and angry. They started to blame each other. I felt embarrassed, but I didn't know what to say, other than to inform the visitors that there was no food. The visitors didn't comment, but one of them said, 'Oooh!'

The villagers requested us to wait for a meal, but it would have taken more than four hours, and we couldn't wait.

After a meeting, we set off leaving the villagers looking ashamed. One of the elders gave me the money back with sorrow on his face. As we were jumping in the vehicle, I heard a voice saying,

'Please come back again.'

By the time we arrived at Belur we were really hungry and tired, and we drove straight to the hotel. Shortly afterwards I discovered that no food had been arranged there. This time I was more angry, and I enquired strongly from the manager why there was no meal for us. He said quietly,

'I am sorry, I forgot that... was it today that you were coming? ...cool down. I will arrange everything now.'

He was upset, and started giving out orders to his staff. The situation was known to the visitors (who did not speak the local language) without their being told, simply by watching what was happening between me, the hotel manager, and his staff.

I didn't say anything to them for a while, but sat on my chair next to the senior officer, and looked at the sky. This time my anger could be clearly read from my face. I broke the silence by saying,

'We have the same problem in this place as in Gadal.'

The senior officer replied,

'Take it easy. Maybe they had some other problems.'

But this didn't stop me thinking about the situation I was caught up in, between two different peoples whose cultures are far apart. When I visit these villages alone I face no problems with food and accommodation. I enjoy camel's milk which is always available, and somebody always invites me to his house. But why did these people not arrange the meals as agreed, and had received the money for?

I ended asking myself who was responsible for this mess — the villagers, me, or the visitors?

Contributed by a Development Studies Course member

▶ *I had found the paper on NK in Bangladesh very positive and encouraging ... This was my kind of development! Generally my feelings were shared by the rest of the group ...*

Discussion papers are teaching materials which contain descriptions or reports of professional work in organizations or communities. In the DSC we used them to help members think about approaches to development work, organizational issues, and the role of the development worker.

Discussion papers can also be used to reinforce the teaching of subject matter. If the current topic is planning, for example, a paper may describe an actual experience of planning and what happened afterwards. The task of the reader is then to identify the relevant principles and issues to do with planning, and to consider how the decisions and actions described in the paper measure up to those principles.

The method is often evaluative. The focus is on role and organization rather than persons and individual experience, on issues and action rather than process, and on 'should and ought' rather than 'why and how'.

Discussion papers have therefore a different character and a different purpose from case studies, although the two methods are sometimes confused. Case studies are exploratory and open-ended; discussion papers are concerned with teaching a lesson. The best case studies have a timeless and universal quality; discussion papers are more topical. Perhaps we can say that we 'look into' a case study, whereas we 'look at' a discussion paper.

The papers can be read by members in advance. They can then be discussed in small groups, and the main conclusions reported back to the whole course group.

The Papers Themselves

Discussion papers may be a few hundred words on a single page, or they may be much longer. The material should be up-to-date, relevant to the course group, and appropriate for the subject concerned. Four examples from the DSC are included as handouts in this section.

 If you wish to prepare your own discussion papers you should look for suitable material in the newsletters of organizations, in journals and magazines, and in books which describe professional work. If you use limited extracts, and edit the material carefully, you may be able to reduce the length without losing important information. You may also want to disguise the material so that the work described cannot be recognized. This prevents members who already know of the work from responding out of preconceptions.

If you use published material you should include a reference to the author and source, and observe the conventions about how the material is used.

Introducing the Papers

One, or perhaps two, papers can be used in a session. Copies can be distributed to members in advance to read and think about beforehand. For the discussion the whole group is divided at random into small groups of five to seven members.

During the early weeks trainers accompany the small groups and assist them by moderating their discussion of the papers. This role is different from the facilitator in a case study. With discussion papers the emphasis is more on the content, less on the process. There may be practice to be assessed, principles to be identified, and evaluations to be made. Trainers may want to lead the discussion to ensure that particular ideas or issues are considered.

After trainers have demonstrated the role during several sessions, they may withdraw and leave the small groups to discuss further papers on their own. This gives members an opportunity to take more responsibility. Each group has to provide the necessary leadership, manage the task, moderate their own discussion and reach conclusions. For the members themselves it is a different experience from working with a trainer, and is another variation within the methodology.

When small groups work on their own they usually return towards the end of the session — perhaps after an hour — ready to share a brief summary of their perceptions and conclusions with the whole group. Trainers may lead this final part of the session.

Working in Small Groups without Trainers

When members work without trainers they can be given a structure for their discussion. This can help them to focus their attention on the material, encourage them to interact with each other, and provide a method for reporting back. The structure should be chosen to suit the material in the paper, the experience of the members, and the subject being taught. Five possibilities are outlined below.

Using Questions

The simplest way to focus attention and deepen the discussion is to add appropriate questions to a paper. Examples of such questions are included with A Viable Scheme and Raising the Price (pages 214, 216). If each of the small groups considers the same questions, it will make reporting back in the whole group quick and straightforward.

A small group discusses a paper

Using Headings

Some papers are longer and more complicated. They may contain a lot of information and ideas, with points and issues to be considered at different levels. Questions alone may not probe or unravel such dense material effectively.

Instead members can be asked to work with certain headings, and to list ideas or points or conclusions under these headings. Well-chosen headings will encourage members to consider each point, each bit of information, and each idea as they decide where to list it. Two general headings which are often useful are 'What Helped?' and 'What Hindered?' Another pair is 'Factors that Encouraged Change' and 'Factors that Resisted Change'. Or three headings can be used, such as 'Essential,' 'Helpful,' and 'Unnecessary.' Another three — which work well with the paper Organizing the Landless in Bangladesh (page 218) — are 'Positive,' 'Negative,' and 'Interesting.'

■ If you want to use headings choose them beforehand, and make sure they are appropriate to the material in the paper. The headings should be broad enough to accommodate ideas, bits of information, aspects of policy or practice, bits of experience, values and attitudes, difficulties, possibilities, and so on.

Explain the task. Ask the small groups to list under the headings whatever points they think belong there. Tell them that at the end they should choose six or eight points which are the most important, and record these on large sheets of paper. Do not clarify further, but leave the members to decide how they understand the headings.

■ When the groups return, ask them to display their most important points. Compare and contrast the lists, and clarify as necessary. The lists are usually similar, but not necessarily so. Different groups may have put the same point under different headings. Such differences should be explored, but do not allow discussions which have already taken place to be repeated or they will become burdensome. Remember also that the purpose is to encourage members to think about the material, rather than to produce lists for the sake of having lists.

Concepts Check

When a paper describes work that seems unfamiliar, members may think it is irrelevant and may not give it their usual attention. Trainers can overcome this by asking members to complete a short check or test of their understanding of the work. Such a check requires the members to interact with the material — however unfamiliar it may seem — and to identify important concepts and features. An example is given with the paper Fisherwomen and Participation (page 226). Members usually enjoy such checks because they have immediate 'right' and 'wrong' answers. The task in the small groups then becomes sharing members' responses to the check, instead of discussing the original paper.

■ If you want to use this method, you must prepare beforehand. For a concepts check of the kind in the example, pick out the factual information in the paper which you want to emphasize, and draft seven or eight sentences or statements based upon the information.

Draft four or five alternative possible 'completions' for each statement. The completions should all appear plausible, but only one completion (or occasionally more) should be correct. A few out of the total of forty-odd possible completions may be deliberately provocative or humourous.

Distribute the paper and the check to the members beforehand. Tell them to read the paper and complete the check individually before the session.

In the session tell the members to work in small groups and to share and compare their responses. When the task is completed ask the small groups to return and report briefly. Take up any issues raised, but do not allow the discussions of the small groups to be repeated.

Still Image or Sculpture

If course members are already familiar with these methods (see pages 266—268), sculpture can be a quick and creative way for small groups to report back their conclusions and perceptions. This works better with some papers than others, and members do need to be practised with the method already.

For example, groups that read Fisherwomen and Participation (page 223), and work through its concepts check, may convey their perceptions more vividly and expressively with sculptures than through verbal reporting. The method works well for that paper because the process and the relationships described are vivid, and because members are already working together on the material as they discuss the concepts check.

■ If you choose the method of sculpture, do not inform the members until they have finished discussing the paper or the concepts check. Then tell them, while they are still in small groups, that their next task is to prepare one, or two, or three sculptures to illustrate their understanding of the situation, or events, or processes described in the paper. Do not allow more than 5 minutes preparation time per sculpture.

When all have returned to the large group ask for the sequence of sculptures from one small group. Allow time for observation in silence, and then check if any clarification is needed. Ask the group to repeat their sculptures as appropriate, and invite the remainder of the group to reflect on what they are seeing, but not to criticize the sculptures. Then proceed with the sculptures of the next small group.

You and the other members can appreciate the 'performance' by clapping at the end of each small group's contribution.

Tag Argument

This method is described on pages 284—285. It can be used after the small groups return as an alternative to reporting back. The method helps members explore issues and roles, especially when a paper deals with disagreement, describes roles or parties with conflicting views, or leads to opposed conclusions.

▶ *...four small teams worked on the 'Fisherwomen' paper... each of the groups were to report their discussions by presenting a sculpture highlighting the processes in which the development worker had achieved her cause. Each group presented completely different sculptures... There was a general agreement that despite the diversity, the meanings of the messages were basically the same.*

Discussion Paper: A Viable Scheme

Viable means 'able to live'; in an economic sense it means feasible or practicable.

A carefully planned scheme for irrigation and agriculture was launched. The scheme was based on co-operation between four different organizations, two of which were voluntary agencies (NGOs).

The first was an agency which was operating well-sinking machinery which had been donated from abroad. The machinery was used for sinking wells for irrigation. The wells could then be fitted with electric pumps to lift the water to the fields.

The second agency was a trust started by prominent local citizens to assist farmers of the area with the development of their agriculture.

The third organization was a commercial company dealing in hybrid seeds. The fourth was a semi-Government agricultural bank, which could offer both long-term and short-term loans to farmers.

Each of these organizations contributed its particular services and skills, so that a complete 'package' could be provided to local farmers. In this way, the sinking of wells, the installing of pumps, the supply of high-yielding seeds, fertilizers and pesticides, agricultural extension services, and long-term and short-term loans were all available.

The scheme was open to small farmers. Large farmers and the landless were excluded. Small farmers could join only if they were 'viable'. This meant that they had to satisfy three criteria.

1. The farmer himself had to have 'potential' as an individual, with a record of 'reliable hard work'. He had to be 'progressive and co-operative', and 'a man capable of devoting all his effort to his fields'.

2. He had to own a 'viable farm', without debts and mortgages, and with sufficient 'potential' in the soil to produce good crops and to be able to repay any loans given under the scheme.

3. There had to be 'viable groundwater' under his farm, so that a successful well could be sunk and his farm could be irrigated.

The scheme was supported with technical and professional expertise. Specialists in crops, agricultural extension and irrigation were employed, and detailed surveys of groundwater, soil, credit needs and so on were made.

Within a year about 100 farmers had been considered for the scheme, and 45 farmers had received loans and agricultural advice. Six new wells had been sunk, fifteen existing wells had been deepened, and twenty-five wells had been fitted with electric pumps. The yields of millet and wheat among the 45 farmers had increased by an average of 50%. Those who grew hybrid cotton had very large increases in yields. One farmer reported that his income had doubled with the sinking of a well and with the new methods recommended in the scheme.

Two years later the scheme had been extended to 400 farmers. More than 200 wells had been sunk and fitted with pumps, and 4,000 acres were being farmed according to the methods recommended in the scheme. As the scheme was extended, Government departments and other organizations contributed directly or indirectly. Among the additional programmes were 1,000 acres of soil conservation; 100 acres of afforestation on common land; 100 kilometres of roads with bridges; the sinking of drinking-water wells, and two weekly medical clinics contributed by a nearby voluntary hospital.

How do you understand the role of the small farmer in the working of this scheme?

Adapted from John Staley, 'Water', in *Growing Out of Poverty*, (ed. Elizabeth Stamp), OUP, pages 74—75

Discussion Paper: Raising the Price

As a result of some simple changes in farming practices, a group of farmers gained large increases in the yields of their crops. Their production of vegetables doubled. At first they were happy, but they soon realized that their hard work to produce more had not improved the condition of their life. This fact disturbed them and during their meetings with a group of animators they had lively discussions.

Challenging questions put to them by the animators helped them realize that the business class controlled the market and fixed the prices. For each basket of vegetables the traders paid a very small amount, but they resold the same in nearby towns for five to eight times as much. Further questioning led the farmers to understand the way that purchases and sales were made in the market.

Ultimately they realized that what they earned after three months of sweat and toil, the traders earned several times over by a few hours of work. In this process of creating awareness, the animators played a key role in stimulating the farmers' thinking and plans for action. The issues were discussed in many meetings, and as the process of exploitation became clearer to them, the farmers felt uncomfortable. A critical understanding of who produces, who buys, where the produce goes, who benefits, and in what proportion, was developed among them. As a result they started exploring ways to tackle this problem together.

In further meetings they realized that the only way for them to challenge the traders was to unite and to bargain for higher prices. The question was whether it was possible to challenge the traders by relying only on the unity and strength of those farmers who were attending the meetings. They decided that everyone who came to the market to sell produce would have to be contacted and involved in the struggle. So they met every seller and explained the issues, and held several meetings of all the sellers at the market site itself. Thus all joined in the struggle.

Finally they decided a day on which everybody would fix a common price for one basket of vegetables. Some members expressed their doubts: 'the traders may refuse to buy our produce at higher rates,' they said, 'and then we will have to carry the entire load back home.' Others said that: 'since the traders would still get huge profits, they would not refuse to buy at the new rates.' Still others were determined to consume the produce themselves rather than sell their hard labour so cheap. They decided that nobody would yield to the threats of the traders, or lower the new price. A penalty would be levied on anyone who gave in to the threats of the traders.

At the next market, the atmosphere was entirely different. When the traders came to collect the produce, the farmers stopped them and told them to pay the new price. The traders were surprised to see the change in the attitude of the people. They moved from farmer to farmer and got the same response. The traders initially did not purchase anything but kept shouting, pressing the farmers to sell at their normal rates, but the farmers stood by their decision. The traders noticed the animators moving among the farmers, encouraging and supporting them, and threatened the animators with physical attack. But all their efforts could not compel the farmers to sell the produce at lower prices. The farmers had fixed the new price and in no case were they prepared to lower it. If the worse came to the worst, the farmers were even prepared to return home with their produce.

As there was no alternative, the traders were compelled to buy the produce at prices fixed by the farmers, especially since they had already made arrangements for its transport. They would still make a profit, but a slightly smaller one.

That was a very happy day in the lives of the farmers. They now felt confident of their ability to do something. The success in action gave them faith in their strength and unity, and they followed the same strategy to secure better prices for their grain and other crops. With every success, their self-respect and confidence increased, encouraging them to continue their struggle further. The process has created problems for the animators and leading farmers who are helping the people because they are often threatened by the traders.

It is amazing how the farmers began to see things differently after they were involved in the process of self-awakening.

One farmer narrated this story:

> The other day when my cabbage nursery was ready, traders asked me to sell the seedlings to them at the rate of 2 coins per 5 seedlings. I demanded two coins per seedling. They kept visiting me with the same offer, and I continued demanding my price. They pointed out that soon the

seedlings would be over-mature and nobody would buy them. But I did not care. At last, when they did not offer me the proper price, I plucked the seedlings in front of them and cooked and ate these seedlings as vegetables. The traders were shocked and went away laughing at my foolishness. But I tell you, eating the seedlings gave me more satisfaction than if I had sold them at such a low price.

What was necessary for the success which is described?
What are the advantages and disadvantages of such an approach?

Adapted from Henry Volken *et al, Learning from the Rural Poor*, MOTT, pages 40—43

Discussion Paper: Organizing the Landless in Bangladesh

Nijera Kori (NK) is a long-established voluntary agency in Bangladesh which is helping the rural poor, both women and men, to organize and assert their rights, and to create a better future for themselves. The words *nijera kori* mean 'we will do it ourselves'.

With 120 workers — of whom 50 are women — NK is working in twenty *thanas*. (A *thana* is the smallest administrative area in Bangladesh, with a population of at least 100,000). NK has helped organize about 1,800 groups of the rural poor, with a total membership of 50,000, out of whom 11,500 were women.

NK is doing this work in Bangladesh where 90% of the population live in the rural areas. About 40% are landless, and they are increasing at an alarming rate. The poor have not benefited from the official development efforts, and continue to lead a dehumanized life of extreme poverty.

The situation of poor women is even worse. They bear a double burden because they are doubly exploited. In addition to suffering from poverty like their menfolk, women get lower wages and have fewer employment opportunities. They suffer from seclusion, beating and desertion by their husbands, and from other social and cultural oppression. Women's and girls' share of food is generally lower than that of men and boys; and their access to health services and education is also less than men and boys.

NK originated about ten years ago, when a Norwegian woman started a training programme to rehabilitate some of the destitute women, victims of the floods, who were flocking to Dhaka in the faint hope of survival. As a result of what they learnt, the women were able to earn a living for themselves.

Gradually the programme expanded. Five years ago some women who were working in a Canadian-sponsored project joined NK, and started projects in the fields. They chose to work with rural women from the poorest strata, particularly from landless households, organizing them into small groups. The programme at this time was exclusively for women and was also run only by women. A year after that 23 more organizers, who had had several years of field experience with another NGO, joined NK which gave a further impetus to the work.

From Organizing Women to Organizing the Rural Poor

Although originally NK worked only with women, gradually it began working with men also. The problems of women are part of a socio-economic and political structure, and can be tackled only by tackling this structure. According to NK, the two struggles — one between the classes and the other between the sexes — have to go on simultaneously. Both women and men have to recognize that there are contradictions between the sexes, that women suffer both from poverty and from oppression from men, and that oppressed men are the oppressors of women within their own class.

Although NK now works with both men and women among the rural poor, it continues to organize separate groups of women and men at the village level. This is because it believes that in mixed groups the special interests and issues of women are not adequately dealt with, nor are women able to assert themselves and develop their leadership potential. But at every other level of decision-making, men and women have joint committees and plan and work together on common issues.

The women's groups, therefore, are not isolated and they do not in any way weaken the organization of the poor. On the contrary, by securing the participation of women in large numbers and giving them an opportunity to develop their understanding, their consciousness and their leadership, the NK women's groups only strengthen the organization of the poor.

Nijera Kori's main objective is to help the rural poor — particularly landless labourers, poor fisherfolk and artisans — to form their own organizations through which they can safeguard their interests and rights. By living with the people in the communities, the NK organizers help them to analyze their own situation, to realize that their strength lies in their numbers, and that therefore they must unite. In the words of one of the workers:

The poor people know they are poor, sick, etc. but often they do not want to examine the situation. Many of them think the problems they face are their individual problems, and that they can do nothing to change the situation. By getting the people to look at their problems together we help them to see that their problems are common. Then they understand that it is the structures which are oppressing them. We want the people to ask for their share, to insist on their rights.

From consciousness-raising the groups move on to specific demands. These may be demands for higher wages, for access to government land for joint cultivations, for proper distribution of food and wages in Food-for-Work Programmes, for action against corrupt officials, and so on. As well as joining with the men on these issues, the women's groups take up others like dowry, desertion, wife beating, and sexual harassment. In one case they protested against obscene cabaret-type dances which are becoming part of some village performances and which, the women felt, excite men to be sexually aggressive.

Mobilizing and struggling for specific demands gives people self-confidence and experience in organization. They learn to shed their fears and to speak up in front of officials and landlords. They feel the strength of unity. Each action makes them stronger, whatever the outcome may be.

Obviously there is backlash against them from vested interests. For example, when groups openly protest against corrupt officials, or demand higher wages, the officials or employers may organize violence against them. There have been several cases of group members and NK workers being beaten up and being accused in false criminal cases. But, as this is to be expected, the group members and workers do not get disheartened by it.

As a matter of principle, NK does not provide loans or grants for taking up development activities. 'We cannot be a funder and an organizer at the same time,' NK workers say. 'Once you get into the relationship of a funder it becomes difficult to organize. Then, as funding is always limited, it ends up by dividing the poor.'

Training within NK

The main focus of NK's work is training programmes. These are of two kinds. First, there is a five-day basic orientation course arranged for men and women separately. The second is an advanced course of three days for both men and women. The training provides the participants with opportunities for critical analysis of their situation and helps them build confidence in their own creativity and capability for action. What is emphasized most is a new way of looking at things, the ability to perceive, analyze and change one's situation.

A mobile cultural team forms an integral part of these training programmes. This team also stages plays and puppet and musical shows for the local communities. This kind of activity is now being strengthened; last year, a two-week training in community theatre was given to 25 NK workers by two experienced women directors. The training programmes are held at the four training centres of NK, all of which are simple, low-cost buildings, constructed in local style.

Most of the 120 full-time workers of NK are from the villages, but there is a small group which is urban-educated and from the middle class. In the past, it has been quite difficult to recruit women workers. When they start, they are given five or six days of orientation, after which they are sent to work with an experienced worker for on-the-job training. Apart from the few who look after administration, fund-raising and overall supervision, who are based in Dhaka (but who travel to villages all the time), all the others are based in the villages. After the first few groups are organized in one area, the group members help in mobilizing others.

NK's Funds and Structure

NK raises funds for its own full-time workers and administration from funding agencies. It is gratifying to see that although NK could get more money from donors it has resisted doing so. It has deliberately retained a simple style of functioning with a modest and egalitarian salary structure. NK owns no cars or motor cycles, which are the first things most foreign-funded organizations acquire.

NK's field operations are divided into four geographical regions. There are also four levels of decision-making. One is the village-level group of the landless, artisans, etc. Representatives from these groups and NK workers of the area form a *thana*-level co-ordination committee. In this committee 50% of the members are expected to be women representing women's groups. The representatives of *thana* co-ordination committees form a regional committee.

For the overall coordination there is a central committee, which includes the four chairpersons of the regional committees, one from the central co-ordination, one central organizer, one central trainer, and two women because none of the regional chairpersons are women. As reflected in this organizational structure, NK emphasizes democratic decision-making.

National Organizations of the Landless

NK has felt the need for an independent organization of the landless in Bangladesh. At present there are small organizations and groups being created by political parties and NGOs, but they have not become a force because there is no co-ordination among them. Along with five other national NGOs, NK is slowly moving towards the creation of a national organization of the landless. Several conventions of grass-root groups, of both men and women, have already taken place.

Some women workers of NK have also been attempting to create a broadly-based women's organization to clarify and highlight women's issues.

Some Problems

The NK team is constantly reviewing its work. They have singled out a number of questions and problems. For example, how to identify their allies at the village level? How broadly based should the organization be? These are constant questions. The leadership of the groups is felt to be somewhat static. A few people seem to be monopolizing these positions, which does not promote democracy in the organization. NK has to he vigilant, encouraging more people to be active and to control their own leaders.

As noted already, it has been difficult to get women organizers, and the participation of women in the training programmes has been lower than that of the men. Much more work needs to be done to get women to participate actively. It is also necessary that the organizers be constantly deepening their own understanding, both of the field realities and their theoretical concepts.

Seeing all this questioning and self-criticism within Nijera Kori, one cannot help feeling that it is an organization which has a long way to go — but that it has the determination and commitment to undertake the journey.

Adapted from 'Nijera Kori: an Attempt at Organising the Landless in Bangladesh', *Ideas and Action*, 157, FFHC/FAO, pages 10—14

In north-east Brazil some 100,000 families live by fishing. Most are poor, with low levels of production and low levels of investment. The people have been organized by the Government to form fishing associations, which are supposed to represent them and to defend their rights. Only men had been involved in these associations.

In some families, women also fish to add to the family income. They fish separately from the men, and are restricted to the swamps along the bank of the river. An observer comments: 'They are condemned to a life in the swamps, on the sticky mud. They leave early in the morning with a basket, a net and a bit of water and food. They head out in boats... It is a life of work, struggle, some hope and a few jokes.' Most of these women are married, but they receive little support from their husbands, and are left with the responsibility for feeding and raising the children. Few of them have any education.

Some years ago a church development worker, who was a trained animator, made contact with these fisherwomen, and began to work with them.

Analysis and Understanding of Participation

The animator's analysis confirmed that the women were totally cut off from any kind of development effort, and that they lacked any resources to change their situation. The animator understood the situation as one where people are unable to influence the forces that direct their lives. In other words, the women were powerless. They lacked any means to have any effect upon the forces that controlled their lives.

The animator saw the objectives for her work as follows:
- that the women should begin to assume responsibility for directing their own lives, and not simply accept the direction of others;
- that the women should regain some dignity in their lives;
- that the women should begin to have some influence upon the fishing association.

The process of participation was developed over time. In the case of these fisherwomen the natural place for their participation was in the fishing association. Yet until now they had been totally excluded from the association; they lacked any voice in the organization that was supposed to represent them.

In these circumstances participation cannot be achieved immediately; it has to be prepared for. In addition participation in the fishing association had to come about as an expression of the women's rights, and not simply as a result of an invitation by the men. Yet without belonging to some formal organization the fisherwomen would never have any hope of improving their lives. So the animator saw her task as working with the women in order that they might establish themselves within this formal organization and have the strength to participate in it effectively.

Method

The first two decisions the animator took were not to impose herself upon the women, and not to proceed according to any particular time-scale. She spent the first nine months only observing the women and being observed by them. One afternoon one of the women stopped and spoke to her after a day's fishing. This was repeated on successive days. Then the animator was invited to fish with the women — 'my baptism in the mud' — and that evening sat and chatted with them. The process had begun — and continues today.

If we examine the animator's approach and subsequent work with the women over a period of seven years, we can see a number of distinct phases:

- a lengthy process of contact and building up of mutual confidence;
- group comes together and meets;
- identification of issues and discussion on particular topics.

Initially there was no structure, and meetings were held with a great air of informality. Little effort was made to hasten or to formalize the group's structure. However, as the group began to get involved in the fishing association, a more formal internal structure emerged to direct this involvement.

The animator herself described her approach as having two main phases: 'discovery', when animator and group established links between each other; and 'waking up', when the group's members began to understand the basis of their miserable existence and decided to do something about it.

Outcome

In numerical terms the work of the animator has resulted in increasing the size and numbers of fisherwomen' s groups in the area. Sixteen women attended the first 'formal' meeting a year after the animator started her work; six years later the original group had grown to 45 and two other groups had been set up, making a total of over 100 fisherwomen involved in group activities. The groups are purposely kept small to avoid the breaking-up which happens in bigger groups.

Some of the original group members have been responsible for spreading knowledge about the group among the local fisherwomen and encouraging new members. In the fifth year the first regional meeting of the different groups was held with 71 participants. But the numerical results hardly reflect the real changes which have taken place.

To encourage such groups to consider the issue of participation actively, and then to undertake some kind of action to get involved, is a discouraging task. When the first formal meeting was held, there seemed to be little on which to build participation. Yet four years later the group felt that perhaps they were now ready to get involved. What took place to bring about this changed situation? For an answer we have to rely on general impressions, informal assessments and observations of changes in behaviour. The animator herself explained how she perceived the fisherwomen's group at the beginning and again four years later:

Group at the first formal meeting	Group four years later
No motivation	Feeling of solidarity
Accepting paternalistic approach	Willingness to make an effort
Passive	Thinking beyond immediate problems
Suspicious	Better organized
Exploited	

As a result of these changes in behaviour, the group grew in strength and began to seek solutions to their problems. First, a widespread movement began to get women registered at the association and to gain legal documentation. Secondly, there was increasing involvement in the association's affairs, leading to the election of two women's representatives to the Board at the end of the sixth year.

These women's groups are part of a wider movement which involves over 5,000 people engaged in fishing in north-east Brazil. The work of the animator and her colleagues has increased these people's participation in their associations and their access to the associations' resources. The associations in turn bring pressure for change. The movement's most notable achievement so far has been Government legislation to control the pollution that poisons the river where they fish.

Adapted from Peter Oakley and David Marsden, *Approaches to Participation in Rural Development*, ILO, pages 51—54

The questions below are to help you check your own understanding of the paper. Please indicate which of the responses you agree with, and which you disagree with. For some statements you may find that you agree with several responses.

1. The animator:

(   ) a. shared the life of the fisherwomen

(   ) b. took technical information to the fisherwomen

(   ) c. told the women how they should solve their problems

(   ) d. told the women that they must confront the men

(   ) e. started from the women's own understanding

(   ) f. managed the women's affairs for them

2. Her general attitude towards the fisherwomen was one of:

(   ) a. pity

(   ) b. respect

(   ) c. understanding

(   ) d. impatience

(   ) e. confidence

(   ) f. concern

3. The animator understood the fisherwomen's problem as being:

(   ) a. that they lacked knowledge of the modern world

(   ) b. that they lacked power

(   ) c. that they lacked any resources to change their situation

(   ) d. that they had no control over their own lives

(   ) e. that they had no access to financial support

(   ) f. that they had no motivation to change

4. The methods which she used were:

(   ) a. asking the women questions about their problems

(   ) b. providing strong leadership

(   ) c. conducting a survey

(   ) d. giving advice

(   ) e. giving the women information about their rights

(   ) f. allowing the women to take the lead

(   ) g. listening

5. The resources which she was using were:

(   ) a. her knowledge of, and conviction about, people's rights

(   ) b. her own skills, knowledge, attitudes, values and convictions

(   ) c. money, aid

(   ) d. her understanding of the ways power is distributed

(   ) e. her contacts with influential people

(   ) f. her knowledge of the local situation

6. Her intentions were that:

(   ) a. the women should identify their problems themselves

(   ) b. the women should make their own decisions

(   ) c. the women should gain more control over their own lives

(   ) d. the women should become aware of injustice and inequality

(   ) e. the process of organizing should spread to other groups of women

(   ) f. she should uplift the women

7. The process of development which took place required:

(   ) a. time

(   ) b. organization

(   ) c. foreign aid

(   ) d. formal education

(   ) e. participation

(   ) f. new understanding

(   ) g. solidarity

8. In the process, the women:

(   ) a. began to understand their situation and their possibilities differently

(   ) b. participated in decisions about their own lives

(   ) c. co-operated with one another

(   ) d. competed with one another

(   ) e. gained greater control over their lives

(   ) f. gained greater self-respect

(   ) g. engaged in confrontation with the men.

John Staley, *Enticing the Learning: Trainers in Development,* University of Birmingham, pages 226-227

Entering into It: Using Simulations

▶ *I will not forget the simulation exercise very easily; a simple lecture comes in through one ear and leaves immediately through the other.*

▶ *I like these exercises. They demand a lot of activity — physically as well as theoretically and emotionally. We are not waiting for each other, but really interacting all together at the same time*

Simulation as a Method

To simulate something is to create a resemblance or representation of it. As a method, simulation represents some aspect of the 'real world' in a simplified and controlled way. So a simulation exercise is a working 'model' of a bit of everyday life. By entering into and experiencing the way the model works, we can perceive and understand that bit of the real world more clearly.

The method is versatile and can be applied to many aspects of life and work and at every level. For example, a simulation can be set in a rural village or in UN agencies' offices. It can deal with a big issue, such as social injustice, or a small issue such as a personnel decision. It can represent a huge system, such as international trade, or a small structure, such as a team of colleagues. It may be focussed on a particular task such as planning, or on a particular role such as development worker, or even on the behaviour of individuals.

Whatever 'bit of real life' is being examined, most simulations start with a structure or situation. Members are allocated to roles within the structure, and are given objectives to work towards. Boundaries are set and rules for interaction are specified. Materials, such as counters and cards, are often used. The emphasis is usually on decision-making by individuals or small groups, and on interaction between different roles within the structure or situation.

The 'action' may continue for up to an hour, and perhaps longer. The action is followed by reflection, often with questions to focus the discussion. Members review their individual and collective experience, examine the processes and behaviour at different levels within the simulation, and share perspectives from the different roles they have played.

The learning comes through changed perception, new insight, the impact of feelings, and use of the imagination, as much as through analysis and understanding.

Simulations work best for groups which are already familiar with action-reflection methods. They can be used in a course during the early weeks, but may be more effective later.

They often become significant events in the life of a course group. Their length, complexity and depth of involvement can make a lasting impression. They provide an experience which all members share. When this becomes part of the life of the group it contributes to the growth of the group itself.

Simulation is usually a popular method. As in role play, it allows individuals to explore roles and to experiment with new behaviour in safety. This is one source of excitement. In addition, many simulations contain elements of fun and 'play'; indeed they are sometimes referred to as simulation 'games' or learning games. The use of counters, cards, building bricks and so on adds to the impression of play.

All this calls for a 'light touch' from the trainer while he/she conducts the simulation. The more serious work may come afterwards, during the discussion and reflection. The final task is relating the experience and the learning to the real world. The learning is often deep and long-lasting.

Simulation and the Trainer

Conducting a large-scale simulation for the first time is a challenge for the trainer. Many prepare themselves beforehand by experiencing the simulation as a participant, or by acting as assistant to an experienced trainer.

Most published simulations contain instructions that are clear and complete, and they can be used with confidence. A few have only sketchy instructions, and some do not give enough guidance for conducting the reflection. Trainers should remember that the reflection is as important as the action.

The connection between some simulations and the real world is close and obvious, but in others it may be more difficult to recognize. Groups already practised in action-reflection methods will make the connections more easily.

Some simulations are predictable, and produce consistent outcomes. Others are less predictable. This does not affect their potential for learning, but trainers should then be prepared for alternative outcomes.

Many simulations are light-hearted and fun, and make the learning comfortable. A few are 'heavier' and lead to outcomes which may be realistic, but which are also disappointing and pessimistic. This does not diminish the learning, but it can be discouraging for an inexperienced group.

Sometimes members become uncomfortable about the way they have behaved in a simulation. They may excuse themselves by saying, 'This was only a game,' or 'It wasn't real,' or 'I'd never do that in the real world'. Trainers will recognize the need for excuses, but should challenge such assertions about the method. A simulation may be a simplified model, but our behaviour within the model is as real as our behaviour anywhere else.

If a group already has pent-up tensions which have not been recognized or dealt with earlier, a simulation may provide the opportunity for release. Then there may be outbursts and exaggerated responses within the simulation. Trainers need to be aware of such a possibility.

Sometimes the dynamic of a simulation can be strengthened by adding 'real' resources, such as the group's refreshments. This adds to the 'real life' quality of the experience, although it can also strengthen feelings and reactions.

None of these possibilities should discourage trainers from using the method. Indeed, they can be welcomed because they bring more of the 'real world' into the training.

Introducing the Method to the Course Group

Before the first simulation is used in a course, the trainer should take 5—10 minutes to introduce the method itself, drawing on the points below.

- A simulation is a simplified model of that aspect of life, or of our work, which we want to study.
- In a simulation each of us is given a role. We enter the model in our role and interact with other people in their roles.
- While we are in our role in a simulation we are given a task to perform. The task may be similar to a task we have in everyday life or work, or it may not.
- Tools or materials may be used in the tasks. Scissors, rulers, cardboard, counters, paper and string are examples.
- While we are in a simulation we have choices. We have to make decisions about how we are going to perform our role, tackle the task, and interact with others. The more we are aware of the way that we and others are doing things and behaving during the simulation the more we shall learn from it.
- A simulation has a set of rules or boundaries. These often represent some of the structures and constraints of the outer world in a simplified form.
- It is a method in which we have the experience first. Then we reflect upon what happened, why and how it happened, how we can understand it, and what we can learn from these things. The core of the method is analyzing the experience we have had in the simulation, and relating that to experience in the outer world.
- Simulations are usually fun.

 # Simulations in the DSC

Eight large-scale (two or three hour) simulations have been used regularly in the DSC. These are well-tried simulations, and some of them are widely known. They are listed here.

1. An Experience of Planning

This simulation can be used to open up the subject of planning and to expose and explore some of the issues around participation in planning. It is described in full, with instructions, in An Experience of Planning (page 446).

2. Programming a Literacy Scheme

This simulation explores detailed decision-making within an overall plan. It is described in full, with instructions, in An Experience of Programming (page 457).

3. Pins and Straws

This simulation reveals the outcomes of different styles of leadership: authoritarian, democratic, laissez-faire and/or bureaucratic. It is described in full, with instructions, in Pins and Straws: Experience of Leadership Styles (page 407).

4. The Trading Game

This is a well-known and much-used simulation. It provides an excellent overall introduction to the world trade system and its inequalities. Instructions for the simulation have been published several times by NGOs.[1] Since the instructions are widely available, they are not repeated in this manual; but suggestions on adapting the simulation to increase its relevance for international development workers are given in The World Trade System: Using The Trading Game (page 308).

5. Starpower

This is a celebrated simulation which is widely known in training circles. It deals with the dynamics of power at society and community levels. The instructions are protected by copyright, so they cannot be repeated here, but they can be obtained from the publishers.[2] Notes for trainers on using this simulation with international development workers are given in An Experience of Power (page 305).

6. BaFa-BaFa

BaFa-BaFa is also a well-known simulation. It gives us an experience of two different cultures, and of moving from one into the other. It helps us to understand what culture is, and to think about how our culture affects our behaviour, our assumptions and our values. It deals with some of the issues of cultural interaction, and is especially useful to those who work as expatriates or with expatriates. Above all, this simulation is fun. It has been much enjoyed by many groups. The diary extract at the end of this section conveys the flavour of it.

BaFa-BaFa is protected by copyright, but instructions are available from the publishers.[3]

The notes on debriefing in the published instructions are sketchy, and more time may be needed for rehearsing the cultures. Allow two hours for the simulation itself and an hour for reflection.

---

1. For example, *The Trading Game*, Christian Aid, London. See www.christian-aid.org.uk
2. R. Garry Shirts, *Starpower: Director's Instructions*, Western Behavioral Sciences Institute, La Jolla, California. See www.stsintl.com/schools-charities/
3. R. Garry Shirts, *BaFa BaFa: A Cross Culture Simulation*, Simile II, La Jolla. Devised by the same author as *Starpower*. See www.stsintl.com/schools-charities/

7. Hierarchy

This explores authority and communication between the levels in a three-tier structure. The workers of the organization have a task to perform, but they cannot proceed with it unless they receive information from the supervisors. The supervisors cannot act without the approval of the managers. The three levels are located in different places, representing Head Office, Regional Office and Field Office, so most of the communication is indirect. The dynamics are those of an organization where work groups are controlled 'from above and afar', a common arrangement in development work. Most players experience tension and frustration. The final outcome depends largely on how the managers play their role. The diary extracts below describe members' experience at different levels.

Instructions for this simulation have been published.[4] Some versions of the instructions are incomplete, and trainers should check them carefully. It is an elaborate simulation, and requires up to four hours altogether.

8. The Aid Committee

This simulation was originally devised to inform the supporters of OXFAM about how the agency makes decisions about grants. Supporters work in small groups as the 'aid committee' of OXFAM, they consider 'applications' from six or seven development organizations working in a particular country, and 'make decisions' about grants to these organizations.

In an adapted and deepened form the simulation is useful in the training of development workers, whose own organizations are often the applicants for grants. The role reversal helps to correct the stereotypes which flourish in aid hierarchies. It reveals some of the difficulties faced by donor agencies, and helps would-be applicants to see how they can improve their own participation in the aid relationship.

For this purpose, up-to-date, deeper, and perhaps more contentious, material is needed. This takes the form of one-page 'applications', each based on an outline of the work of a real organization in a particular country. There should be applications from six to eight organizations, but all names should be disguised and the organizations should not be known to course members.

The country should not be represented among the members; but it should be somewhat familiar, and film material from the country may be used to prepare the 'committee members' for their task.

The 'committee papers' can be distributed for reading before the committees meet. If the applications represent a range of development work, the discussions in the committees become a useful review of members' present thinking about development.

---

4. For example, John Adair et al., Hierarchy, A Handbook of Management Training Exercises, Volume I, BACIE, London, pages 69—77. Another version is Communications and Problem Solving in a Hierarchy, published by The Institute of Finance Management, pages 196—205. The simulation seems to have originated at the University of North London.

After their deliberations the 'committees' compare their decisions. These are usually different, which is a useful insight in itself. The committees' decisions are often accompanied by requests for more information, further requirements, conditions, postponements, partial grants and so on, which are the very kinds of donor agency behaviour that applicants complain about.

Members take time to 'get into' their roles as committee members and to deal with the written material, so allow two hours for the simulation itself and one hour for reflection.

The diary extracts included below convey some of the insights gained from this simulation.

BaFa-BaFa: entering another culture

▶ *I was appointed to start my cultural adventure in a very friendly and relaxed Alpha culture... we lived happily in our culture, loving and caring of each other. We enjoyed our friendships within a fairly strict set of rules... we lived in a beautiful harmony.*

But all of a sudden the door was opened and a stranger came in. He approached straight our female members. The Alpha-men reacted immediately by throwing him out of the community. However, he kept coming back, behaving the same way. The peace of the Alpha community was then disturbed by the continuous stream of visitors of the Beta group...

Our Alpha community also paid visits to the Beta group. While I was still checking the cards in my hand there were some greedy, money-hunting Beta members around me trying to cheat and exploit me. I couldn't concentrate to learn their culture since all my energy went for protecting my cards...

Hierarchy: an organizational structure

▶ *I was in the workers' group. We had to work hard to fulfil the instructions of our supervisors and managers. Our managers and supervisors were sitting comfortably in the top floor and sometimes coming to see us for their so-called surprise visits...*

▶ *We dealt with feelings yesterday and it was interesting to note that for some, the simple ordinary simulation exercise was turning rather sore as feelings of frustration and anger from the workers' group began to surface. N said twice that the whole thing was becoming rather real...*

▶ *The exercise continued over lunch, and there were some rumours of strike action and compulsory redundancies...*

▶ *I started my work in development as a manager in a top-down organisational structure. The exercise has helped me to understand my role, and it provides an opportunity for self-criticism. It has helped me to understand the staff at other levels by putting me in their place.*

The Aid Committee

▶ *Earlier in the day I sat down in a group of six as an Aid Committee, to decide on whether or not to support seven projects recommended by our representative in Brazil. For all of us it was a big jump from one side of receiving Aid to the other (deciding where the Aid should go) and showed me some of the processes involved in the decision-making. We had a considerable discussion as to what was our Committee about. We wanted to define ourselves, which we felt necessary so that we become able to decide our priority areas. The other interesting debate that we had was about criteria ... The fact that we, the Aid Committee, laid down criteria put us in a very powerful position in relation to the people involved in the Projects. They were not involved in the decision; and although we said we wanted to support projects that empower people I wondered whether our very action in this respect was disempowering.*

▶ *We were divided into four groups and played an Aid Committee meeting ... We had seven applications to consider and only two were accepted fully in all committees. The other five applications were responded to differently by the different committees. Some refused them, others accepted only part ... Some asked for more information and breakdown ... In many ways we acted in the same way as many donor agencies act, a behaviour we very often dislike ... But when you look back, and see it from the donors' point of view, you can understand the donors' doubt ... I see the importance in working for trust and equal power between donors and recipients.*

▶ *I have discovered that donors are human just like me.*

Looking at It: Visual Material

▶ *Have you been to rural Egypt? ... similarities like bread-making, oven, children and their natural play-ground, milking goats, chasing flies while eating... Familiar sights can lead us to misinterpret the picture: 18 people saw the same picture, but came up with different ideas and meanings. Don't know where to start? Sit down, listen and observe was the advice given...*

Visual material such as photographs, drawings, film or video is widely used in education and training to convey information, raise issues, illustrate situations and demonstrate professional work.

In the DSC we used films from many sources and on many subjects, from world poverty to re-afforestation, from the evolution of a development programme to the working of a women's trades union. Such films make a significant contribution to members' knowledge, and the change of medium is usually welcomed.

However this use of visual material to support the teaching of subject-matter belongs more to an academic approach, and so it is beyond the scope of this manual.

What can be done here is to describe how we can also use visual material as part of an experience-based approach.

More Real Life

Small numbers of suitable photographs or short lengths of film can be used as 'visual case studies'. If the material shows us everyday life — people at work, people in their community, people at home — it becomes another means to bring more real life into the classroom, with the added stimulus of a visual dimension.[1]

Suitable material illustrates situations or communities comparable to those where course members themselves work. In other words the people in the film or in the photographs should be in similar roles to the people whom the members meet in the course of their daily work. Examples from development work could be a family in a village, a group of farmers, women in a shanty town, a child playing, a committee of elders, some local officials, another development worker, a community meeting, or an organizational committee — more or less ordinary people setting about more or less ordinary everyday life.

Ideally this kind of material should be open and non-committal, without an obvious message or principle. Material which promotes a point of view, or teaches us a lesson, or leads us to certain conclusions — however valid these may be — does the work for

---

1. The medium chosen must be appropriate to the training venue and circumstances as well as to the group concerned. Photographs and illustrations can be handled easily. More can go wrong with film and video. They require equipment, reliable electricity, blinds or curtains, suitable storage, technical support and so on. Film may seem exciting to members, but the excitement may come from seeing films as entertainment. It takes time to adjust to the discipline of using film for learning.

us, instead of allowing us to work with the 'raw material' and arrive at our own questions or conclusions. There are parallels here with the development process itself.

A few appropriate photographs or a short length of film will be enough to generate a lot of useful sharing and discussion. The material should be accessible, digestible and stimulating. Photographs and illustrations should be large enough, so that several members can see and work with them at the same time.[2] If a collection of photographs or illustrations is available, a small selection should be made, either by the trainer or by the members. Between 8—12 enlarged photographs may be enough for half a session of discussion, whether in the whole group or in small groups.

Likewise, a complete film or video of 50—60 minutes may be too discursive, too indigestible and too passive. Instead an extract of 10—15 minutes can be selected. Even that may be better seen in two or three sequences, interspersed with discussion.

Photographs can be looked at for any length of time, and can be referred to again, just as a case study or discussion paper can be read again. Films, on the other hand, move at a predetermined speed, and those who are watching cannot adjust this. As we watch a film we see more than we can take in or remember, so we make a selection according to our own interests, experience and preconceptions. This makes it all the more important that film material is thoroughly discussed afterwards. If the material is shown again after the discussion, it allows members to review their earlier selection and to check their perceptions in the light of the discussions.

The broad task of the members is to observe and gather whatever information they can about the people shown, and about the situation and the relationships, to recognize the reactions which the material produces in themselves, to make links with their own experience and, by sharing perceptions and interpretations with each other, to consider alternative understandings and possibilities.

The task of the trainer is to raise appropriate questions about the material. For example, after looking at a photograph of people in a family, some questions might be:
'How do you imagine the relationships between the people in the photograph?
'Do you think that the family was happy or sad at that time?
What makes you think so?'
'We can see the content of the picture. What do you imagine is the process?'
'For you does the photograph illustrate development or underdevelopment?'

After 15 minutes of film material from a community, some questions might be:
'What struck you most in the film? Why did that strike you?'
'Did the physical setting (or situation or culture) seem strange or familiar?'
'What did you see which you did not understand?'
'If you could visit the community shown in the film and meet one person there, which person would you choose to meet? What questions would you want to ask that person?'

---

2. A suitable size for pictures is 12 × 16 inches (30 × 40 cm).

We are closer to reality with photographs and film than with writing, and their impact is more immediate. The responses members make to them are often quick and strong. Such responses are rich material for further work.

▶ *The only sounds we heard were the sounds of the village... as the film was only 15 minutes long, we realised that we couldn't make value judgements but understood that this was a trap that development workers often fall into. ...as a Westerner, who is used to getting to grips with problems immediately... my desire to rush forward was mirrored in our desire to suggest improvements to the Egyptian village, immediately, without gathering further information. We realised our fault.*

▶ *...a film which projected picture-memories of our childhood, of relatives and friends back home, living in their village, which is so similar to the one we saw. O and A saw themselves in the film returning to their village, being greeted, being hugged in a real local way, being respected, being welcomed, being really understood and being themselves. B and R saw themselves milking a goat, or was it a sheep? What a pity we could not see it for real. A film which made us think about our roots and dreams. I looked at W's face. The sun was shining through the window and made his whole face shine. We don't need to watch any more films, just look at each other and find out about the stories behind the different faces.*

Programmed methods use written material — either on paper or on a computer screen — and require continuing interaction from the reader. At frequent intervals the reader is asked to make some kind of response, either within the written material itself or in discussion with other readers. The response has to be made before the reader is permitted to continue using the material. The purpose is to reinforce the learning in a more active way than happens with straightforward reading.

When the content of the material is information and ideas, the method belongs more to an academic approach. When the content poses situations and problems, and calls for decision-making and sharing with other readers, then the method can fit an experience-based approach. Four variations of the method are described below, three of which belong to an experience-based approach.

The difficulty with either approach is that materials have to be prepared. Writing the appropriate material — or even adapting existing material — and then laying it out is a big task. The instrument has to be finely tuned to the users. Both the content itself, and the instructions for working with it, have to be clearly understandable.

After it is written the material has to be tried out informally, perhaps two or three times, before it can be introduced to a large group or used as a course event. If some readers are working in a second language those who prepare the material will have to keep this in mind too.

For the trainer who enjoys writing, all this may present an interesting challenge and a creative opportunity, but for others it may seem a daunting task. Attempting the work is obviously more worthwhile if the course or training event will be repeated, and the exercise can be used again.

When a programmed exercise is used during a course the trainer's task is to introduce and explain it, to set up small groups, announce the timing, and so on. The trainer then withdraws, and makes only an occasional visit to check on progress and timing while the members and groups work on their own. Both trainers and members may welcome this in itself, partly as a further change in the methodology, but also as a break from each other!

Programmed Learning

Here information and ideas are imparted in small pieces.[1] The content is broken down into a sequence of small items, each typically a short paragraph with one piece of information or one idea. Members study this material individually and in their own time.[2] As they read each item, they are required to work with it, usually by answering a

---

1. Not to be confused with An Experience of Programming (page 452). Both are concerned with breaking a large whole into small steps.

question about what they have read. Two or three alternative answers to the question are offered, and the member chooses one and records it. The correct answer then follows, the member compares that with his/her own answer, and then moves on to the next item.

Although this belongs to an academic approach it can be used alongside experience-based methods to convey content which is otherwise lacking. For example, in the DSC we found that some course members had received only a limited scientific education. Yet unless every member had a basic knowledge of the earth's natural cycles, and of the impact of human activity on the earth, it was not possible for the group as a whole to deal with environmental issues in relation to development. So alongside the DSC we ran a weekly programmed course entitled 'Exhausting the Earth'.

Members worked through a section of 'Exhausting the Earth' each week. They did this individually, outside normal DSC hours. This meant that those who were new to the information could take as much time they needed for the task, while those who were already informed could work faster. This weekly learning was reinforced by discussion in small groups, during which members also shared opinions and relevant experience.

The discussions enabled those who had more knowledge and understanding to assist those with less. In this way a wide range of content could be conveyed to course members without using up course time, and without resorting to lectures.

Decision-Making Exercises

The method comes closer to an experience-based approach when the items in the written material are problems to be solved and decisions to be made. Course members are asked to imagine themselves in a familiar role, such as development worker. In that role they read about a situation or a problem from professional work, and are then asked to make an appropriate response. In practice they are usually asked to choose one among several possible ways of responding. Then they go on to read comments on each of the alternative responses, and find out how their own decision is evaluated within the exercise. The procedure is then repeated with the next situation or problem.

Such exercises can bring more 'real life' into the classroom, as well as providing a change of method, and they are generally well-received. Some members appreciate being given 'right answers' for once!

When the exercise includes periodic discussion in a small group the learning is enriched by members' differing views. A group that 'gets its teeth' into such an exercise may learn a lot, as well as having fun.

In the DSC we used an interactive exercise called Chikkanahalli.[3] Members work in role as village development workers in small groups of five or six. They alternate every five

2. And sometimes at a distance, hence the term Distance Learning.
3. Chikkanahalli is set in India, but has been adapted for use in other countries such as Tanzania.

or ten minutes between working on their own and working with the small group. At each stage in the exercise they are presented with a situation or problem, and are asked to make and record their individual decision from among six alternatives. They are then asked to discuss the matter in the small group and to make a group decision. After that they read comments on the alternatives, and assess their own and the group's decisions.

Members then move on to the next situation, again working individually at first, and afterwards collectively. This switching from individual to collective work provides valuable alternation within the learning process. It also leads to the sharing of experience, opinions and organizational practice between the members at each stage as they try to reach agreement on the group decision.

For the sake of more structure the exercise includes scores, and members are awarded these according to which alternatives they choose. However, 'the purpose is not to achieve high scores, but to take away as many ideas and insights as you can'.

The Action Maze

Problem-solving and decision-making can be taken further when the successive situations in the exercise form a continuing sequence, and when members are confronted by the consequences of their decisions at the next stage in the exercise.

In the variation known as action maze, the member — again in role — reads about a situation and makes a decision from among alternatives. Depending on the decision, he/she is then directed to another page in the exercise and there reads what has happened as a direct result of that decision. He/she is now asked to make a further decision in the light of the new situation, and so on. This continues until the member achieves one of the several possible outcomes, some favourable and some unfortunate. At this point the member is released from the exercise.

The close linking of decisions and their consequences gives this method an imaginary structure which the member 'enters into', as with role play and simulation. The members 'perform' in the role given, but because decisions are made individually, and the path taken through the exercise is determined by those decisions, each member works alone.

In the DSC we used an action maze called Ana Amed's Posters, an exercise in managing a personnel difficulty in a development organization. The exercise contains a variety of situations that members may or may not have to face, depending on the decisions they make. The situations range from infringements of organizational practice to grumbling among the staff; from distress and tears to an unexpected and formidable visitor; and from the loss of a valued employee to intervention by the Chairman.

All the difficulties can be avoided however, and a happy ending can be achieved, by careful explanation, patient listening, the acceptance of feelings, and an understanding of the person!

The In-Tray Exercise

This is another variation which again involves decision-making and problem-solving. Members are asked to imagine that they have been appointed to a new job, such as a manager in an organization, and that they have just arrived at their new office, but without a handover arrangement from their predecessor.

As they start their new work, they discover that their in-tray already contains a dozen items — letters, memos and notes. Some of these represent opportunities, but most seem to be problems. Some are big problems and others trivial; some are internal to the organization and others external; some are procedural and others concern policy or broader issues.

The task of members, in this role and situation, is to decide what should be done about each item: what is urgent, what can be left until later, who should be consulted, what response should be made, what additional information is needed, and so on. The in-tray is worked through individually, and the decisions are later shared in small groups.

In the DSC we used an in-tray exercise called 'Mr Sen Moore'. Mr Moore has just been appointed Director of APSA, a development organization...

Chikkanahalli, Ana Amed's Posters and Mr Sen Moore were prepared for use in the DSC. They are too lengthy and too specialised to be included here, but are mentioned as examples of the kinds of material which can be written to meet particular training needs.

Chikkanahalli

▶ *...an exercise on decision-making that needed lots of imagination... What will you do to start your work? How will you approach the people? How will you respond to their interruptions? Do you think they were lazy and ignorant? Be careful! Don't be prejudiced. Don't have pre-conceived ideas. We worked for the whole morning and part of the afternoon on our own. We didn't see our tutors...*

▶ *Don't take the score seriously — it's not a competition. We are self-regulated again. The first stage is done. The delicate task of introductions in Chikkanahalli is so important, and A's experience is shown to be an advantage. My score does me credit on the first question, but not on the second — scores are only important when I get a good one. Our group is working well together under I's leadership. We are hurrying to finish. The final questionnaire is completed and I am the perfect development worker! Or is it that I have discovered how the person who set the questions thinks, and gave the expected answer? I am far too conscientious to take a holiday and have gone back to Chikkanahalli.*

Ana Amed's Posters

▶ *I found myself as a qualified supervisor in a rural development programme facing a conflict with Ana Amed, my team secretary. It was not an easy task but at last I managed to keep her in her working position.*

▶ *Problem-solving like this helps me to know a lot more about myself. It is characteristic for me to have difficulties in careful explanation but I am a good listener, and so after Mrs Ana Amed stopped crying she told me a lot and quite intimate problems of her life. That helped! I believe it also helped because I didn't have a quick, good and right solution of this problem. In going the way together, Mrs Ana Amed could develop her problem for herself.*

Mr Sen Moore

▶ *It was indeed quite a revealing experience how different people reacted differently in the same given situation. Each one of us was bringing his/her values, culture, and experience in making decisions. Some of the decisions we took were conditioned by the law of the land of our domicile or expatriation and the local traditions. Whereas I could easily endorse the idea of a teacher becoming a member of a teachers' union, a friend from Sudan could not stomach it. Some could not see anything wrong in obliging the Police Officer...*

...The experiences in the smaller goups were later shared with the whole group. A question was raised whether it was right to open the envelope with the superscription 'Personal and Confidential' and addressed to (the former Director) by name. The consensus seemed to be that as long as the word 'Private' was not there Mr Moore could open the letter and deal with it.

6.8 How Are We Doing? Widening Evaluation

▶ *In the interim evaluation it is interesting to listen to course members' opinions and suggestions, not only about development as a subject, but also as a course: its structure, methods, etc. It was useful feedback for both tutors and course participants.*

The evaluation and monitoring of participatory training happens at three levels.

Future Performance

Ultimately training must be judged by the future performance and effectiveness of the people who receive training. This can be tested only after they have returned to their work, and perhaps only some time later.

Continuous Monitoring

A second level is monitoring of the learning within the course itself. Ideally this is happening all the time. The trainers follow the process and interactions, they observe the climate in the group and the roles members are playing, and they listen to feedback from the course diary and other events. For an experienced trainer this process — which is partly internal and partly discussed with colleagues — becomes automatic. The result is continuous adjustment to an always-changing situation. Flexibility in role, iterative planning, an evolving timetable, and a repertoire of alternative inputs and events make such adjustment possible.

Periodic Evaluation

The third level involves more deliberate and more explicit evaluations of progress. Both trainers and members are formally involved, and the results are used, both by the trainers who have organized the course, and by the members who share responsibility for it. Most courses include an evaluation at the end, by which time it is too late to change that particular course. If an interim evaluation can be arranged early in a course, the results can be used immediately.

Interim Evaluation

Obvious items to be evaluated include the extent of progress towards the objectives, the levels of satisfaction, the usefulness of particular sessions and events, the effectiveness of methods, how far expectations are being met, how much the learning is relevant to members' work back home, and practical arrangements.

It is more difficult to evaluate the role and work of individuals, both members and trainers. In a participatory methodology, members share responsibility for the course.

Each has a contribution to make to the life and learning of the group, and each is in charge of his or her own participation, role and learning. So any course evaluation should at least invite members to reflect on themselves, and on their role, commitment, contribution and learning. Widening the evaluation in this way reminds members that progress and satisfaction do not depend only on the trainers.

Trainers may have to decide how far they are willing to submit their own performance for examination by the course members. To do this they need confidence in themselves and trust in the judgement of members. The principle here is that we should not expect others to change unless we ourselves are willing to change. Trainers need feedback for their own growth and change, even if this is sometimes painful. The more they are willing to receive it, the more evaluation serves as a model for participatory evaluation in development work.

The course group, as a whole, also shares in the responsibility. So there should be questions about the process in the course group, the growth of the group, the climate, the levels of participation, the observance of norms, and any current difficulties. The responses to such questions are necessary before the members can even consider whether they want to change the way their group is functioning. This also has parallels in development work.

Using a Questionnaire

One way of finding a balance between encouraging openness and retaining some control is for the trainers to draft an evaluation questionnaire and distribute it to each member for a written response.[1]

Members should be told that the results will be shared in the course group, and that they will be expected to take responsibility for what they write. The principle here is to keep responsibility close to the members, and not allow them to blame others and 'walk away'. They should be ready to support and justify their opinions, and should have suggestions for improvement. A written evaluation is also an opportunity for members to practise giving feedback in writing.

When trainers use a questionnaire it becomes their responsibility to see that the responses are collected, collated and reported back. Yet another principle of development work is relevant here, which is that data should not be taken away from a community to be used elsewhere, but should remain available to the community for its own purposes. If members find that the reporting back is complete and frank, they will gain trust in the trainers.

When trainers report back on the responses to a question it does not mean that individual members are exposed. 'Three people wrote that the session on underdevelopment

---

1. Another possibility is that course members are given the task, partly to evaluate the course and partly to obtain experience in evaluation.

was disappointing' allows those individuals to take responsibility and explain their view further; but it also allows them to remain silent. Nonetheless, it is difficult to maintain anonymity in a course group, even if this is desirable.

Members can be asked to discuss their responses to certain questions in small groups, and then to share conclusions or recommendations in the whole group. Questions which produce diffuse responses can be dealt with in this way.

However the reporting back is done, members find it is helpful to to see how their own responses and perceptions match others in the group. They may discover that their perceptions and feelings are more widely shared than they expected.

Members' opinions about levels of progress, achievement, satisfaction, etc can be graded on a scale. If the course group is large they can also be scored. A scale with an even number of points — perhaps four or six — forces members at least to choose above or below the mid-point. When a scale has three or five points, too many members may choose the mid-point.

Scores can be transformed into averages and percentages, but trainers should be cautious about this. The numbers in most courses are small, and small samples do not support averages or percentages. It is more useful to report actual scores.

The information and opinions which emerge from an interim evaluation may lead to changes, so the sooner it can be done the better. On the other hand members must be given enough course time to adjust to the methodology and to form their views clearly. An interim evaluation may be conducted at the end of three weeks in a three month course.

Some useful interim evaluation questions are:

- 'How has your understanding of development (or other topic) changed since the beginning of the course?'
- 'What have you learned about yourself which you did not know before the beginning of the course?'
- 'How do you assess the progress the group has made so far towards achieving its objectives in the course — disappointing/adequate/good/very good?'
- 'How do you see your own contribution in assisting the group to achieve its objectives?'
- 'Do you think that the course group has any difficulties at present? If so, what are they, and what do you think can be done about them?'
- 'Reflecting on your experience of the course so far, what has been — more useful/less useful/frustrating or disappointing?'
- 'How do you see your learning in the course as being relevant to your own work?'
- 'Can you make any suggestions to the trainers about their role/s which will help them to increase the learning?'

End of Course Evaluation

By the end of a course the attention of members begins to move towards departure and back home. The amount of time and energy which they are able to give to evaluation may be limited. Yet there will be opinions and feelings about the course which they need to express, individually or collectively, and they will want a considered reaction from the trainers. They may also want to know the trainers' assessment of their group.

If, after a three month course, the concluding evaluation is started at the beginning of the final week, there should be time for responses to be collected, collated and reported back by the middle of the week. If this can be done a day or two before the members depart, there is still time for reflection and discussion of the outcome within the course group, and still time for members to make recommendations for the future.

▶ *It was followed by discussion of results of the evaluation. There are two things I appreciate about this activity. First, we had it in the middle of the term, and secondly for discussing its results. Often, in my experience, evaluations are done at the end of the activities, which do not give opportunity anymore to discuss the results, nor the chance for changes for learning to the fullest extent. In general, the result of our interim evaluation is very good and I believe we all deserve congratulations from ourselves.*

▶ *The afternoon session touched a lot of raw nerves. This was the interim evaluation session. The power of tutors, linguistic imperialism, domination in sessions, the validity of course activities, the way we challenge or fail to challenge each other, were all touched on with some passion. At times I felt uneasy — was I suddenly aware that we had shifted quadrant, from low challenge and high support to high challenge and low support? On reflection the criticisms of the course seemed balanced — some felt the tutors were giving too many facts and answers, others wanted more ... There were serious issues raised, things all of us have to be aware of. For that alone this difficult session was worthwhile. As F said, 'We all lose when anyone feels unable to contribute.'*

▶ *I suggest that it would be more appropriate if we ourselves set the evaluation questionnaire and method next time, so it becomes our own evaluation and a learning process too.*

6.9　Ending the Week

▶ *...V invited reflections on the week's activities... Finally everyone presented a word as a 'gift' to the group. Flow, affection, interaction, co-operation, solidarity, keep smiling were some of the words.*

Marking the end of each week gives a sense of completion, both to content and process. One or more 'snapshot' exercises can be used for the purpose. Examples are given below. Some of the exercises invite members to make only a brief response, while others have more depth. All are short and simple.

Trainers must expect that in the early weeks the depth of reflection and discussion will be limited. They must also expect that some initial responses will be evaluative, and should be ready to point out the difference between reflection and evaluation.

Such exercises may be more useful for the early weeks, before the course group has gained its own momentum. Later in the course the members themselves may take responsibility for ending the week.

Exercises to End the Week

1. Completing Statements

 Give the members 4 to 6 incomplete statements which are appropriate for that week. For example:

'As I look back over the week...
a) something that has surprised me is...'
b) something that I have enjoyed is...'
c) a difficult moment for me was...'
d) something that I have appreciated about myself is...'
e) I think that we, as a group, are...'

Ask members to complete the statements individually, and then to share their responses in groups of four or five.

Listen to the responses to e) in the whole group. Allow 30 minutes altogether.

2. Reflections on the Week

Ask the members to review the events and experiences of the week individually, and to reflect on their own roles and responses. Ask them to concentrate on the process of the course and sessions, rather than the content. Ask them to jot down notes. Allow ten minutes for this.

■ Then ask them to share their reflections and conclusions in groups of four or five. Allow 20 minutes for this. Collect some of the reflections (but not evaluations) in the whole group. Allow another ten minutes for this.

3. A Word for Myself this week

Tell each member to take some minutes for thought, and to choose a word they would apply to themselves as they have been during the past week. Ask them to write the word down. Then go around the whole course group, one by one, and invite each member to share their word. Allow the words to be clarified if necessary, but not discussed. Allow up to 30 minutes altogether.

4. A Symbol for Myself this week

Ask each member to identify and name an object that symbolizes their experience of themselves during the week — how they have been, and how they have imagined themselves during the week. Allow a few minutes for individual thought. Members then share the symbols in small groups of three or four, but do not discuss them in the whole group. Allow 15 minutes.

5. Sharing Feelings

Invite all members, one by one around the circle of the whole group, to share what they are feeling at that very moment. If some share thoughts instead of feelings point that out gently — 'That's what you are thinking. Can you say what you are feeling?' — but do not press them. If anyone expresses strong or unexpected or negative feelings invite the person concerned to explain. If this exercise is done as an ending to the week, many of the feelings expressed will relate to that, but some may be connected with other matters or issues. Allow up to 20 minutes.

6. A Symbol for the Group

Tell each member to choose a word or a symbol to describe the course group, as they see it at the present time. Ask them to share and discuss these in groups of three or four. Collect some in the whole group, and be ready to discuss them briefly. Allow up to 30 minutes.

7. What Are You Learning?

Tell members to work in pairs with a simple role play. A is himself or herself as a member in the course. B is a colleague from back home who is visiting the course briefly. B wants to know what A is learning from the course. Allow 15 minutes for the role play.

Bring members back to the whole group and invite them to report from either role on their experience of the visit — how it went, how the colleague seemed, and so on

■ — but without repeating the content of the discussion itself. Allow 15 minutes for the reporting.

8. Enabling Questions

Tell members work in groups of three or four. Their task is to share some of their recent reflections and learning, and to frame two enabling questions based on these (For enabling questions see page 376).

Then ask each small group to offer their questions to the whole group. Allow at least 30 minutes.

9. What Roles Have I Been Playing?

This exercise is for later in a course, and should be used only after work on feedback has been done (see page 330). Tell the members to work in groups of three, preferably with two others they feel they know more closely. Their task is to give feedback to each other as each individual requests it, but with a focus on the roles that individuals have been playing during the week (see also The Individual in the Group, page 148—149). The usual rules for feedback apply. Confine the results to the small groups. Allow at least 30 minutes.

10. A Sculpture of the Group

This exercise can be used if the method of still images or sculptures has already been introduced (see page 266—268). Tell members to work in groups of five or six. Using the method their task is to represent the functioning of the whole course group as they see it at the present time. Allow only ten minutes for the small groups to create the sculptures.

Invite each small group to show their sculpture in silence. Invite the remainder of the group to reflect on what they are seeing, but not to criticize or challenge the sculptures. Finish by appreciating the sculptures, and inviting any overall reflections.

▶ *At the end we tried to write the key words of the whole week — reflection... decision-making... sharing... understanding of underdevelopment... what is the good life?... interdependence... feelings... poverty and aid... listening.*

▶ *...ended with cheerful words of the week... like solidarity, sensitivity, optimistic people, time, trust, cooperation...*

▶ *We end our third week with words to describe how we feel now. 2 are unclear, 4 are weary or stressed, 17 are progressing or learning. Quite a good balance, I'd say.*

CHAPTER 7

A Fresh Look
(contributed by Sue Mayo)

▶ *J introduced us to S, an action lecturer ...*

▶ *What we do with S is very different from what we usually do. It's more physical ... I like it.*

The whole of this chapter is based on work contributed to the DSC by Sue Mayo who also supplied the written material for the chapter. The chapter has been edited by John Staley.

The methods described in this chapter can help us to re-examine some of our professional experience by bringing work situations alive through drama. We work with 'real life' in the course room. We also benefit from the observations and interpretations of others, which extend our own perceptions and understanding.

The work is an effective way for members to convey their own experience and to enter into the experience of others. This is especially valuable when members come from different cultures and different work settings. Indeed the work often transcends these differences and reveals universal human relationships and dynamics.

It brings course members into close collaboration with each other, which contributes to cohesion and solidarity within the course group, and strengthens the learning process. And, perhaps as important, the methods are exciting and enjoyable.

The work is divided into five phases, each representing a stage in the methodology. The sequence is designed to build up skills and confidence, and to provide progressive learning opportunities. Exercises at the beginning raise awareness about communication, improve skills in observation, and help members to distinguish observation from interpretation. This is preparation for drama work in the later phases with still images, sculptures and role plays.

The phases should be followed in sequence. Some of the exercises could be used separately, but the drama work should not be attempted without the preparation.

This work is best done after a course group has gained cohesion and the members are working together effectively. The fifth or sixth week has often been a suitable time in three month courses. The complete sequence requires about nine course sessions, depending on the number of role plays in the later phases. If all the work is done in consecutive sessions it may occupy three days. Alternatively, the work could be undertaken, in one or two sessions a day, on consecutive days. Whatever the practical arrangements, it is important that the momentum of the work and the continuity of the learning is not broken.

Objectives

- to provide opportunities for members to re-examine experiences and relationships in their work back home, to become more aware of their own roles and responses, to consider possibilities for change, and to prepare for future action;
- to enable members to share aspects of their work situations, and personal and professional experiences, with other members of the course; and to hear the perceptions, interpretations and insights of others;
- to improve awareness and skills in observation, to distinguish observation and description from interpretation, and to raise awareness about the workings of interpretation;
- to raise members' awareness of inter-personal, organizational and community relationships and communication; of power and powerlessness; and of leadership;
- to give members practice in looking before concluding, describing before interpreting, seeing the possibilities in a situation, recognizing alternatives, identifying moments when change occurs or becomes possible, and trying out new approaches;
- to encourage imagination, creativity, communication, and flexibility among course members and within the course group.

Materials and Rooms

A soft leather ball or small bean bag is generally used in Phase One for Playing Ball. An extra eight or nine lightweight and moveable chairs will be needed in Phase Three for Top Chair and Top Person. Otherwise the only furniture needed are the usual moveable chairs. Alternatively the work can be done sitting on the floor. Either way, open floor space will be needed for the active work.

Separate rooms will be needed in Phase Five for small groups to prepare their still images and role plays.

Generally props, costumes, furniture or other aids to performance are not encouraged in this work because they distract us from direct observation.

Using Drama Methods

Drama methods are experience-based, and follow the familiar alternation of action and reflection. They are participatory, and all members of the group are involved. Even those who have the temporary role of observer are active participants.[1] Members'

---

1. Many of the drama methods are drawn from the work of the Brazilian Theatre Director, Augusto Boal, who originated 'The Theatre of the Oppressed.' Boal coined the word 'spect-actor', meaning a fully active and engaged spectator.

feelings are engaged, as well as their thoughts, and it is important that the group has already done some work in recognizing and sharing feelings.

There are parallels with the case study method (page 164). Both allow us to examine, or re-examine, personal experience. Both allow to bring our own perceptions and experience to bear on a 'story' contributed by another person. Both methods rely on observation, analysis and an imaginative 'entering into' the world of the other. Both encourage differing perceptions and interpretations, and second thoughts. Both are as likely to lead to divergent thinking as to convergent thinking.

Yet drama methods have a more vital quality than written methods. They offer us a different — and living — medium, and a greater depth of experience. Some have compared it to working in a different dimension, or in a different language, a universal human language which is physical and visual.

Although parts of the work are based on the personal experience and work situations of individuals, it is not possible to recreate these exactly in the course room. Yet much that is authentic from their experience and situation can be shown. After using the methods, members often comment that they feel they have really 'been in that situation' or have 'met the people there'.

Working with the methods encourages members to balance observation of the present with imagined possibilities for the future; and to balance attention to issues with a concern for persons. In such ways drama methods have a wider reach than other methods. They are vivid because they happen literally 'before our eyes', and they are immediate because they take place in the 'here and now.' They are also more complete because they work at the emotional level as well as at the thinking and analytical level.

While there are important skills which support the usefulness of the methods, members are not required to like or to be interested in theatre and performance. Like any methods, they will suit some people better than others.

The 'rules' of each exercise or method provide important boundaries. They may sometimes seem restrictive, but their purpose is to create a focus and a common purpose. Trainers may need to remind members from time to time of the focus and the boundaries of a particular piece of work.

In all the exercises there are certain outcomes that often occur. However it is best never to count on particular outcomes. One of the exciting things about these methods is that they open up a whole range of possibilities and alternatives.

▶ *By the use of lectures, many a mind went out to venture. By the use of role plays, many a mind imagined reality ...*

Phase One:
Paying More Attention to Other People

▶ *S, a visiting tutor, led the course participants through a soft but very careful analysis ...*
using a tool known as drama.

This phase contains exercises to increase awareness of others, and to improve skills in observation and communication. Introducing the work as a whole, followed by the exercises in this phase, takes about 1¼ hours or most of one course session. For some of the exercises members work in pairs.

Playing Ball

This is a simple game which brings to the surface many aspects of communication. It is usually played with a soft leather ball or small bean bag. It can also be played with an imaginary ball, which makes the game accessible for members with restricted mobility. Allow 15 minutes for the exercise altogether.

■ Ask the members to stand or sit in a circle. Trainers should take part. Members throw the ball across the circle to one another, first making sure they have eye contact with the person to whom they are throwing.

Once members are throwing and catching freely, ask them to say their own names as they throw.

When a real ball is used some members who are games players may show off their skills at the expense of those unfamiliar with throwing and catching. If this happens you should gently discourage it, and remind the group that the aim is to throw the ball so that the other person can catch it, rather than making it difficult for them.

Wait until the group establishes a smooth rhythm, saying their own names as they throw, and including everyone in the circle.

Then ask them to continue making eye contact, throwing and catching, but now to say the name of the person to whom they are throwing the ball.

Let this continue for a few minutes until a smooth rhythm is again established.

Then indicate that you want the ball to be thrown to you, and so bring the exercise to an end.

Ask members to remain in the circle, and invite reactions, feelings and reflections.

Throwing and catching are metaphors for speaking and listening. It quickly becomes clear that if people are not ready for the ball — if eye contact has not been made —

they often fail to catch it. So it is with communication: most people do not hear the communication if they are not ready for it, and if contact has not first been established. One problem in communication can cause other similar problems. For example, if one person drops the ball, it will often be dropped again several times before a rhythm is again established.

■ If the members do not recognize such parallels themselves you can point them out. You can refer back to this exercise if the issue of communication comes up later.

Sticky

This exercise gives members an experience of leading and of following. It requires concentration and teamwork. It links with Images of Leadership in Phase Three.

■ Ask the members to work in pairs. If the numbers are odd a trainer makes up one pair. In each pair one person chooses to lead, and the other to follow. The leader holds out one hand, palm down. The follower holds out their own hand, palm up, underneath the leader's hand and close to it but not touching. The follower must keep this distance between the two hands constant. As the leader moves the follower will therefore have to follow, with the pace, scale and direction of the movement decided by the leader. Ask the group to work in silence. After five minutes ask partners to swap roles.

Allow members time to share and reflect after the exercise:
'How did you feel about leading? Following?'
'How was the relationship between you?'

Sometimes people have very strong feelings about leading or following, being in control and being controlled. Some members may subvert the game, for example by leading too fast for their partner to follow, or by refusing to follow. These aspects are also worth exploring.
Allow 15 minutes for the exercise altogether.

Groupings

This is a light-hearted exercise which encourages members to observe more actively. In the course so far they may have gained only a general visual impression of one another. This exercise requires members to look at each other more closely and in more detail, which may lead them to discover unexpected similarities and differences.

■ Call out certain features of appearance or dress, appropriate to the group, and ask members to get into groups accordingly, and without talking. For example,
those wearing glasses and those not;
those wearing watches or rings and those not;
the colour of shoes or certain clothes;
those with the same eye colour.

■ After several such groupings, ask for any comments or reflections. Some possible questions are:

'What were the sizes of the different groupings?'
'How did it feel to be the only one in a group? Or to be in a big group?'
'Did you discover anything about others that you did not already know?'

Allow 15 minutes for the exercise.

Three Changes

This exercise is about the careful observation of other people, and becoming aware of changes in what we see.

■ Ask members to find a partner quickly, and stand back to back without touching. Tell them that both partners are to make three minor changes to their clothes or appearance. They are then to turn and face each other. Each is now to try to work out what changes the other has made. Allow a few moments for reactions and comments.

The exercise may take ten minutes altogether.

Mirrors

This exercise is about observing a partner and anticipating the partner's movements and gestures. The work involves continuing eye contact between the partners, so trainers should decide whether single sex pairs are more appropriate.

■ Ask members to find their partners and to sit facing each other. One is A and the other B. A makes a series of gestures and facial expressions, and B copies these as though he/she is a mirror. So when A moves the right hand B makes a corresponding movement with the left hand. A's task is to make it possible for B to mirror effectively, not to make the movements difficult for B. B's task is not only to follow A's movements, but to anticipate them, so that the movements of both partners become simultaneous.

After several minutes ask the pairs to exchange roles. The exercise can then be extended by using both hands. Finish with reactions and comments.

Allow 10—15 minutes altogether.

▶ *When S suggested that the people who didn't wear glasses should be separated I thought it will be for checking our eyes ... When she started to separate the same colours of eyes, same shoes, and wearing rings I understood there is a different meaning. Then S explained about a very small (imaginary) ball in her hands: but unfortunately I could not see the ball, and I thought I have really a problem with my eyes ... We started to play with the ball. It was very interesting with contact of eyes, and saying our name, and throwing the ball to the person who had already contact with eyes. It was a good way to more awareness in communication.*

▶ *Everyone seemed to have enjoyed the sessions with S although some people commented that it would have been better to have some time after every game to reflect on instead of having them all in a row.*

7.3 Phase Two: How We Respond to What We See

▶ *I personally learnt that it is very important for me to make a careful observation of what I see before jumping on to interpretations and conclusions.*

In this phase course members begin to work with still images, and learn to separate description from interpretation.

This phase takes 1¼ hours, or most of one session.

Change the Image

This is a non-verbal exercise in looking at images which helps us to separate observation and description from interpretation. This is important preparation for using these drama methods.

■ Ask the whole group to sit together at one end of the room. Ask for two volunteers to stand up in front of the group. Ask them to take up simple positions in relation to each other, for example shaking hands. They should then stand still in this position.

Now ask the other members what they see. Different people will see different things.

Often members will give interpretations. For example, 'Someone is saying goodbye to a friend at the station,' or 'It is a new staff member being welcomed by their boss.' You may hear many interpretations, as people see characters and a story in even the simplest image.

The members who are creating the image may want to 'correct' the interpretations by sharing their own thoughts or intentions. You should discourage this. The 'actors' should remain silent, so that the image remains just an image.

Now ask one person in the pair to remain 'frozen' in their position, and the other person to sit down. Invite someone else to stand up, and to take up a different position in relation to the person already there. The new volunteer might, for example, choose to stand alongside and also extend a hand. Then the image immediately changes.

Again ask the rest of the group what they see. They are likely to offer interpretations again, but now based on the new image, and perhaps quite different both in meaning and in feeling.

At this point you should help the group to differentiate between describing and interpreting. Ask the members in the audience to describe what they see, but without interpreting it. They may find this much more difficult than it sounds!

Using the example above, a description might be: 'A man is standing, his right hand extended, his weight forward on his right foot. He is looking ahead. Beside him is a woman. She also has her right hand extended, her feet are together, and she is looking straight ahead.'

The focus of this statement, with its descriptive language and factual observation, is quite different from the assumptions of interpretation.

Individuals will more or less agree on the description, but there can be many interpretations. Interpretations of this image might be: 'They are the parents waiting to greet their child', and 'Two health workers are greeting people as they arrive at a clinic'. These are only two examples, and there could be as many interpretations as there are members watching.

Description and Interpretation

■ Emphasize the importance of these and the difference between them. Draw on the following points.

- Description and interpretation are both important. Describing enables us to share our observations with others. It helps us to clarify and identify what is actually there, without forming conclusions. Interpreting gives us the opportunity to bring our own experience to bear on what we see. Hearing the interpretations of others helps us to gain deeper insight into the situation that we are all observing.

- Most of the time we tend to skim over observing and describing, and go immediately to interpretation. We draw on our past experience, and on images and ideas which are already stored in our memories, to help us make sense of what we are seeing. We do this almost automatically, and mostly without being aware that we are doing it.

- Yet we need to be aware, not just for this method, but in any work involving other people. As development workers we need to look and listen carefully and thoughtfully. We need to avoid making assumptions, jumping to immediate conclusions, reaching premature judgements. So we need to be cautious about making immediate interpretations.

- Most of us have had the experience of misinterpreting something that we have seen, sometimes with unfortunate consequences. On other occasions we may have been looking at a situation in a certain way, and then have changed our understanding of it because we have been given more information.

- As this work continues, individual members will be sharing some of their experience through visual images, while other members will be looking at the images and commenting on them. When we make comments on the images of other people, we are actually offering them interpretations based on our own experience. We need to recognize that our interpretations are not objective — they are always subjective.

- This is not to say that interpretation should be avoided: it is both necessary and inevitable. But it is important that we become aware when we are making interpretations.

- Using these methods helps us to become more aware of all these issues.[1]

Change the Image, continued

■ You should remind members as often as necessary about the difference between description and interpretation, the need for both, and about the advantages of separating them.

Continue the process of asking one person in the image to sit down, and another to go in and take up a new position that will change the image.

Help the members to see how certain changes, even in small details, can profoundly affect an image. For example, if two people look at each other, or if they look away from each other, or if one person looks at the other, while the other looks away, it can change the way in which the observer interprets the situation.

Giving the image a context also makes a big difference. For example, suppose there are two women sitting on chairs, facing the same direction, but looking at each other. Give those watching an opportunity to describe and interpret the image. Then ask them to notice how their interpretation changes if they are given additional information. Tell them, referring to the same example, that this scene is taking place in a prison yard. Ask them how they see it now. Who are those people? What are they both thinking or feeling?

Then ask them to imagine that the scene is in a refugee camp, or that both the women are four years old, or that they are mother and daughter. Every time new information comes in, we see the image differently.

Bring the exercise to a conclusion after about eight changes, and after exploring these issues.

30—45 minutes will be needed altogether.

The exercise is a building block for drama methods. It needs to be given adequate time, so that members become familiar with creating images, and with looking at them.

Members will benefit later if they already appreciate the importance of detail in an image, for example the direction in which someone is facing and looking. The distinction between description and interpretation will be needed again in the later work.

---

1. Some members may be interested in the idea of 'Body Language' where meanings and interpretations are attached to particular gestures or to particular ways of standing or sitting. Body Language tends to assume that there are fixed rules, for example, that crossed arms always represent a closed and defensive attitude. Such assumptions are not useful with drama methods because they encourage conclusions to be made too quickly, whereas a careful and detailed examination of an image will reveal much more. The assumptions are particularly unhelpful for international and cross-cultural groups because the same gesture can have different meanings in different countries and cultures. Trainers should be ready to challenge any assumptions based on the 'rules' of Body Language.

All this will help communication within the group as members become more sensitive to the way in which we interpret what we see.

Joining Mime

This exercise continues with the themes of observation, description and interpretation.

■ Ask the whole group to sit together at one end of the room. Ask for a volunteer to step forward in front of the group and silently mime some familiar activity which they do frequently when they are back home.

The remainder of the group watches. Tell them that when anyone thinks that he or she has recognized the activity, they should step forward and begin to mime it too. Continue with this invitation until all those who believe they recognize the activity are miming alongside the first person. Suggest to those still watching that they look for the similarities and the differences in what the volunteers are doing.

Then stop the miming, and ask each person who has joined the activity what they are doing, and where they imagine they are. Ask the original volunteer the same questions, but at the end.

Sometimes you will hear similar answers, although they may differ in detail. But sometimes members say that they have been miming an activity which was quite different from the original. Make it clear that this is not a guessing game, and that there is no 'right answer'. Any contribution we have made to the miming will have depended on our interpretation of what was already being shown.

Repeat the exercise a few times with new volunteers, and then ask the group to discuss what has come out of the experience.

Sometimes members will recognize an activity, such as washing dishes, but while they are miming it themselves they imagine that they are in their own home. So then they do the washing up as they usually do it at home. They have recognized the activity of washing the dishes, but have translated it to their own past experience.

At other times members will not recognize the activity, either because it is outside their experience, or because it is being done in a way that they do not recognize. For example, a course member mimed chopping wood, and sat on a stool to do this. Some other members could not imagine sitting down to chop wood, so they could not recognize what activity the mime showed.

This exercise underlines how we interpret what we see, and how we use our own past experience to help us interpret it. There may be many interpretations of the same activity. There are also situations and activities that we simply cannot interpret at all because we have not experienced or witnessed anything like it.

Allow 30 minutes for this exercise.

▶ *The second half of the morning involved practising the discipline of observation... our interpretations of what we saw varied from person to person and changed radically if part of the picture we were observing changed... it only took a small amount of additional background information to radically change our interpretations again.*

▶ *First we learned to look at everything as something that contains information. Then we had to learn how to describe something. For some of us this was harder than we thought, sticking to the facts without making assumptions or placing our 'interpretation' on something. At one point we had to imagine M as a prison officer! It was much easier to imagine O and S as four-year-olds playing...*

Phase Three:
Power, Leadership and Our Work Back Home

▶ *We need to understand the power relationships and structures before we attempt to make changes in any situation.*

This phase uses still images or sculptures to explore expressions of power and leadership, and to consider the principal relationships in members' work situations. The phase requires 2½ hours, or most of two sessions.

Top Chair

This exercise deals with the issues of power and status. The exercise also helps members to develop skills in 'reading' images and understanding situations.

■ Ask everybody to sit down at one end of the room. At the other end place eight or nine lightweight chairs. Identify one of the chairs in the middle as the most important chair, with the highest status among the chairs. Refer to it as the 'Top Chair'.

Ask for a volunteer to come and re-arrange all the chairs in a way that will make it clear that this particular chair is the 'top chair'. When the volunteer has finished, ask him or her to sit down again, and invite the other members to comment on the image which the volunteer has created:
 'Is it clear which is the top chair?'
 'What makes this clear to you?'

Then ask for a second volunteer to demonstrate the status of the top chair using a different arrangement, and again invite members to comment:
 'How do you react to this arrangement?'
 'Does it feel comfortable or is there tension in it?'
 'Does the top chair seem 'safe' in its status?'

Repeat this several times with different volunteers. Each volunteer may offer a new arrangement. One member may put the top chair at the top of a stack of all the other chairs. Another may make an image where the top chair is leading a line of the other chairs. A third might have the top chair out at the front, facing the other chairs, and so on.

There are many possibilities. Raise some corresponding questions, for example, if the top chair has been placed out in front of the others:
 'Does the top chair look isolated?'
 'Is it in command? Or is it in front of an interview panel?'

If it has its back towards the other chairs:
 'Does the top chair seem vulnerable?'
 'Can you also see it as the bottom chair?'

■ If it is at the top of a pile:
'Does it seem well-supported from below?'
'Could it be undermined?'

As the exercise proceeds, and five or six arrangements have been tried, the discussion will go faster and questions may no longer be necessary.

As the uncertainty of some images becomes apparent, some members may look for more striking ways of showing which is the top chair. For example, they may turn all the other chairs upside down in front of the top chair.

Stop the exercise whenever you think that members have understood the issues.

This may be after 20 or 30 minutes.

The intention of the exercise is not to arrive at the most effective way of arranging the chairs. The purpose is to explore the images, to recognize differing interpretations of the same reality, and to begin to think about how power and leadership are manifested and how we respond to them. Are we aware of the power relationships in our own work in development or training?

Top Person

This exercise follows after Top Chair, and also deals with the issues of power and status. It introduces some ways in which people demonstrate and assert their power, and helps members to develop skills in 'reading' images and in understanding situations and relationships.

■ Ask the whole group to sit at one end of the room. Place eight or nine spare chairs together in a circle at the other end, but leave aside the one that was 'top chair' in the previous exercise.

Ask for a volunteer to come into the circle and to take up a physical position which will show that they are the 'top person'. After they have taken up their position ask the other members to comment. Again the purpose is not to evaluate, but to share descriptions and interpretations.

While the first volunteer stays in the circle and maintains their position, invite someone else to come in and show greater importance and power. Then ask the remaining members to comment. If they offer a lot of interpretations immediately, ask them to describe the image first, to say what they are seeing, before they give interpretations and comments. Make sure that descriptions include the direction in which individuals are facing and where, and at whom, they are looking.

Tell the two volunteers to remain in their positions, and invite a third person to come into the circle and show even greater status. Again discuss the new image:
'How is status being shown through posture, gesture or symbol?'
'How is status being shown though the individual's position in relation to others?'
'How does someone express personal or inner confidence?'

■ This process continues until all or most the members are in the picture, or until the group agrees that the process cannot be taken further.

Conclude with comments and reflection. Some suitable questions may be:
'How do we ourselves express our own power back home in our work?'
'How is power seen in the organization or community where we work?'
'How do we deal with the power of those we work with?'

The exercise may take 30 minutes.

How members choose to express power and status may differ according to the setting and cultures represented. There may be gender considerations also. In an international group some members may draw on the religious, military or political symbolism of their own background, but generally this can be understood by other members. There seems to be an underlying language of power that is universally recognizable.

Images of Leadership

This exercise allows us to explore ideas and images of leadership, and to compare our own perceptions and expectations with those of others.

■ Ask the members to get into small groups of four to six. Their task is to create a still image which shows their idea of leadership.

The members of each group will need to talk this over first, and to exchange their ideas, thoughts and feelings about leadership — and perhaps about followership too. They may conclude that there are many kinds of leadership, but they should choose one idea to work on. Allow up to ten minutes for this discussion.

Tell them to draw on their work in the previous exercises, to choose the physical positions and postures of each person carefully, and to decide which way they are to face in relation to the group. For example, is leadership about someone in front showing the way? Or is it someone at the back, pushing others forward? What other configurations represent leadership? Allow another five minutes to prepare the images.

When the groups have decided on their images, ask one small group to get into position and to hold it for two or three minutes. Invite the other members to walk around the image, and to look at it carefully. Ask them first to describe what they see and then to interpret it. Give the group concerned a chance to respond briefly to what they have heard, and then go on to the next image. Working with each image may take about five minutes.

Once all the images have been seen, invite the whole group to reflect on what they have seen and heard. Connect the experience with varying ideas and ways in which leadership is exercised, and received by followers.

Finish the exercise by helping the group to make connections between the earlier work on power and status, and this work on leadership.

■ 'Which image will represent our own style of leadership back home?'
  'Which will represent leadership in our organizations? Our communities?'
Allow 45 minutes altogether.

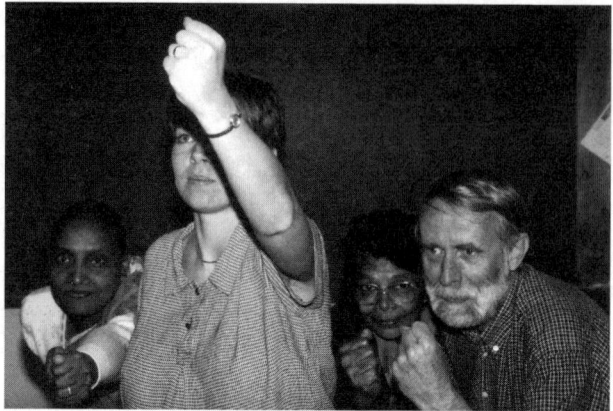

Two images of leadership

There are other issues here for development workers, who may be working with communities that experience themselves as powerless. The development worker may be seeking to work in a way that empowers others, but from a position of relative power him- or herself. How does the development worker who has power encourage leadership in others who have less power? At other times development workers themselves may feel powerless, even when they are in positions of leadership.

 ## Using Still Images or Sculptures

These exercises use the method of still images. Still images are also sometimes referred to as pictures or scenes or sculptures. Creating a still image requires the member or members concerned to select a particular focus, and to choose precisely what they want to show and how they will show it. When used in the training of professionals who

Another image of leadership

work with other people the focus is usually on relationships, communication, structures, power, leadership and so on.

The member or members concerned take up their positions and postures to create the image, and stay absolutely still while those watching examine the image. The image becomes like a moment frozen in time. Members may be asked to remain still and silent for several minutes, so that those who are observing can look at all the detail, and can speak about what they see.

The trainer may encourage the observers to move around the image so that they see it from every angle. Only after the observers have offered their descriptions and interpretations does the trainer invite those who have created the image to respond.

A situation or moment can be conveyed in a single image. An experience or 'a story' can be told through a sequence of images. These images then resemble the frames of a film which has been slowed down. Members move from their positions in one image to those in the next, usually when asked to do so by the trainer. The story can be told in this way without any words, which helps those who are watching to see it with fewer preconceptions, and without knowing what 'the author's' own judgements or conclusions are.

An image or a story can also be shown without giving names or labels to the characters and without providing background information. This allows those watching more freedom when they make their observations and interpretations. Too much information interrupts this process.

For example, if a character has already been labelled Development Worker, or Village Leader, or Donor Agency, the observers will view him or her according to that role or label. Similarly if they are told in advance that the image shows a conflict they may not look for any other dynamics. So those who are watching need not be given background information, but simply encouraged to speak about what they see and how they interpret it. In this way we may learn much more.

It may be that different observers will make quite different interpretations. Yet all of the interpretations are valuable. For example when all are looking at the same character in the same image, and one person sees a father, another sees a bishop, and a third sees an aid worker, we learn both about the story shown in the image, and about the experience of the people responding to it. Had the character been labelled or costumed, we would not have had the opportunity to hear this rich diversity of interpretation.

When we become observers ourselves, and look at someone else's still image, we often see our own stories reflected there, and can make connections to our own experience in a way that is helpful to the whole group.

Work Sculptures

This exercise allows some members to show their work situation back home as a still image. We can link this with Me and My Work (page 90). The emphasis here is on structures and relationships, including power and leadership.

■ Split the members into small groups of five to seven. Any members who appear to work well together can be allocated to the same group, but any from the same organization should work in separate groups.

Explain that each small group is to show some aspect of a member's work back home by means of a still image or work sculpture. The focus should be on routine work and everyday relationships, not on unusual situations or exceptional events.

Tell the groups that their first task is to find a volunteer, or choose the member whose work is to be shown. Ask them to consider the possibilities briefly, and to make a decision. The person whose work situation is to be shown becomes the 'author'.

After the small groups have reached a decision, explain that the author should be present as him/herself in the sculpture. The other members of the group are to represent colleagues, the boss, community groups, the donor agency or whoever is relevant and significant to the work of the member concerned. Make it clear that the author is in charge, and that the other members in the sculpture must accept his or her 'direction'.

Explain that the author can choose to show the actual physical setting, for example, the layout and relative positions in which people sit in the office back home. This can be useful, in that power relationships, communication problems, and so on, may be revealed.

But also explain that it is not necessary to show the physical setting or layout; it is much more important to represent the relationships. The group's task is to create the sculpture in whatever way best reveals the relationships, the structure, the power, the leadership, and the communication channels. Position, posture, spacing, direction and attention are all important. In other words, the image may be a symbolic representation rather than a reconstruction.

So, for example, a boss who works nearby, but who is preoccupied and unsupportive, might be shown as being further away or as looking away. Conversely, a community leader

■ with whom the member works closely, but who does not even belong to the organization, might be shown standing nearby. Or the donor agency — which in reality is thousands of kilometres away — may be closely monitoring the work, and therefore might be shown sitting nearby and watching.

If there are difficulties between the staff in a team, or between colleagues, these can be shown by considering very carefully how people should be positioned in relation to one another, the distance between them, what postures they are using, which way they are facing, and whether they are looking at one another or not.

In short, the sculpture should give the flavour, or tell the story, of the work situation rather than trying to represent it literally.

Allow the groups five minutes to choose whose situation is to be represented, and about ten minutes to prepare the sculpture.

Then ask the members of each group in turn to show their sculpture, and to remain static and silent while the other course members examine it. Encourage the other members to walk all round the sculpture and to notice all the detail in it. Ask for observations and descriptions first, and then interpretations.

Allow five minutes for looking at each sculpture.

If necessary remind members that this is not a guessing game. The task of those who observe is not to guess at what the sculpture is intended to illustrate, or to agree or disagree with each other, but to say exactly what they themselves see and how they interpret that. Some of the interpretations may not be true to the reality of the author's situation back home. Yet every interpretation brings the insights of someone else's experience, adds its own possibilities, and throws light on the situation.

After the observers have made their interpretations, allow the author an opportunity to respond to what he or she has heard. He or she may have gained new insights, but may feel a need to correct 'misinterpretations' or to rebuff certain comments.
  'Is what you have heard what you expected, or is it unexpected?'
  'Do you want to give us any additional information?'
  'Have you gained any new insights?'

At this point you may conclude the exercise with reflections in the whole group.

Or you may encourage some discussion about the possibilities of change. Ask the author:
  'Would you like to see any changes in the situation you have shown?'

If he or she would like to see changes, ask:
  'How would you show such changes in the sculpture?'
  'What would look different in the sculpture?'

Then invite the author to rearrange the sculpture accordingly. This may involve changing some people's postures and positions, bringing them closer or moving them apart, changing the direction they are looking in, and so on.

Ask the observers what they see now. Then ask the author:
  'What would need to happen for there to be such a change?'

■ Remind members that in this work we are not trying to decide how a member's organization back home should be improved. We are using the member's experience and perceptions as our raw material, and together we are exploring the dynamics, the difficulties and the possibilities it offers, and contributing our own perceptions, insights and experience. We are not changing work situations back home, but we are changing our perceptions and thinking about those situations, and exploring possibilities for the future.

Conclude the exercise with reflections in the whole group.

The exercise requires members to show only limited aspects of their work situation. For those who work in very complex situations it can be hard to choose what to show. Sometimes, when we talk about a work situation, the complexities can seem overwhelming. But when we represent them in a sculpture the choices we have to make may reveal important truths.

For example, we may place ourself away from colleagues in the sculpture, and only then suddenly realize how alone we feel in our work. When we try to put some other people concerned into the places we would like them to be in, we may realize that certain relationships are simply not possible. Or we may suddenly be able to see how things could be changed and improved.

So learning may come from the direct insights of the member concerned, as well as through the contributions of others.

▶ ... *we played with six black chairs. I didn't realize that there could be so many ways to give importance to one chair. I alone could find three ways ...*

▶ *We discovered that the power of the top chair lay in the structure, the position ascribed to it by others. The same is true in real life. The exercise taught us to be keen observers of what we see in real life.*

▶ *S asked for a volunteer to represent a person with power. And C was there!!, sitting with folded arms and a proud look on his face, like a real Inka or Mandinka. He didn't keep his power for long because an African King came and took the power. Then, Mother Britannia sent her representative to control this situation, but a man from far off Pakistan arrived and began to stare at the others wisely?! Later a Scottish development expert arrived and tried to keep the power until a representative of the World Bank showed money. And, dear Diary, she was so sure that nobody could beat her, but a warrior of justice came and destabilized her high, high position!!*

▶ *A group exercise in picturing leadership produced many different images — cattle being herded to market, an injured man being helped to hospital, a children's Sunday School outing, and a puppet show.*

▶ *It amazes me how much can be communicated in silence. It seems to me, as portrayed in the still pictures, that silence makes a lot of communication without needing to say anything. It is important for me to realise that in role plays, like in case studies, one can only deal with the information given at that point in time and place; and that in discussions and different understandings and analyses there is no single answer or conclusion.*

Phase Four:
Power and Powerlessness

▶ *It was very interesting and meaningful to see the power and powerlessness enacted without any motion.*

▶ *Each story became real and touching ... Whether myself, falling into bureaucratic procedures in passport office and submitting to cultural domination of eldest brother; or E as a discriminated refugee child in school; or M as eye-witness to a gunshot killing: all experienced powerless situations submitting everything to the powerful.*

Members work with images and sculptures to explore ideas of power and powerlessness, and to re-examine some of their own experiences or stories. By now members should be familiar with using still images and sculptures, and with describing and interpreting what they see. They have usually recognized that many relationships in development work are mediated through power.

The work in this phase takes about 2½ hours, or most of two sessions.

Images of Power and Powerlessness

■ Ask the members to form pairs. One partner is A, the other B.

Ask the pairs to stand back to back and a short distance apart.

While they are back to back, A is to adopt a physical posture which shows his or her interpretation of power. At the same time B is to adopt a posture which shows his or her interpretation of powerlessness. It works better if the partners do this without reference to each other.

When they are ready, ask the pairs to face each other, to move if necessary so as to be in relation to each other, and to take up their postures.

Now split the whole group into two. Tell half the pairs to relax their positions, and to look at the pairs in the other half. Ask them to comment on what they see. Ask them to look at the detail, and to look for similarities and differences among the pairs. Some useful questions are:
'What is common among those showing power?'
'How is power being expressed?'
'Which postures and gestures are the powerful tending to use?'
'Where do they look?'
Ask similar questions about those showing powerlessness.

Then ask the pairs who have been observing to take up their postures. The other half of the group now observes, comments and considers the questions.

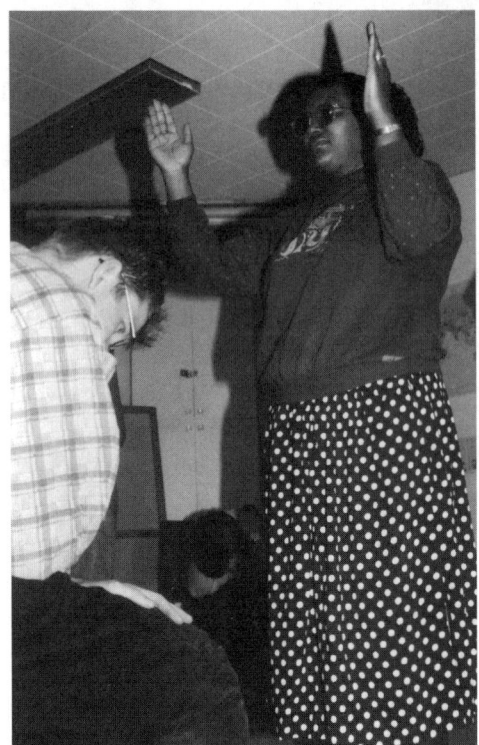

Images of power and powerlessness

■ Tell the whole group to return to their pairs, to reverse roles in the pairs, and to repeat the exercise. A is now to show powerlessness and B is to show power.

Again split the whole group and look at the sculptures in two halves, with further comments and the questions.

Now invite the As and Bs to reflect together in their own pairs:
'How did it feel to be powerful or powerless?'
'What did you feel in relation to each other?'
'How was it to move from one to the other?'
'Did one feel more familiar?'

Sometimes members feel more comfortable in one position than in the other:
'Which was comfortable, and why?'

Then bring the whole group together for reflection and comments.

Strong feelings may be expressed, which may come from the personal experience of members, or may arise as a result of working with oppressed and powerless people.

It is important to avoid any assumption that power is always 'bad'. If it seems useful, go back and look again at some of the sculptures to see how power is being expressed. Some of them may convey a sense of energy and optimism and support. Look at them again in relation to powerlessness, and see if members' views change.

This exercise may take 30 minutes.

Sharing Stories of Powerlessness

This exercise allows some members to share an experience of powerlessness through a series of still images or sculptures.

■ Divide the members into small groups of four to six members.

Tell the small groups that each member can share an experience — or 'story' — of an occasion in their work when they have felt powerless. Make it clear that members are not obliged to share, but that all should have the opportunity. The sharing may take 15—25 minutes.

Tell the small groups to choose one story to show to the rest of the group. Making this choice can be difficult, so suggest that groups choose the story that all or most of the members can relate to and clearly understand. Explain that the task will be to show the chosen story through a series of still images, and that some stories may suit the task better than others. Making the choice may take five or ten minutes. After the small groups have chosen their stories, the 'author' of the story being shown is to lead the group and create up to five still images that tell the story. The author should be in the images, and each image should show an episode in the story. Creating the images in the small groups may take 15—20 minutes.

The small groups now take turns to tell the stories through the images, while the rest of the course group watches.

Ask the first small group to show the whole of their sequence of images quickly, to provide an overall impression. Then ask them to start again and go through the images one by one, remaining static and silent in each image until you tell them to move on. Invite the rest of the group to comment on and interpret what they see in each image.

Encourage the observers to move round so that they see all angles. If you think that the observers need to be clearer and more objective insist on the discipline of describing before interpreting.

Remember that this is not a guessing game. Do not allow the observers to debate among themselves as to who has the correct interpretation of the images.

Invite the observers to notice how power is being expressed. Is it through position, through gestures or symbols, through the expression of confidence, or by the support or dependence of others? Many of these will have been identified when reflecting on Top Person (page 264).

Ask the observers to look particularly for any point in the images at which things might have changed or gone in a different direction.

The author of the story should not respond or 'make corrections' while other members are still offering their interpretations. However, it may be helpful to ask the author factual questions if members are uncertain or confused.

Once all the observers' interpretations have been heard, invite the author, and other members of the small group which has made the images, to share their thoughts.

■ Some questions may be:
  'What have we learned about the situation which was represented?'
  'Was there a moment when things could have turned out differently?'
  'If so, what was it, and when? What prevented it?'

If appropriate remind members again that when we think about change we are not expecting to 'solve the problem', but are exploring possibilities and alternatives. If necessary discourage them from passing judgement on the author, such as, 'You should have ...' or 'Why didn't you ...'

After finishing the reflection with one small group, continue with the next.

Looking at each of the images, hearing the descriptions and interpretations, and discussion with the author and small group members, will take up to 20 minutes per small group.

After seeing the work of all the small groups and discussing the content of the images, conclude with reflections on the process and the method.

Some possible questions at this point are:
  'How did it feel to share a story in the small group and then in the whole group?'
  'What did the author or the small group members learn by doing so?'
  'What was particular about sharing it by this method?'
  'How did it feel to give and receive interpretations?'

Using Images from Work Experience

When course members start to share situations from their own experience, the question may be asked: how true is this representation of that situation and experience? However it is not intended, nor is it possible, to recreate any situation from back home in all its detail. Our information is always limited, and is 'chosen' by the person bringing it. Yet by their very simplicity still images can bring the essence of a situation into the course room.

The observers have to deal with what they have been shown in the images. Trainers should be cautious about any discussion or analysis that moves away from what has been shown. As with the discussion of case studies, members' attention may need to be directed back to the material in hand.

The 'correct interpretation' of images is irrelevant because those who are observing and interpreting cannot know everything that is going on in the images, and even less what has actually gone on in the situations which are being represented.

Those who contribute their stories have authorship during the preparation of the still images and role plays. In the whole group we value every story that is brought, but once a story is shown in the whole group it becomes common property for all the members to work with. It may be helpful to explain this.

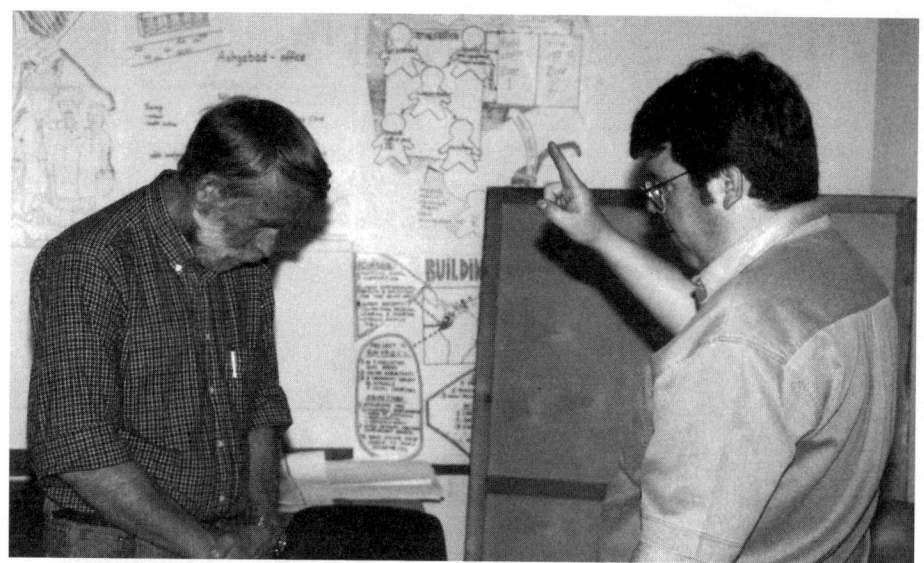

Image from a story of powerlessness

When we make an interpretation we do so out of our own experience. We bring our experience to bear on whatever we are seeing, and in this way we may shed light for others on the story being shown. At the same time we may add to our store of experience and learning.

Sometimes course members imagine that a problem which they are sharing can be 'solved' by an alternative means to that shown in a sculpture or a role play. If necessary trainers should correct such expectations. Members must remember that although these methods are so vivid, and bring so much real life into the course room, they remain representations of the stories that members bring. Problems back home will have to be dealt with back home. What we can do in the course room is to bring the experience and insight of everyone to bear, to look for ways to understand the problem better, and to explore the possibility of 'doing things differently'.

Those who are the authors of the stories, those who work at the images in the small groups, and those who observe and interpret, can all gain new understandings of the situations and events being described, and can make strong connections with their own experience.

▶ *Later we worked in pairs and the skill was to represent power and powerlessness. Mo represented the authoritarian father's role; and I was a blind, chained person who was dependant on others. I saw (my husband) kneeling down in a very modest position. I never saw him like this before. (I enjoyed it!!!) I could also see J lying on the floor, but because I was a blind person I couldn't see more. Then, we changed our roles and we, the powerless became powerful, but we were kind. So, dear diary, we had a good time and now we have a lot to reflect on.*

▶ *I tell you, Mr Diary, you cannot easily interpret each group's still images. M and gang, I thought they demonstrated Mafia movements, but it was a scene in Nepal showing how powerless M was ...*

E's group's still image was all about how powerless E (felt) when he faced a difficult situation in the British Embassy. F's group tried to show how F became powerless when accidentally caught up with malaria and brought into a large hospital. Thank God he is not dead.

▶ *Mind you, these different activities really were a great help to our communication levels — imagine the eye contact in it, the different relationships being made, establishment of basic trust and confidence, especially in dealing with our true stories, experience and situations.*

Image of power and powerlessness

▶ *Salaam. Today the theme was what it means to be powerless. What a question to put to a disabled person!*

... We first worked in twos and then in fours. Groups of two (each playing the role of powerful/powerless), and groups of four to explore personal experiences related to the two positions. I confirmed that in my life I played both roles: but some couldn't recall being in a powerful position in relation to others. S then asked if we could think of some personal experiences where we felt powerless. I decided to tell the group of my first day at school and this was later played by all the group together in three different pictures. This was followed by a discussion on what could be done (either practically or imaginary) to help or change the situation ...

... We then noticed two things: that the dividing line between the state of being powerless and the state of being powerful is very thin, and that some people look powerful or are powerful only because others are powerless. It was interesting in the discussions we had so far that power was only once shown as 'positive'. To me that was very significant as to how power is associated with oppresson, exploitation, cheating etc. ...

... As a disabled person, the whole discussion on power and how people use it is a very central issue. People don't normally see how powerful they are in relation to the disabled. It wasn't a moment in life

that I could go back and remember, it is something that I live with every day. If we define 'power' as taking decisions that affect other people's lives, then you can imagine how many such decisions were taken for a disabled child/man/woman ...

... The observation made earlier that some people become powerful only because others are powerless is very important. We sometimes create monsters for ourselves by allowing others to climb over our shoulders ...

... Power is at the centre of any discussion on Development and it is in the centre of the behaviour of human nature. We cannot do without it, and its excesses will bring us down. The only way is to find how power can be shared by all, or at least that is the way I see it.

Phase Five:
A Fresh Look at Work Experiences

▶ *... people who do not express themselves using words can express themselves strongly in role play.*

▶ *... this morning's role plays. For me it was like a reality. For example, I was very revolted when E received the dismissal letter ... it was not easy for me to be N in his Thailand story ... congratulations for 'Bishop' A from Zaire ...*

Members work in small groups and use still images and role play to re-examine events or situations arising directly from professional experience.

The objective of this phase is to re-examine real-life problems in development work away from the heat of the moment, and to explore possible solutions. 'Scenes' are acted out with movement and words. Those observing and interpreting are again active participants or 'spect-actors'. The work assumes that course members have participated in the earlier phases and are familiar with the methods.

Members work in small groups of five to seven. One session is required for preparatory work, and the small groups will need separate rooms at this time.

Showing and reflecting on the images and role play will then take half a session for each small group. If this is followed by interventions a further half-session or more will be needed for each small group.

From Still Images to Role Plays

Sharing 'Stories' from Work Experience

 Divide the whole group into small groups of five to seven. Those who work well together can be allocated to the same small group, but those from the same or related organizations should work separately if possible.

Tell the members in each small group to start by sharing experiences of any unresolved problem or issue in their everyday work situations. Later the group will work on one of the stories.

Explain that there are the following criteria for the 'stories':
● no one is obliged to bring an experience, but everyone should have the opportunity;
● the setting should be members' routine work and everyday relationships.
  They should not share an unusual situation or an exceptional event which is unlikely to occur again;

- the experience should be an event or occasion — something that happened — rather than a general problem or issue. For example, if a member wishes to explore a problem of poor communication, he or she should choose a clear example of when this made an impact, rather than describing the problem in general terms;
- the experiences must have happened to the person concerned. They should not be the experience of anyone else, however significant;
- the problem must be unresolved. If it has already been resolved — however successfully — there will be no role later for the spect-actors!

■ When all who wish to have contributed their 'stories', ask the small groups to choose one story to work on further. Suggest that they choose an experience that all or most of the group members can understand clearly and relate to.

Explain that they will be presenting the story to the rest of the group in two ways. First, they will show it as a sequence of up to five still images. Secondly, they will perform the story, with words and movement, as a role play. Ask them to choose a story that they think will suit this task. Sharing such 'stories' in the small groups, and choosing one of them, may take 45 minutes.

Preparing the Still Images and Role Plays

Now the task of the small groups is to prepare their still images and role plays.

Advise the small groups to start by creating the still images. Doing this will help them to identify the key moments or incidents in the story, and will make them think carefully about individual, structural and power relationships. After they have created the still images, they can go on to develop the role play, with words and movement. The role play should start with the first still image and end with the last.

Remind the other members that the person whose story is being told is 'the author of the play', so he or she should be asked about details before decisions are made.

Ask the 'actors' to limit themselves to asking for information and clarification about their role and character. As small group members they may make suggestions, perhaps about how something can be shown, but they should not offer advice or tell the author what he or she should decide. It is the author who must be satisfied that the images and the role play convey what he/she wants them to convey.

The author will tell the 'actors' who they are to represent. The author should give each character a central attitude in the situation being shown, and make it clear what that character seems (to the author) to want from the situation. The actors should then hold to these attitudes, not only during the role play, but during any interventions afterwards.

Advise the small groups as follows:
- concentrate on showing power structures, relationships, communication channels, groupings, and images of power and powerlessness;
- keep all the work simple so that it is easily understood and can be repeated;

- avoid props, costumes and labelling characters. Remember that the method works best when people are not told too much!
- pay attention to detail — eyes, hands, gestures, postures, distances, direction;
- the role play should last for about five minutes;
- it should incorporate the still images. It should start with the first image and end with the last;
- the work should show the problem, but not suggest possible solutions;
- they should work quickly and avoid polishing the role play. This is a learning method, not a performance.

■ At this point the small groups should move to separate rooms so that they can work undisturbed. Visit the groups in their rooms as they work to encourage them, to deal with queries, and to remind them of the time. If members have already practised using still images they may need only 30 minutes to prepare the images and the role play. Some groups may need 45 minutes.

Members observe a role play

Showing the Still Images and Role Plays

Prepare the course room so that a small group can work at one end and the rest of the course group can observe from the other.

Ask one small group to show their five still images.

Invite the observers to make their initial responses. By now members should move easily between describing and interpreting, and should accept a diversity of interpretations.

■ Showing the still images and responding to them may take 15 minutes.

Then watch the role play. Tell the observers to look for power structures, relationships, communication channels, groupings, gestures and symbols of power, and the appearance of powerlessness. Notice whether the earlier responses and interpretations of the still images correspond with what is revealed in the role play. Even any misinterpretations may have relevance.

Then ask the small group concerned to remain silent and to listen to the observers.

The observers' task now is to identify what they see as the problem or issue. At what point do they think the problem becomes inevitable? What might be possible moments for change?

Identifying the problem can take some time, as the first impression may not be the most accurate. For example, a member may have brought an experience of a communication difficulty between two colleagues who work at the same level. When the images are shown, and the role play is done, it may become clear that the problem originates somewhere else, for example with managers at a different level.

Allow the observers to discuss the problem and see if they come to a conclusion. Then consult with the group which has brought the role play, and reach an agreement on the problem.

Showing the still images and the role play of a small group, and responding to them in this way, may take 30—45 minutes.

Members observe a role play

281

Using Interventions

Now the small group is going to work further on their story through the use of interventions. This may take a further 45 minutes to one hour.

An intervention is a method that allows a group using role play to:

- learn more about the situation or problem, and to think around it;
- be clearer about where the problem really lies;
- bring their own experience to bear on the situation;
- consider some possible action or solutions;
- consider what we can actually change;
- try out alternatives.

An intervention cannot solve the problem, but it may reveal more possible ways forward, and allow us to try out different options before making decisions.

The best way to describe interventions and their use is to show how they have worked in particular role plays.

Role Play 1

The Interventions Used: 'Groupings' and 'Stepping In'

A member with the job of Nursing Director at a hospital showed a role play of a situation in her work. She had had to speak to a colleague of hers, who was the Senior Doctor, about his behaviour towards the Midwives. The Hospital Director was present and heard what she said. He responded angrily to what the Nursing Director said, and the situation was still unresolved.

We used two interventions to explore this problem. Firstly, we were aware that there were several *groupings* in the role play, and we asked the characters to stand in their various groupings (see Groupings as an exercise, page 256).

In one grouping there were women (the Nursing Director and the Midwives) and men (the Hospital Director and the Senior Doctor). In another grouping there were senior staff (the Hospital Director, the Senior Doctor and the Nursing Director), while at a junior level there were the Midwives. There were also ethnic groups: the Nursing Director was an expatriate, the others were all from the 'host' nation.

By looking at these different groupings we could see that there were already tensions between the different groups to do with gender, status and ethnicity. We discussed these issues in some detail, obtaining additional information when necessary from the author of the role play, but also adding in other experiences from the group that could shed light.

Having got a better picture of these complexities, we moved on to *stepping in*. In this intervention, all those watching are first invited to think how they would have handled the situation, and what they would have done in a different way.

Then, rather than giving advice or making suggestions, volunteers are invited to 'step in' to the role play and take on the role of the author — in this example, the Nursing Director — and to try out their suggestion by playing her part in a different way. The other characters in the role play are asked to stick to their roles as they have understood them, but to respond to the different ways in which the new actors now approach the situation.

Continuing with the example, one volunteer now playing the Nursing Director may tell the Midwives that she cannot pass on their complaints and that they should go directly to the Hospital Director. Another may show the Nursing Director speaking in private to the Senior Doctor. Another may show the Nursing Director first asking for advice from the Hospital Director, and so on.

This method underlines an important truth in development work: that we cannot directly change the behaviour of others, we can only change our own behaviour.

When using the method it is helpful to remember that we are not searching for a single correct solution, even if that was practicable. If a volunteer steps in and claims to have 'solved' the problem, the trainer can point out that the author's back home situation is much more complicated than the role play, and that there are issues which we know nothing about. Our task is to explore possibilities in the 'here and now', in the group as we are, working with the information we have.

The trainer acknowledges each suggestion as it is tried, but goes on inviting further volunteers to step in and come up with more. Each of the different possibilities which are offered may help everyone to expand their thinking, to consider alternatives and to gain in understanding.

Role Play 2

The Intervention Used: 'Images of Power and Powerlessness'

A development worker gave the example of a community of villagers who resisted his efforts to encourage them to become more independent. As he described the situation, they wanted aid, not development.

We returned to the version of his experience shown in his five still images, and asked to see the images of the villagers only. We noticed that the villagers were kneeling, lying down, sitting on their hands, hiding their faces. These were like the images of powerlessness we had made previously (see page, 271—272).

Some members then entered the images and demonstrated the postures they would like to see the villagers in. These showed people standing up, looking confident and empowered. We then thought about the transition from the powerless position to the empowered one. What was needed to move from one to the other?

We looked next at what was keeping the villagers in their powerless positions. Volunteers from the rest of the group took up postures and positions to represent war, apathy, poverty, low self-esteem, and dependence. We discussed the ways in which these could be confronted. The development worker was encouraged to find ways of getting the villagers to stand up. We observed that this was difficult, but it seemed to work when he made direct contact with them, established trust, and went very slowly.

This was a description of physical action, but it describes well the process of development in the role play. Those members who were representing war, apathy, poverty etc, remarked that they felt much less powerful when all the villagers were standing up. The development worker noticed that his own role seemed to change slowly as he got all the villagers onto their feet. Their change meant a change for him also.

Role Play 3

The Intervention Used: 'Tag Argument'

A woman development worker who worked in a rural setting showed us her experience of trying to increase literacy among women. Many of the women were interested in learning to read and write, but their husbands opposed this. The development worker did not want to force the issue, but she could see benefits for the whole community if the women had access to literacy. The development worker was not from the same cultural group as the community, and herself came from a culture in which men and women had equal access to literacy.

Many in the course had experience of this problem, and we decided to share experience in the whole group by using *tag argument*. We asked all the members to form pairs and sit facing each other. One was A and the other was B. We told them that all the As were now in the role of husbands, and all the Bs in the role of wives. This was regardless of the sex of the members. We asked the Bs to explain to their husbands that they wanted to join the literacy classes. The As were then to respond. All the pairs were talking at the same time; it was noisy and fun!

After about five minutes, we asked all the As to sit together on one side of the room, and all the Bs on the other. We placed two chairs in the centre of the room, facing each other. We asked one A to sit in one chair, and one B in the other. This pair were to start to discuss and debate the issue, while all the other members listened. At any time, another A might come and 'tag' (touch lightly) the A who was speaking. The latter then had to get up and go back to the As' side of the room, while the newcomer replaced him in the chair and carried on the discussion without a break. The Bs were to do likewise.

In this way the whole range of arguments on both sides of the issue could be stated and heard. When any A or B found that they were losing the argument or running out of ideas they could put out a hand to their team, and someone else would come and replace them.

After using tag argument in the whole group, we returned to the role play in the small group. The development worker was then able to try different ways of approaching the problem, having gathered a whole range of information and insights from the group.

Tag argument personalizes a proposal or issue. As a method it works in relation to a specific situation with concrete details, and is helpful for airing the pros and cons of opposing views and for practising the arguments. It is unlikely that either side will win the argument, though this can happen. The different strategies that emerge from the exercise can be tried out in the role play, or they can be noted as a range of possibilities for back home. The method is less useful as a means for debating general issues.

Tag argument (Sue Mayo observes)

Role Play 4

The Interventions Used: 'Speaking Your Thoughts' and 'Seeking Advice'

One member spoke about his responsibility for the administration of a small NGO. He felt constantly overwhelmed by paperwork, and was aware that colleagues and people in the local community felt frustrated by his lack of efficiency. He showed us a scene in which one colleague was waiting to obtain some paperwork, another was trying to help him locate the paperwork, and a local person was waiting to see him. He described himself as 'drowning in paperwork'. We stopped the action and asked each character to tell us *what they were thinking* at that moment. The development worker was thinking that he needed some help with organization. One colleague was thinking about whether he would obtain a permission slip in time; the other was hoping to be able to get on with her work. The local person was hoping her wait would not go on for too long. We wondered if there might be a way for all the people concerned to get what they wanted.

We sent the development worker out to sit with the 'spect-actors,' in order *to seek their advice*. The development worker then replayed the scene, trying out in turn the different pieces of advice he had been given. So now we could see each piece of advice being tried out in action, and observe how well it worked. All the actors had been given a description of how the development worker saw their character, and what motivated them as far as he knew. This gave them enough information to know how to respond when the development worker tried out the new approaches.

It could be tempting for the group doing the role play to come up with some instant solution; but if everyone sticks to the information they have been given about their role, it is possible to try out a variety of suggestions. For example, to make the development worker suddenly more effective at administration would be unrealistic, but to try out steps towards that could be very useful.

Role Play 5

The Interventions Used: 'Identifying the Moment for Change' and 'Seeking Advice'

A development worker described interviewing a man from the local community for a job as a plumber in the development centre. The man was not qualified in plumbing, and so did not get the job. Soon afterwards, the man returned, threatening violence against the staff in the centre. The development worker immediately appointed armed guards for the centre.

The development worker expressed his dismay at the way things had escalated so quickly. The spectactors were asked to see if they could *identify the moment* when a different course of action might have changed the outcome. Most of the group felt that the crucial moment was when the development worker told the local man that he had not got the job.

At this point we sent the development worker to *seek advice* from the 'spect-actors'. He tried out two suggestions: the first was that he should offer the man another job that suited his skills; the second was that he should offer to find the man some training to gain the skills he needed. Both pieces of advice avoided leaving the man feeling completely rejected, and allowed him to maintain his dignity.

While the detail of the advice may not have been appropriate in the real circumstances, the whole group learned something very important about anticipating difficulties, taking action at the right moment, and avoiding the escalation of tension.

Choosing the Intervention

Seven methods of intervention are described above, and there are others. It can be difficult to decide which is the most appropriate intervention to use in a role play.

The trainer is likely to have to make this choice during the session itself, and at a moment when the course members are deeply involved and excited. To begin with, it is helpful to keep a list of the methods to refer to, so as to avoid overlooking any of the possibilities.

Some starting points and criteria for choosing the intervention are:

- to look for ways which will help us understand the situation shown in the role play better;
- to identify the possibilities for change in that situation, and to test these out;
- to consider and explore alternative ways of dealing with the problem or issue shown;
- to pick up echoes of work done in previous phases, and to apply methods and learning with which the group is already familiar.

Interventions are used in small groups, but the other course members who watch and listen are as actively involved as those in the small group. With the whole course working together, everyone will learn.

Observing role play

▶ *We were actually tasked to explore some problematic situations in our place of work ... and then make a role play out of it. As an audience, we will not only be listening and watching, but be 'spect-actors' which means as spectator you will also be expected to act, in short, an active participant is needed out of you! ...*

... As we were intently watching the others do the playing, my dear diary, we tried to identify what is really the problem. We look at the different relationships, at those who have power over those who are powerless, and of course the communication channels — how does it flow — to whom and what? We tried also to unfold the many possibilities of finding the solution ... by giving some suggestions,

changing somehow the approach, or making some interventions ... Trying ourselves to be more objective in times of crisis! Oh my dear diary, if you'd only watched us performing ...

▶ *From my group we had the role play on drinking water problem in the slum and how it was handled. The second group conducted a role play of an office situation ...*

▶ *We learned that role play can be very useful to find out what is really going on under the surface. To think out the solution of a conflict or a problem we must first find out what is going on under the surface.*

▶ *The role plays represented the actual situations in the following people's work: M, Jy, Sr and myself. It was interesting to see how easy it was to interpret the still pictures as opposed to the actual role playing with words and actions. I was challenged personally to see visually how much responsibility I have ... Could I possibly carry so much? Therefore a need to re-look at myself and the burdens.*

▶ *... we all watched. At the end of each we looked for alternatives and possibilities of solving the conflict. Generally the role plays were exciting to me, especially Group Three's, because it reminded me of the conflict that happened in one of our Districts.*

▶ *Today, during Je's role play in which I participated, I was forced to look back at my own situation ...*

▶ *We presented 'the ID card problem in Pakistan'. This was Sa's story ... When I became a Pakistani woman and stood behind more in the demonstration march, I could understand their culture more clearly and experience the reality. And I felt I was in a scene from the women's history.*

CHAPTER 8

Thinking About Our World

Win as Much as You Can

▶ *I enjoy these games because they often show how things work and how people act in reality.*

This exercise deals with the dynamics of trust, co-operation and competition within an interdependent system.[1] The learning is relevant at all levels for development — group, organization, society and international.

As the exercise also deals with attempts to benefit at the expense of others, it can be used to illustrate Dependency Theory.[2] The exercise can also be used to illustrate the effect on the environment of pursuing 'national interests' or 'company profits' without regard for global interdependence.

It is suitable for the early part of a course, perhaps during the second or the third week.

It is a lively exercise, and despite the sombre learning, it is fun to play. Altogether, with the discussion afterwards, it requires one session.

Objectives

- to explore the dynamics of trust, co-operation and competition;
- to experience the effects of competition within an interdependent system;
- to raise members' awareness of their own attitudes and behaviour when working in a small part of a larger system;
- to introduce the concepts of interdependence, multiple identity and superordinate goals.

Preparation and Materials

■ Prepare small slips of paper of four distinct colours, one colour for one sub-group. Ten slips per sub-group will be needed. Have a copy of the handout (pages 296—297) ready for each member.

Before the group members enter the room move the chairs into four small circles in the corners of the room. As members come in invite them to sit in whichever small circle, or sub-group, they choose. The sub-groups should be far enough away from each other so that their members can confer without being overheard.

---

1. The exercise is well known in some training circles. It has been published elsewhere, sometimes under names such as Win-Lose and Competition or Co-operation? The earliest source seems to be J. William Pfieffer and John E. Jones, *A Handbook of Structured Experiences for Human Relations Training*, Volume II, University Associates Press, Iowa, pages 66—70.
2. Dependency Theory is an attempt to explain underdevelopment. It suggests that underdevelopment is an active process of impoverishment caused by exploitative relationships.

Introducing the Exercise

■ Introduce the exercise by saying that it is relevant to relations between groups. Examples could be groups in a community, or departments in an organization.

Tell the members that the object in the exercise is to 'win as much as you can', and 'to score as many points as you can'. If any members ask who 'you' refers to, tell them to decide that for themselves.

Distribute the handout (pages, 296—297) and use it to help explain the exercise.

Tell the group that there will be ten rounds. Each round will last two or three minutes.

In each round, each of the sub-groups is to make a choice between two alternatives, X or Y. The consequences of choosing X or Y are shown in the first table (page 296). Take the group through the possible combinations and the scores. Show them that the second table (page 297) is for keeping their sub-group's score in each round.

Give each sub-group ten small slips of coloured paper. Tell them that their sub-group will be known by the colour of its slips, for example, the blue group, the red group, etc.

Conducting the Exercise

Tell the members that Round One is starting, and ask them to make their first choice between X and Y. You should be ready to allow five minutes or more for this first round, especially if there are members who are unfamiliar with such exercises.

Each sub-group writes its decision on a slip. Ask them to write the Round Number on the slip also, and then collect the slips. When you have all four, announce how many sub-groups have chosen X and how many Y. This will tell members the number of points their sub-group has scored in that round. Do not reveal which sub-group has made which choice.

Proceed immediately to Round Two, repeat the process, and then go on to Rounds Three and Four.

In Round Five inform the members that the gain or loss of points will be multiplied by three. Tell them that single representatives of each sub-group can meet each other in the centre of the room to consult on the choices the sub-groups will make in this round. Allow some minutes for such consultation. Then ask the representatives to return to their sub-groups before the decisions for Round Five are made.

For Rounds Six and Seven proceed as before. In Round Eight any member of any sub-group is permitted to meet the members of other sub-groups for consultation. Allow time for this if required. Scores in Round Eight are multiplied by five.

Round Nine is as before.

Inform the members that the exercise ends with Round Ten. In Round Ten, members are again permitted to meet and consult. If there is little or no response, check whether they want to meet or not. Scores are multiplied by ten.

In most groups the sub-groups compete throughout the exercise, and the level of trust becomes lower and lower. Sometimes members negotiate an agreement in Round Five or Eight, but it is seldom kept by all sub-groups. A few course groups have ensured that an agreement works in Round Ten by marking all slips with Y during their negotiations and giving the slips directly to the trainer.

Conducting the Reflection

■ At the end of the exercise ask the sub-groups to work out their total scores. Invite them to take a couple of minutes to exchange reactions to the experience in their sub-groups.

The reflection is done in the whole group, but members should remain sitting in their sub-groups. If the reflection is conducted in a light-hearted manner, it helps members to deal with their feelings.

Invite any immediate and general reactions. Be prepared for strong expressions. Some sub-groups may cast blame immediately on others for what they see as betrayals of trust. Others may want to defend their actions.

Some individuals may be disturbed by their own behaviour. They may express guilt because they tried to gain at the expense of others. If so, encourage them to look at the system as a whole; the issues in the exercise go beyond individual behaviour.

Put a table on the board (see opposite page) listing the rounds and sub-groups. Leave space for two additional columns to the right.

Ask the sub-groups to reveal their choices in the first round. If there is any uncertainty you have the slips for verification. Then ask them to explain their choices and intentions, and invite comments on their experience during that round. Repeat for subsequent rounds. Explore what happened in the rounds when negotiation was permitted. Focus on any expressions of feeling and on statements about motivations, attitudes and decisions, but do not allow the discussion to become laboured.

When all ten rounds have been reviewed, and the choices explained, enter the total score of each sub-group. Then put a heading over the next column: Total Of Sub-Group Scores.

Show the group that the scores can be added 'sideways' to give the whole group's score round by round. Discuss these figures (which may total zero in many rounds), and make an overall total at the bottom of the column for the whole group. Point out that this is what the whole course group has scored in the exercise.

Put a heading over the remaining column: Possible Scores. Calculate these on the basis of four Y choices in every round, and show that the possible overall total for the whole group is 10,000. Make sure that everyone understands that the way for the whole group to achieve the maximum is for all sub-groups to choose Y in every round. (This corresponds to a Win-Win outcome.) Invite members to compare this maximum with the actual score of the whole group, and explore the difference, assuming there is one.

Group Scores

Round	Yellow	Pink	Blue	Green		
1						
2						
3						
4						
5						
6						
7						
8						
9						
10						
Total						

Learning and Application

Some members may immediately make connections between the exercise and many situations in the real world, organizational, national and international. Others may find the links less clear, especially if the exercise comes in the early part of a course.

As the discussion proceeds the ideas of interdependence, multiple identity, and super-ordinate goals can be introduced (see glossary, page 471). These can help to make sense of the dilemmas in the exercise, and show ways out of them.

■ The title and object of the exercise was Win as Much as You Can:
'How did you understand 'You' in that situation?'
'Did you think of yourself as a member of your sub-group, or a member of the whole group?'
'If you identified with your sub-group, what was your sub-group's relationship with the other sub-groups?'

Point out that in the exercise the decisions of each sub-group affected all the other sub-groups, and the group as a whole. Point this out as an example of 'interdependence'. Explain the idea further if necessary by referring to other examples, such as the family.

If the sub-groups competed with each other — as they usually do — the following questions may be useful:
'What will happen to the group as a whole if sub-groups try to win at each others' expense?'
'In an interdependent system can one part go on 'winning' at the expense of other parts of the same system? What happens in the long run?'

In the long run all parts of such a system will suffer and 'lose'. Win-Lose (some win, some lose) will become Lose-Lose (all lose).

Make the parallels with other situations:
'If a department in an organization tries to benefit itself at the expense of the organization as a whole, what will happen in the long run?'
'If companies try to benefit themselves at the expense of the environment what will happen to the environment — and to the companies — in the end?'
'If countries try to benefit themselves at the expense of the rest of the world, what will happen to the world in the end?'

Ask members of the sub-groups which were competing:
'Did you sometimes prefer to lose rather than allow others to win?'

If so, then everyone is already losing! (= Lose-Lose).

Yet we have seen that it was possible for the whole group to score the maximum number of points, and for all the sub-groups to share in that total.

Everyone then wins! (= Win-Win).

'What were the difficulties in achieving this?'

■ 'How were the levels of trust between the sub-groups?'
'What caused any loss of trust, and what were the effects?'
'When trust is lost, and we are are competing at each other's expense, are
we helpless, or can we change things? How do we restore trust?'
'What did we do in the exercise? What can we do in our situations back-home?'

This can lead on to issues of identity and superordinate goals:
'Can we be members of sub-groups and of the whole group at the same time?'
'Can we have multiple identities?'
'Can we identify with our own department at the same time as we identify
with the whole organization?'

'Can we be nationals of our country and citizens of the world simultaneously?'
'Can we work for the development of our communities, and for the protection
of the global environment, at the same time?'
'Can we share the same overall or 'superordinate' goals, which will give us
our overall direction, while we work towards our specific goals at our own level?'

▶ *Our afternoon exercise was* Win as Much as You Can. *The attractive title hides many meanings behind, when winning usually means lose, and lose means lack of trust. Really we were different uncooperated units rushing to win the game at the expense of the others. We did it and this was satisfactory to us for a while, but it was big disappoinment when sorting the global result, to discover that all lose.*

▶ *We all seemed to take this game very seriously. I hope F and L are now speaking to one another again ... Instead of co-operating for the common good of all, we schemed so that only one group really benefited at the expense of all others.*

▶ *We explored our interdependency in the game. The Blue ladies' group ended in extreme discouragement over the loss of more than 4000 points — mainly due to terrible Pink group that on purpose cheated and lied ... Also the Yellow group was deeply disappointed that our group — the Green one — and the terrible Pink one didn't stick to the agreement. But they concluded the game saying they remained poor, but with a slightly cleaner conscience anyway ...*

... The discussion afterwards was fascinating and also, when we extrapolated to a world view, very thought-provoking. How many of our governments only want what is best for themselves? How will the world ever dig itself out of the mess of distrust, greed, jealousy, downright malice and misunderstanding that it is in? How soon will we all be losers? As A said, the world is already a long way through the game: How many people are prepared to change the way they play? If I really think hard about it, despite my principles, am I prepared to change the way I behave?

You will be working in one of four sub-groups.

For ten successive rounds you and your partners in your sub-group will choose either an X or a Y. The scoring for each round will depend upon the pattern of choices made, as shown in the table below.

4 Xs = each sub-group loses 100
3 Xs = these sub-groups win 100 each 1 Y = this sub-group loses 300
2 Xs = these sub-groups win 200 each 2 Ys = these sub-groups lose 200 each
1 X = this subgroup wins 300 3 Ys = these sub-groups lose 100 each
4 Ys = each sub-group wins 100

Adapted from J. William Pfieffer and John E. Jones, *A Handbook of Structured Experiences for Human Relations Training*, Volume II, University Associates Press, Iowa, page 69

You are to consult with your partners in the sub-group during each round and make a JOINT DECISION. During rounds No. 5, 8 and 10 you may also consult with the other sub-groups.

Round	Consult With	Choice	Won	Lost	
1	Your sub-group partners				
2	Your sub-group partners				
3	Your sub-group partners				
4	Your sub-group partners				
5	Other sub-group representatives. Your sub-group partners				Scores x 3
6	Your sub-group partners				
7	Your sub-group partners				
8	Members of other sub-groups. Your sub-group partners				Scores x 5
9	Your sub-group partners				
10	Members of other sub-groups. Your sub-group partners				Scores x 10

▶ *... it was interesting to note how my view about the poor people has matured-up with my growing-up and being involved in development work.*

This exercise encourages course members to reflect on their attitudes to poverty and poor people and on how these attitudes may have changed as a result of being involved in professional development work.

The exercise is conducted in the whole group, but what is shared are generalized impressions from the group as a whole, rather than individual attitudes. So the exercise is not threatening and is suitable for the beginning of a course, as part of an introduction to underdevelopment and development.

The exercise requires half a session, and can be used before Factors in Underdevelopment (page 301), the two together forming one session.

Objectives

- to explore links between perceptions and attitudes towards poor people and approaches to development;
- to encourage course members to consider their own attitudes towards poor people and poverty, together with the assumptions of their organizations;
- to help members reflect on whether their understanding of poverty (and underdevelopment) has changed, and if so what caused it to change.

Conducting the Exercise

■ Start by making the links between the way we understand underdevelopment and the kind of development work we tend to do.[1] Explain that for the purpose of the exercise you will use the more feeling word 'poverty', and the more common idea of 'poor people', rather than the cold and technical term 'underdevelopment'.

Ask the members to think back to the time before they came into development work. It may be easier for them, and give a common reference point, if you ask them to think back to the time when they were children, either at home with their families or at primary school.

---

1. Poverty is usually understood as an economic condition. Underdevelopment is a broader term, and includes economic, social, political, societal, psychological and cultural deprivation.

■ Ask them:

'What sort of words did you hear being used about poor people in those days?'

'What did the adults in your family say about poor people?'

'What did your teachers say about them?'

'What words did your classmates use?'

'Why were poor people thought to be poor?'

'Did you hear any local proverbs or phrases which referred to poor people?'

There may be members in the group who are themselves from poor families. You may not know this, but acknowledge the possibility without asking, and point out that poor people themselves have ideas about why they are poor.

'How did poor families understand their own situation?'

'What words did they use?'

'What did people think were the reasons for their own poverty?'

Ask members to think back for two or three minutes and to jot down the words that occur to them. In an international group invite them to refer to their own language. Then ask them to share the words and their meanings with their neighbour for three or four minutes.[2]

Bring attention back to the whole group and invite members to contribute any of their words, but do not insist that everyone contributes.

Write all the words contributed on the left side of the board, without comment or classification. Add words of your own if you wish. Go on listing words until contributions stop, or half the board is used up. You should have a list of 15—25 words.

Ask the members what words they would use now, as adults, as development workers, and as individuals with direct experience of poverty and poor people.

Again ask them to share briefly with neighbours. Then collect words from the whole group, and list them on the right side of the board.

Ask the members to consider the two lists, and to discuss with their neighbour how the lists differ. Emphasize the task:

'What strikes you about these two lists?'

'Do the lists say much the same? Or is there a difference? If so, what?'

'What about *these* words, as a whole? ... *those* words, as a whole?'

'Comparing one list with the other, what are the differences?'

Invite thoughts and suggestions, and collect these on another board. Invite any observations.[3]

If the members recognize significant differences between the lists go on to ask them:

'Have your own ideas or attitudes about poor people changed since childhood?'

'If so, when did that happen? What caused them to change?'

---

2. The writing down first and then the sharing in pairs helps to reduce any awkwardness.

3. If the lists are similar, or if members do not perceive them as different, explore the reasons.

■ Ask them to think about this for a minute or two, and then to share with a neighbour. Invite anyone to explain in the whole group what caused their own ideas to change.

Conclude by exploring parallels between changes in members' own ideas and changes in understanding at professional and organizational levels:

'Have your own organization's ideas changed?'
'Has the general understanding of poverty and underdevelopment among NGOs changed?'
'How has this affected their understanding of development?'
'What does it mean for the role of the development worker?'

▶ *... a list was drawn up on what the poor people were named — e.g. lazy, sinners, rubbish, spongers, its their own fault etc, just to mention a few. The same process was carried out to list how a development worker might describe poor people — powerless, trapped, marginalised, exploited, etc.*

▶ *Unlike those words ... which imply individual's fault, the words we use today suggest that some forces are responsible.*

▶ *The whole group agreed that there was indeed a difference between the first and the second sets of answers. Some points were: the second set of answers was more political; it has more terminologies; it recognises a second party, force or power that causes such conditions; and looks at the issues in a societal dimension or perspective. While the first set was putting blame on the people; was more judgemental; and looked more to individuals rather than the people in general. One last comment was that, in the first set, the people are the problem, while in the second, the problem is upon the people.*

8.3 Factors in Underdevelopment

▶ *We found it difficult to agree over common causes of underdevelopment.*

▶ *I think many of us realised that we all have theories about development, or at least elements of theory.*

We all make assumptions about what development is, and how it can be achieved. These assumptions will depend what we think are the causes of poverty and suffering. Or, using a colder and more technical word, what do we think are the causes of 'underdevelopment'?

Poverty is usually understood as an economic condition. Underdevelopment is a broader term which includes economic, social, political, psychological and cultural deprivation. How do we understand the problem of underdevelopment? What assumptions are we making about that?

Unless we understand a problem correctly our work on the solution may be ineffective, if not damaging. So the sooner we become aware of our assumptions, and the more we can test them in training, the better.

This exercise opens up discussion between members about underdevelopment. It includes a questionnaire about factors which may contribute to underdevelopment, or may result from it (pages 303—304).[1]

The exercise can be used at the beginning of a course, as part of an introduction to underdevelopment and development. It can be used immediately after Perceptions of Poverty and Poor People (page 298).

Objectives

- to explore differing assumptions and opinions about factors linked with poverty and underdevelopment;
- to make course members more aware of their own assumptions and opinions, together with those of their organizations;
- to demonstrate that a development organization's understanding and approach must be appropriate to the community and situation it is working in.

---

1. Questionnaires are a convenient method for turning minds in the direction of an issue or topic, and opening up discussion of it. The disadvantage is that they may suggest an agenda and boundaries, and appear to discourage creative enquiry beyond these. They may offer comfort to members — and even to trainers — rather than challenge. So it is important that questionnaires such as this are used only as starting points.

Conducting the Exercise

◼ The exercise begins with the questionnaire which members complete individually. Make a point of inviting them to add more factors if they wish. Some members may be familiar with the ideas and will need only ten minutes. Others may need up to 20 minutes.

Members then discuss and compare their responses in small groups of four, or five if necessary. If they have already been working in small groups, ask them to change the groups. The discussion may take another 30 minutes.

At the end of that discussion ask each group:

'Which factors were identified most often as causes of underdevelopment?'
'How much agreement was there? Can we expect agreement? Do we need it?'
'Do we expect the factors to be the same for all countries and all communities?'

The factors which are chosen most often give an indication of the group's general understanding of underdevelopment at this time.

Reflecting on the Process[2]

◼ Conclude by enquiring about the process of the discussion in the small groups:
'How did you start the discussion?'
'How did you share your responses?'
'What do you think helped your discussion? What made it more difficult?'

'Did anyone change their minds? If so, why? Were you really convinced?'
'Who spoke more at the beginning?
'Had everyone spoken by the end?'

'Was the energy level high or low? Did it change? What affected it?'
'What was the mood? Tense or relaxed? Co-operative or competitive?'
'Did anyone take on a leadership role?'

▶ *It seems clear that one's understanding of underdevelopment depends on one's values, beliefs, view of oneself, view of other people, own experience, other people's ideas, etc. This understanding will in turn determine one's understanding of development, the kind of development work one does, and how one will understand one's role as a development worker.*

▶ *Questioning is important for everyone. The poor remain poor until they start to ask why ...*

---

2. The task and the procedure in the exercise here are similar to those in The Task and the Process (page 128). If that exercise has already been used, the learning from it may assist the members here. It may be worth exploring this and reinforcing the learning.

Questionnaire: Factors Related to Underdevelopment

Work individually to start with. Below is a list of factors which are related in some way to poverty and underdevelopment. Go through the list and indicate those factors which you consider to be basic causes of poverty and underdevelopment. Add other factors to the list if you wish. After indicating those factors which you consider to be causes of poverty and underdevelopment, identify the three which you think are the most important.

When other members are ready form small groups of four. Compare and discuss the three factors which you have each identified. See if the group agrees on the three factors which are the most important.

Discuss in your group which factors are symptoms of poverty and underdevelopment, rather than causes.

	overpopulation
	out-of-date technology
	international trade policies and practices
	lack of personal initiative and self-confidence
	relationships of dependency
	the failure of rich countries to give enough aid
	unfavourable climate
	the colonial past
	lack of strong leadership and discipline
	inequalities of power
	lack of education and training
	transnational companies
	armed conflict

	too much government control
	ignorance and superstition
	socialist economic organization
	expenditure on arms and the military
	lack of roads, railways, hospitals, schools etc
	corruption
	lack of trades' unions and peasants' organizations
	domination and exploitation by some over others
	shortage of land and natural resources
	feelings of apathy and hopelessness
	not enough job opportunities
	capitalist economic organization
	lack of hard work
	unrest caused by subversives
	international debt
	damage to the environment

John Staley, *Enticing the Learning: Trainers in Development*, University of Birmingham, pages 303—304

▶ *The experience of power we each had lives on in our hearts as if it were today ...*

▶ *The game clearly emphasised how people with power in hand can abuse the power they have for their own sake at the expense of the powerless people.*

Starpower is an acclaimed and 'powerful' simulation which has been widely used to explore the dynamics and structures of power in society and in communities. It provides a valuable experience in the use of power and its effects, and raises awareness of the workings of power in human relations.

The simulation is especially useful for development workers because it offers an insight into the difficulty of using power in ways that are 'developmental' for others. It also demonstrates how complex our attitudes and feelings towards power are, not only among those who have power, but also among those who do not.

At the personal level the simulation challenges us to reflect on our own values and behaviour. One of the insights we may gain is that, whatever our ideological claims, we tend to use power to secure our own advantage. This realization may lead members to individual heart-searching.

Trainers must start by obtaining the instructions for Starpower. These have been published, but they are protected by copyright and so they cannot be included here. Instructions, and materials for using the simulation, are available from the publishers or suppliers.[1] However, as this simulation is widely known in training circles, copies of the instructions can sometimes be borrowed, and suitable materials can be found locally.

The simulation is best used towards the end of a course, after more basic issues of power have already been raised and recognized. There is then already a context in which to embed the new learning. There should also be a level of cohesion by then which will help the group to contain any confrontations. However there should be enough time left before the end of the course for the issues to be engaged with, and the new learning to be incorporated into the members' understanding of development.

The process within Starpower is less predictable than in some other simulations. At a certain stage in the process the trainer transfers power to one sub-group within the simulation. What follows will then depend on the behaviour of the sub-group. This may vary from outright exploitation of the rest of the group to benevolent attempts at 'sharing'; but whatever the sub-group attempts is likely to be resisted by other sub-groups, and strong feelings and reactions may be expressed.

---

1. R. Garry Shirts, *Starpower: Director's Instructions*, Western Behavioral Sciences Institute, La Jolla, California. Or see http://www.stsintl.com/schools-charities/

Although the resulting situation may seem chaotic and even disturbing at times, there is rich material for learning; and the excitement and unpredictability should not discourage trainers from using this simulation.[2]

The unpredictability makes it more difficult to use a standard sequence and structure for the 'debriefing'.[3] When the debriefing begins members may need time to re-live the process, and to share heated feelings, before they are ready to move on and reflect analytically and objectively.

For less experienced groups it may help to split the debriefing and conduct it in two stages. The first stage, immediately after the action, is focussed on what happened, who did what and to whom, the feelings, the decisions, and the consequences.

The second stage, which may be later that day or the following morning, is to reflect on the dynamics, the issues raised and the applications to professional work. A further stage is to encourage individuals to reflect on their own reactions, behaviour and role.

When the simulation is used in an international development group with an awareness of North-South issues, the experience tends to be interpreted and discussed in North-South and international terms. While this can be useful, such issues may be better dealt with by using The Trading Game (see page 308).

The particular contribution of Starpower is in exploring the dynamics and structures of power within national societies and within communities. When it is used with a group whose members belong to the same national society, and whose reflections are deep, this simulation can transform members' understanding of the workings of power.[4]

▶ *The wealthy group, which was in a position to dictate terms, was only concerned to consolidate its position. In their effort to keep the other two groups dependent, they changed the rules drastically to suit themselves ...*

▶ *We all know what happened. We in the Squares were given power and misused it ... I ended up taking a central role. Its quite a shock that I could enter the role so easily ...*

▶ *What have I learned about power this morning? Power is a big temptation for human beings.*

---

2 Usually the sub-group which is given power will 'abuse' it, and this offers rich opportunities for learning as indicated in the published instructions. However among development workers who are aware of the issues, some sub-groups may attempt to 'share' power. This can be disconcerting for the trainer who is expecting the more usual exploitative behaviour; but as a learning opportunity it is equally valuable because it opens up the issues of paternalism and dependency, which are central in development work.

3. The published instructions for Starpower suggest a total time of two hours, but at least three hours should be allowed. If this is divided into two sessions, the first is used for introducing the simulation and playing it, and the second is for the 'debriefing' and reflection. The exercise can be tiring, so refreshments are welcome between play and 'debriefing'. If these are being arranged by the trainer in the same room, they can even be incorporated into the game, and given to the sub-group with power for them to distribute in whatever way they choose. This adds additional — and real — stakes into the experience.

4. An exploration of power structures within their own society may feel uncomfortable, or even alarming, to some members. They may take refuge from such a challenge by turning the discussion towards the international system and blaming those 'further from home'. Trainers should be ready to challenge this.

Though I think I don't like to oppress people in my life, I change my mind right after I was put into a group possessing big power. This game is an important challenge to me. It gives me the chance to evaluate my energy towards oppression. Since my attitude towards oppression changed easily, I realise that I have not yet enough energy to struggle against oppression at the present time. I feel helpless. Fortunately I discover it earlier.

▶ *I'm still feeling the distress of 'Starpower'. The decision, at the end of the long afternoon, to share power and resources equally among all, was laudable. But I did not trust this so-called equality. It came down from the top as a 'gift'. One can't be given equality; one must feel equal. I felt I had been manipulated ... My distress is not related to the game alone, but to the realisation that my cherished ideals — equality and sharing — had been forced on the group, and (was) therefore, meaningless. I was reminded that the way you go about reaching your goal is as important as the goal itself.*

▶ *S emphasised on the simulation ... we had a very fruitful and long discussion ... questions were raised:*

1. What kind of power do we have as development workers? How can we use it best?

2. If real development depends upon capturing and using power, in what way are development workers different from politicians?

▶ *I suspect most of the course members occupy positions of some power in their organisations. We should all be careful that we are not seduced by power.*

The World Trade System: Using The Trading Game

▶ *This game is true to real life. The control is within the system, but if the system is bad who can change it?*

This simulation enables a group of 15—30 people to create and experience a trading system which has many parallels with the world system. The simulation is widely used among the supporters of donor agencies in some Northern countries to raise awareness about injustice in the world.

It can also be used in the training of development workers who may be aware of the injustice already. Their need may be to understand more clearly how the world trade system works, and how such trade may be affecting the prospects for development in the countries, and even the localities, where they work. To meet this need the exercise can be modified so that it 'simulates' the real world more closely.

Detailed instructions for this simulation have been published, and cannot be included here. Trainers should start by referring to the published instructions.[1]

It is assumed, from this point onwards, that the reader has access to the instructions and is familiar with the simulation. Some modifications follow which increase the accuracy of the simulation and make for closer realism. As the world trading system continues to change, further modifications will be needed in the future.

Preparing the Room

■ The room for the simulation represents the world in which international trading takes place. Before the group assembles you should prepare the room to represent some of the physical, technological and economic realities of the world.

Provide a table for the International Market in front of the main chalk-board or flip chart. Place the tables for the two 'Northern' countries near the International Market. This reflects the reality that the markets are mostly located in the North and are closely linked to the Northern countries. Provide a chair for each member at these tables.

Locate the Southern countries at the other end of the room, away from the Market, 'on the margins'. Do not give the Southern countries tables. You can also give some of them less chairs than members. This represents lack of infrastructure in those countries.

---

1. *The Trading Game*, Christian Aid, London. See www.christian-aid.org.uk

■ Put the information about shapes and current prices on a portable board or chart, and place it so that those in some of the Southern countries cannot see the information. This represents the communication difficulties of some Southern countries, and their difficulties in keeping in touch with changing international markets.

You can place any surplus furniture in the room between the Southern countries to represent the oceans, mountain ranges, or deserts and consequent difficulties of communication.

Adjustments to the Simulation

International Market

In the published version one of the organizers or trainers is instructed to play the role of banker. Change this role to International Market, and if necessary explain to the group during the briefing that the International Market is a system, not a person.

Tell the group that the International Market will accept shapes only in multiples of five. This represents the economies of scale of automated manufacturing, and makes the task of the trainer playing the role easier.

Provide the trainer playing the International Market with a set square and a protractor identical to those given to groups A and B. This makes checking those shapes easy. Instruct the trainer to be strict over the quality of shapes offered, especially by the Southern countries. This represents some of the difficulties Southern countries have in breaking into international markets.

If some Southern countries are able to borrow rulers or set squares and make their own templates of the shapes, you can alter the sizes specified on the board. This represents change in the market, and the outdating of technology.

From time to time during the game, adjust the prices of shapes according to the level of supply. This represents the fluctuations of real markets. Write the new prices on the portable board.

Trading Years

Tell the group that time in the simulation will be divided into trading or financial years. Each 'year' lasts approximately 10 minutes, and you will announce the end of it.

Ask the trainer playing the International Market to be ready with the accounts of each country at the end of each year. Either you or he/she should put these on the main board as running totals. This allows members to see how their own country is doing, compared with others, as the simulation progresses.

If any country does not earn, point out that their economy is failing and that part of their population may be in distress and starving.

■ Each country starts with a sum of 'money'. This represents the country's reserves, and is much larger for the Northern countries. These reserves may be used for transactions between countries. The published instructions specify 'money' in the form of pounds sterling. Change this to units of money or trade, and do not specify any currency. If you calculate these units at the same value as units earned from trading, you can include them in the accounts at the end.

The simulation can usually be concluded after four years of trading, i.e. approximately 45 minutes.

Country Groups

Allocate four or more members to each of the two Northern countries.[2] Designate these countries A and B. Do not name them after real countries: that will be done during the reflection.

Allocate three or more members to each of the Southern countries. There should be at least three Southern countries, preferably four or five. Designate them C, D, E and so on. Do not name them after real countries.

Materials

Give countries the following raw materials and technology:

A

2 sheets of paper
1 pair of scissors which cut cleanly
1 ruler
1 compass with pencil
1 set square
3 pencils
1 pencil sharpener
10 x 100 'units' of currency

B

1 sheet of paper
1 pair of scissors which cut cleanly
1 ruler
1 compass with pencil
1 protractor
3 pencils
1 stick of glue
8 x 100 'units' of currency

C

8 sheets of paper
half a sheet of coloured sticky paper
2 x 100 'units' of currency

D

4 sheets of paper
half a sheet of coloured sticky paper
1 unsharpened pencil
2 x 100 'units' of currency

---

2. If they have fewer members the country will not have 'a sufficient labour force to make use of all its technology', and its technology should be scaled down.

E

3 sheets of paper
2 pencil ends, one with a broken lead
a piece of a broken ruler (not long enough to use)
2 × 100 'units' of currency

F

10 sheets of paper
a piece of a broken ruler (not long enough to use)
2 × 100 'units' of currency

■ Any additional Southern countries can be supplied similarly to E and F.

Emphasize that members may not use any of their own materials, pens, knives or rulers during the game. Tell them to put these away.

Simulating world trade: the rich and the poor

During Play

Remember that the purpose is to simulate the world trade system as it is, and not as we might like it to be. You should be ready to favour countries A and B so that they retain their advantages. This represents their greater influence in the world. Do not make adjustments that favour the Southern countries.

The published instructions describe the use of coloured sticky paper to represent raw materials unrecognized by their 'owners'. Examples in the real world are ores and minerals. The instructions also describe introducing new supplies of 'raw materials'. Include both of these.

■ Another intervention which favours countries A and B is to introduce synthetic substitutes. If A or B has difficulty in getting paper from the Southern countries you can supply them with sheets of a different paper. Explain that this represents a synthetic substitute which their greater research abilities have discovered. Examples in the real world are artificial fibres and plastics.

If you, or any other trainer, is playing the role of United Nations you should intervene only if all the countries request it and if they all give you the necessary authority. Such agreement is unlikely, and demonstrates the limitations of the UN.

Discussion and Reflection

The simulation recreates the inequalities and dependency of the world trading system in an immediate and visible way. Those who represent the Southern countries usually describe feelings of anger and apathy, and reactions during the discussion may be strong.

The published instructions include some guidelines for trainers for leading the discussion of the system as a whole with its general difficulties and injustices.

More specific features of the system also sometimes emerge during this simulation. They may include:
- the preoccupation (busyness or business) of Northern industrial countries;
- terms of trade and changing market prices;
- disparities in scientific and specialised knowledge;
- commodity agreements, and the difficulties of making them work;
- temporary immigrant labour and its subordinate status;
- export-processing zones;
- aid as grants, as loans, or as technical assistance;
- dumping of outdated technology;
- the exploitation of ignorance;
- tendencies towards breaking the rules, confrontation, violence, war.

Only some of these features appear on any one occasion, depending on the actions of the course group involved, but you should ensure that any such features have been recognized by members and are discussed.

Whenever experience in the simulation is discussed one important question is:
'Who was controlling the system?'

If members of the Southern countries indicate that A and B had control, ask the members of A and B if they felt that they were in control.

If members suggest that you, as organizer, had control, point out that, although you introduced the structure, you were not controlling the dynamics or the decision-making or the ways that members played their roles.

■ Another question is:

'Should such a system be changed?'

If there is agreement in the group that the system should be changed, ask:

'Who is going to change it?'

'Will the Northern countries change it?'

If there is any tendency to blame the outcome on those members who happened to play roles in the Northern countries, ask the group if they think the outcome would have been different if other members had played those roles. Help them to see that individuals tend to act according to their roles in the system.

Your final question can be to invite names for the countries. By this stage the names suggested will reflect the experience and insights which members have gained from the simulation.

Thinking about our world: an informal discussion

▶ *I must say this is part of the human nature. I myself was in the rich group in the simulation exercise, and acted precisely as the rich would act in the real life.*

▶ *We had three papers, a pencil, and two broken pieces of a ruler. One of the industrial countries didn't even want to speak to us. One man there said, 'We have everything. We don't need anything.' The other industrial country suggested buying our papers, the most valuable items we had ... I think power was on their side.*

▶ *It's surprising that people (or these development workers) could adopt the roles so quickly and behave as what would have happened in the reality ... Yesterday, I was feeling 'powerless' during the simulation. I have seen the necessity of co-operation amongst poor countries. But we couldn't persuade them and ended up by adopting the rules of competition — sacrificing others and being satisfied by the result where we are not the last.*

▶ *The simulation exercise helped me to witness the trade imbalances in a tangible way. The simulation leaves me tired and exhausted. I ask myself whether I am a development or underdevelopment worker ...*

... I also hear of IMF, World Bank and multinational companies:
    how do these animals look?
    where do they graze?
    what do they eat?
    how big are their stomachs?
    how do they reproduce?

▶ *It was interesting to hear that the groups representing poor countries felt powerless, and felt that power was given to countries A and B. A and B, on the other hand, felt that they had no influence upon the international market. Nevertheless, they both finished the game with a really nice surplus.*

▶ *The question is still yet to answer — can the system be changed? If so who will change it?*

CHAPTER 9

Thinking About Ourselves

A Window on Ourselves

▶ *... each of us is endowed with the basic tool of development work which is the self. So it is just, fitting and right for us to know this tool very well.*

The principal 'resource' or 'tool' that any of us has, as a development worker, is his or her own self. This is the tool we must work with, whatever our role, and whatever the task. To produce the best results with any kind of tool, we must know how to use it. We must understand how it works, what it is capable of doing, and what its limitations are. We must know when it will work more effectively and when it will work less effectively. We have to know how to maintain it, and even make improvements to it. So each of us needs to give attention to our own self.

The Johari Window is a well-tested model for thinking about the self. It is simple and easily understood, and is not threatening or evaluative. It is especially useful with groups whose members have not yet begun to reflect upon themselves or upon relationships in their work.

The model also provides an excellent framework for team-building through self-disclosure (see page 325), and for increasing effectiveness through feedback (see page 330).

It can be used during the first half of a course, after the group has gained experience in working together. By this time the members should be ready to consider not only 'the role', but 'the person' as well (see pages 123—124).

The material which follows requires one session, or it can be shortened and used with Self-Disclosure (page 325) to make up one session.

Objectives

- to encourage individuals to reflect on their own selves as the principle resource in their working relationships with others;

- to introduce a simple model of the individual self or personality, and to raise members' awareness of the impact of personality on behaviour, communication, management and leadership;

- to introduce methods by which members can increase their openness and effectiveness in relating and working with others.

Introducing the Model: The Johari Window

■ Draw on the first paragraph of this section and emphasize the importance of understanding the self as the principal resource of every development worker.

■ Introduce the Johari Window as a simple way of thinking about ourselves, making use of the following points. Check if any members are already familiar with the model.

● The Johari Window offers a way of thinking about the self or personality, especially in relationship to others. It is a greatly simplified model — the personality is much more complicated — but it is a useful starting point.

● Johari is taken from the names of the originators, Joe (Luft) and Harry (Ingham).[1] Their model is described as a window with four panes of glass between the self or personality inside and other people outside.

● Part of this window (one of the panes) is described as being 'open': I can see through this myself, and other people can see through it too. This is the *Open* or *Public Area* of my self or personality. It is known to me and to other people.

● Another pane is 'closed' or opaque: I cannot see through it myself, and neither can anyone else. This pane of the window conceals the *Unknown Area* of my self or personality. Neither I nor other people know this part of my personality.

● The other two panes have one-way glass: one allows looking out and the other allows looking in. I myself can look out through one pane, knowing what is inside; but other people cannot see in. This is the *Secret* or *Private Area* of my self or personality, known to me but not to others. It is also known as the *Hidden Area*.

● The fourth pane is opaque to me; and I cannot see out through it. But other people can see in through it. They see things which I do not see, so it is known and usually referred to as the *Blind Area*. This represents aspects of my self or personality which other people know about, but which I am not aware of myself.

The Four Window Panes

■ Use the diagram (see page 318) to focus on each Area of the Self — or each pane of the window — and describe them in more detail.

Start with the Open Area and its characteristics which are described below.[2]

● <u>In The Open Area</u> other people see me as I see myself:

I feel free to be myself and to express myself;

I feel able to say what I mean, and what I feel;

communication with others is open and direct;

relationships are straightforward, without stress;

I am available and receptive to others;

I can be spontaneous, genuine and intimate with others;

1. The earliest version seems to be: J William Pfeiffer and John E Jones, 'Johari Window: An Exercise in Self-Disclosure', *A Handbook of Structured Experiences for Human Relations Training*, Volume I, University Associates Press, Iowa, pages 66—69.
2. Note that in this context 'openness with others' refers to the personality. It is not to do with confidential information or personal data such as salary. If this is misunderstood, members may be dubious about the prospect of 'openness'.

my activity is open and comfortable;

my motives and actions are known to me and to others;

and I have greater contact with the 'real world'.

- There can be negative behaviour in the Open Area. For example, a person may be impatient or rude. Yet if this is 'out in the open', and is admitted by the person concerned, it may be tolerated by others and does not become such a difficulty.

	Seen by myself	Not seen by myself
Seen by other people	Open Area	Blind Area
Not seen by other people	Hidden Area	Unknown Area

- In the Hidden Area (also called the 'mask' or 'façade') I know much about myself, as a person, that I do not reveal to others:

I hide aspects of my personality which I consider to be weaknesses or failings;

I hide feelings and attitudes that I do not feel free to express;

I hide what I fear may be judged, criticised or attacked;

I keep things hidden in case I get hurt because of them;

There are times when I remain silent, although my head or heart may be full;

I conceal aspects of myself that I think are too sensitive, embarrassing, or risky to share with others;

I have a hidden personal agenda;

keeping behaviour and knowledge hidden uses up my energy, which creates anxiety and tension for me.

- In the <u>Blind Area</u> (or 'blind spot') others are aware of things about me that I am not aware of myself:

  I see myself differently from how others see me;

  I may have a style of personality — for example, arrogant or withdrawn — that, unknown to me, makes me less accepted by other people;

  I may be exposing my own feelings or behaviour, and imposing these on others, without being aware of them myself;

  I may use gestures or mannerisms or habits of speech that I am not aware of, but which limit, or even damage, my communication and effectiveness;

  I may make impressions on others, and create resentments, that I am not aware of;

  I may have weaknesses that I do not recognize, but which are spoiling my work;

  I may have strengths that I do not recognize, and therefore I am not making use of them.

- The <u>Unknown Area</u>: in this 'pane' of the window there are things about myself that no one knows. I do not know them, and neither do other people. They include memories, experiences and feelings that affect my behaviour and relationships, but which are unconscious, and are not recognized by me or by others.

  I have unknown abilities and potentials there which may emerge and 'save the situation' in a crisis, or when extreme demands are made on me;

  there may also be destructive and violent tendencies, which may break out under extreme stress or conflict;

  these are the times when I may discover how brave, or how effective, or how violent, I can really be.

- The Unknown Area will never be known fully, but some of it may be progressively revealed during the individual's lifetime. There are many mechanisms which contribute to keeping it unknown, some individual, and some social and cultural. Sometimes people say that this is the Area that 'only God knows'. It is an important Area, more so than the diagram suggests.

Changing the Window

■ After describing the four Areas, explain how the size of each can change.
Draw on the following points.

- The model is not static, and the relative sizes of the panes in the Window may change. In a newly-formed group the Open Area of each member is likely to be small to start with. As the members get to know each other, they begin to form friendships. As they trust each other more, they have less need to hide things from each other. Then they reveal more of themselves, and so relationships and trust are further strengthened. The Open Areas become larger and the Hidden Areas are reduced.

- Such changes happen naturally, but the Window can be 'remodelled' more consciously and deliberately. As individuals we can make an effort to increase the size of our Open Area and to reduce the size of the Hidden and the Blind Areas.

- To enlarge the Open Area and reduce the Hidden Area, we can use the method known as Self-Disclosure. This is a process by which we reveal aspects of our lives and personalities, make ourselves known to others, share personal information, tell others about our feelings and opinions, and help others to get to know us.

- To enlarge the Open Area and reduce the Blind Area, we can use the method known as Feedback. Feedback is information about ourselves which is given to us by other people. They tell us, for example, about how they perceive us, or how our behaviour is affecting them. When we receive such information we can choose whether to act on it, or not. We can decide whether we will make changes in our behaviour, or not. If we wish to enlarge our Open Area and reduce our Blind Area we can deliberately invite Feedback from others.

- Both Self-Disclosure and Feedback require openness, acceptance of oneself and other people, and mutual trust. Mutual trust encourages self-awareness; whereas lack of trust, or a feeling of threat or insecurity, generally tends to reduce awareness.

- Self-Disclosure and Feedback are linked to one another. Self-Disclosure tends to encourage Feedback. Any change in the Window will affect all the four Areas.

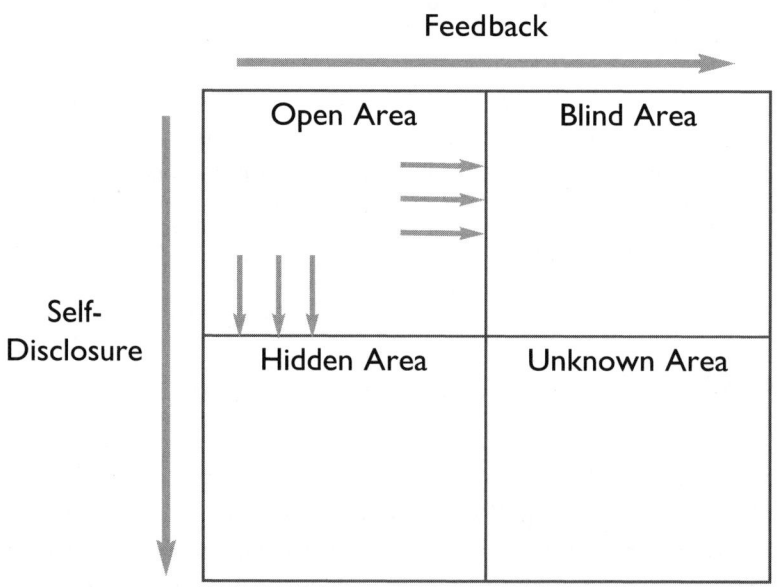

- If we succeed in increasing the Open Area, we can 'become ourselves':

  being more authentic and more relaxed;

  communicating more clearly and directly;

  making better use of our personal resources and abilities;

  having more energy, skills and personal resources available;

  being capable of greater intimacy and spontaneity;

  meeting our own needs more effectively;

  having greater and more effective contact with the real world;

  more clearly perceiving other people as they really are;

  working and co-operating more effectively with other people;

  and being a more effective team-member.

Using the Model

■ After the explanation and clarifications tell the members to work individually. Tell them to draw their own Johari Window to show their everyday relationships with other people generally.

Ask them to share their Windows in pairs or threes, and then consider the following questions:

'How large is your Open Area?'

'In general, do you think you have a larger Hidden Area or a larger Blind Area?'

Ask them to think of someone close to them, a relative or friend. Tell them to draw their own Window to show how they relate to that person. Ask them to share this with their partner/s, and then consider:

'Is the Window for this relationship changing or static?'

In the early life of a course group Hidden Areas are large. As the course progresses the Open Areas usually become bigger and the Hidden Areas become smaller. Raise the following questions for discussion:

'How would you draw the Window of this course group at this time?'

'What can you do to increase your own Open Area in this group?'

Such questions help members to absorb the ideas underlying the Johari Window. The following exercise has the same purpose.

Such a Person ...

Tell the members to change partners or groups. Draw the three diagrams shown on the next page, one by one, on the board. Ask the members to discuss each situation in their pairs or small groups.

■ Imagine that you meet someone with a large Hidden Area, like this:

How will you experience such a person?

What would you expect in that person?

How would you relate to him/her?

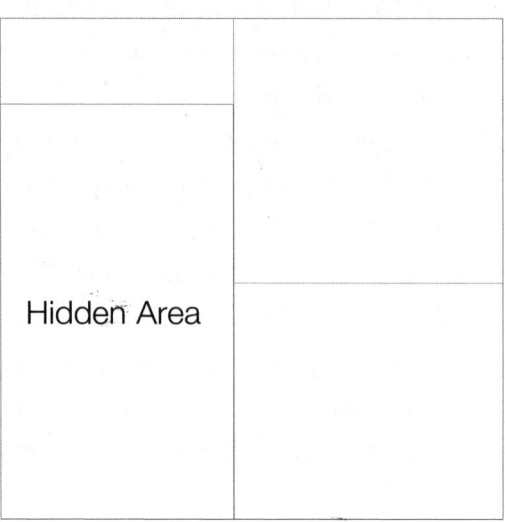

Hidden Area

Blind Area

Imagine that you meet someone with a large Blind Area, like this:

How will you experience such a person?

What would you expect in that person?

How would you relate to him/her?

Imagine that you meet someone with a large Blind Area and a large Hidden Area, but a tiny Open Area, like this:

How will you experience such a person?

What would you expect in that person?

How would you relate to him/her?

Open Area

Blind Area

Hidden Area

The Window at Work

■ Our relationships in our work back home with our boss, our colleagues, and our subordinates are critical, not only to the success of their work and ours, but also to the work of the organization. There is usually a connection between these relationships and the relative sizes of the panes in our Window.

Ask members to draw their Windows for their relationships with their boss, their colleagues and their subordinates, and to discuss these with their partner/s.

'Are the three Windows similar or different?'

'Is this helping or hindering my work and organization?'

'Should I do anything about them?'

Point out that most of us have a large Hidden Area in relation to our superiors, a large Open Area in relation to colleagues at the same level, and a large Blind Area in relation to our subordinates.

In conclusion remind members that the Johari Window is intended to convey concepts rather than reality.

The Unknown Area

The description may suggest that the Unknown Area can also be reduced and remodelled; whereas much of this Area will remain unknown, even to the end of a lifetime. Indeed the Unknown Area can be thought of as part of the individual's unconscious. This can be suggested by drawing the diagram as shown below.

Open Area	**Blind Area**
Hidden Area	
	Unknown Area

■ Finally suggest to the group that if we apply the model more widely we can imagine that the Unknown Areas of poor and powerless people are relatively large. Such people have had little opportunity to realise their strengths or to experience their capabilities. Enabling them to discover these strengths and capabilities, and to achieve their potential as human beings, is one of the challenges of development work.

▶ *People were opening 'little windows' — but cautiously and rightly so. Maybe 'bigger windows' will be opened as trust develops. The sense of supporting one another, being positively critical, was very real ...*

▶ *I am more complex than this window — my lines are not all straight. Some secrets I reveal to those I love and trust but not everyone. I am so practised at hiding some secret areas that I think even I cannot see them any more — are they in the secret or blind area? And are not some things in the public area only counterparts (like opposite sides of a coin) of things in the secret area? ... perhaps friendliness and team spirit is linked to a fear of conflict?*

▶ *What are the hidden areas and blind areas for North and South, and rich and poor? Perhaps the North has the largest blind area. So many are ignorant of the consequences of our life-style and our history.*

9.2 Making Ourselves Known: Self-Disclosure

▶ ... *learning about others' lives ... led us into deep understanding of each other ... it is an endless process, full of adventure and fun.*

Self-Disclosure is a process by which we make ourselves known to others, reveal aspects of ourselves and our lives, and share personal information, feelings, and opinions. In such ways we make ourselves more accessible, and help others to understand us more clearly as persons.

It is a process which happens naturally in friendships, or in groups that are functioning effectively, but it can be deliberately encouraged in a training group as an aid to learning.

The potential benefits are higher levels of trust, greater group cohesion, team-building, greater personal effectiveness and individual growth and satisfaction. These, in turn, favour learning. A training group provides an ideal opportunity to practise self-disclosure.

The introduction to the topic is followed by two exercises, and further exercises are included. All this work will require one session.

Self-Disclosure follows naturally after A Window on Ourselves (page 316). If it is necessary to shorten these events, both can be taken in one session.

Objectives

● o provide an opportunity for members to practise self-disclosure within the training group, to gain in personal confidence, and to experience the effect on inter-personal relationships;

● to add to the levels of acceptance, support and trust within the training group and thus to encourage team-work and co-operative learning.

Introducing the Topic

■ Introduce the concept by drawing on the first three paragraphs above.

Explain that the overall task for each member is to share with others some personal information, as he/she chooses, which will help the other members to know and understand him/her better. If members talk about their childhood, their family situation, their school experience, their likes and dislikes, or their interests outside their work, then this is likely to lead to self-disclosure.

■ Emphasize that self-disclosure does not mean that we expose everything to others, or that we have to deal with anything which is uncomfortable. It does not mean revealing secrets and confidences; to do that could be naive.

Make it a rule that what is disclosed is the choice of the person concerned, and that he/she takes responsibility for it. Similarly members can refuse to talk about anything they do not wish to reveal, and others should not press questions.

If it is a heterogeneous group point out that there are varying cultural attitudes towards personal information and individual differences. Information which is openly shared in one culture — such as religious or political convictions, or salary level — may be guarded in another. In some cultures individuals are not expected to be 'different' from the norm; in others 'individualism' is expected and valued. Despite such complexities in a multi-cultural group, self-disclosure may be all the more useful in helping the members to function together effectively.[1]

After explaining self-disclosure, it may reassure members if you make links with experiences that they have already had together in the course. Photolanguage (page 101), Merry-go-Round (page 104), Me and My Work (page 90), My Life Road (page 344) and some exercises in Ending the Week (page 247) all include self-disclosure.

 ## Using the Exercises

Disclosure in Pairs

Tell the members that they should now work with their neighbours in pairs and each disclose a bit of information about themselves that the other does not already know.

Then invite a few members to share their reactions to doing this. Keep the focus on reactions and feelings, not on what was shared, and make it brief. This helps to set the scene for the more deliberate exercise.

Who Am I?

This exercise is done individually to start with. Tell the group that each member is to write ten answers to the question 'Who am I?' In other words, they should ask themselves the same question ten times, and write down a different answer each time.

Point out that it will not be useful if members give answers which are obvious or already known to others. Statements such as 'I am a man,' 'I am a Sri Lankan,' or 'I am the director', will not contribute to self-disclosure. Even apparently personal information such as 'I am married', or 'I am a father', or 'I am talkative', may be known already. What will be useful are statements about what is not already known.

---

1. Self-disclosure is not the same as self-exposure! This is a pitfall of the English language, and in a multi-lingual group you may need to clarify the difference.

■ Ask members to list their ten answers to the question in order of importance.

Tell them that they will now work in groups of three or four. Each member is to disclose as much, or as little, of his/her own list as feels comfortable. The task of the other members is simply to listen and to accept whatever is shared. They should not ask questions unless for clarification, should not discuss what they hear, and certainly should not challenge or evaluate it. If there is not already a norm of confidentiality, you could propose it for this exercise.

After sharing, and if time permits, the following question can be asked:
'If the first item on your list was removed — i.e. was no longer true —
what difference would it make to you and to others?'

Members should reflect on this individually and share answers in the small groups if they wish.

Then ask the members to rejoin the whole group. If time permits and the climate seems favourable, invite some members to share any of their own information in the whole group. Make it clear that individuals are to speak only for themselves, and are not to repeat anything they heard from others in the small groups. This sharing in the large group is voluntary, and the response may indicate the general climate in the group.

Finally call for any comments on the process, and on the feelings experienced during the exercise. Some useful questions here are:
'What was this experience like for you?'
'Did you have any strong feelings at any point?'
'Did the way that others in your group spoke affect what you were willing to disclose yourself?'
'If one person is open, what effect does this have on others?'

'How much depth was there to the sharing in small groups?'
'Do you think you took any risks in what you disclosed?'
'Do you feel you know anyone else any better after this exercise?'
'Do you feel you know yourself any better after this exercise?'

'How do you find the climate in the group at present?'

Additional Exercises

Finding Symbols

Tell members that they are to work individually to start with. Tell them that they have two minutes to find and bring an object from within the room — or from within the building (five minutes) or from some wider area (ten minutes) — which in some way represents themselves. After they have returned with their objects, they should join others in groups of three or four. They should show their object to the other members and explain in what ways it represents them. Finish the exercise with any comments on the process in the whole group.

Completing Statements

■ Give members the beginnings of five or six statements which they should complete individually. Examples of statements are:

'When I was a child I often ...'

'A difficulty I had as a teenager was ...'

'When I get time off I like to ...'

'When no one is nearby I sometimes ...'

'Something I enjoy in my personal life is ...'

The statements should be appropriate to the group and to its stage of growth, and should form a sequence, rather than leading in different directions.[2]

Conclusion

■ Conclude the session by reminding members that self-disclosure happens as people learn to trust each other and as friendships and relationships grow.

A training course is often a favourable setting.[3] It can happen informally at almost any moment during a course and in the life of a group, and it contributes to the learning process. As members become more aware of it, and of its advantages, they can make more deliberate choices about how much they disclose of themselves.

The task of the trainer is to create conditions which encourage trust and favour disclosure, but the members themselves must continue to be responsible for whatever they disclose.

In the wider world we may be less generous in how much we disclose. In a course group self-disclosure can and should continue.

▶ *We also looked at how we can make the Open Self bigger and then we had an exercise on Self-Disclosure. It says a lot about the level of trust in the group that many of us felt able to be so frank during this exercise. However I also felt a degree of caution ...*

---

2. This is similar to Merry-Go-Round (page 104).
3. Other settings may be less favourable. Trust may not develop and relationships may not grow. There can be obstacles, some of which we create ourselves, such as:

I find it difficult to talk about myself in front of others;
I do not understand or trust the other person sufficiently;
I fear that the other person may not like what I disclose;
I fear that he/she may use whatever I reveal against me later on;
I want to be seen in a particular way;
I do not want to reveal any 'weaknesses';
The climate in the group (or organization) is not open and accepting;
The culture in the organization (or society) is competitive and critical.

▶ *It's hard to believe that we've known each other for only one week. It's not that the time seems longer, but the degree to which we've gotten to know each other is much higher than usual after sharing the same classroom for one week ... In the process of getting to know each other ... I've realised how rich a group we are.*

▶ *I feel that as I get to know the group I get to know myself. The image of exploring the darkness was a powerful one. The feelings I have when I get to know others remind me of who I am and areas of myself that I need to understand and develop. I wonder if the others in the group feel this way too?*

▶ *Together we talk about feedback to help each other grow. The group reckons we are okay at positive feedback but not so honest about negative.*

▶ *I wonder if we are really able yet to offer feedback that is useful, or are we all still too afraid of upsetting our colleagues to say what we really feel? I do not think that as a group we are reaching our full potential.*

In human relations training 'feedback' is information about the effect our behaviour has on other people.[1] The purpose is to raise our awareness of how far our behaviour is appropriate and effective. This puts feedback at the centre of improving the quality of our work with others, whether in the organization or in the community.

Feedback may happen naturally during the life of a training group, but it is often deliberately introduced as a learning experience. Some trainers argue that feedback is the principal means — perhaps the only means — through which individuals can change and grow as persons, and that it should form part of any training for people who work with people.

In addition to the potential for individual growth and greater effectiveness, favourable experience in handling feedback can add to members' confidence in themselves, and encourage them to adopt more open and reciprocal relationships.

Feedback will be more accepted and more effective after members have built up trust in each other, so it should be used in the second half of a course. It is linked with A Window on Ourselves (page 316) and Self-Disclosure (page 325) and should be used after them.

One session will be needed to introduce the topic, followed by exercises and practice in small groups. The exercise Are You Someone Who ...? will need a second session.

Objectives

- to introduce feedback as a method for stronger teamwork, open communication, and greater effectiveness in work with others;

- to raise members' awareness of how their behaviour is perceived and experienced by others;

- to raise members' awareness of how appropriately their behaviour serves their intentions, and whether any of their behaviour is dysfunctional or inappropriate for their role as development worker;

- to provide members with experience of giving and receiving feedback, and to increase their confidence and skill in doing both.

---

1. Feedback is usually understood in interpersonal terms, but it can also be used between small groups.

Feedback and Course Groups

Feedback should be used with care, and at an appropriate stage in a course. Generally the higher the level of trust between members and the greater the cohesion of the group, the more members will welcome feedback and the more useful it is likely to be. In most courses it will be appropriate after the half-way point, by which time there should be sufficient group cohesion and a suitable balance between support and challenge. Yet there should be enough of the course remaining for givers of feedback to feel that there is still something at stake, and for receivers to try out new behaviour if they wish.

A partial or limited experience can be introduced first — perhaps positive feedback only — and then a week or so later the experience can be taken further. It is important to generate a feeling of safety. If the group is going through a period of conflict it may be better to wait.

In a multi-cultural group there are likely to be varying attitudes to direct feedback, and trainers need to be sensitive to these. Members who come from hierarchical or competitive situations may understand feedback more in terms of authorized correction by a superior; feedback from a peer group may seem more threatening. Others may come from cultures where direct confrontation is normally avoided, and they may feel uncomfortable unless a clear structure and sanction are given. Others again may come from cultures where interactions are normally direct and even abrasive; and they may already be waiting for an opportunity to tell others in the group some 'home truths'.

 ## Introducing the Topic

■ Introduce the topic, drawing on the points below.

- The word 'feedback' comes from electrical engineering and computers. It refers to the linking of an output to the mechanisms which produce it, in order to make adjustments.

- At a personal level feedback is information from others, such as colleagues, teammates or course members, about the impact that our behaviour is having on them. This is an interpersonal process among peers, and is different from the formal guidance or supervision which may be given by a superior or boss.[2]

- We are most likely to be given feedback when our behaviour is causing others irritation, anxiety or difficulty. This may be due to behaviour we are not even aware of. Or we may be aware of it, but not realize the way it is perceived and experienced by

---

2. Few organizations have mechanisms for deliberate interpersonal feedback among peers. Hierarchy is usually an obstacle to feedback. Staff in an organization seldom give feedback to their boss, or receive it from their own subordinates. Subordinates usually grumble instead!

other people.[3] Unless we receive feedback we shall continue to rely on our assumptions about how others perceive us and our behaviour. Such assumptions are often mistaken.

- Feedback does not require that we do things differently. It is simply information which adds to our understanding of ourselves in relation to others. It is then for us to decide whether we want to make changes in our behaviour. Feedback is an opportunity for change, but it does not require change.

- Feedback is not all negative, but includes behaviour which is appreciated by others, and strengths and potential which we have, but do not recognize. Feedback which is affirming and appreciative is called positive feedback. Feedback which is pointing to difficulties or to the need for corrective change is called negative.

- We all need affirmation, appreciation and positive feedback. If we receive these, it helps us to listen to negative feedback, and to accept it. Negative feedback alone can seem too critical and hurtful, even if we recognize it as accurate. When feedback is included in training, there is a general principle of balancing negative with positive.

- If it is appropriately given, and well-received, feedback is a powerful tool. Through it we can gain a much more accurate picture of ourselves in relation to others. Without it we may never make the adjustments that could transform parts of our lives, and bring us greater personal happiness, as well as increasing our professional effectiveness and satisfaction.

■ As you introduce the topic, check with members how feedback is seen in different cultures.

Ask members whether they have heard themselves on tape, or seen themselves on film? If so, were they as they had imagined themselves?[4]

Ask members to share with a partner any previous experiences of positive and negative feedback from colleagues (not superiors), co-workers, or other peers including friends.
'How did you feel at the time'
'Was it useful or not? If so, why? If not, why not?'
'Was it done with care and skill?'
'What helps to make feedback useful?'
'What are some of the guidelines to observe when giving feedback and receiving it?'

Stress that there are certain attitudes and skills needed for giving and receiving feedback successfully. General guidelines with explanations are set out in the handout Interpersonal Feedback (page 336). This can be given for individual reading.

---

3. The range of behaviour which can upset others is all too great. It can include personal habits, habits of clothing, failure in personal hygiene, distracting mannerisms, habits of speech, a misplaced sense of humour, gender and other insensitivities, interrupting, failure to listen, authoritarianism, lack of punctuality ... The concern here is with behaviour which relates to our work and hinders our being as effective in our working relationships as we could be.
4. If members have not heard their own recorded voices, or seen themselves on film, it may be helpful if this can be arranged.

Practising Feedback

■ If you are going on to introduce the exercises below, give the members a few immediate rules to follow, such as the following:

- Before giving feedback, think of the needs of the other person and of what may be useful to him/her. Comment only on behaviour, but not the person him/herself.

- When giving feedback, stick to descriptions and observations. Focus on the specific actions of the other person, and give examples.

- Avoid judgement or evaluation. Avoid 'You should ...' and 'You ought ...' Do not interpret the other person's intentions or motives.

- Take responsibility for your own reactions and feelings. Describe these by using 'I' statements. Explain 'I' statements if necessary (see Taking Responsibility for Our Feelings, page 372).

- When you receive feedback, whether positive or negative, listen without comment until the speaker has finished.

- If you receive feedback that is general or vague, ask for particular examples.

Alternatively — if the members are already experienced with feedback — ask them to draft their own rules, and add to these where necessary.

Affirmation of Each Other

This is an exercise in positive feedback only. It can be used with a group of ten or twelve, but becomes unwieldy with larger groups. It generally has the effect of increasing group cohesion.

Ask the group members to sit in a circle. Ask them to consider every other member in turn, and to identify two (or three) positive and affirming contributions, qualities, or characteristics which they observe or experience in that person. They should then list the items in the form of a brief memo to the person concerned. The memo must include the name of the receiver and the name of the sender. After every member has written all their memos, the memos are given or 'posted' to the receivers to be read privately. When all have read them, invite some responses and reactions.

Negative and Positive Feedback in Small Groups

This is a structure for deliberate interpersonal work.

Invite members to form small groups of three or four, according to their choice. Ask each group to identify a volunteer to be the first to receive feedback. Tell the other members to be ready to take turns to give the volunteer negative feedback.

Tell them that they must use a set form of words:
'An observation which I have made about you, (name the person), and which I do not like much is...'

■ After hearing a member's feedback the volunteer repeats the meaning immediately, beginning with the words:

'What I think you mean to tell me is ...'

The volunteer then adds his/her response to the feedback, again using a set form of words:

'... and my response to that is ...'

The volunteer then receives negative feedback from the other members in the small group, using the same procedure. Then a second member becomes the volunteer, and the process is repeated, until all have received negative feedback from each of the others in the group and have made their responses.

After the round of negative feedback the process is repeated by a round of positive feedback. The wording now is:

'An observation which I have made about you, (name the person),
and which I do like is ...'

The receiver responds with the same set words as before. By the end every member should have received negative and positive feedback from all the other members of their group.

Visit the small groups as they are working and check that they are following the forms of words. The exercise should not become heavy. Watch for tension or anxiety. Use cheerful observation, informal enquiry, and an attentive smile to reduce tension.

Alternative Words

Similar exercises to the above can be used with groups of three or four, while changing the form of words to suit the group and circumstances.

One alternative form of words is:

'(Name), I like you because ...'
'(Name), I like you but ...'

Another, perhaps more comfortable, is:

'Something I would like you to start doing is ...'
'Something I would like you to stop doing is ...'
'Something I would like you to go on doing is ...'

Another is especially useful when two people with conflicting roles are working together:

'The things you are doing which help me with my own work are ...'
'You make my work more difficult by ...'
'It will help me do my work better if you ...'[5]

---

5. This last form of words is also useful between colleagues in organizations, especially if a subordinate is invited to give feedback to an immediate superior.

Reflecting on the Experience of Feedback

■ After such exercises ask the members to return to the large group and to share any reactions. The purpose is to review the experience, and express feelings, but not to repeat or discuss anything that has been said in feedback itself. Some possible questions are:

'How was it? What was the experience like?'
'Do you think you have learned anything new about yourself?'
'Was there depth to what people said? Or was any of the feedback trivial?'
'Did you find it more difficult to give feedback or to receive it?'
'Was that what you had expected? What were the difficulties?'

Explore members' feelings during the exercises:

'What feelings did you have while you were giving feedback to others?'
'How was it to give positive feedback? Negative?'
'What feelings did you have while you were receiving feedback?'
'How was it when the feedback was positive? Negative?'

Record the responses on the board under the headings:

Negative Feedback		Positive Feedback	
Giving	Receiving	Giving	Receiving

The results often indicate that anxiety over giving negative feedback is greater than anxiety about receiving it.

If the feelings about positive feedback — both giving and receiving — are themselves positive, ask the members why we do not use positive feedback at least, more often?

We can give feedback within a training group, but it may not be so possible in the outside world. Conclude with some of following questions:

'As a manager, leader or development worker how open to feedback are you?'
'Do the norms of your culture and organization allow direct feedback?'
'If not, are there other ways of sharing interpersonal perceptions and helping colleagues to grow and become more effective?'
'Would it be useful if managers received feedback from subordinates?'

Are You Someone Who ...

This is a more elaborate exercise in feedback, which is done in small groups of three (or four) members. It takes the form of a questionnaire, each member sharing perceptions of the other members in relation to 54 statements. Instructions are included in the handout (see page 340).

The 'interpretation' at the end of the exercise refers back to the Johari Window (page 316) and assumes that members are familiar with that.

The advantage of this exercise is its 'safety' which stems partly from its structure and rigid boundaries, and partly from the statements themselves.

While it may be bland, it is a useful initial experience, and helps to encourage feedback in a heterogeneous group.

■ Use the exercise as preparation for more direct feedback. Allow a whole session and invite general comments in the whole group at the end.

▶ *I am really grateful for the session on feedback, and I could have gone on exploring this for some time ... What a potential constructive feedback holds! I realise how I have come to know a great respect for those who, in the past, have given me feedback in a caring, sensitive way.*

▶ *The comment that people don't often give Feedback upwards made me think: What is the best way to reflect and gain 'true' feedback and not just the feedback that you want to hear?*

▶ *... how strange to see oneself on TV ... I think I shall try to look more cheerful in future and I ask the group to give me feedback.*

▶ *S and F helped me to discover previously blind areas like: I am someone who would let my wife be responsible for the family's money, I am someone who is likely to take little interest in my own appearance ... The exercise so impressed me that I went immediately for a haircut to somehow compensate — I hope you have all noticed!*

▶ *... if we want to make our feedbacks helpful for others we should observe rules ... J gave us some exercises to practise these rules. Most difficult was an exercise with a rude secretary at donor's agency. Some feedbacks were not according to the rules, as hurt and indignant persons are often unable to control themselves.*

Guidelines: Interpersonal Feedback

Feedback is clear, non-judgmental information given to another person about how his/her behaviour affects you. If feedback is given in a positive and skillful way it can be helpful. But if it is handled without sensitivity and skill, it may not be helpful, and may even be damaging. It is therefore important that certain principles and procedures are followed, both in giving and in receiving it.

A. Giving Feedback

1. It is appropriate to consider giving feedback to another person if you think that some part/s of that person's behaviour is unsuitable for a situation or a relationship, and especially if you think that he/she is not aware of this.

2. Before starting, think of the needs of the other person and of what may be useful to him/her. Feedback should be offered out of a wish to help, and given in a caring and supportive way. Check your own feelings and motives. If you suspect that you want to speak from your own need to control the other person, or to retaliate, or to punish them, then you had better keep quiet!

3. Speak directly to the other person, face to face, either in privacy or with one other person who can provide support. Remain calm, take your time, and make yourself clear. Dropping hints, making jokes, small-talk etc. are not feedback.

4. Always give positive as well as negative feedback. If you have difficulty in giving positive feedback to a particular person, it may indicate that you are not perceiving them accurately, and you should not give them negative feedback either!

5. Your focus is on the behaviour or specific actions of the other person. Give specific examples and exact data. For example, 'When you interrupted me just now, I felt annoyed,' or 'I felt uncomfortable when you put your feet on my chair during the discussion.' Don't make general statements, such as, 'I feel annoyed with you because you often interrupt me,' or 'I feel uncomfortable with you because of the way you behave in discussions.' Unless you give specific and concrete examples the other person may not understand what you are telling him/her.

6. Stick to observations, facts, what is said, and what is done. This is what you actually know. Do not try to describe or interpret the other person's intentions or motives. You do not know what these are. A statement such as 'You expect other people to agree to everything you propose,' is not useful because it is only your guess or interpretation.

7. Take responsibility for your own feelings and reactions, and describe them by making 'I' statements. For example, 'I felt hurt when you laughed at me.' Avoid making 'You' statements, which tend to blame the other person, and may provoke a defensive reaction. 'You wanted to hurt me when you laughed at me...' will probably be denied or rejected. Statements which begin, 'You always ...' or 'You never ...' are likely to be resisted.

8. Stick to descriptions and observations. Avoid judgement or evaluation, either of the action or of the person. If you judge the other person's action, for example, by saying, 'You were wrong to shout at me,' it will probably produce a defensive reaction. If you judge the other person's character, for example, by saying, 'You are dominating and inconsiderate,' it will almost certainly produce a defensive reaction!

9. Avoid 'You should ...' and 'You ought ...' Do not give the other person advice unless he/she specifically asks you for it. Your task is to give information so that the other person can decide for him/herself what to do about it, and what changes to make, if any.

10. Speak only of behaviour which the other person could change, for example, his/her habit of yawning loudly whenever someone else begins to speak. Such behaviour is within his/her control. Do not speak of behaviour over which he/she has no control, for example, a habit of stammering. To comment on that will only increase anxiety and frustration.

11. Choose the appropriate time and situation to give feedback. Generally it is most useful immediately after the event concerned while this is fresh in both minds, and so long as neither person is upset or agitated. Don't give feedback long after the event has taken place, in some other situation, or with some other group of people.

12. The best time to give feedback is when the other person asks for it. If that happens, ask him/her exactly what he/she wants to know. One of the worst times to give feedback is when the other person has made it clear that he/she does not want to receive it. It will then be ineffective, if not damaging.

13. Give an amount of information that the other person can deal with at one time. You may want to give much more, but if you give too much feedback all at once, he/she may be overloaded and unable to use any of it.

14. After you have given your feedback, check with the receiver whether he/she understands what you have said, and whether he/she accepts it or not.

B. Receiving Feedback

1. When you receive feedback, whether positive or negative, listen without comment until the other person has finished. Do not let your feelings get in the way of the information you are being given, and do not interrupt with denials or defences or explanations. Give yourself time to think about what has been said. Ask yourself whether the information seems accurate or not.

2. It can be helpful if you summarize the feedback that you are being given, whether you agree with it or not. 'What you are telling me is that ...' This allows both you and the other person to check that you have understood it correctly, and also makes a space for assimilation and consideration. It is as important to summarize positive feedback as negative.

3. It may increase the sense of structure and safety for both people if the receiver uses a set form of words. One such is, 'What I hear you telling me is ... and my reaction to it is ...' The same form of words should be used for positive and negative feedback.

4. When you receive positive feedback, accept it and enjoy it. Do not dismiss it or brush it aside. Recognize your strengths, and own them. An exercise or experience in feedback is an unusual opportunity to take the help of others to focus on your strengths and improve your own perception of them. 'Tell me more.' Recognizing strengths is as important for personal growth as recognizing weaknesses.

5. If you receive feedback that is painful or which you have doubts about, check its accuracy with other people. Do they see your behaviour in the same way? A training group is the ideal opportunity for such clarification. If similar feedback is given consistently by a number of people, it should be considered more seriously.

6. If you feel that the feedback is 'loaded' in some way, or biassed, or given out of hostility, do not immediately become defensive, or attack the other person, or withdraw in dismay. Instead, express your feelings about what has been said: 'I feel upset/misunderstood/hurt when you say that.'

7. If the feedback is general or vague, ask for particular examples. 'What exactly did I do which upset you?'

8. If you are given feedback on your personality, ask for comments on your behaviour: 'You say I am dominating. Can you give me an example of this?'

9. After hearing the feedback, decide whether you will do anything about it. It is your choice to change your behaviour or not. Take responsibility for deciding whether you will do anything differently, and if so, what. Small, achievable and specific changes are more realistic than a wholesale transformation! If you think it will help you, tell the other person/s what you plan, and ask for their help in monitoring your (different) behaviour in future.

John Staley, *Enticing the Learning: Trainers in Development,* University of Birmingham, pages 336—339

Introduction

Form groups of three (or four). Each member should know the others fairly well. Do not sit with people you do not know.

On the following pages are statements which may or may not describe you. In column A mark your initial/s opposite those statements which you feel *do* describe you, i.e. which are true about you. If they are not true, or if you are not sure, then leave a blank.

Then fold back column A so that only columns B, C and D are visible and pass the copy of the exercise to the person on your right in the small group. It is important that all the copies are circulated to every member in the group, so do not simply exchange copies with anyone.

You will be given another copy by the person on your left. Put your initial/s in column B opposite those statements which you think *do* describe the person concerned. If they are not true, or if you are not sure, then leave a blank. Do not look at column A.

Now fold back column B so that only C and D remain visible. Again pass on the copy to your right, and receive a copy from your left. Repeat the process for the third person in the group. Do not look at columns A or B. If there is a fourth person in the group, fold back column C and repeat the process again.

Each member should now take back his or her original pages, unfold them, and compare his/her own perceptions with those of the other members in the group.

Your Name: ....

Are you someone who...?

A __ B __ C __ D __   1. ...keeps trying until you reach your goals?

A __ B __ C __ D __   2. ...listens carefully to others?

A __ B __ C __ D __   3. ...actively takes a leadership role?

A __ B __ C __ D __   4. ...is supportive and encouraging of others?

A __ B __ C __ D __   5. ...often interrupts others?

A __ B __ C __ D __   6. ...tends to make very quick judgements?

A __ B __ C __ D __ 7. ...is task orientated?

A __ B __ C __ D __ 8. ...tries to make others feel comfortable?

A __ B __ C __ D __ 9. ...waits for someone else to say 'hello' first?

A __ B __ C __ D __ 10. ..allows the mind to wander and daydreams a lot?

A __ B __ C __ D __ 11. ..is very competitive?

A __ B __ C __ D __ 12. ..prefers to work by yourself?

A __ B __ C __ D __ 13. ..does what you want to do, has fun, and worries about the future later?

A __ B __ C __ D __ 14. ..tries to get the approval of your supervisor?

A __ B __ C __ D __ 15. ..tells jokes?

A __ B __ C __ D __ 16. ..would take the blame for a subordinate's mistake?

A __ B __ C __ D __ 17. ..has a high level of commitment to any group offering opportunities for new learning?

A __ B __ C __ D __ 18. ..would let your husband/wife/partner be responsible for the family's money?

A __ B __ C __ D __ 19. ..would discuss personal matters with your children?

A __ B __ C __ D __ 20. ..believes that most people can be trusted?

A __ B __ C __ D __ 21...will let people take advantage of you?

A — B — C — D — 22...takes time and trouble over relationships?

A — B — C — D — 23...would be a difficult person to be married to?

A — B — C — D — 24. ..always has something to say?

A — B — C — D — 25. ..asks colleagues for help when you need it?

A — B — C — D — 26. ..is satisfied with yourself?

A — B — C — D — 27. ..is extremely dependent, always needing support from others?

A — B — C — D — 28. ..is likely to take little interest in your appearance?

A — B — C — D — 29. ..volunteers to help others?

A — B — C — D — 30. ..gets disturbed under pressure?

A — B — C — D — 31. ..pushes to get things done?

A — B — C — D — 32. ...is likely to agree that abortion is sometimes necessary?

A — B — C — D — 33. ...will work for social change even if it means considerable sacrifice for you?

A — B — C — D — 34. ...wants things done in your own way?

A — B — C — D — 35. ...makes friends easily?

A — B — C — D — 36. ...is a considerate friend?

A — B — C — D — 37. ...has difficulty to say 'no' when invited to do something you don't want to do?

A — B — C — D — 38. ...tries to live for today, enjoying the present and not worrying about the future?

A — B — C — D — 39. ...is warm and friendly?

A — B — C — D — 40. ...does things suddenly without previous planning?

A — B — C — D — 41. ...reveals little of yourself to others?

A — B — C — D — 42. ...does only the minimum necessary to get by?

A — B — C — D — 43. ...prefers to work with other people?

A — B — C — D — 44. ...likes hard physical work?

A — B — C — D — 45. ...can't keep a secret?

A — B — C — D — 46. ...is emotional?

A — B — C — D — 47. ...is serious?

A — B — C — D — 48. ...can play children's games and enjoy them?

A — B — C — D — 49. ...is highly motivated to achieve a lot in your career?

A — B — C — D — 50. ...is willing to consider and accept alternatives?

A — B — C — D — 51. ...takes personal responsibility for what happens to you?

A — B — C — D — 52. ...if often defensive?

A — B — C — D — 53. ...finds it difficult to relax?

A — B — C — D — 54. ...dominates situations?

Interpretation

Referring to the Johari Window, those statements which you marked as true, and which the other members have also marked as true, can be regarded as being in your 'Open Area'.

Those which you marked, but which the others did not mark, can be regarded as being in your 'Hidden or Secret Area'.

Those which the others marked, but which you did not mark, can be regarded as being in your 'Blind Area'.

Reflection

Now discuss the results in your small group. Take the opportunity to explore how you perceive and experience each other.

Attention may be given to the 'Blind Areas'; or to statements marked by one member only which the concerned person may want to verify. Those responding should be precise, giving examples of specific behaviour whenever possible.

Adapted from an unattributed secondary source

9.4 My Life Road

▶ *Yet another non-easy task was there for us. To draw and tell someone else your 'life road'. Quite not easy for me ... In my life I have never bothered to write or tell the whole ... only told some bits of it. It is a new experience for me today.*

This is a powerful exercise which has helped members of many courses to deepen their understanding of themselves and of each other, and has enriched their group.

Each member is invited to 'draw' his or her life, from birth to the present, using the symbolism of a journey. They share these drawings in small groups and later reflect upon them. Such work is sensitive and requires care from trainers and members.

It is more useful in a course group whose members are already comfortable with each other, who are practised in reflection, and who have expressed a wish to deepen their relationships and understanding of each other. It is less appropriate for a group whose interest is mainly professional role and practice, or where the group climate is unsupportive.

The exercise is best done in the middle of a course. It should come after other personal work such as Attending to Our Feelings (page 362). The work itself needs thought and care, so a time when the group is relaxed, and the course is without external pressures, will be suitable.

Members can be given the task and asked to prepare their drawing overnight or over a week-end. They will each need A3 size paper and coloured pens or pencils.

The work links with Making Ourselves Known: Self-Disclosure (page 325) and What Are Our Values? (page 347).

Objectives

- to encourage course members to reflect on their past life and to relate that to their present life;
- to help them to identify significant events and influences in their lives;
- to help them to recognize trends and patterns in their lives;
- to encourage them to explore their personal goals, values, roles and decisions;
- to increase their understanding of themselves and of others.

Introducing the Exercise

 Start by explaining that the exercise involves personal work, and ask course members to be respectful of each others' confidences and sensitive to their feelings.

■ Explain that the task of each member is to 'draw' or symbolize their life, from the time of their birth up to the present, in the form of a road or path. In other words they are to make a drawing or diagram of their individual journey through 'the landscape of life.'

Add a few suggestions about other symbols which could be used. This will help to make the main idea clearer. For example, significant events might be represented by milestones or signposts along the way; significant people might be shown as companions or meetings on the journey; directions taken or not taken might be shown by crossroads, junctions or turnings; and difficult periods might be shown by steep slopes or pot-holes. Suggest that members could use colours to represent their feelings about particular periods and events.

Avoid giving too many or too specific suggestions. The best results will come when members have understood the basic symbolism, and then work on drawing their roads in whatever way is meaningful to them personally. Some people prefer to represent their life's path as a river. Accept any idea that will help members to complete the task.

Explain to members that later the drawings will be shown to others in small groups. Some may feel uncomfortable at this prospect, especially if their past has been painful. Allow for this by saying that if anyone does not wish to share, he/she will not be under any pressure to do so, but that every member should at least complete the drawing of his/her life road. Sometimes, after other members have shown their drawings and talked about their lives, those who were reluctant will be ready to take their turn in sharing.

The drawings are best made overnight or over a weekend. This allows members sufficient time, both to work on the drawing and to reflect on their lives. Point out that the greater the depth and 'quality' the members give, both to the drawing and to the reflection afterwards, the richer their learning.

 ## Reflecting on the Exercise

Some members may spend much time and care on the drawing, and may adorn their road with many symbols and figures. Others may draw a few bleak lines. Some drawings may be colourful: others may be drab. Some may express happiness; others pain and distress. Members who have lived through violent conflict, or who have been refugees, may show parts of their lives as blank or blotted out.

■ Invite members to share their drawings in small groups of three or four. Tell the small groups that their task is to focus on what individuals have chosen to show and are willing to share. Questions may be asked for clarification but should not probe beyond that. Allow sufficient time for the sharing: 20 minutes for each member is a rough guide.

If additional trainers are available, they can accompany the small groups during the exercise. The trainers should then come prepared with drawings of their own life roads and share these in the small groups. They can help the members of the small groups to focus attention on what they are being shown, and may perhaps ask questions for clarification:

■ 'Why is there a bend here?'
   'What do these marks mean?'
   'Why have you used this colour?'
   'Can you clarify what happened here?'

If additional trainers are not available you should circulate among the groups yourself, listen to and monitor their discussions, and again encourage the focus on what is being shown and what is visible. If you want to ask further questions, or offer insights or challenges to individuals, you may do so privately later.

Even if attention is kept to what is visible, the exercise can have a powerful impact, especially for those who have not previously reflected on their past, nor thought about the way that influences, events and decisions from their past are influencing their present. Strong feelings are sometimes released, and you should be ready to accept these.

After the sharing in small groups invite the members to reflect again individually on their life roads. To assist this reflection offer some of the following questions:

   'Look again at the way you have drawn your life road. Does anything strike you, or surprise you, about the way you have shown it?'

   'Can you see any patterns or trends in it? Are any features repeated?'

   'Which have been the most important events in your life?'

   'Who or what have been strong influences in your life? How do you feel about them?

   'What major choices have you made, and why? What alternative paths did you decide against?'

   'Who has given the direction and shape and impetus to your life road? You yourself? Your parents or family? Other people?'

   'How does your past life link with your present work?'

   'How far are you yourself giving direction to your life at present, and how far are you simply "letting it happen"?'

   'How do you measure and evaluate your road?'

   'Can you imagine the direction your journey will take in the future?'

9.5　What Are Our Values?

▶ *My values are the basis of creating the future. How can you promote change if you can't recognize values?*

Our values are reference points for the kind of future which we are are trying to bring about. They guide the future we are striving for, whether for ourselves and our families, or for our community and our society. Since the task of development is to bring about a new future — a future that is different from the present — values are at the core of development work.

Our values are what seems to us important, right and desirable. They are the principles and ideals we uphold. They are the criteria by which we judge our own conduct and the conduct of others. Whenever we have freedom to choose, they guide us in behaviour and decision-making. They set the priorities for our lives. They give us direction and consistency as we make important choices.

So the concept of values is an important tool for thinking about development, and about ourselves as development workers.

The topic can be introduced in the third or fourth week of a three-month course. The work in this section requires two sessions. Additional material follows in More About Our Values (page 356) and will require a third session. The work links with many other topics, most directly with My Life Road (page 344).

Objectives

- to introduce the concept of values, and to raise members' awareness of the role of values in development, culture and other aspects of human life;
- to encourage members to use the concept of values as a tool for analysis and for deeper understanding of human relationships and motivations;
- to encourage members to identify some of their own individual values and to consider how these relate to their choices in life, society and work;
- to encourage members to consider their personal values with respect to their commitment to development, their aspirations for development, and the motivation for their work day by day.

Introductory Exercise

The idea of values is abstract and may be unfamiliar to some members. An introductory exercise offers members an experience of how their own values work in practice, which helps to make the idea more concrete, accessible and easier to introduce.

The exercise takes one hour. If it is followed by the introduction to the topic a session will be required altogether.

The Story of Petal.[1]

■ The story has five characters who are named. Before the session check that the names are not represented in the group concerned. If necessary substitute more suitable name/s.

Ask the members to sit in small groups of five or six, including men and women in each group if possible. Tell them that you are going to read a story to them, and that you will then ask them questions about it. Read the story, word for word.

> Once there was a young woman called Petal. Petal was 19 years old and very beautiful. She was also very poor. She lived in a village on the bank of a big river.
>
> Petal was engaged to be married to a young man called Thomas. Thomas lived in another village on the opposite side of the river. The river was very wide and fast, and there were crocodiles in it.
>
> One day Petal heard that Thomas was very ill, and might even die. She became very anxious about Thomas. She loved him very much, and she wanted to go and be with him if he was sick, and especially if he might die.
>
> So she went down to the river, where there was a ferry boat. The ferry boat used to be rowed by a ferryman called Roger. When Petal said she wanted to cross the river, Roger asked her for a large fare. Petal said that she did not have any money but that she would pay Roger later. Roger refused. Then Petal pleaded with him to take her across because Thomas was so ill, and might die. Roger refused again. Then he said that he would take Petal across, but on one condition — that she should go to bed with him first.
>
> Petal was very upset about this, and went back to her village wondering what to do. On the way she met her cousin Arthur, and she told him what had happened. 'That's nothing to do with me,' he replied. 'It's your problem. I can't help you. Don't involve me in it. I don't want to have anything to do with it.' Then Arthur went off leaving Petal helpless.
>
> Petal didn't know what to do. She hated the idea of going to bed with Roger, but she loved Thomas so much and thought that if he died she might never see him again. She had to get across that river somehow. So finally she went back to Roger, and went to bed with him. Then Roger took her across the river, and she rushed to Thomas's house.
>
> At Thomas's house Petal nursed him and looked after him. Soon Thomas felt better, and was out of danger of dying. After some time Thomas asked Petal how she had crossed the river, and where she had got the money. Then Petal told

1. Thanks to Henry Nunn for the original story.

Thomas what had happened. Thomas was furious. He shouted at Petal and abused her for having gone to bed with Roger. He told her he'd never forgive her, he would never marry her now, and that she should get out of his house for ever.

Petal went sadly down to the ferry again. On the way she met a neighbour called Colin. She told Colin everything that had happened. Colin was very angry when he heard it, and he rushed straight to Thomas's house, pulled Thomas off his sick-bed, and beat him up very badly.

■ Having told the story, ask the members to work individually, and to decide which of the five characters behaved worst and which behaved best (or least badly). Ask them to rank the worst at 5, the best at 1, and the other three in order from 2 to 4. The ranking must be written down. This is done without discussion, and may take five minutes. Make it clear that it is the behaviour described in the story which is to be judged.

Ask the members to share their ranking in the small groups and see if they can reach a consensus. After the discussion has continued for 10 or 15 minutes, tell them to stop and ask if they are reaching agreement. If not, ask them what they think the prospects of agreement are. Usually there is little agreement.

Tabulate some examples of ranking from individual members, or from small groups, on the board to show the variety. Add your own ranking, and ask:
    'Who is right?'
    'Which is the right answer?'
    'Can there be a right answer?'

Point out that the different judgements and rankings depend on the member's perceptions and values.

Some may see Petal as a victim who sacrificed herself for the sake of her love, and who is the least to blame. But some may condemn her behaviour outright because she gave up her chastity. Others may see her behaviour more as ill-considered and irresponsible in those circumstances.

Among development workers the ferry-man is often blamed as an exploiter; but in other groups, perhaps less idealistic, he may be seen as conducting his business in the way he knows. For some people, family obligations may be a very strong value, and the behaviour of cousin Arthur is most to be blamed. For others non-violence may be more important, and they may condemn the neighbour Colin for beating Thomas. The way Thomas's behaviour is judged may depend on the values and expectations members have about gender roles and loyalty.

The rankings will reflect individual values, but cultural and religious values will also play a part.

■ Ask the members to report on the process of their discussions in the small group:
    'What was it like?'
    'What was the quality of the discussion?'
    'Did everyone feel their view was heard?'

■ 'Did anyone feel they had to give in to the majority view?'

'If anyone changed their ranking, were they really convinced?'

Discussion of this exercise may continue at length. A short break will help the group to move on.

Introducing the Topic

■ Introduce the idea of values, drawing on the first three paragraphs at the beginning of this section, and on the points which follow below.

- Making judgements about human conduct, as demonstrated in the Story of Petal, is one way we use our values. But the idea of values is useful in other ways.

- The idea can help us to understand other people and their motivation and choices. We can even use the idea to help us understand our own behaviour and choices.

- At wider levels the idea can help us to understand political, cultural and religious forces. Values are a central part of theories of underdevelopment and development.

- As individuals we act according to our own values. They are the criteria we refer to whenever we make an important decision. We direct our lives by them, and respond to the world and to other people according to them.

- Most of the time we take our values for granted. As we grow up we acquire them from our family, social class, culture and society. We seldom question them or the effect they are having on us and others.

- Someone has said that our values are like our kidneys: we are not usually aware of them, at least while all goes well. But when something goes wrong, and they become disturbed, we realize how important they are to us!

- Values are an abstract idea. We cannot see or touch values, but we see the effects of them in people's decisions and actions.

■ At a suitable point in the introduction, ask members for their own everyday definitions of values. Check that different aspects are included, for example:
- what we think is right and wrong;
- what is important to us in our lives, what we value;
- what we believe will give us happiness;
- what we want for the future;
- the goals we strive for;
- the basis for important choices we make in life;
- the beliefs or principles on which we act.

Ask members to give examples of some values. If necessary add some yourself, such as the following:

politeness	children	modernity
justice	efficiency	wealth
security	punctuality	cleanliness
tradition	respect for age	independence

■ Conclude the first session with discussion in the whole group.

Thinking about Our Own Values

Start by inviting members to deepen and extend their understanding of values. Draw on the following points.

● We can say that values are long-lasting beliefs that a particular kind of conduct (for example, politeness, honesty or kindness) is preferable to the opposite (rudeness, dishonesty, cruelty); or that a particular state of affairs (peace, security or salvation) is preferable to the opposite (war, insecurity, damnation). When we think about values in this way we can see how they guide our lives, give us goals to strive towards, and lead us to principles that we uphold.

● We then use these beliefs or values as moral standards by which we judge our own and other people's behaviour. They tell us what is good and what is bad; which actions are right and which are wrong. They serve as the reference points by which we allocate praise or blame. The Story of Petal gave us an experience of using our values like this.

■ Invite members to consider some of the following statements:
'I thought N behaved properly.'
'I blame M for what happened.'
'Q is looking after his family very well.'
'The government's policies are unjust.'
'He is lazy.'
'She is a good woman.'
'Those children are so rude.'
'This community has become too money-minded.'
'That organization treats its workers fairly.'

These are examples of judgements based on values.

Ask the members to share with their partners in the group a few short statements which reflect their own values.

Go on to explain that we can claim values as our own only if we act on them. Draw on the following points.

- We must distinguish the values which we do have from those we would like to have. We all have wishes and intentions — behaviour we would like to change, ways we would like to be, qualities and abilities we would like to have. But unless we act on these, and do so consistently, they remain wishes and intentions, and we cannot claim them as our values.

- We can claim a value as our own when it is reflected in our life and actions. When we want to identify our values we must look at what we have actually done, at the choices we have made, at the priorities in our life. If it is our value it will have guided our choices consistently, and will be apparent in our behaviour and in our life. In other words there must be evidence to support our claim to any particular value.

Some Personal Values

The theme can be continued with the questionnaire Identifying Some Personal Values (pages 354—355) which focusses on life goals. The work in small groups is also an experience in self-disclosure, and contributes to cohesion in the group.

■ Tell members to sit in groups of three or four, and distribute the questionnaire.

Some members may feel that this is an examination of their virtue, so reassure them that it is for their own use only. Tell them that the questionnaire will be useful only if they can be honest with themselves.

What are our values? Sharing in groups of four.

■ Tell them to start by working individually. Remind them that they can identify items as values only if they have consistently chosen and acted on them. There must be evidence if it is a value.

The individual work may take 20—30 minutes. Then members work in the small groups for another 30 minutes.

After the small groups have completed their discussions, bring the whole group together for any general sharing or clarification.

Conclude the session by giving two or three of the following questions for individual reflection:

'What are the main influences or sources that have contributed to my values?'

'How have my values affected important decisions I have made in my life?'

'How do my values fit with my understanding of development?'

'Which of my values help me in development work, and which hinder?'

'Do I see any contradiction between the future I want for myself and the development I envisage for other people and for society?'

▶ *... we discussed about the behaviour of five characters in the story. We ranked all the characters. As a result, there were thirteen types of different order. It means each of us put different judgements based on different values. It is amazing for me, but it is very natural. Long after the session the discussion continued. It seems to me personal values are very fixed and deep in each of us.*

▶ *As we discussed the questionnaire on values I felt myself fighting with myself on some occasions. I felt the questions helped me to discover part of myself.*

Below is a list of personal goals or life values relating to work in development. You may add to the list if you wish.

For each item in the list, assess how important it is to you in your life and in your work. Do this by using the scale opposite each item.

> The scales run from 1 to 5:
>
> 1 represents: not at all important to me; unimportant to me; not a value or goal or principle for me.
>
> 5 represents: very important to me; a guiding value, goal or principle in my life and work.
>
> 2, 3 and 4 are intermediate positions on the scale.

Circle one of the numbers on each scale, depending on how you assess the unimportance or importance of the item in your own life and work.

Remember that goals and values have meaning only if they are acted upon; so rate high only those values which have actually influenced your decisions or actions in the past.

1. Spiritual growth	1 2 3 4 5
2. Wealth, prosperity, earning a lot of money	1 2 3 4 5
3. Power and influence over other people and their lives	1 2 3 4 5
4. Freedom and independence to make choices for myself	1 2 3 4 5
5. Guiding, teaching, advising other people who are not so skilled or knowledgeable as I am	1 2 3 4 5
6. Using to the full my own talents and potentials	1 2 3 4 5
7. Being recognized and respected for my work	1 2 3 4 5
8. Bringing about greater justice and equality	1 2 3 4 5
9. Working with people who are completely dependent on me	1 2 3 4 5
10. Having an interesting and challenging life	1 2 3 4 5
11. Participating in a worthwhile cause or movement	1 2 3 4 5
12. Meeting the expectations of those who have authority over me	1 2 3 4 5
13. Having an important and responsible job	1 2 3 4 5

14. Doing what I think God wants me to do	1 2 3 4 5
15. Being promoted or moving to jobs with higher status	1 2 3 4 5
16. Peace of mind, freedom from anxiety	1 2 3 4 5
17. Duties and commitments to my family	1 2 3 4 5
18. Getting my work done effectively and efficiently	1 2 3 4 5
19. Avoiding any kind of conflict with other people	1 2 3 4 5
20. Having control over money and other resources in my work	1 2 3 4 5
21. Sacrifice of my own needs	1 2 3 4 5
22. Being liked by other people	1 2 3 4 5
23. Getting a secure job and a regular income	1 2 3 4 5
24. Achievement, a sense of accomplishment and successful completion	1 2 3 4 5
25. Seeing other people take control of their own lives	1 2 3 4 5
26. Care for living things, plants and animals	1 2 3 4 5
27.	1 2 3 4 5
28.	1 2 3 4 5
29.	1 2 3 4 5
30.	1 2 3 4 5

After rating all the listed items:

a) Look at the ratings and reflect on them. Are you generally satisfied or dissatisfied with what you see? Are there any contradictions? Do any of the ratings surprise you? Do you see any patterns? Do you want to bring about any changes in your goals or values which are listed?

b) Identify the five goals or values which are the most important to you and which have most influenced decisions or actions in your life and work.

c) Consider these five goals or values. Do they show a pattern, or have a common basis? Are they consistent with one another?

d) Ask yourself why they act as guides in your life and work.

e) Work in groups of three or four and share these five goals or values and your reflections on them. Share the evidence that these are important goals and values in your life.

John Staley, *Enticing the Learning: Trainers in Development*, University of Birmingham, pages 354—355

More about Our Values

▶ *... what are the values of development? The responses from the course participants were human dignity, justice, equality, self-confidence...*

Many development workers have found values an idea which is helpful in their work, both in explaining some of their own dilemmas, and in making sense of other peoples' ideas and efforts to achieve development.

This section extends the themes which were begun in What Are Our Values? (page 347). The method is brief presentations of concepts, alternating with discussion in pairs and threes and the sharing of experience. It requires one session.

Values and Ideology

■ Show briefly how some familiar political ideologies can be related to values. Draw on the following points.

- We have already identified some of our own individual values. We can extend the idea of values beyond the individual, and use it as a tool for analysis in systems. We can identify the values which prevail in a community, a culture or a political movement. Similarly, professions, organizations and families will have their shared values. Indeed any cohesive group will share values.

- Values are at the base of every belief system, or 'ideology'. Each political ideology gives importance to particular values. For example, four of the values of capitalism are: enterprise, efficiency, competition and individualism. Four of the values of social democracy are: community, co-operation, interdependence and social justice. Depending upon our own values we shall be attracted towards, or repelled away from, certain ideologies.

■ Ask members to identify some of the values of two or three systems familiar to them, such as the international trade system, the international women's movement or formal education. Collect some responses on the board.

Go on to discuss values and development theories. The different ways in which development is understood can also be linked with different values. One programme may emphasize social justice while another emphasizes modernisation. One approach gives importance to broad participation, another gives importance to managerial control. One organization values efficiency, another values consensus.

Ask members to identify some of the values of the development (or aid) programmes of their government. Remind them to think about what is done, rather than what is claimed.

Now ask them to think about their organization. Do they think the values are the same as the government's or different?

Collect some responses.

The Strength of the Evidence

The topic continues with the need for 'evidence' of our values. The work is likely to appeal to more self-analytical members, but all members can be reminded of the principle, and introduced to the criteria below.

■ Remind members that it is simply not enough to claim that we have certain values. We must be able to prove it. We must be able to demonstrate our values by our actions and choices. Words, wishes, hopes and aspirations are not enough.

Values which are strong and deep will not only be reflected in our actions, but will also give direction and energy to our lives. The more strongly we hold a value the clearer the 'evidence' will be.

We can use the following criteria to measure how strongly we do hold a particular value.

- Are we happy with that value, and do we appreciate and esteem it? If a value seems to be a duty or a burden, it may have been imposed on us, rather than being something we have willingly accepted. Values which other people tell us we 'ought to have', but which we do not appreciate, belong to the realm of preaching.

- Have we accepted that value for ourselves, or has it been inherited from others? Parents, elders and teachers often impose their own values while they are bringing up children. When we become adults we can reconsider the values we have received, and can accept or reject them for ourselves. We will act on those values that we have accepted for ourselves more clearly and more comfortably than those which we have passively inherited.

- Have we chosen that value for ourselves, or did we receive it as part of our culture? We are often unaware of the values we receive from our culture. We may have to visit and live in another culture before we recognize this. Then we can perceive our own culture more clearly, and can accept or reject some or all of its values.

- Do we speak out and speak up for the value publicly? If we are committed to it — if it really is our value — we shall be prepared to speak up for it, or to write in support of it. We shall be ready to use our resources and energy, and to accept stress, for the sake of it.

- Are we are prepared to take risks for the sake of the value? For example, are we willing to risk the disapproval of parents or relatives or friends — or boss, colleagues, donor agency, or even government — for the sake of what we value? Will we risk damage to our reputation, or to our family's reputation?

- Are we ready to confront other people on the basis of the value? Are we ready to 'stand up and be counted' for the sake of values we hold? In our development work, for example, are we willing to show solidarity with the poor and to confront the powerful? Are we ready to oppose, to protest, to demonstrate?

- Are we prepared to make sacrifices for the sake of the value? Will we give up our job for it? Are we willing to be arrested for it? Will we go to prison for it? Some people devote their lives to a cause they believe in, including political and religious movements intended to benefit the poor. Some people even sacrifice their lives for strongly-held values.

■ Invite members to reflect on their own, and to apply the criteria or questions, one level at a time, to the values which they believe they hold strongly. Remind them that there must be evidence at the level of each criterion.

Values and the Personality

The criteria suggest that the values which we hold strongly are deep in us. One simple model of the personality puts values near the centre.

■ Introduce members to the model shown here, but emphasize that it is an over-simplification.

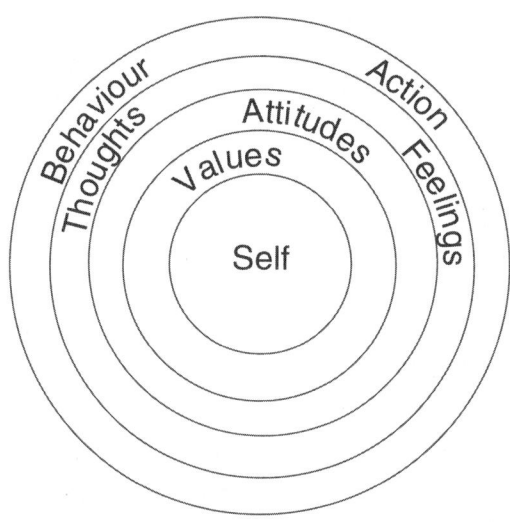

Nonetheless the model may be helpful to members who have not given much thought to the person, and have not considered how different aspects of the personality can affect our behaviour and action and therefore our work and our commitment.

Conflicts among Our Own Values

Introduce the idea of conflicts among our own values. Members may have already identified some conflicts in their own values from the questionnaire, Identifying Some Personal Values (pages 354—355).

- Ideally our values fit together and reinforce each other. A set of consistent and compatible values will help to give a clear shape and direction to our life and work. But sometimes we find that values cannot be reconciled with each other. When we are faced with a dilemma or 'a difficult choice' this may be due to values pulling in different directions. For example, we value our traditional dress, yet we are drawn to modern fashions. We want to spare the environment, yet we want to travel. We value 'the simple life', yet we want to earn a high salary.

- When two of our values are in conflict we feel an internal tension, often with a sense of being pulled in different directions. If the tension continues we experience stress. A common conflict of values for development workers is between the demands of their work and the needs of their family. Another is between getting things done to meet organizational needs, and giving time and attention to people in the community and their views.

- If values seem to be pulling us in different directions, we can look at what we actually do in order to know which values are stronger. That is 'the evidence' we have referred to earlier.

- Generally the more we become aware of such conflicts, the better we shall be able to deal with the resulting tension and stress.

■ Ask members to work in pairs or threes, to share examples of internal conflicts from their own experience and lives, and to tell each other how they deal with the resulting tensions.

Conflicts with the Values of Others

Introduce the idea of conflict between our own values and the values of others. It has been suggested that it is when our values are opposed or threatened that we become more aware of them.

We all know that some of our values differ from those of other people, including people who are close to us. This can be a cause of conflict, even within families. For example the younger generation may adopt values which are different from those of their parents. We then have conflicts between 'modern' and 'traditional', and a so-called 'generation gap'.

■ Ask members to work in pairs and share three important values of the older generation in their own family or culture.

Then ask in the whole group if members hold those values as strongly as the older generation does.

We have seen already how political ideologies are based on differing sets of values, which represent alternative visions of how society should be organized. As individuals we refer to our own values when deciding which political movement or party we will support. Other people, with different values, will support another party. Then we find ourselves 'in opposition' to them.

■ Ask members to work in pairs and identify the values of any political party or movement which they feel comfortable with and are willing to support. Then ask them to identify some of the values of a party which they do not support, or which they oppose.

Ask them to give brief examples from their work in development of how their values have clashed with those of other people. If this is done in the whole group you can monitor the examples. Not all clashes are due to differences in values!

One of the challenges of development work is that we often work with other people whose values are different from our own.[1] Ask members to reflect on some of the following questions:

'Can we understand and respect the values of other people when those values are very different from our own?'[1]

'How well do I understand the value system of the community where I work? Can I enter into that value system?'

'How similar or different are my values to those in the community? Can I work for change there without imposing my own values?'

'How do I work with people whose values are very different from my own?'

Questions such as these are central to our role as development workers.

Values and Change

Do our values change? Most people will say that they can and do change, but that it is a slow and sometimes painful process. As children we tend to absorb our parents' and family's values uncritically. But as we grow into adulthood, in a world which itself is changing, our experience may lead us to reconsider those values, and either to re-affirm them or to adopt new values.

There are certain circumstances which encourage that process of reconsideration and may lead on to change. These include:

- our educational experiences (especially when these differ from life at home);
- experience of another culture, as in higher education or training;
- entering a new profession, such as development work;
- exposure to different value systems or beliefs;
- a deep personal or family crisis;
- a new political or religious understanding;
- important relationships with people who have different values.

---

1. Using role play or still images to explore different, and even opposed, value systems can help members to understand and appreciate the other viewpoint. The methods allow us to 'act out' from different or opposed values, but without compromising or threatening our own values. This can be very illuminating, and can contribute to a deeper understanding of difference.

■ Invite members to reflect individually on the questions:
'Are any of my values changing?'
'What is causing them to change?'

In conclusion, widen the question to the level of the community, or even society.
'Are some of our long-held values changing?'
'Can we have development without changing our values?'
'Which of our values have to change?'
'Which of our values will we hold on to?'

This may lead into discussions about the preservation of cultural identity.

▶ *The values we value most are those we have chosen ... Sometimes values are given to us through suggested or forced ways ... This raises an interesting question as to whether development workers are able to allow freedom of choice in projects according to community values, or whether we believe we know the right values for all. Development workers could be tempted to control, manipulate or change people according to their own values ...*

▶ *Last year I had an opportunity of visiting my home country. During my time there I found that what people give more value to is not valuable for me. I could see my staying abroad for the last 15 years has changed my values gradually.*

▶ *... it's in our values that we find our commonality and humanity, and from them that we shall carry forward our work.*

Attending to Our Feelings

▶ *It is still much more easy for us to talk about a topic or an issue than to talk about our feelings. Why is that?*

▶ *Something very important happened today when P invited us to reflect upon feelings. A number of rather quiet friends started to talk ...*

Our feelings play a central part in our responses to other people and to the world around us. They affect our motivation and behaviour, our relationships and communication, our effectiveness and, indeed, our happiness.

As 'people working professionally with people', development workers need a basic sensitivity and competence in recognizing and dealing with feelings, both their own and those of others.

There is also a group dimension. A group which deals with its members' feelings openly and sensitively becomes more cohesive and more energetic. It becomes a mature and effective group. In a training group this supports the learning.

The topic can be taken up in the third or fourth week of a three-month course. It requires at least two sessions. Material for a first session, part conceptual and part experiential, is included here. The remaining work Going Further with Feelings (page 369) should be done soon afterwards.

The work links with case studies (page 164) because any well-chosen case study has a feeling dimension. It links with reflections on process, including the daily diary (page 72), and with many topics. More generally, there is a feeling dimension — whether conscious or unconscious — to every moment throughout a course, just as there is at every moment in our lives. So feelings can be explored at any suitable opportunity, whatever the topic or content happens to be.

Objectives

- to raise awareness and understanding of personal feelings and their role in human behaviour and action;

- to encourage members to become more in touch with their own feelings and to accept them as a natural part of everyday life;

- to help members to make more use of their own emotional energy, and so improve their effectiveness as leaders, managers and agents of development;

- to increase the confidence and skill of members in dealing with their own feelings, and the feelings of others, at individual, organizational and community levels;

- to enhance the cohesion, effectiveness and maturity of the course group.

Introducing the Topic

The way we learn about feelings is through recognizing and understanding our own, and this is the theme of the work in this section. The work is intended to increase members' effectiveness as leaders, managers and development workers. It is not included for the sake of personal growth.

Such work may be familiar, even self-evident, to some course members, but others may not have given conscious attention to their feelings previously. Trainers should allow for some course members being out of touch with their own and others' feelings. In some cultures men in particular may seem to be 'emotionally illiterate'. Even the words to identify feelings may not be known.

Other members may recognize the realm of feelings, but give importance only to rationality, dismissing feelings as irrational or irrelevant. Yet failure to attend to the realm of feelings has been the downfall of many development programmes.

So the importance of the topic will be self-evident to some members, but not to others. Those who do not see its importance immediately will need an explanation and rationale.

■ Acknowledge this by asking the members::
  'What do you *think* about giving attention to feelings during this course?'
  'What do you *feel* about that? Are you pleased? Irritated? Uncomfortable? Surprised? Excited?'
  'What other feelings do you have?'
Ask them to share briefly with their neighbours; and then invite a few responses from the whole group. This may provide an opportunity to distinguish thinking from feeling.

Rationale for the Topic

Then introduce the topic briefly, drawing on some of the points given below. The introduction may take 15 minutes.

- The principal resource — the main tool — of the development worker is himself or herself. This is more important than any technical or material resources.

- When we use any tool we need to know how it works, what its effects are, what its limitations are, how to maintain it, and so on. In the same way, as development workers, each of us needs to understand how our own self functions.

- In other words, we need some insight into the human person and personality, a large part of which is emotional. So we must give attention to feelings, trying to understand our own better, and trying to be sensitive towards those of others.

- Feeling is literally the sense of touch; but it generally refers to the emotional side of a person's nature. 'Feelings' are the affections or emotions; the consciousness of pleasure or pain, and so on. Happiness, anger, disappointment and anxiety are other examples of common feelings.

- Whether we like it nor not, feelings play a large part in the process of every human activity, and influence every relationship between people, at every level from individual to international.

Relevance to Development Work

- Competence in dealing with feelings is required in many professions. It is especially necessary when the behaviour of 'clients', whether individuals or communities, is influenced by feelings.
- In the development field the reactions and behaviour in a community — and the possibilities for development — are constantly affected by currents of feeling. Essential aspects — such as leadership, participation, commitment and 'ownership' of the process — are all driven by emotional forces.
- When the development worker's role is not clearly defined or clearly understood — which is often the case — the worker needs sensitivity to other people's emotional reactions to his/her presence and activities. Without that sensitivity the development worker may not recognize what is going on in the community, and the work may fail.
- Competence with feelings is even more necessary where there is poverty and powerlessness. The victims of long-term disadvantage may suffer from a lack of self-esteem which obstructs development. This may not be apparent at an everyday level, and it needs emotional sensitivity to recognize it and deal with it.

Learning about Feelings

- The most effective way of gaining fluency with feelings is to recognize and understand our own. Working with feelings among other practitioners during a training course is an ideal opportunity to increase our awareness and skill.
- In a training group, as in any community, currents of feeling are always present, and are always having an effect on the process and on the group climate. This in turn affects the group's communication and decision-making, its co-operation and participation, and its effectiveness in achieving its objectives. All this provides constant opportunities to study the effect of feelings on us as individuals, and on the group.
- Members who can already handle a wide range of feelings will find this an easy topic. Others who are less comfortable at dealing with feelings may find it more puzzling. Such differences may be due to personality, education, and cultural or gender expectations.

 ## Recognizing Feelings

■ Continue with the following exercises which are intended to help members recognize feelings, both in themselves and as concepts. Allow sufficient time, especially

■ at the beginning, so that members work in a relaxed mood. Keep the discussion matter-of-fact, accepting, interactive and cheerful.

Naming Feelings

Ask the members to give examples of feelings. Collect these on the board. Some may not be feelings. Refer these back to the group — 'Is that a feeling?' — and help them to distinguish thinking and feeling.

If the group has difficulty in identifying feelings, add some — pain, pleasure, impatience, amusement, excitement, fright, shame, surprise, frustration, triumph and worry are all everyday examples. Love and hate may be included.

Ask if the feelings listed can be roughly grouped under main headings, such as Happy, Sad, Angry, Afraid, Surprised, Disgusted? Do this on the board with the participation of the members. Allow 15 minutes altogether.

Naming and listing feelings in this way begins to remove some of the mystery which surrounds this topic for some people.

Sharing Feelings

■ Tell the members to sit in groups of three and each share a time during the last few days when they felt happy. Then another time when they felt anxious (or surprised). Then a time when they felt angry. The discussion is completed in the threes and not reported to the whole group. Allow 15 minutes altogether.

It is important to include anger, because this is the emotion most often denied or suppressed, especially perhaps by development workers! The exercise gives members an opportunity to talk about anything that may be troubling them.

Your Thoughts about Feelings

This is a questionnaire which can be used to extend the introductory discussion. A questionnaire is conceptual rather than experiential, but it helps some members to feel more comfortable in engaging with the topic.

■ Tell the members to complete the questionnaire individually, which will take about ten minutes. Then tell them to share their responses in groups of four (20 minutes).

Then lead a brief discussion in the whole group. The statements with odd numbers are said to be True, and those with even numbers are False. Do members agree?

If time runs out the session can be ended here. The follow-up session can then continue with the remaining two exercises before moving on to Going Further with Feelings (page 369).

Thinking or Feeling?

In present-day English the words thinking and feeling are often mixed up. You hear people saying, 'I feel ...' when they mean, 'I think ...'

■ In an international group ask about the words in other languages and cultures. Are the meanings clearly separated?

Ask members to use the words below, and to complete the statements out of their own experience in ways that will illustrate the difference between thinking and feeling:

'I feel ...... because I have been thinking about ......'

'I think I ought to ...... but I feel ...... about it.'

'I am feeling ...... today, and I think the reason is ......'

Ask them to share their statements in twos or threes.

Then ask for a few examples to be shared in the whole group, and check that the difference is clear. Allow ten minutes.

The Head and the Heart

In an international group ask:

'In your culture, which part of the body is believed to be the home of feeling?'

'Which is the home of thinking?'

Usually the heart and the head are identified.

Suggest that some of us, as individuals, tend to be guided mainly by our hearts, or our emotions. Others of us give more importance to our heads, or our thinking. Ask members, as individuals, to identify which they are more often guided by.

Tell them to imagine a line or continuum across the longest dimension of the room. At one end is heart; at the other end is head.[1] Ask them where they see themselves on this continuum.

After they have considered the question, tell them to get up and stand on the line wherever they think their place is. Place yourself or indicate your own position on the line.

After all have taken up their positions, invite some members to state briefly why they have put themselves there. After a few have spoken, ask all the members if they are happy about where they are. Would any of them prefer to be somewhere else on the line?

If some say 'Yes', tell them to move to where they would like to be. Ask those who move why they want to make the change, and what would help to make the change possible.

Part of the value of this exercise is that it requires us to 'take up a position'. But the exercise should not be prolonged or allowed to become 'heavy'. Ten minutes should be long enough.

This is the most suitable stage at which to end the session.

---

1. See Continuum (page 108). If other parts of the body are mentioned, such as the guts, they can be added into the discussion and the exercise.

▶ *Are we aware of our own feelings? Did you know what you felt, or didn't you, when V asked us about our feelings? Or perhaps you felt the question irrelevant. Do we have words to express our feelings? Do we feel too naked when we reveal some of our feelings? Are we afraid of hurting somebody? I hope that we will be able to recognize and talk about some of our feelings in this group. I think we need to develop our ability in this. When we are going to work in a community, the members of the community will have lots of different feelings towards us and our projects. How can we deal with these feelings if we are only vaguely aware of our own feelings?*

▶ *It was also good to get words/adjectives to the feelings each of us have in this part of the course. Sometimes it's difficult to say why we feel as we do. Is it the personal side of our lives, the course topics, the other course members, our work at home — or a mixture of these things — which makes us feel as we do? Maybe we all should stop a minute sometimes and feel where we are and why we are feeling as we do.*

▶ *I am impressed by the tutors' concern for thoughts and feelings as well as for knowledge. This has been strange for me but very positive, and is helping in the development of my own personality.*

Questionnaire: Your Thoughts about Feelings

At every moment of our conscious lives there is a 'current' of feelings which runs within us. The current may be giving energy to the whole of our being, or it may be only flickering at a low level, but that current is always 'live' at some level.

What do you think about your 'feelings'?
Put a T (for True) or F (for False) against each statement in the following list:

1. At every moment in time my feelings are part of 'the real me'.   (   )

2. Becoming aware of my feelings means being ruled by my feelings.   (   )

3. Paying attention to my feelings helps me to understand
   who and what I am   (   )

4. If I ignore my feelings, and try to forget them, they will
   simply disappear.   (   )

5. I can learn about myself by becoming more aware of my feelings.   (   )

6. There are no risks in revealing my feelings to others.   (   )

7. If you can never feel angry with other people, you may never
   be able to feel affection for them either.   (   )

8. Hiding 'negative' feelings is necessary for close and deep
   relationships.   (   )

9. Many of us hold on to 'negative' feelings; we store them up
    inside us.   ( )

10. Disagreement always leads to a bad relationship.   ( )

11. If I keep all my 'negative' feelings stored up inside me,
    I may have little capacity left for 'positive' feelings.   ( )

12. Women may discuss feelings, but it is not proper for
    men to discuss feelings.   ( )

13. When a friend shares feelings with me, he/she is
    encouraging a deeper friendship.   ( )

14. In training for development work, feelings need not be
    given any attention.   ( )

15. The best way of understanding other peoples' feelings is
    to study your own.   ( )

Based partly on E. H. McGrath, *Basic Managerial Skills for All*, Prentice-Hall, New Delhi, page 202

Going Further with Feelings

▶ *I have learned to trust my feelings as an important resource ...*

This section is a continuation of Attending to Our Feelings (page 362) and should follow soon afterwards. It combines the presentation of ideas and issues with discussion and exercises. The purpose is to continue raising awareness about the importance of feelings in any work with others, and to improve members' confidence in dealing with their own and others' feelings. The work requires at least one session.

Culture, Feelings and Education

This is a large subject area. What can be done here is to raise members' awareness of how influences and experiences from their past may be affecting their present-day work and attitudes.

■ Suggest to the group that some families, and some cultures, give more importance to thinking and intellectual achievement, while others also recognize feelings and the role of the emotions. Ask members to share with partners in the group how it is in their own family and/or culture. Which is given importance?

Go on to formal education. Here thinking is usually given more importance, and feeling is often ignored or dismissed. Ask members if that was true in their own education.

Circulate the short extract Feelings And Education (page 374). After members have read it, ask some of the following questions:
   'How were feelings dealt with in your education?'
   'Were you ever told to "Control yourself" or "Use your head" or similar?'
   'Were you told "Keep your temper" or "Don't cry" or "Stop sulking"?'
   'Were boys and girls given the same messages?'
   'How do you think your experience as a child affects the way you deal with feelings now as an adult?'
Introducing the ideas and discussing the extract may take 20 minutes.

Feelings as Energy

We often experience our feelings as a kind of energy, as an impulse to action, or as the source of our motivation. An obvious example is fear of a danger, which causes us to prepare for the danger, and either confront it, or avoid it, perhaps by running away. Another example is affection, which draws us towards those we love and encourages us to do things for them. Anger is another feeling that generates a lot of energy.

■ Introduce the idea of feelings as energy.

Ask members to work in pairs or threes. Ask them to share an example from their own

■ life during the last few days of a feeling they have acted upon, i.e. done something because of the feeling. The example may be an everyday matter, and of no great significance, but it is a further opportunity for members to recognize and 'own' their feelings.

Go on to suggest that, if the energy which arises from feelings is not expressed or released, it may accumulate, like water in a reservoir. Eventually this pent-up emotional energy may overflow or burst out, just as the water may overflow or burst the reservoir. The result may be disturbing, and can even be violent.

A sudden release of feelings can happen at the individual level. It can also happen at a community or national level. Ask members to share in their pairs or threes an occasion in their life:
- when their own feelings burst out. What was the feeling? What happened?
- when another person's feelings burst out, or were vigorously expressed;
- when the feelings of large numbers of people were expressed.

Ask the members to discuss whether such outbursts are a problem or an opportunity in development work.

Introducing these ideas, and the discussions in small groups, may take 20 minutes.

Feelings: Good or Bad?

In some cultures certain feelings are branded as good or 'positive', while others are branded as bad or 'negative'.

Such words can be misleading. Feelings are neither good nor bad in themselves. Fear and anxiety, for example, are often described as negative but they can be most positive. Our fear of a wild animal may save our life. Our anxiety about an event may lead us to perform well. Anger can be destructive, but it too can be constructive. When anger is directed at injustice it is a powerful force for change.

When we evaluate a feeling as bad or negative we may then dismiss it, or even deny it and suppress it. Feelings which are ignored or denied like this tend to accumulate inside us and then burst out later. We would do better to accept that any feeling which occurs in us is natural. Our task is to recognize a feeling when it arises, to work with it and to manage it. It is the way in which we manage our feelings — what we do with them, and how we use them — which becomes 'positive' or 'negative'.

■ Introduce the members to these ideas. Ask them which feelings are considered 'acceptable' — or positive — in their own families or cultures:
   'Are children allowed to express feelings which adults should not express?'
   'Are there gender differences? Are men expected to express certain feelings, but not others? Is it different for women?'

There are similar expectations related to professions. For example, priests are not expected to show anger. Soldiers are not expected to show fear.
   'What about development workers? Which feelings are they expected to keep hidden?'

Introducing and discussing these ideas and issues in the whole group may take ten minutes.

Expressing our Feelings

■ Introduce this part of the topic to the members by drawing on the following points.

- For many of us the pros and cons of expressing feelings are confused.

- Some of us, as individuals, find it natural and easy to express our feelings, while others tend to keep our feelings to ourselves. We each have our personal inclinations. We are also affected by our upbringing as children, and by cultural, gender and professional expectations. What seems important is to become more aware of our feelings, and more skilled in working with them, whether we then express them or not.

- While we remain conscious, feelings are always flowing in us, even if we are not aware of them. If we act on feelings unconsciously, without being aware of them, our communication may become confused and contradictory. We may behave in ways which are inappropriate without realising it, and even damage our relationships and undermine our work.

- A familiar example is the development worker who believes him/herself to be endlessly patient at community meetings, but whose impatience is obvious to the community. People may be attending the meetings only to see if there is an explosion!

- When we become aware of our feelings we have the opportunity to choose what we will do about them. It is the awareness which gives us a choice. We can choose whether we hide the feelings, or whether we express them. If we choose to express them we can further choose whether we express them strongly or mildly, and then whether we act on them or not.

- To continue with the same example, if we attend a community meeting and realize that we are becoming impatient, we can consider the alternatives we have and choose the one which seems most appropriate in the circumstances.

- This is not to argue for always expressing feelings or for always acting on them. Sometimes it is more constructive, and indeed safer, to keep them hidden. At other times more may be achieved by revealing them, and even by expressing them strongly! But unless we have the awareness we do not have the choice.

- If we can recognize our own feelings and make an appropriate choice, we can take care of our own needs while being responsive to others' needs. These are skills, and if we learn them we will increase our effectiveness in our work and in our lives.

Statues

This is an exercise in the expression of feelings. It usually produces a light-hearted mood in the group.

■ Tell members work in pairs of the same sex. One partner is to be the Sculptor, the other is the Clay. The Clay remains passive and allows the Sculptor to direct or arrange his/her posture, gesture and facial expression to portray a particular feeling.

Give each pair a different feeling to portray, such as Joy, Grief, Astonishment, Disgust and Anger. While the pairs are working you should check that they are working only with the feeling you have given them, and are not adding stories or situations — the exercise is not a role play. After working together for five minutes the Clay should be able to 'step out' of the portrayal and re-assume it at will. When all are ready, ask the Clay of each pair in turn to portray his/her feeling. Ask the other members if they can identify the feeling.

Then reverse or change the pairs, and ask the new Sculptors to choose a feeling for their Clay to portray. Follow the same procedure, again checking that each pair is working with a feeling only and not with a story.

Even if the portrayals are hesitant, and the identifications are not clear, the process is usually fun, and it gives members more confidence to talk about feelings.

Introducing the ideas may take ten minutes, and the exercise a further 15 minutes.

If time runs out this is a suitable place to end the session. However the remaining work on 'I' statements is important, and it should be taken up soon afterwards.

Taking Responsibility for Our Feelings

Give importance to this part of the work. It is a central issue in human relationships, and not least in development organizations. Introduce the issue by drawing on the following points.

- We often hear remarks such as:
  'He made me angry ...'
  'You always upset me!'
  'She usually cheers me up ...'
  'Somehow they make me feel guilty ...'

- In each statement the speaker is blaming (or praising) someone else for what he or she is feeling. In reality, our feelings are our own. Other people may speak or act in all kinds of ways that stimulate or stir our feelings, but the feelings themselves are in us and belong to us, and we must take responsibility for them.

- When I take responsibility for what I am feeling, I can learn about myself. If I ask myself why I am feeling angry or upset or sad, I give myself the chance of finding the answer, of understanding myself and my reactions better, and perhaps of changing the way I deal with such situations in future. But if I continue to attribute *my* feeling to *other* people, I do not give myself any possibility of learning or changing.

- When we take responsibility for our own feelings, it allows us to make 'I' statements. An 'I' statement is a statement of fact about our own feelings and the reason for them. The intention of an 'I' statement is to give information — specific information — and to avoid blaming the other person. It is then easier for the other person to accept the statement, to learn from it and to make a change in future, if he/she chooses.

- Notice the difference in the following examples. Which are the 'I' statements?
  a) 'You always interrupt ...'
  b) 'I felt irritated when you interrupted me just now.'

  a) 'You always go by your own experience. Why can't you take other peoples' experience seriously?'
  b) 'I am disappointed because I do not think you are taking our experience seriously.'

  a) 'Don't you dare talk about the role of women like that!'
  b) 'I feel uncomfortable when I hear you talking about the role of women like that.'

- So we need to be aware of the words we are using, at least in the English language. A more careful use of words can help us to gain a more accurate view of the situation and of our role and responsibility in it.

- As our view changes, we may change our behaviour. And it is the changes in *our* behaviour which may influence others to change their behaviour. This is also the reality of development work, though it is seldom understood. We cannot make other people change their behaviour; we can only change our own.

- At the very least, 'I' statements can help us avoid unnecessary conflicts.

■ Tell the members to work in small groups of three or four, to share their reactions to the principle of 'I' statements, and then to produce one or two examples of their own, real or imaginary.

When the members of a group are able to share their feelings and reactions through 'I' statements it contributes to a more open climate, it raises the level of challenge in an acceptable way, and it contributes to the process of feedback. All this adds greatly, both to the quality of life in the group, and to the learning and abilities of the individual members.[1]

Introducing the idea of 'I' statements, together with the discussion in small groups, may take 25 minutes altogether.

This is a topic that never ends. Feelings are part of every moment in a course, and trainers should use suitable opportunities to express their own feelings and to reinforce members' learning.

More particularly, trainers should look for opportunities in the course to use and affirm 'I' statements, and to challenge expressions of blame.

---

1. In homogeneous groups the skill of recognizing feelings can be taken further with empathy exercises. These can help members to 'listen to the feelings' when others speak, which is an invaluable skill when working in any community.

▶ *I was arrested by L's claim of anger as a natural emotion, coming out of somebody who feels being exploited. And the thought brought me to the situation at home about the richness of anger that moved people to bring about change.*

▶ *I think T did something important yesterday, when she shared her feelings in the group. And also J who dared to pick it up for discussion. I do not know how to express this, but I think that if we are willing to let others see some of our feelings then we may get a better contact with each other.*

▶ *... the group went on discussing the feeling of guiltiness which has arisen in the minds of some participants who try to help solve the problems in underdeveloped countries, understanding that their help could do very little for the cause. Later it was found that many of the group members carry the similar feeling in different situations and at different levels, and become inactive due to the pressure of feeling. ... it was suggested that, instead of getting paralysed with the feeling, we must overcome (it) by looking for the cause of this feeling.*

▶ *The fun part of the day was 'sculptures and clay'. First M had to make me appear afraid by moving me about into an appropriately shrinking position. Then I had to make M look happy — easy with such a naturally happy-looking person anyway. The serious side of this was to think about how people express feelings, and become aware of both our own emotions and reactions and those of other people. The final stage of the day was about taking responsibility for our own feelings rather than blaming someone else. So now every time someone irritates me I will have to analyze why — it will take me hours!*

▶ *FEELINGS, FEELINGS and FEELINGS. Feelings seems to dominate the whole Development Course. I think the time has come to deal with FACTS ...*

Extract for Discussion: Feelings and Education

As children the first thing many of us remember having learned about feelings is to 'control them'. At school the message that feelings are socially unacceptable was confirmed: 'Use your head', we were told. For many of us this resulted in an imbalance between emotions and intellect which was further re-inforced in later years.

Now, as leaders and managers, we may find that this imbalance complicates our attempts to make personal contact with others. We may find it difficult to build up satisfying and effective relationships in our work, our communities, our organizations, and with our families and friends. Perhaps these difficulties reflect the even more basic problem we have, which is to accept our feelings ourselves, and come to terms with our whole selves.

Based on R.P. Lynton, *Introduction to Feelings*, SIET, page 90

CHAPTER 10

Thinking About Our Role

▶ *I think we begin to learn and grow by the questions we ask.*

Questions are powerful because they call for answers. Asking questions is one of the principal tools of the development worker. It is also one of the principal tools of the trainer who works with experience-based methods. It may also be one of the principal tools of the course member who is clarifying his or her own convictions and commitments.

There are many categories of question, but for practical purposes it is helpful to distinguish closed, open and enabling questions. Course members will be familiar with closed questions, which are characteristic of much teaching in schools. The purpose of this session is to encourage members to use open and enabling questions.

The use of appropriate questions is a skill — and, perhaps even more, an attitude — which trainers should practise and demonstrate, and encourage among members, throughout the course as part of the methodology.

The topic should be included early in a course. If the handout can be given for preparatory reading, half a session may be enough to introduce the topic.

Objectives

- to raise members' awareness of the role of questions in training and development work;
- to distinguish between closed, open and enabling questions, and to recognize their usefulness in different situations;
- to give members practice in using open and enabling questions;
- to encourage members to adopt the attitudes and skills which support open and enabling questions.

 ## Introducing the Topic

■ Introduce the topic in general by drawing on the points above and the introduction in the handout (page 378).

Closed Questions

Ask the members to work in small groups of three or four. Explain the nature of closed questions, and tell the members to frame a closed question for the other members of their small group. Tell them to ask their questions and listen to the answers.

■ Discuss the nature of closed questions with the whole group. Point out that they are an essential tool for discovering and collecting information, but that is also their limitation. The answers they produce tend to be information only. They do not stimulate wider thinking.

Open Questions

Go on to explain open questions. Tell the members in their small groups to frame and ask each other open questions. Members who are used only to closed questions may find this difficult, so invite some examples for discussion in the whole group. Some of the examples may turn out to be closed or evaluative questions. Others may be vague. Help the members identify a level of question that stimulates thinking and carries the communication forwards. Point out that when open questions are used in a group or in a community, they encourage participation.

Enabling Questions

Go on to enabling questions. Tell each member to frame an enabling question about the work back home which they could 'take home' with them after the course. This could be a question for their organization as a whole, or for their colleagues, or for themselves.

Review a few of these questions in the whole group, while avoiding discussion of possible answers. Some of the questions which are proposed may turn out to be evaluative, rather than enabling. Members are likely to be familiar with evaluative questions, and these may occur easily to them. Point out that such questions can be useful but that they belong to a different process.

Remind members that evaluation is essentially a closed process — a measuring of achievement against expectations which have already been decided upon. Evaluative questions are usually asked for the benefit of the person doing the asking. An enabling process is more open and exploratory, and is more for the benefit of the person or people being asked.

Enabling questions stimulate thought, reflection and discussion. They can also challenge perceptions and assumptions, generate dynamism and energy, and lead to action and change.

▶ *I can apply questions to my situation, but I would find it difficult to apply someone else's answers.*

▶ *I'm afraid I'm going to have an indigestion of questions ... I need someone with whom I could share my thoughts on what's going on ... I shared my worry with a fellow resident.*

The conversation went something like this:

Me: You know, I'm getting worried about my progress on the course.

He: You mean you're losing interest?

Me: I'm not losing interest. The truth is I'm beginning to super like it. My only problem is that I seem to question everything lately. Questions: they keep coming. I even dream of questions ...

He: ... why worry? Isn't this the reason you came to study here in the first place? This means that you are getting what you came here for. You are being developed.

Me: Am I? Thank God!

▶ *I shall ask the question 'Why?' again and again ...*

▶ *In future I shall take nothing for granted. I shall keep questioning — especially myself.*

▶ *I think I've gained a lot of self-confidence, maybe because we have had a lot of questioning ...*

Guidelines: Asking Useful Questions

Asking questions is one of the principal tools for development work.

When we ask questions in everyday life, we usually do so for our own benefit, in order to have more information, to increase our knowledge, or to understand something better. As we go through the course, we shall probably ask questions of this kind about all sorts of things in order to satisfy our own need for more information and understanding.

But we can also use questions to help the person who is being asked. In a training course, or in our work back home, well-chosen questions from us can help colleagues to think more widely and more deeply about issues, problems and situations which they face. Similarly, if our colleagues ask us appropriate questions, they can help us to analyse matters more fully, understand a situation more completely, consider more alternatives, and even make better decisions.

Questions require answers; and that is why they are such an effective tool. But some kinds of question are more useful in development work than others.

Closed Questions

Some kinds of question require a particular answer. There is only one correct answer to each of the following questions:
- what do 2 plus 2 add up to?
- which city is the capital of Namibia?
- how many course members are there in this room at present?
- how much is this Government's aid budget?
- who is the Secretary-General of The United Nations?

Such questions are sometimes called closed questions because they are closed to everything except the correct answer. They do not lead to anything else.

Closed questions are often questions about known facts. This is the style of question many of us were asked in school when a teacher wanted to test whether pupils had learned certain facts. Closed questions may be important during the course in order to gain factual information. For example, we may need to ask another course member questions about his/her work:

- what is your designation?
- what are your organization's objectives?
- how many villages does the organization work in?
- how much was the rainfall last year?
- which are the staple foods in the villages where you work?

Factual information may be essential for our own understanding of a work situation or a community, but such questions do little to stimulate any further thinking by the person who is being asked.

Open Questions

Questions which do not have a 'right' or 'correct' answer are sometimes called open questions. We can think of open questions on a scale.

At one end of the scale are questions which lead to the answer 'Yes' or 'No', or which offers two choices only:

- are you going to the meeting this evening?
- do you prefer tea or coffee?
- shall we meet at eleven o'clock?
- will you do this work today or tomorrow?

Such questions are 'open' only a little way.

At the other end of the scale are questions that may be 'too open' to be useful. Questions such as:

- how do you like living in this country?
- what do you think about the problem?
- does aid help in development?
- does the World Bank do any good?
- are there any difficulties in your village?

may be too vague to be helpful. Vague questions may lead to vague answers.

Enabling Questions

But somewhere in the middle of the scale are questions which stimulate and challenge the thinking of the person being asked.

The following are possible examples of such questions:

- can you explain that problem more deeply?
- how do you think the organization can deal with this situation?

- why do you think the director reacted in that way?
- in which ways could the manager get out of this difficulty?
- what do you mean when you say 'they wouldn't co-operate'?
- how do you think the leaders were feeling during that period?
- what was your role?

Such questions are not always easily answered. There may be no answer, or no single answer. Or the answer may be complicated. Or there may be more than one answer. To some questions there can be alternative answers, or possible answers, or suggested answers or speculative answers ...

Such complexity has to be accepted, and even welcomed! Single answers in complex situations are usually inadequate, often wrong, and sometimes dangerous.

What is important is to be clear whether the answer given is based on facts and knowledge, is the result of analysis and deduction, is an estimate, or is just a wild guess.

As we gain experience in using questions, and gain more skill with them, we shall become more effective in helping other people to analyze their own situation more sharply, to reflect more deeply, and to reach a more complete understanding of how to deal with their problems:
- how do you understand the nature of that relationship?
- you have described what is happening, but what do you think the
  real, underlying, problem is?
- what are the possible causes of that?
- what are the other enquiries you should start to make now?
- which of the possible courses of action would be the best to take
  at this time?
- are there any conclusions we can draw from our discussion?

Such questions can be described as enabling (making possible) or facilitating (making easier) the thinking and understanding — and action — of the other person.

If questions are effective, and are used with skill and concern, they can even empower other people, and increase their self-reliance. In a community they can encourage divergent thinking and generate alternatives for the future. In these ways we can think of enabling questions as an instrument in the development process itself.

Choosing an open and enabling question, and asking it in an appropriate way, is a skill that comes with practice, listening and reflection. As you go through the course, be aware of the kinds of questions you are asking. You will certainly need to ask questions for your own benefit and to satisfy your own curiosity, but you can also ask questions which will help to deepen the learning within the course group, and will encourage other course members to take their own thinking to wider and deeper levels.

Finally, remember that, in order to use questions efficiently, you must also listen well. The two skills go together. You will not be able to choose useful and appropriate questions if you do not listen actively and effectively.

John Staley, *Enticing the Learning: Trainers in Development,* University of Birmingham, pages 378—381

What Do We Say? Our Responses to Others

▶ *Even though acceptance of others is the best method, in our practical life many times we blame or give advice to others.*

When we are in a professional role the kinds of response which we give to other people sometimes becomes habitual. When the task is a routine one, we may respond to others without giving either the task, or the people, much attention.

In our role as development worker, we may even be in the habit of making responses which are inappropriate to development, but without being aware of this. When we are working with vulnerable or powerless people, the way we respond, and what we say, can have more impact than we realize. One kind of response will confirm another person's powerlessness; a different response will challenge it. As development workers we should be aware of how we tend to respond to others, especially people in the community.

This is an exercise to raise awareness of the kind of response we tend to make. The purpose is to raise awareness rather than to diagnose behaviour.

Such an exercise has an artificial — and even facetious — quality, and it should not be taken too seriously. Nonetheless it is useful preparation for role plays, simulations and discussions. Members usually enjoy doing it. It also serves as an informal check for trainers on levels of awareness in the group.

The exercise is done individually, and then in small groups. It should be used after the course members have gained experience of the methodology and are working effectively together.

Part 1 can be given for individual preparation in advance. Discussing Part 2 in small groups of three or four takes at least half a session.

Objectives

- to raise awareness among members of their individual tendencies when responding to other people in professional work;

- to help members, as development workers, to consider whether the ways in which they habitually respond and reply to other people are appropriate to development.

▶ *... it was only after finishing the exercise I realized that sometimes I can judge, blame and criticise others; but most I listened to others and responded both to their words and feelings.*

▶ *The exercises were practical to our work back-home ... we found that most of us take the acceptance approach — as listeners, responding to other people's feelings which helps to encourage a person to say more and to explore the problem further.*

This exercise is to help us think about how we respond to other people, especially when they share a problem with us.

Consider each of the 15 situations below. How would you respond to what the other person says? Four possible responses are given; choose the one nearest to your natural response. If none of them fit at all, then write your own response opposite (e). When you have completed this, we will go on to Part 2.

1. Imagine that you are to chair a committee meeting one day. While you are waiting to start the meeting, a member you do not know well comes in and sits next to you. He/she says, 'I've had such trouble in getting here today. So many problems came up on the journey. Anyway I've made it!'

Which of the following responses are you most likely to make to him/her? Which would be the most 'natural' response for you to make?

a. ☐ 'Perhaps you could leave your office earlier when you are coming to a meeting here.'

b. ☐ 'Something really does need to be done about our transport system.'

c. ☐ 'Other people seem to manage to get here alright.'

d. ☐ 'It's good that you've got here! What problems did you have?'

e. ☐ Other (specify).

2. Imagine that you are in a small group in a training course and the moderator of your group says, 'There's a bit of a problem, because I can't understand the task the trainers want our group to do today.'

Which of the following responses do you think you are most likely to make?

a. ☐ 'Well, you are the moderator. It is really your responsibility.'

b. ☐ 'If it's important, the trainers should come and tell us what to do.'

c. ☐ 'Why not go and find the trainers and ask if they will explain it again?'

d. ☐ 'Would you like us to see if we can work it out together?'

e. ☐ Other (specify).

3. Imagine that you are visiting a community and a poor old woman there says to you: 'Life is miserable for our family now. My son has given up his job. My grandchildren are not getting enough to eat. My daughter-in-law is sick and

can't do any work.' Which is your most natural response?

a. ☐ 'The first thing is to take your daughter-in-law to the doctor, and the second is to tell your son to get another job.'

b. ☐ 'You must be wondering how you are going to manage. What do you think you can do now?'

c. ☐ 'Life must be miserable for you all! I hope someone will give your son another job soon.'

d. ☐ 'Why on earth did your son give up his job?'

e. ☐ Other (specify).

4. Imagine that you are employed as a trainer in a course. A trainee has been in the training group for three weeks. During a discussion with you he says: 'I don't know why it is, but I just don't feel as though I am one of the group. They are all nice enough people, but somehow they seem to have a closed circle and make me feel like an outsider. Maybe there is something wrong with me; I don't know.'

Which response would you be most likely to make?

a. ☐ 'Perhaps we should ask the Course Director to speak to the group about it.'

b. ☐ 'It seems to you that the group does not accept you. Do you see anything you can do to change that?'

c. ☐ 'Well, either you have made a mistake in coming on this course, or the other people have.'

d. ☐ 'Cheer up! I think you should just give them more time to realize that you are a nice person: then they will accept you.'

e. ☐ Other (specify).

5. You are the leader of a team of development workers. During an interview with you, a worker states: 'I don't want to work with R any more. He is lazy and is taking a superior attitude. He complains about the rest of us not helping him. He thinks he is too good for this kind of work. I am fed up with being in the same team as him.'

Which response are you most likely to make to the worker?

a. ☐ 'The Committee ought to discipline R.'

b. ☐ 'Do you know that R has a reputation for being unco-operative?'

c. ☐ 'Do you think R realizes the effect his attitudes are having on you? Have you talked to him?'

d. ☐ 'There are always problems like this when we work with other people. You should not be surprised if you have difficulties from time to time.'

e. ☐ Other (specify.)

6. You are at a conference. Someone you have met there says to you: 'Our organization has a lot of problems over planning, especially when the plans go to our Board for approval. Our local Pastor is Chairman of the Board.'

In which way are you most likely to respond?
a. ☐ 'That's what often seems to happen when pastors get involved.'
b. ☐ 'What you should do is to raise the matter with the Board itself.'
c. ☐ 'Does the Bishop know? Shouldn't he do something?'
d. ☐ 'What actually happens at the Board meetings?'
e. ☐ Other (specify).

7. A colleague, whom you don't know well, suddenly dashes into your office, gives you a big smile, and says: 'I'm feeling very happy. I spoke to someone about a problem and felt fully understood. I feel as though a big burden has been lifted from my shoulders. It is great!'

How will you respond to your colleague?
a. ☐ 'What was the problem? Perhaps I can help with the solution too.'
b. ☐ 'Hooray! You must be feeling wonderful!'
c. ☐ 'Please tell me who you spoke to, so that I can get that feeling too.'
d. ☐ 'Why do you let things become such big burdens?'
e. ☐ Other (specify).

8. You are attending a training course. During a group discussion one day a fellow-trainee remarks, 'I don't want to think about my work and my organization back home. It's all too painful.'

a. ☐ 'Would it help to discuss some of the painful things?'
b. ☐ 'Sooner or later we have to learn how to face painful things in our work.'
c. ☐ 'Well, we have all come here for training so that we will be more useful when we go back home.'
d. ☐ 'Don't you think your management will put things right soon?'
e. ☐ Other (specify).

9. You are the manager of a project. The work of a young male member of staff has fallen in quality, and there are complaints. He has been sent to you for an interview. On arriving he says, 'I don't know why I should be asked to talk to you about my work. I haven't complained, and I haven't time for this kind of chat. So tell me what you want to say and let me get back to my work.'

a. ☐ 'I would like you to tell me you how you think you are getting on. You have come to see me because you have been sent, and not because you feel any need to discuss matters.'

b. ☐ 'Some of the experienced senior people in the project should be able to help you deal with whatever is going wrong for you.'

c. ☐ 'You may not have complained yourself, but other people are complaining about you. How do you think they are feeling?'

d. ☐ 'I suggest you do not jump to conclusions. Often people need help even when they are not aware of the need.'

e. ☐ Other (specify).

10. You are acting as a consultant to a development organization. Your task is to help the organization improve its effectiveness. A manager in the organization mentions a problem of unsatisfactory staff meetings.

a. ☐ 'You should get some expert to come and tell you how you can improve the meetings.'

b. ☐ 'When there are repeated problems in meetings, it is usually due to the style of the chairperson.'

c. ☐ 'I suggest you prepare a report for the trustees on the quality of meetings in the organisation.'

d. ☐ 'Tell me more about what happens.'

e. ☐ Other (specify).

11. You are a development worker, and you go to meetings with the staff of other organizations. One day a worker from another organization, whom you do not know, sits next to you. After introducing himself, he tells you, 'I'm a bit out of touch with what's going on. I have been absent from my office a lot lately. To tell you the truth, I'm getting fed up with the job I have in my organization. Day in and day out, week after week, one month after another — it's getting me down. So I have been staying away, and I've missed some of these meetings.'

a. ☐ 'Perhaps you should ask for a transfer to another department?'

b. ☐ 'Have you discussed these feelings in your own organization?'

c. ☐ 'I suppose we must be thankful that at least we have jobs — so many people haven't got a job at all.'

d. ☐ 'It sounds as though the management ought to make some changes in your organization.'

e. ☐ Other (specify).

12. You took your vehicle for repair, The mechanic assured you that it would be ready by 5.30. At 5.30 it is not ready, and you are angry. The mechanic says: 'You are angry with me.'

a. ☐ 'Why are you so late? You promised it for 5.30. You have let me down.'

b. ☐ 'Next time I bring my vehicle you must plan the work. Then this won't happen again.'

c. ☐ 'Yes, I am angry. When will it be ready?'

d. ☐ 'People in this country don't know how to keep to time. They must be taught. Otherwise we shall never make progress.'

e. ☐ Other (specify).

13. One of your subordinates has been late for work three times in the last week. You ask why, and he replies, 'I just can't seem to get going in the morning. To be honest, I have lost my enthusiasm for the work. It just doesn't seem to interest me any more. And when I do get up, I have to rush to get here.'

a. ☐ 'Perhaps you should talk to a counsellor.'

b. ☐ 'It's rather unfair on the organization if staff come late.'

c. ☐ 'Can you say why you have lost your interest?'

d. ☐ 'Isn't it possible for you to go to bed earlier? Then you could get started earlier in the morning.'

e. ☐ Other (specify).

14. You are the head of a department. One of your workers, who was recently appointed, and has not made much progress with her work, tells you: 'I just can't seem to get started with this work. I can't get into the way of it. I try to find out what I should be doing, but no one has time to talk to me. The other workers all

seem to be too busy to explain things to me.'

a. ☐ 'It is never easy to start in a new job. Do you think you have been trying hard enough?'

b. ☐ 'Other people ought to be giving you more help. We could speak to someone about it.'

c. ☐ 'Well, I am sorry you haven't had more help. You had better make a plan and timetable for getting started, and then discuss it with the others.'

d. ☐ 'You feel you are being ignored. Is there something you can do about this yourself? Or would you like to discuss it further with me?'

e. ☐ Other (specify).

15. A colleague comes back from lunch smiling and says, 'I just saw a peacock in the garden outside. Oh, it was so beautiful. Such colour on his neck, and the tall feathers on his head! And while I was watching him he spread his tail.'

a. ☐ 'How beautiful it must have been!'

b. ☐ 'Peacocks are not so common. We ought to have more peacocks in the garden.'

c. ☐ 'The peacock is the male bird. Don't forget to look out for the female bird too. Remember gender equality!'

d. ☐ 'They say that peacocks are rather stupid birds.'

e. ☐ Other (specify).

Some situations suggested by Gopal Valecha, unpublished MS; and E.H. McGrath, *Basic Managerial Skills for All*, Prentice-Hall, New Delhi, pages 149—150

Circle your responses to the questionnaire in the table below. For example, in situation 1, if you chose (c), put a circle round the c in line 1 of the table

	I	II	III	IV	V
1	c	a	b	d	e
2	a	c	b	d	e
3	d	a	c	b	e
4	c	d	a	b	e
5	b	d	a	c	e
6	a	b	c	d	e
7	d	a	c	b	e
8	c	b	d	a	e
9	c	d	b	a	e
10	b	c	a	d	e
11	c	a	d	b	e
12	a	b	d	c	e
13	b	d	a	c	e
14	a	c	b	d	e
15	d	c	b	a	e
TOTALS					

Add up the number of responses circled in each column.

Notice how your score is distributed. Have you got a higher score in one or two columns than others? Then read the comments which follow.

After reading the comments, discuss your results with other members in small groups of three or four.

Blame

The answers listed in Column I are those which pass judgement on others, blame others, or criticize them. If you have a high score in this column you should ask yourself whether you have a tendency to blame others, and whether such a tendency helps you in your relationships and communication.

Generally it is not useful only to blame others, partly because it seldom leads to any change. By blaming other people, we avoid taking any responsibility for the situation or problem ourselves, and defend ourselves from having to take any action. If the other people are aware that we are blaming them, but do not accept that blame, they may become defensive, and even hostile. The result may be conflict. In any event nothing useful will be done about the situation or problem, either by them or by us.

Advice

The answers listed in Column II are those which give advice. The limitation of advice is that it comes from the experience of the advice-giver and not from the experience of the advice-receiver.

If you have scored high here, you should ask yourself if you have a tendency to give advice. If so, do you give more of it — and more often — than is useful and appropriate? Many development workers tend to give a great deal of advice, especially to the poor and powerless, who seldom find it relevant or useful.

However good our advice may be, and however well-meaning we may be as advisors, if the advice is not wanted — or not wanted at that time — it will not be useful. People may hear it passively and say 'yes, yes,' but that does not mean that they are accepting the advice, and even less that they will act on it. Advice which is given insistently may even be resented.

The best time to offer advice is when we are asked for it. Then we know that the other person is motivated to receive it and is ready to listen to it.

Looking Outside

The answers in Column III are general appeals to some person or group in authority and perhaps far away, saying they should do something to solve the problem. It is a defence which we use to save us from having to do something ourselves.

We make responses of this kind when we ourselves feel powerless, or when we feel trapped in a rigid hierarchy, or when we do not want to become more deeply involved. We take refuge in an attitude of dependence and, like children, try to push the problem onto some substitute for our parents. So we pass the problem on and upwards to another level in the hierarchy — whether it is the management, the trainers, the trustees, the bishop, the director, the Government, or even God — saying that they should do something.

Such responses often contain the words *should* or *ought*. Do you tend to use a lot of *shoulds* and *oughts*? Generally these tendencies do not lead to action. In fact the *shoulds* and *oughts* are not even passed up to the person or group being invoked. So nothing gets done at any level.

Acceptance

The answers in Column IV represent acceptance of what has been said. They suggest that you have listened to the other person, and are responding both to their words and also to their feelings. The other person is more likely to feel that he/she has been understood, and this will encourage him/her to say more.

Many of these responses are in the form of an enabling question. This helps the other person to explore the problem further, and perhaps to begin to recognize what he/she can do next.

Other

If you have written your own responses (Column V) you may be able to assess them for yourself in the light of these comments.

▶ *I realised that I need to be very cautious about how I interact with other people when I am asked to assist them. If not, I will steal their problem.*

This exercise demonstrates in a light-hearted way some of the difficulties, both of helping, and of being helped.[1] In particular it offers an experience of the delicate balance between offering help and taking control. It is so easy for us, as development workers, to slip from supporting other people into making them dependent.

The learning from the exercise can be related to entering a community and the expectations which that raises, to the role of the worker in the subsequent decision-making, to power and dependency, and to the ways in which aid is given and received.

The exercise is best used in the first half of a course while members are becoming aware of the issues of role and power in development and aid-giving.

Objectives

- to explore the process of helping and to examine the relationship between those who give help and those who receive it;
- to experience and identify issues in this relationship, such as effective and developmental ways of helping, and control and dependency;
- to encourage individuals to identify and reflect on some of their own tendencies in giving help, and their preferences in receiving help.

Materials

The exercise is done in pairs, sitting at tables. Each pair will need 20 wooden blocks or cubes of the kind sold as toys for small children. The blocks should be about 2 inches (5 cm) square on each side. The sides should be flat and smooth so that the blocks can be stacked above one another. Full matchboxes are a possible alternative. Each pair will also need a blindfold.

 Introducing the Exercise

■ Tell the group members to sit in pairs at the tables. Start by reminding them that simulations and exercises often take the form of games, and sometimes children's games.

In this exercise they are going to use children's building blocks.

1. The original version of this exercise, which focuses on expectations and targets, has been attributed to Udai Pareekh.

■ Tell them that in each pair there are two roles.[2] One is the person who has a task to perform or a job to do; he/she will be referred to as the Worker. The other is the Helper, whose role is to help the Worker with the task.

The task is to build a tower of blocks, as tall as possible, using single blocks placed one above the other. This may seem straightforward but, as in real life, there are constraints.

The constraints for the Worker are that he/she:
   cannot see — he/she will be blindfolded;
   cannot speak, and must remain silent throughout the exercise;
   must work with the left hand (or if left-handed, with the right hand).

The Helper may see and speak, but must not touch the blocks. (Do not suggest it, but if anyone asks you, the Helper *is* permitted to touch the wrist or hand of the Worker.)

Tell the group what is the average achievement, i.e. the average height of the tower which previous pairs have built.[3] Tell them that if the tower falls its height cannot be counted.

Ask for any clarifications, and then tell the Helpers to tie the blindfolds for their Workers.

When all are ready, tell them to begin. Check that they are following the rules. As the exercise proceeds much of what the Helpers say to the Workers falls into four categories.

● Warnings:
   'Gently!'
   'Don't knock it!'
   'It'll fall if you aren't careful.'
   'Not like that!'

● Directions (clear and unclear):
   'Move it 2cm to your right.'
   'Bring it down now, very slowly.'
   'Turn it the other way.'
   'Twist your hand and straighten the block.'

● Information:
   'The tower is ten blocks high now.'
   'That last block is not straight.'
   'There's a loose block lying to the left of your hand.'
   'There are five more blocks we can use.'

● Encouragement:
   'Well done!'
   'It's going up fine!'
   'You are doing well!'
   'Give your arm a rest before you do another — there's no hurry!'

---

2. A third possible role is that of Observer. This role is useful if the group is already practised in observing and in giving feedback.
3. This will depend on the blocks. For well-cut two inch blocks the average is 14.

■ Some Helpers may also 'take a hand'. The rules do not permit them to touch the blocks, but they can touch and guide the hand of the Worker. As the task becomes more difficult, some Helpers may help in this way, so that a taller tower can be built.

Some pairs may stop building at the average height you have given them. Others may go further, perhaps until the tower falls down.

As the pairs finish — usually after 15 or 20 minutes — ask them to remove the blindfold and then sit silently to watch those still working. When all have finished, or when you judge it is time to call a halt, ask the members to take a minute's break, to return the blocks to their boxes, but to remain sitting in their pairs.[4]

Helper, observer and worker

 Reflecting on the Exercise

Every pair will have had a somewhat different experience, so there will be a lot of information to deal with. Using a structure for the discussion will help to get the information into order, which will help the members to contribute and to learn.

4. If the blocks are left out on the tables some members are likely to go on building with them during the discussion, which is a distraction.

■ Begin by asking for any general reactions. This allows immediate concerns to be aired and strong feelings to be expressed.

Giving Help

Now tell the group that the first part of the discussion will be confined to the Helpers. The Workers are to remain silent and listen. Ask the Helpers to state how they helped:
    'What did you do?'
    'What kinds of help did you give?'
Much of what they report will fit the categories above. Help the group to distinguish the categories for reference later.

Encourage and explore any expression of feelings, such as frustration over the Worker's difficulties and not being able to help more, or anxiety over the greater speed or higher towers of other pairs.
    'What was it like to be helping? How did it feel?'
    'How do you feel about what was achieved? Are you satisfied?'
    'Did you feel that you were competing with the other pairs? What effect did this have on the way you tried to help?'

Receiving Help

Now tell the Helpers to listen in silence while the Workers speak:
    'What it was like to receive help? How did you feel in that situation?'
    'What kinds of help were you given?'
    'What kinds of help were most useful?' (Refer to the earlier categories.)
    'Was any kind of help not useful?'
    'What would you have liked your helper to do?'

Often the Workers' perspective is very different, which is a surprise — and even hurtful — to the Helpers. Workers may say that some kinds of help they received were not useful. Generally information, encouragement, and clear directions are appreciated, but warnings, unclear directions and 'taking a hand' are not.

Invite all members to reflect on their own tendencies when helping others, and their preferences when they are being helped.

Sometimes Workers say that they would have preferred silence from the Helper. This can lead into a discussion about the need for Helpers at all:
    'Could the Workers have performed the task on their own?'
    'How much could they have achieved?'

As the tower becomes higher the task becomes more difficult:
    'Is it only then that the Workers need help?'
    'Should the Workers stop building when it becomes difficult?'

Explore the quality of the helping relationship, as the Workers experienced it:
    'Did you feel in control of your task, or were you dependent on the Helper?'
    'When you stopped building, which of you had decided you should stop?'

■ 'Did anyone stop at 14 blocks? Did 'the average' become the target?'
'What do you feel about what was achieved?'
'Whose achievement was it?'
'What percentage was your achievement? What percentage the Helper's?'

If members avoid these last questions, and describe the work as a partnership or team-work or a 50—50% achievement, you should challenge them.

Go on to ask:
'How would you describe the relationship between you and the Helper?'
'Who had power in that situation?'
'Would you say it was a developmental relationship?'

If any Helpers took the hands of their Workers and guided them, you should help them explore that experience in terms of comfort (for whom?), control and dependency, achievement, and developmental quality.

The delicate balance between helping and taking control

Learning and Application

Some final questions for the whole group are:
'How does this experience relate to what we do as development workers?'
'Does the Helper have to make some of the same choices as the development worker?'
'Which kinds of helping are more useful?'
'Do I need to change my own style of helping?'
'Was the attention of the Helpers upon the Workers and their possibilities? Or was it on the blocks and getting the tower built?'

■ 'Was attention on the partner or on the task?'
'Where is my attention when I am working back home?'

'Was there some "competition" with other pairs? What effect did that have?
In my work back home do I compete with others?'

'What can we learn from this exercise, and how can we apply the learning?'

There may be a few members who do not easily recognize the parallels between the exercise and the practicalities of development work. You may need to elaborate on the similarities between the roles in the exercise and roles in the field.

▶ *During the exercise one could hear the crash of poorly-constructed towers smashing down upon the wooden tables when efforts failed. When success was achieved, applause rang out. Either way, laughter was spontaneous and indicated the enjoyment of the participants.*

▶ *Through the simulation we have realised the kind of relationship between the 'helper' and the 'helped' person. Sometimes for the sake of help we control people's creativity, wisdom and make them more vulnerable and dependent on us. If we are not aware, all of our good intentions may slip on controlling and instructing people.*

▶ *We were reminded how our haste to help, and our anxiety to achieve results, can so easily reduce other people to dependency — and underdevelopment. We talk of the people controlling their own development — but it was the helpers who were in control yesterday ...*

▶ *... those of us who would be expatriates in the developing world formed an inner circle. We discussed our attitude to our receiving countries, and they discussed their attitude to us. We then 'visited' and compared notes. By the end of the session we were all still friends — I think.*

The method which is described below can be used to share perceptions, and to give feedback, from one role to another role within the same system. It is particularly useful if perceptions and feedback are not normally shared. For example, it can be used to allow field staff to give feedback to head office staff within the same organization. It can be used to allow aid recipients to give feedback to donors. It can also be used to explore issues such as gender roles. The method is useful when roles come into conflict and the relationship between them is contentious.[1]

One of the opportunities of the DSC has been bringing together members from interacting roles in the voluntary aid system, but without the usual constraints of those relationships.[2] We have used the method to explore some of those relationships. In particular we have used it to explore the role of expatriates in voluntary agency and NGO development work. That example is used here to illustrate the method.

Such issues and the method itself belong to the later part of a course. By that time a course group should be ready to contain its differences, and to benefit from them. It should come after work on feedback (see page 330), and after Bafa-Bafa: Entering Another Culture (page 231) if that is used.

Most of a session will be needed.

Expatriates and Counterparts

In development work expatriates are individuals who undertake such work in a foreign country, usually in some expert capacity. Most expatriates come from another continent; but some may come from a neighbouring country, especially at times of conflict. Some may be refugees.

Counterparts are local development workers, nationals of the host country, who have the role of relating to an expatriate, and of working alongside him or her and learning from his/her expertise.

---

1. Other methods can be used, such as Image-Sharing. This is a well-known method for sharing perceptions, but it is more elaborate and more time-consuming, and can be intimidating. We did not often use it in the DSC, and it is not included here.

2. One of the constraints on learning within the voluntary aid system is hierarchy and control. When aid is given it is usually accompanied by reporting requirements and accounting procedures, and often by cultural assumptions and external values. These flow 'down' with the aid from donors to recipients, but most of the time — and despite so-called partnership — little flows back up again, and least of all feedback. Self-correcting mechanisms are therefore lacking, and so distortions arise. Eventually a crisis may erupt, the recipients' perceptions may suddenly be expressed — and the result is shock, pain and disappointment for the donors.

When the method is to be used with expatriates, the trainer identifies the course members who have the roles of expatriate and counterpart within the aid system. If there are members who relate to each other in their own roles back home, they should be allocated to separate small groups. There will also be members who have worked neither as expatriates nor as counterparts.

In many DS Courses it happened that in a group of 18—20 there were about six members who were working as expatriates, and there were often about six nationals of receiving countries with the role of counterpart back home. These numbers are assumed here for the sake of the description.

 ## Introducing the Method

The method starts with a questionnaire. In the present example this is about perceptions of the role of expatriates in development work (see page 401).

The purpose of a questionnaire is to provide a framework for discussion and to set some boundaries. It encourages members to think about roles rather than particular people, encourages them to be specific, and provides a basis on which they can share perceptions. At the same time it excludes the extreme or eccentric, and discourages the assertions and anecdotes and blame that may otherwise obscure the discussion. The questionnaire contains ready-prepared statements, but members can add their own statements.

■ Introduce the topic briefly. Distribute the questionnaire and ask all members to complete it individually. This takes 15—20 minutes.

Tell the expatriates to form a small group, representing the 'sending countries', in the centre of the room. Most course members accept such a separation according to back home roles, but if cohesion in the group is weak, or there is sensitivity over the roles, some may be reluctant. Trainers should be ready to offer support if necessary.

Divide the counterparts into three groups and ask these groups to sit towards the walls as 'receiving countries'. Tell the remaining members, who are not counterparts and perhaps have limited experience of work with expatriates, to make up the numbers in the three 'receiving country' groups.

Tell all members to work now in their small groups, to share their responses to the questionnaire and see how similar they are, and briefly to compare experience.

Allow up to 15 minutes.

Then tell the expatriates that they will shortly travel to 'the foreign country where they will be working'. Tell members of the receiving groups that they are about to 'receive expatriates to work with them'. Such pretences add humour and help to keep the mood light.

Divide the expatriates into three pairs and send them to the three counterpart groups.

■ The task in these combined groups is to inform those in the other role of the responses which have been shared in the original groups. Allow 10 minutes.

Now tell the expatriates that they 'are going on leave to their home country'. Ask them to return to their own group, and to share what they have been told in the counterpart groups. Ask the counterpart groups meanwhile to prepare some recommendations for improving the quality of the work of both roles. The expatriates will consider these recommendations 'when they return from their leave'. Allow 10 minutes.

Tell the expatriates to return to their 'host countries'. Ask them to listen to the counterparts' recommendations, and make a brief response. Then they should 'bid farewell' to their counterpart colleagues, return to their home country, and share the recommendations in their own group. Allow 15 minutes.

Finish the exercise here by asking all members to join the whole group, and inviting any final reflections and comments.

Alternatively, finish by asking each small group to prepare a statement, addressed to the other role, using the form of words:

'It would make our work easier if you ...'

Ask for a member of each counterpart group to make the group's statement directly to the expatriate group. Then ask the expatriate group to make their statement direct to the counterpart groups. Each statement should be heard by the whole group. Allow 10—15 minutes.

The issues are often contentious, and the method should be handled with care and with humour. Expatriates — and donors — are often unaware of the strong feelings their role excites. It is important to focus the discussion on role, rather than allow it to become an opportunity for complaint and blame directed at individuals.

When there are criticisms of a role some individuals may take exaggerated personal responsibility upon themselves for what are actually systemic or organizational difficulties. Trainers should be sensitive to this.

▶ *Is it true that the very presence of an expatriate in a community is power in itself? Does he consciously or unconsciously feel that he is superior to the 3rd World? Are those feelings the remains of the past colonialists? These were some of the questions raised by the group ...*

▶ *... we must accept the fact that expatriates are individuals, and it is not fair to generalise or compare him/her with a past experience or to another person.*

▶ *We found out that our own perception of ourselves differed from how the others see expatriates. In the small group where M and myself were sent, it was said that expatriates are representatives of the interests of the donors who give confidence to the donors that the money is well used. They don't speak out about injustice and oppression, they do not give enough importance to local culture, and they don't promote solidarity. I have to listen carefully to all this, although it hurts me.*

▶ *J's questionnaire produced an awful lot of thought among us potential expats. Trying to separate what our experience told us was the actual role of expatriates, and what our hearts/minds told us should be the role of expatriates was incredibly difficult. Finally we came to some agreement, before being dispatched to talk to groups of nationals to discover their views, which I would have to report as various! Some didn't want expatriates at all, or would tolerate them to keep donors happy, while others would accept them for certain tasks and provided the expats obeyed certain rules.*

... The afternoon finished on a positive note with statements from the groups of nationals and expatriates — although all were slightly different, a central theme was the importance of listening, learning and understanding.

Questionnaire: The Roles of Expatriates

In your own experience, or from your own observations and understanding, what are the main roles that expatriates are most commonly playing in the development programmes of NGOs in the 'third world'?

Please note that the question is about the expatriates who go to work with voluntary agencies, NGOs, Churches, etc. We are not concerned here with expatriates working for other organizations such as the UN, governments or commercial companies.

Sixteen statements follow about the roles that such NGO expatriates may be playing.

You may add more statements if you wish.

Please mark five statements which, in your experience or from your observations and understanding, reflect most accurately the roles that expatriates are playing.

Then please mark two of the statements which, in your experience, they are *not* playing.

- ☐ a. representing the interests of foreign donor agencies
- ☐ b. providing additional commitment and motivation for change
- ☐ c. exercising power and influence which they might not have at home
- ☐ d. exercising leadership and management skills where these are needed
- ☐ e. providing technical expertise and services where these are lacking
- ☐ f. introducing ideas and practices not previously known locally
- ☐ g. using their access to aid to get things done
- ☐ h. contributing different perceptions and values to local decision-making

- [ ] i. informing people in 'the North' about the problems and perceptions of people in 'developing countries'

- [ ] j. speaking out about situations of injustice and oppression

- [ ] k. giving confidence to donors that their money is being well used

- [ ] l. enjoying a higher standard of living than in comparable work at home

- [ ] m. supporting the work of local colleagues through training, advice and discussion

- [ ] n. facilitating local groups to meet their own goals

- [ ] o. giving importance to local culture and values, and seeking ways to strengthen and preserve these

- [ ] p. promoting international contact, understanding and solidarity

- [ ]

- [ ]

- [ ]

John Staley, *Enticing the Learning: Trainers in Development*, University of Birmingham, pages 401—402

10.5 Questions about Leadership

A questionnaire is a convenient way to introduce a large topic such as leadership. It can help to turn members' minds towards the topic, and gives them an opportunity to clarify and compare their existing ideas. It can also help members to become more aware of their usual assumptions, and begins the process of challenging some of these.

The questionnaire which follows contains 24 statements about the effectiveness of those who become leaders in the context of development work. It can be used as a starting point for the topic, but should be followed up by further work such as Leadership: Which Style To Use? (page 416).

Objectives

- to introduce the topic of leadership in development work;
- to raise issues about the role of leader and aspects of leadership;
- to provide an opportunity for members to share experience and discuss their assumptions and preferences in relation to leadership.

Using the Questionnaire

■ Distribute the questionnaire Effective Leaders (see pages 404—406) to each member and ask them to complete it individually without discussion. This may take 15—20 minutes.

Then tell the members to form small groups of three or four. If there are colleagues from the same organization ask them to join different groups.

Tell the groups to work through the questionnaire, sharing their individual responses in their group and explaining their reasons.

The task is not to reach consensus, but to uncover differing assumptions and ideas. The discussion may take 20 minutes.

Bring the work back into the whole group, and take up any statement in the questionnaire that you want to emphasize, or which members want to discuss further. Some of the statements are deliberately ambiguous.

Remember that the purpose is to stimulate thinking rather than to reach conclusions. As far as possible avoid repeating the discussions which have already taken place in the small groups. The whole procedure may take 45—60 minutes.

All of us have some basic ideas and assumptions about leaders and leadership. Below are 24 statements about the effectiveness of those who become leaders. Think about the statements and indicate whether you agree or disagree with them. Add comments if you wish.

	Agree	Disagree	Comments
1. An effective leader sees the strengths and weaknesses of individual members of the group or team.	☐	☐	
2. An effective leader treats each member of the group or team in the same way.	☐	☐	
3. An effective leader varies his or her use of authority according to the group and situation.	☐	☐	
4. An effective leader thinks of duties and activities, not of objectives and results.	☐	☐	
5. An effective leader makes a distinction between doing things in the 'right way' and choosing the 'right things' to do.	☐	☐	
6. Effective leaders are people who are born with special personal abilities.	☐	☐	
7. An effective leader must have an impressive appearance.	☐	☐	
8. An effective leader can always 'put on an act', or pretend, in order to convince other people.	☐	☐	
9. Effective leaders can be discovered, but they cannot be developed.	☐	☐	
10. An effective leader must be able to control other people.	☐	☐	

	Agree	Disagree	Comments

11. An effective leader makes sure that he or she is popular with other members of the group ☐ ☐

12. An effective leader realises that people have mixed feelings towards authority; i.e. they both like it and do not like it. ☐ ☐

13. Effective leaders tend to smooth over or avoid conflict. ☐ ☐

14. An effective leader encourages honest disagreement in order to find better solutions. ☐ ☐

15. An effective leader is careful never to make mistakes, and never allows other members of the group to make mistakes. ☐ ☐

16. An effective leader gives importance to humour, and uses it to keep a sense of perspective when the group is struggling with a problem. ☐ ☐

17. An effective leader considers the members of the team, and their potential and growth, to be more important than materials or money. ☐ ☐

18. Besides the authority of his/her position an effective leader tries to develop other forms of influence, i.e. personality, competence and skills. ☐ ☐

19. An effective leader is one who usually gets whatever he or she wants in a group discussion. ☐ ☐

20. Effective leaders make clear the values they believe in. They act on these values, and stand up for them whenever necessary. ☐ ☐

21. An effective leader uses his/her authority or influence within a group to help it achieve its goals. ☐ ☐

22. An effective leader is sensitive both to group and individual needs, as well as to the demands of the task and the situation. ☐ ☐

23. Someone who is an effective leader in one situation will be an effective leader in all situations. ☐ ☐

24. An effective leader should sometimes become an effective follower. ☐ ☐

Based on E. H. McGrath, *Basic Leadership Skills*, XLRI, pages 88—89; A. J. Britto, *Leadership Quiz*, HODCONTS; and other sources

Pins & Straws: Experience of Leadership Styles

▶ *I come from an authoritarian tradition, and I am reflecting deeply upon the way in which I should exercise my leadership role in future.*

This simulation gives small groups experience of different styles of leadership.[1] The principal styles are authoritarian and democratic. Others are laissez-faire and/or bureaucratic. The discussion afterwards reveals the consequences of each style and compares them, enabling members to reflect on how appropriate they are for development work.

Members work in groups of four to seven. All groups have the same task of making a construction out of pins and straws. One member of each group is invited beforehand to take on the role of leader. He or she is given instructions for a particular style of leadership and is asked to behave accordingly. Other members of the group are 'themselves'. During the simulation they respond to the style of leadership in their group, and work at the task, according to the impact the leadership is having on them.

The simulation is appropriate for the second half of a course, by which time a course group should be able to contain any strong reactions. It requires at least two consecutive sessions. It is generally enjoyed and appreciated.

If four or more sessions are allocated to the topic of leadership, a useful sequence is:

1. Questions about Leadership (page 403), followed by the material under the subheadings Ideas about Leadership and Functional Leadership (pages 417—418). One session.

2. This simulation and the reflection afterwards. Two sessions.

3. The material under the sub-headings Styles of Leadership, and Choosing the Appropriate Style (pages 418—421). One session.

Objectives

- to demonstrate and dramatize different styles of leadership;

- to explore the effect of different styles of leadership on the motivation, participation and behaviour of followers;

- to explore the effect of different styles of leadership on the performance of the task, both the amount of work achieved and the quality of the work;

- to consider the suitability of different styles of leadership for development work.

---

1. An early version of this simulation is given by J William Pfeiffer and John E Jones, 'Pins and Straws: Leadership Styles', *A Handbook of Structured Experiences for Human Relations Training*, Volume V, University Associates Press, Iowa, pages 78—84.

Preparation

Small Groups and Their Leaders

The principal styles to be demonstrated are authoritarian and democratic. Laissez-faire can also be included, but this style is seldom seen in development work. The bureaucratic style is seen in some kinds of development work and can be used as a third style. If numbers permit, all four styles can be demonstrated. So course members work in three or four small groups, each with four to seven members, including the leader.

The success of this simulation depends partly on the trainer's choice of the individuals who will act as leaders and demonstrate the styles. Not every member will be able to take on such a role, act it out according to the instructions given, and if necessary hold on to the role under pressure from other members of the small group.

Beware of 'typecasting'. For example, if there is a member whose habitual style is recognized in the course group as strongly authoritarian, that member should not necessarily be invited to act as the authoritarian leader. Instead another member with a different habitual style, but who will be able to assume the authoritarian role and demonstrate it effectively, may be invited. The simulation is an opportunity for the leaders to behave in ways they would not normally do. The invitations to act as leaders should be made — and accepted — before the session, and their instructions given in advance so that they can prepare themselves. The remaining members, who will become the followers, can be allocated to the small groups in advance or chosen at random at the time.

Rooms

For the first session, during the simulation itself, each group will require a separate room with a table to work on. The rooms can be arranged beforehand to help 'set the scene' for a particular style. For example, notices such as NO TALKING and NO IDLING can be put up in the authoritarian leader's room, and the leader can be given a desk and a special chair from which he/she can oversee and supervise. In the democratic leader's room all the chairs can be arranged round the table, and there can be some shared facilities, such as a jug of water and glasses. For the bureaucratic style some RULES AND REGULATIONS can be put up on the wall to inform members, for example, that if they want to leave the room (perhaps to go to the toilet) they must submit a written application and so on. Such preparations may seem frivolous, but they reinforce members' experience in the simulation, and they can be fun in themselves.

Materials

The materials recommended are drinking straws and tailor's pins, which are cheap and readily available in many parts of the world. Each small group should have 100 straws and 100 pins. If necessary, other materials suited to the task could be used instead.

Instructing the Leaders

The instructions for the leaders describe the behaviour required, but do not identify the style. They follow below in the order Authoritarian, Democratic, Laissez-faire and Bureaucratic. The Rules and Regulations belong with the Bureaucratic Style. Each member of that small group should be given a copy of these Rules and Regulations.

PLEASE DO NOT SHOW THESE INSTRUCTIONS TO ANYONE ELSE

Instructions for Leader

1. Your job is to be the leader in your group. Use the style of leadership described below without informing the group members of what you are doing.

2. The task is to build a construction out of straws and pins. Constructions will be judged after the exercise for height, strength and beauty.

3. The construction is to be built entirely according to your ideas.

4. Do not confuse the members of your group by telling them your ideas, or giving them information about how the finished construction will be. Simply give them their tasks and orders. Do not accept any suggestions, nor allow them to choose what to do; that will only lead to complications and difficulties.

5. Do not allow the members to waste time talking to each other. If they have anything to say they can speak directly to you.

6. Remain somewhat separate from the group. Do not mix with the members too much, and do not join in the work yourself. Your job is to control everything. You can give praise or blame to individuals according to how well you feel they are following your instructions.

7. When you join your group members you should tell them that you have been appointed as their leader.

PLEASE DO NOT SHOW THESE INSTRUCTIONS TO ANYONE ELSE

Instructions for Leader

1. Your job is to be the leader in your group. Use the style of leadership described below without informing the group members of what you are doing.

2. The task is to build a construction out of straws and pins. Constructions will be judged after the exercise for height, strength and beauty.

3. The construction is to be the product of the thinking and work of the whole group.

4. You should encourage a complete discussion of the task and of how the work is to be divided between the members. As far as possible you should allow the members to choose how the work is to be divided and what each will do.

5. During discussion you should act as a moderator. When any suggestion is made, you should take it seriously, and find out how far other people agree with it. You should encourage the group to reach a consensus before decisions are made.

6. You should encourage the members to talk with each other while they are working, and should join in the work yourself. You can give praise and criticism according to the way the group as a whole has agreed to set about the task.

7. When you join your group members you should tell them that you have been appointed as their leader.

PLEASE DO NOT SHOW THESE INSTRUCTIONS TO ANYONE ELSE

Instructions for Leader

1. Your job is to be the leader in your group. Use the style of leadership described below without informing the group members of what you are doing.

2. The task is to build a construction out of straws and pins. Constructions will be judged after the exercise for height, strength and beauty.

3. The construction can be the result of the members' individual creativity and work.

4. You should inform group members of the task, and give them the pins and straws, but you should not direct the group in any way, nor try to help them in deciding how to set about the task.

5. Avoid making any suggestions about what is to be done, how it is to be done, or who is to do it. Leave the members free to experiment with whatever ideas seem best to them. Let each of them decide what they will do. There is no need to praise or criticize anyone's work.

6. If members prefer to work individually and separately on the task, and each make his or her own structure, that is up to them.

7. When you join your group members you can tell them that you have been appointed as their leader; but you should not call them together nor organize them in any way.

PLEASE DO NOT SHOW THESE INSTRUCTIONS TO ANYONE ELSE

Instructions for Leader

1. Your job is to be the leader in your group. Use the style of leadership described below without informing the group members of what you are doing.

2. The task is to build a construction out of straws and pins. Constructions will be judged after the exercise for height, strength and beauty.

3. The construction is to be built according to the division of work which is specified, and the rules and regulations which are given.

4. You should inform the group members of the task, and supervise the appointments specified. Make sure that they all read and sign the rules and regulations.

5. Your job is to see that appointments are made, that the rules and regulations are observed, and that everything is done in an orderly and systematic way. If there are any questions you are not certain about, you should refer them in writing to a higher authority.

6. You can praise and criticize individuals according to how well they perform the particular jobs they are appointed to do; and how well they observe the rules and regulations.

7. When you join your group members you should tell them that you have been appointed as their leader.

Rules and Regulations

1. The oldest person in the group (apart from the leader) must be appointed to design the construction.

2. The two youngest people in the group must be appointed to make the construction.

3. One person must be appointed to maintain the stocks of straws and pins.

4. All straws used must be equal in length.

5. Straws must not be bent or creased in any way.

6. The pinning of straws must be done at the furthest ends of the straws.

7. Each joint must be strengthened with extra pins.

8. If straws are pinned together, straws of a related colour must be used.

9. It is the responsibility of the leader to see that these rules and regulations are observed.

 Introducing the Simulation

■ Tell members that the simulation will provide them with an experience of leadership. Explain that they will be working in small groups in separate rooms, and that the leader for each group has been appointed. They should think of the leaders as managers or bosses, and of themselves as followers or subordinates.

Tell them that the task will be given to them by their leader, and he or she will also tell them about the resources and time available.

Split the course group and ask the followers to go to their rooms and wait for their leader.

■ Check with the leaders that they have understood their instructions and are clear about what they have to do.

Inform the leaders that when you visit the groups you will reinforce their style by adopting that style yourself.

Inform the leaders of the time limits, give them the pins and straws for their groups and ask them to start work. Wish them luck!

Introducing the simulation, dividing the whole group, and checking with the leaders may take 15 minutes. Allow 45 minutes for the simulation itself.

Conducting the Simulation

The leaders of the small groups should follow their instructions and be responsible for the work of the small groups during the simulation itself.

Your task is to visit the groups from time to time, and to reinforce the leader's role and style by acting in the same style yourself. For example, adopt an authoritarian style towards the authoritarian leader and speak only to him/her; whereas you might talk with both leader and followers in the democratic group.

At the end of the simulation ask each group to bring their constructions back to the course room. The democratic group often requests extra time, so if a whole session is available this allows a little flexibility.

A break at this point also makes it easier for groups to finish at different times.

Any time remaining in the session can be used to compare the constructions made in the small groups.

 ## Conducting the Reflection

Ask the members to sit in their small groups with their leaders. Start by thanking the leaders for having taken on their roles. Explain that each small group has had a different experience, so the first part of the reflection will be in the small groups.

However before the groups begin their discussions you should explain the differences in the leaders' instructions. Read paragraphs 1, 2 and 7 of the leaders' instructions to the whole group. Point out that the task was exactly the same for each group and that each had the same materials. The difference was in the way the leader was asked to behave. Ask each of the leaders to read out to the whole group paragraphs 3—6 of their instructions.

If feelings have run high during the simulation it is important that members recognize that the leaders were acting according to instructions.

Distribute the questions for small group discussion (see page 415), and ask the groups to work through these on their own for about 30 minutes.

	Authoritarian	Democratic	Laissez-Faire	Bureaucratic
Behaviour of leader: what did he/she do? Not do?				
Effect upon followers: their feelings, motivation, behaviour, satisfaction?				
Performance of task: amount and quality of work completed?				

■ Then ask for one member of each small group to summarize their discussion on the board, using a column in a table such as the one above.

A table allows members to quickly grasp the experience of the other small groups, and provides a summary of the outcome of the simulation. The alternative is to ask each small group to produce a poster using the sub-headings.

Allow time at the end for members to exchange questions between the small groups and between leaders and followers. Ask which style made best use of the members' resources and skills? Which style produced the 'best' construction?

Conclude by pointing out that each style is appropriate in some circumstances. Ask the members which style they think is generally appropriate for development work? Invite them to reflect on how this relates to their own styles of leadership in their work back home.

Authoritarian Style

▶ *When five members of our group settled in a room, our 'appointed' leader entered. Two of us stood up and showed respect towards him. But the reaction was cold and followed by strong orders mentioning the task. No request, no co-operation, no questions from members and no smile on the face! Then the struggle started. After starting with polite suggestions, the discussion ended with strong arguments and finally non-cooperation and strike! With this authoritarian leadership I don't have to explain what happened to the task ...*

▶ *In the exercise I was under By, who was demonstrating authoritarian leadership. It was awful. I really got upset and irritated by the way he treated us ... I had to tell him afterwards that I was glad that I knew him from before. I know that By wouldn't act like this in real life. But from being in his group, I learnt how insecure I felt and how passive I became in just following orders.*

▶ *When I used my Authoritarian style upon my group ... my group felt that they did not have any motivation, and they concluded that this kind of leader is not good for development work.*

▶ *Maybe this style is good for situations of emergency where the people don't have time for discussion.*

Democratic Style

▶ *In the second group the leader informed the instructions informally, became friendly, co-operative and also a part of the group, so that the climate in the group was more open. The members seemed to be satisfied about their task due to democratic style of leadership.*

▶ *Our task was to construct a tower or building with the pins and straws. We spent a lot of time in the beginning but finally the building had beauty, height and strength ... people felt included ...*

▶ *The group in room 212B reported a democratic style — they were satisfied, and it allowed them to be creative and effective in development work.*

Bureaucratic Style

▶ *... our group was Bureaucratic, or 'everyone must follow the rules'. At first it was quite nice to do exactly as I was told, but after a while the rules seemed to become more important than our task. Everybody was very eager to obey and that really provoked me ... in my work I am usually rather obedient and quiet. It made me very happy that it was possible to try another behaviour, to see myself from another side in this secure atmosphere where we know and trust each other.*

▶ *The group in room 208B reported a Bureaucratic style, rigid and not useful in development.*

▶ *This style of leadership is good for accounts and records, but not for development organizations.*

Laissez-Faire Style

▶ *C was our leader. He just asked us to make a structure. But he did not order us ... He did not tell us anything about what kind of structure he wanted us to make. When I asked him if he is ready to accept any kind of structure that we make his answer was yes. At that moment I take him as leader by designation only ...*

▶ *The third group, laissez-faire, had no specific direction, and the question arose whether they really were a group ...*

In Conclusion

▶ *It was good to see that different styles are needed in different situations ...*

Questions for Discussion: Experience of Leadership Styles

Discuss your own and your small group's experience, using the following questions as guidelines.

At the end of the time allotted (approximately 30 minutes) please be ready to record your group's main observations and responses under the three sub-headings.

The Leader

— how did the leader inform the members about the task?

— how did he or she behave towards the members?

— how was the work divided up?

— how were decisions made?

— what difference would the leader's absence make to the achievement of the task?

The Members

— how was the members' behaviour affected by the leader's behaviour?

— how satisfied were members with their own participation?

— how did they feel about the style of leadership being used?

— how did they relate to each other?

— what was the climate of the group?

The Task

— how much work was done?

— what was the quality of the work?

— how did the members feel about doing the task?

— how much satisfaction do they feel about what they achieved?

— did anyone give praise or blame for the work done? On what basis?

— what are the advantages and disadvantages of this style of leadership?

John Staley, *Enticing the Learning. Trainers in Development,* University of Birmingham, page 415

Leadership: Which Style to Use?

▶ *We came back to styles of leadership, with the concern about meeting the people, and concern with the task and getting the work done. Which is more important to us? Is it the task? Or peoples' feelings, thoughts and the human aspects? To me it is a very difficult question ...*

Leadership is one of the central issues in development work. Development workers are in leadership roles, and how they practise their leadership affects the process and prospects of development. Success and failure in development programmes are often due to the quality of leadership, both in organizations and in communities.

Leadership is a huge subject, with a vast literature. New theories are constantly appearing, many of which are little help in day-to-day practice. In a training course it is necessary to narrow the subject down, and to use an approach which course members can apply to themselves and their work.

It is also a vexed matter. Myths and misconceptions abound, complicated by differing cultural expectations. One of the advantages of studying experientially is that some preconceived ideas can be discarded.

If four sessions are allocated to the topic of leadership, a useful sequence of material and events is:

1. An introductory questionnaire (see Questions about Leadership, page 403); followed by the material under the sub-headings Ideas about Leadership and Functional Leadership (pages 417—418). This makes up one session.

2. The simulation Pins and Straws (page 407). This requires two sessions.

3. The material under the remaining sub-headings, Styles of Leadership and Choosing the Appropriate Style (pages 418—421). This requires one session.

Objectives

- to raise the issue of leadership in development work, including functional leadership;

- to experience and recognize functional leadership and its importance in informal situations;

- to consider alternative styles of formal leadership and their suitability for development work;

- to encourage course members to reflect on their own preference, style and practice;

- to encourage course members to make their own leadership more effective and more appropriate for development work.

Ideas about Leadership

■ Introduce further ideas about leadership to the group, drawing on the first three paragraphs above and the following points.

- There is confusion and controversy in development organizations about leadership and what is appropriate for development work.

- Each of us has our own ideas and assumptions. How we understand the role of leader will be affected by our culture, our training, our organization, our boss, and even the management fashion of the moment.

- Our individual ideas will also be influenced by the kind of leadership we experienced in our own families when we were children. (At a suitable moment the trainer can ask members to speak briefly to their neighbour about the 'leadership style' of their own parents or older siblings and other adults in their families.)

- We also have personal preferences. Some kinds of personality are comfortable with hierarchy and the clear exercise of authority. Others are comfortable with more individual independence, or with more inclusion and consultation.

- Our ideas about leadership are formed in particular situations. Inherited leadership is common in a traditional clan or tribal structure. Elected leaders may seem more appropriate in mixed urban communities. Our ideas may change as the society we live in changes.

- Our ideas about leadership also change with the needs of the moment. For example, during a period of national crisis we want strong leaders, whereas during a period of peace we want leaders to be more accountable.

- There is an old saying, 'Leaders are born, not made'. This suggests that we must have a certain kind of personality to become a leader, and that leadership is a gift that cannot be learned. Research into leadership does not support such assumptions.

- The research does not reveal a clear pattern of personal traits in those who become leaders. Leaders generally have self-confidence, energy and intelligence, but many people who have these qualities do not become leaders.

- When we study leadership, we must give attention to those who are being led. The followers — staff, subordinates, members — should be taken into account as much as the leader.

■ After introducing these ideas, invite comments and discussion before going on to a discussion about functional leadership.

Functional Leadership

■ Introduce the idea of functional leadership, and give importance to it. This may be a new idea to some members, while others may tend to dismiss the 'informal' as insignificant, and give importance only to designated leaders who have been appointed or formally chosen in some way. Draw on the following points.

- In small and informal groups, where no one is designated as the leader, we can observe leadership as a 'function'. This function gets passed around, from one person to another, according to the current needs of the group, the task to be performed, and the skills, experience and inclinations of individuals in the group. One person may lead during work on the task, another may lead when the group is dealing with the outside world, another when technical skills are needed, and yet another when the group's social life is concerned.

- Much day-to-day leadership among human beings is of this informal, undesignated and functional kind. The leadership in many social situations, among friends, in a training group, between colleagues at the same level, or within a family or community, is usually of this kind.

- Members need to be aware of such functional leadership in any interactions with other people, and especially when they are working in the community. The way that leadership is exercised in the community, both formal and informal, will determine the prospects for development there.

■ Some members may be steeped in the assumption that only designated leadership has to be considered. Others may accept the idea of functional leadership, but not recognize it in practice.

Functional leadership can be made more clear and concrete to members by referring to the life of the training group. At a suitable moment ask members to identify examples of such leadership in the life of their own group.

Styles of Leadership

However most members work for much of their time in established organizations or institutions. Then leadership is formal and established, and the individual is given a designation, for example, director, supervisor, team-leader or manager. In that situation it is helpful to think about styles of leadership.

The simulation Pins and Straws: Experience of Leadership Styles (page 407) demonstrates three or four styles of leadership and members are able to experience these directly. The simulation allows members not only to understand the styles in action, but to observe how each affects the group being led, and how that affects achievement of the task. Members come to their own conclusions about how appropriate each style is for development work.

The material below follows on from the simulation, but can be used without it.

■ Explain to members that three styles of leadership can be seen as a continuum of the the use of authority:

Authoritarian ——— Democratic ——— Laissez-Faire

The Authoritarian Style is one where all the authority is held and used by the leader:
  'You do what I say.'

In the Democratic Style the leader shares authority with the followers:
  'Let's decide together about what we are going to do.'

In the Laissez-Faire Style the leader exercises very little authority and hardly leads the followers at all:
  'You do whatever you like.'

This style is useful in some spheres, but is rare in development organizations and is not considered in detail here.[1]

Elaborate briefly on the two principal styles as follows:

● The Authoritarian Leader

  makes the decisions;

  gives orders to the followers/subordinates/members;

  controls their work;

  does not allow them any choices;

  communication is one-way, downwards, from the leader;

  the leader evaluates the work of followers by his/her own standards, giving mostly criticism and blame.

● The Democratic Leader

  involves the followers in decisions, using consultation, consensus etc;

  allows the followers to make choices and to control their own work;

  encourages team-building and trust within the group;

  gives praise or criticism according to shared standards;

  communication is two-way, down and up, and is open.

Alternative Styles

These two styles, and the contrast between them, may raise doubts and questions for those in leadership roles:

  'How do I choose between being directive and being democratic?'

---

1. The simulation may also have included the Bureaucratic Style. This can be regarded as a 'depersonalized' Authoritarian Style. It is not dealt with here.

'I must get the work done, but I want everyone to be consulted ...'

'I want others to participate in the decision-making, but time is limited ...'

'If I make decisions it is less work for me, but if we discuss decisions we get better results ...'

'I do want to be democratic with my followers, but I must keep control ...'

'Do I have to choose between authoritarian and democratic?'

■ Discuss this kind of tension with the course members. Ask if it seems familiar from their own work back home.

Distribute the handout Appropriate Styles of Leadership (page 422) and use it to show that there are intermediate positions between authoritarian and democratic.

No one style is going to be appropriate for every situation, every group and every task. We should not expect to be able to choose a particular style and then always stick to that. Emphasize that the most effective leaders vary their style, using different styles at different times, and choosing the style which is appropriate.

Go through the handout with the members. Suggest that if we could go further to the left, beyond the diagram, we would reach dictatorship. If we could go beyond the diagram to the right, beyond laissez-faire, we would reach abdication. Either extreme seems a violation of responsible leadership.

Show how, as the leader moves further along the scale from a fully authoritarian style towards a more democratic one, he or she makes the decisions but is allowing the followers increasing influence over those decisions.

Then show how a point is reached where the leader no longer announces the decision, but begins to share the problem with the followers, inviting them to find solutions. Even then the leader may continue to control the boundaries and limits. A fully democratic style, where the leader becomes one of the group, is rare in formal organizations. An example of that style being used in a community is given in the discussion paper, Fisherwomen and Participation (page 223).

Emphasize that every style and every intermediate position has its usefulness. Even the fully authoritarian style may be appropriate in a crisis.

Ask members for examples of the styles and the intermediate positions from their own experience back home and from within the course.

Choosing the Appropriate Style

The most effective leaders can vary their style, can use different styles in different circumstances, and can choose the style which is most appropriate.

As leaders ourselves we should also be flexible. We should be able to move up and down the scale, and choose a position that is:

a) feasible for us personally;

b) appropriate for the group, followers or subordinates involved;

c) suited to the task that has to be done, and the situation we are working in;

d) compatible with the process of development.

■ Distribute the handout, Choosing a Leadership Style Within An Organization (page 423). This indicates some of the factors and forces we must take into account when we choose a leadership style. Tell members to work through the handout, either in the session or overnight, and to think about their answers to the questions.

Then ask them to work in groups of three, and to share their thoughts on the first part.

Suggest that it is the democratic style which supports development. This is usually the members' own conclusion after the simulation. Development workers must be able to lead with a democratic style if they are to be effective in promoting development.

Even within a formal organization the democratic style has advantages. The research shows that as we move towards this style:

● there is an increase in the commitment of subordinates to their work;

● they find it easier to accept change in the organization;

● the quality of decision-making in the organization improves;

● teamwork and morale are improved;

● there is growth in the group and in individuals;

● there is growth in the leadership potential of others.

All of this is 'developmental'.

Conclude by raising some questions for members to reflect upon:

'Do you tend to rely on one style of leadership only?'

'Can you become more flexible, and vary your style more?'

'Can you be democratic for most of the time, but directive if required?'

'Can you strengthen your democratic and developmental style?'

▶ *We always look at a leader as somebody who lords it over others: they are ahead and others, the led, follow. But in examining informal functional leadership I found that any kind of positive initiative that a person takes is an act of leadership. My experience of this kind of leadership is that it does provide a challenge to those whose assumption is that they are born to lead, and others must follow. The fact that other people can also be leaders can be very dislodging to us when we understand leadership as dominance and control of others.*

▶ *Sometimes the real leader is the one who has the courage to ask that 'stupid question' that nobody else dares to raise.*

▶ *I now realize that in the past I have done my work in an extremely authoritarian style. I have not been able to trust people. Now I have discovered a new way of looking at people. When I go back home I realize I must decrease my power, and no longer claim the last word on every occasion. Only in this way can the people around me develop for themselves.*

Guidelines: Appropriate Styles of Leadership

GREATER USE OF AUTHORITY BY LEADER OR MANAGER

GREATER SHARING OF AUTHORITY BY FOLLOWERS OR SUBORDINATES

Authoritarian Leadership

Democratic Leadership

Laissez-Faire Leadership

| Leader makes decision, announces decision, and gives orders to followers | Leader makes decision, explains reasons, and persuades followers to accept decision | Leader presents own ideas, invites advice and questions, then makes decision | Leader proposes a possible decision to followers, but is willing to change that decision | Leader presents the task or problem, collects suggestions from followers, then makes decision | Leader presents the task or problem, defines limits, and joins followers to make decision together | Leader participates as a member of group, group sets its own limits, and makes decision |

Adapted from Robert Tannenbaum and Warren H. Schmidt, *How To Choose A Leadership Pattern*, Page 3

How effective a style of leadership is will depend on the other people with whom it is used, and the situation in which it is used.

An effective leader is able to choose and use a style which is appropriate, both to the followers or subordinates concerned, and to the particular situation.

At the same time, we each have our individual preference for a style of leadership which we are generally comfortable with.

So in deciding 'how to manage', and which leadership style to use, you should think about three sets of factors or forces:

- the forces you recognize in yourself, and your own individual preferences, as the leader or manager;
- the forces which operate among your subordinates or followers;
- the forces in the task and situation which you have to deal with.

To help you consider these factors or forces systematically, read the three sections below, and answer the questions.

As you deal with each question consider how your answer will affect your choice of leadership style. Some answers will push you in the direction of a more authoritarian style. Some will encourage you to use a more democratic style.

Discuss the questions in Part 1 in small groups of three.

1. Forces in you, as the leader

Your motivation and values:
- how much do you value efficiency and the rapid completion of work?
- how strongly do you believe that people should participate in decisions which affect them?
- how important to you is the growth of potential and leadership in other people?

Your preference in leadership:
- are you comfortable to work with others in a team? Or are you more comfortable to be in charge and give orders?
- what has been your previous experience of leadership by other people, such as your parents, teachers or bosses? What 'models' of leadership have you experienced?

- Which kinds of leadership are you comfortable under? Which make you feel uncomfortable?

Your tolerance of uncertainty:
- how much do you trust other people generally?
- how much risk and uncertainty can you cope with?
- how far can you allow decisions to be out of your own control before you feel insecure?

2. Forces among your subordinates or followers

Their needs and expectations:
- do your subordinates need or expect to be directed? Or do they expect to be independent?
- how much do they expect to share in decisions?
- do they have enough confidence and understanding to participate in decisions?
- are they ready to assume responsibility for their decisions?

Their previous experience of leaders:
- what will they expect from their leader?
- how much confidence will they have in you as a leader?
- how much uncertainty and insecurity can they tolerate?

Their motivation:
- do they understand the objectives or task? Are they committed to them?
- how much did they participate in setting the objectives or choosing the task?

The group:
- what size is the group? How many people are involved?
- do they work well together, or are there communication or other problems among them?
- are there cultural factors and preferences to consider?
- do you work with several groups? If so, do they have similar or different needs and expectations? Will the same style of leadership suit all the groups?

3. Forces in the task, the organization and the situation

The task:
- can everyone be involved? Can the decisions be shared?
- is it a technical matter? Can everyone understand the decisions?
- who is going to be affected by the result?

The organization:
- the organization's purpose, values, and usual style of leadership,
- the physical arrangements, where people work, the buildings and sizes of rooms, the distances involved, transport, the means of communication,
- the frequency of meeting together.

The situation:
- is there pressure of time?
- are there external factors to be considered, such as government policy, donors' requirements, the state of law and order?
- are there expectations in the surrounding communities to be considered?

Adapted from Robert Tannenbaum and Warren H. Schmidt, *How to Choose a Leadership Pattern* pages 7—12.

10.8 A Perspective on Conflict

▶ *'Conflict:' someone said that the word itself is too strong and too big.*

▶ *... we have found out that in general conflict is negative, but if it is kept within limits and managed effectively it will have advantages also ...*

Conflict is an inevitable part of change. It is the other side of the same coin. We cannot have any change — or any development — without some amount of conflict.

Conflict is always a concern in development and for development workers. When it is managed and used with skill it can be a prime tool for development. When it becomes violent, and degenerates into warfare, it can be the greatest obstacle to development.

Conflict is increasing in the world. Competition for resources, rising expectations, plural values, and changes in relationships are contributing to it.

Even as a subject to be studied, it is huge and intractable. Whole courses, and countless training events and books, attempt to grapple with it. Here the topic is introduced, in a limited way, mainly at interpersonal and organizational levels. Even at these levels the subject may seem disturbing to some course members.

The approach is to recognize conflict at different levels, and to show that some level of conflict is inevitable in development work, and indeed in daily life. Members are invited to consider their own attitudes and behaviour in relation to conflict at this level, so that it may be seen as less of a threat and more as an opportunity. The approach is partly conceptual and partly experiential.

The material below requires two sessions. The topic links with many others, including Cosy Or Challenging? The Climate In The Group (page 86), More About Our Values (page 356) and Puzzling It Out: Using Case Studies (page 164).

Objectives

- to explore the topic of conflict, to demystify it, and increase the ability of members to approach conflict with increased understanding and objectivity;
- to demonstrate that conflict is a fact of life and of all relationships, and to help members distinguish the levels of conflict which may be useful from those which may be harmful;
- to demonstrate that conflict is inevitably linked with change, and to consider this in the context of working for change through development work;
- to encourage members to share their experiences of conflict at work and within their own organizations, and to recognize individual styles of dealing with it;
- to increase members' confidence in using conflict as a tool for change.

Introducing the Topic

■ Explain that conflict is a huge subject, and only introductory work is possible. The intention is to provide some starting points for further study, and to make the whole subject seem less daunting.

One way of putting conflict into perspective is to recognize that the word itself means different things to different people.

Ask the whole group what words they associate with conflict. As they offer words, write them across the board roughly according to the level of conflict represented, from the 'normal' tensions of everyday life — hesitation or dilemma — on the left side, through argument and disagreement in the centre, to violence and warfare on the right.

Collect at least 20 words. If necessary contribute words yourself to ensure that the spread from left to right is complete.

Examples are: hesitation, dilemma, uncertainty, misunderstanding, difference of opinion, contradiction, disagreement, argument, competition, confrontation, shouting, abuse, struggle, force, violence, battle, cold war, and hot war.

Focus on the words, starting from the left, and discuss them with the group:
'Do we sometimes have internal tensions? What happens in our minds when we are faced with a difficult choice? Is this a kind of conflict?'
'Is a misunderstanding between two colleagues a kind of conflict?'
'Are the words and levels of conflict on the left side ordinary and everyday? Do we all experience them? Are such levels of conflict acceptable?'
'Do the words as a whole represent a continuous sequence?'
'At what point in the sequence does the level of conflict become stressful?'
'Is violence the problem? Can we distinguish violence and conflict?'
'Does it help to consider different levels of conflict?'

By this stage members may agree that conflict is part of everyday life, that there are different levels of conflict, and that not all of these are threatening. They may identify violence as the problem rather than conflict.

Ask members to think about any changes they have experienced — in their own lives, in their work and organizations, or in their communities or nations. Have any of these changes been without some level of conflict? Is it possible to have change — or choices, or decisions, or actions — without conflict? Is development possible without conflict?

Useful Levels of Conflict

Introduce the idea that within an organization some level of conflict may be necessary and useful. Conflict can be an opportunity to bring about change in organizations — and also change in communities.

Tell the course members to work in small groups of four or five. Ask them to refer back

■ to the words on the board and identify the levels of conflict which may be useful within an organization, together with some of the possible benefits.

If necessary, mention possible benefits such as bringing issues into the open, clarifying what people think and feel, showing where change is needed, 'clearing the air', and so on.

Ask members to share experiences or examples of conflict which they think were beneficial.

Illustrate the general point with the simple graph shown below.

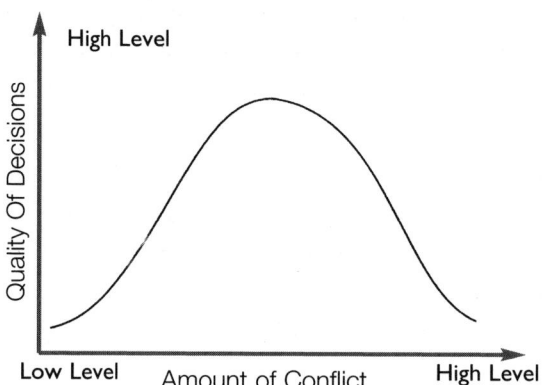

Managing Conflict

Suggest to the group that, when conflict occurs in an organization, the objective is to keep it within the limits where it may be useful, and to prevent it from growing out of control. In other words conflict has to be managed.

Distribute the questionnaire Managing Conflict in an Organization (see pages 431—432) and ask members to complete it individually. Then ask them to work in groups of three or four and compare their responses. Invite any comments in the whole group.

Introduce the idea of 'warning signs'. For a manager or team leader one of the most useful skills is to recognize the early signs of conflict and be able to act early enough to keep it within bounds. Ask members what they think are some of the early warning signs of conflict within an organization or a team. List these on the board.

If necessary contribute to the list yourself. Examples are individuals withdrawing, difficulties over decisions, arguments about minor issues, gossip, grumbling, factions forming, individuals absent, short tempers, and abuse.

Ask the members to discuss the list briefly.

The work outlined above will occupy roughly one session.

Our Attitudes to Conflict

■ Continue the work in a further session by inviting members to consider how they themselves react when faced with interpersonal conflict, and how they deal with it.

Where Do We Stand?

Ask members to stand on a continuum line (see pages 108—109) to demonstrate their own attitudes towards interpersonal conflict. One end represents tendencies like not confronting others, disliking arguments, avoiding conflict, maintaining harmony and so on. The other end represents enjoying argument, being able to confront others, accepting some conflict and so on.

The categories may not be exactly defined, but members will be able to take up approximate positions. When they have placed themselves, ask them to talk with those standing near them and to compare notes. Invite them to adjust their positions in relation to others if that now seems appropriate.

Ask questions to the group or to individuals:
'How do you react to the way the group has arranged itself?'
'Is this how you see the group?'
'Are you surprised by where you see anyone else standing? If so, who and why?'
'Are you happy about where you stand yourself? If so, why? If not, why not?'
'Would you prefer to be in another position? If so, why?'

Invite anyone who would like to change his/her attitude towards conflict to move to the position they would prefer. Ask those who move to explain the difference, and to say what they think holds them back.

How Do We Deal with Conflict?

The questionnaire Dealing With Conflict (pages 432—440) offers another way for members to think about interpersonal conflict and their own attitudes and behaviour. Distribute Part 1 of the questionnaire and ask members to work at it individually. This may take 20 minutes. If time is short members can be asked to to complete it overnight.

When Part 1 has been completed, distribute Part 2 for members to score their own responses. Check that they understand the procedure and the results. Explain that the questionnaire gives a rough indication rather than an accurate assessment. It is to provide food for thought, but should not be taken too seriously. If necessary explain the five styles and the diagram.

Distribute Part 3, which explains the five styles in more detail and suggests their advantages and disadvantages. Joint Problem-Solving may be ideal, and Compromising may be realistic, but the other styles also have their uses. The question is whether we can vary the ways in which we deal with conflict, and can choose the style that is appropriate to the situation.

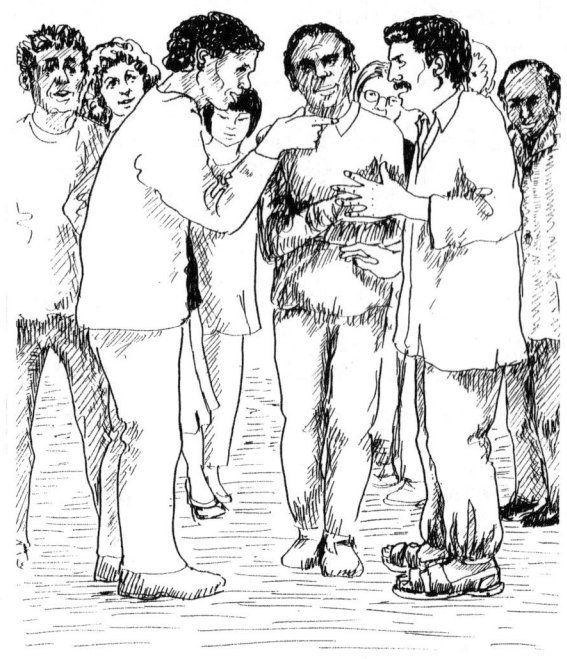

Exploring conflict with role-play

A Conflict with a Colleague

■ This is a light-hearted exercise which gives members an opportunity to try out these different styles while in role.[1] Ask members to work in pairs, and to decide who is A and who is B. Distribute the role outline (page 441).

After members have read the outline ask them to take up their roles and see if they can reach any agreement within the pairs. Tell them that the As are to adopt a Dominating style and the Bs an Avoiding style. After a few minutes ask them to continue in the same A and B roles, but to exchange the styles. After a few more minutes ask them to stop, to give their attention to the whole group, but to remain in their places. Collect some reactions from both As and Bs.

Then ask the Bs to move and work with another A. This time, if the As are Dominating, the Bs should be Smoothing Over. Then both A and B should be Dominating at the same time. Again check for reactions and share in the whole group. Now ask the As to move to new B partners.

Other combinations of styles can be tried, but before ending both A and B should use Compromising at the same time. The exercise can finish with both using Joint Problem-Solving. Bring the members together and ask them to share further observations and insights.

1. With acknowledgments to Simon Fisher.

The exercise demonstrates the styles and their effects, and gives members an experience of being on the receiving end of different styles. More important, it gives members a safe opportunity of using styles which are new to them. This can be enriching in itself.

▶ *... the group was given the opportunity to spread themselves along a conflict continuum line, the extreme ends being avoidance of conflict and active participation or desire for conflict. Naturally I sited myself at the side which avoided conflict ...*

▶ *... the questions led us to see our tendencies ... I was not sure of how the others felt, but I felt good and the result seemed to be showing what I know of me. There was one thing I seemed to see in common among us — that the Smoothing Over seemed to be more than the Dominating.*

▶ *The discussion ... developed into a conversation about handling conflict. We looked at how, as development workers, we may well have to engage ourselves in situations of conflict in order to generate change. I know from a personal point of view this is not something to which I look forward, as confronting such situations has never been one of my strong points.*

Questionnaire: Managing Conflict in an Organization

To reduce the likelihood of damaging levels of conflict within an organization, there are many preventive actions that can be taken. Some more or less appropriate suggestions are given below.

Imagine that you are the director of an organization, or the manager of a team or department. Which will you consider the most important and useful suggestions? Which suggestions are not useful at all?

_____ a). encourage a working climate where sharing, co-operation and consultation are expected, but where differences can also be expressed.

_____ b). clarify structures, procedures, responsibilities and authority within the organization or department.

_____ c). give all the staff a strongly-worded talk every week on working peacefully together.

_____ d). increase your own awareness of the mechanisms of conflict and your skills in managing and resolving it.

_____ e). anticipate in advance where and when conflicts are likely to arise, and keep watch for the early signs of any conflict.

_____ f). encourage staff-members to put forward their own views without attacking or blaming those with different views. Encourage 'I' statements.

_____ g). use an authoritarian style of management and take all decisions yourself so that there will be less reason for others to quarrel with each other.

_____ h). make sure that all staff (including yourself) share their expectations of each other's roles and work, and especially when new staff are appointed.

_____ i). give time and attention to listening to what other people say about their work and problems, listening to their words and to their feelings also.

_____ j). arrange informal meetings without any particular agenda where staff members are free to bring up anything that concerns them, including any clashes with colleagues.

_____ k). arrange regular formal staff meetings about important issues and problems, and encourage staff members to express their viewpoints and differences of opinion openly.

_____ l). when a problem or conflict arises, ask those involved what they think is the underlying cause.

After ranking the suggestions, compare and discuss your conclusions in small groups.

Exercise: Dealing with Conflict, Part 1

Each of us has our own way of dealing with conflict; and we may tend to use that way, or style, whenever we are faced by conflict. The exercise is to help us identify which is our preferred way, or style, of responding to and resolving conflict.

Below are 30 pairs of statements. For each pair circle 'a' or 'b' to indicate which statement more closely fits the way you tend to deal with differences between yourself and other people.

Although the statements themselves are repeated, each pair of statements is a different combination. You should therefore continue to think carefully about the pairs of statements as you complete the questionnaire.

1. a. I am usually strong in pursuing my goals.
   b. I try to get all concerns and issues immediately out in the open.

2. a. I put my cards on the table and invite the other person to do the same.
   b. When conflicts arise I try to win my case.

3. a. Once I decide on something I defend my decision strongly.
   b. I prefer not to argue but to look for the best solution possible.

4. a. I sometimes give up my own wishes for the wishes of the other person.
   b. I feel that differences are not always worth worrying about.

5. a. I accept the views of the other, rather than rock the boat.
   b. I avoid people with strong views.

6. a. I like to cooperate with others and follow their ideas.
   b. I feel that most things are not worth arguing about.
      I stick to my own views.

7. a. I try to find a compromise solution.
   b. I am usually strong in pursuing my goals.

8. a. When conflicts arise I try to win my case.
   b. I propose a middle ground.

9. a. I like to meet the other person half-way.
   b. Once I decide on something I defend my decision strongly.

10. a. I feel that differences are not always worth worrying about.
    b. I try to find a compromise solution.

11. a. I propose a middle ground.
    b. I avoid people with strong views.

12. a. I feel that most things are not worth arguing about.
       I stick to my own views.
    b. I like to meet the other person half-way.

13. a. I am usually strong in pursuing my goals.
    b. I sometimes give up my own wishes for the wishes of the other person.

14. a. I accept the views of the other, rather than rock the boat.
    b. When conflicts arise I try to win my case.

15. a. Once I decide on something I defend my decision strongly.
    b. I like to co-operate with others and follow their ideas.

16. a. I try to find a compromise solution.
    b. I sometimes give up my own wishes for the wishes of the other person.

17. a. I would accept the views of the other, rather than rock the boat.
    b. I propose a middle ground.

18. a. I like to meet the other person half-way.
    b. I like to co-operate with others and follow their ideas.

19. a. I feel that differences are not always worth worrying about.
    b. I am usually strong in pursuing my goals.

20. a. When conflicts arise I try to win my case.
    b. I avoid people with strong views.

21. a. I feel that most things are not worth arguing about.
       I stick to my own views.
    b. Once I decide on something I defend my decision strongly.

22. a. I try to get all concerns and issues immediately out in the open.
    b. I feel that differences are not always worth worrying about.

23. a. I avoid people with strong views.
    b. I put my cards on the table and invite the other person to do the same.

24. a. I prefer not to argue but to look for the best solution possible.
    b. I feel that most things are not worth arguing about.
       I stick to my own views.

25. a. I try to get all concerns and issues immediately out in the open.
    b. I try to find a compromise solution.

26. a. I put my cards on the table and invite the other person to do the same.
    b. I propose a middle ground.

27. a. I prefer not to argue but I look for the best solution possible.
    b. I like to meet the other person half-way.

28. a. I sometimes give up my own wishes for the wishes of the other person.
    b. I try to get all concerns and issues immediately out in the open.

29. a. I put my cards on the table and invite the other person to do the same.
    b. I would accept the views of others, rather than rock the boat.

30. a. I like to co-operate with others and follow their ideas.
    b. I prefer not to argue but to look for the best possible solution.

Exercise: Dealing with Conflict, Part 2

(i). Circle your responses to the questionnaire in the table below. For example, with pair 1, if you chose statement 'a' as more closely fitting for you, then again circle the 'a' in the first line of the table.

	A	B	C	D	E
1				a	b
2				b	a
3				a	b
4	b	a			
5	b	a			
6	b	a			
7			a	b	
8			b	a	
9			a	b	
10	a		b		
11	b		a		
12	a		b		
13		b		a	
14		a		b	
15		b		a	
16		b	a		
17		a	b		
18		b	a		
19	a			b	
20	b			a	
21	a			b	
22	b				a
23	a				b
24	b				a
25			b		a
26			b		a
27			b		a
28		a			b
29		b			a
30		a			b
TOTALS					

435

(ii). Add up the total number of responses circled under each of the columns A, B, C, D and E.

(iii). The maximum score in any column is 12; and the total in all columns should be 30. Check your own totals; and see if there is any discrepancy.

(iv). The five columns represent five different styles of dealing with conflict:

A = avoiding
B = smoothing over
C = compromising
D = dominating
E = joint problem-solving

A score of more than 6 for any style indicates that you may prefer to use that style. A score of less than 6 suggests that it is a style you do not prefer.

(v). The five styles are shown in the following diagram. The characteristics and advantages and disadvantages of each style will be described separately.

(vi). After hearing the five styles discussed, reflect on how the questionnaire came out for you. Do you think it indicated correctly your preferred style/s of dealing with conflict? Do you always use the same style/s? Are you satisfied with the way you deal with conflict?

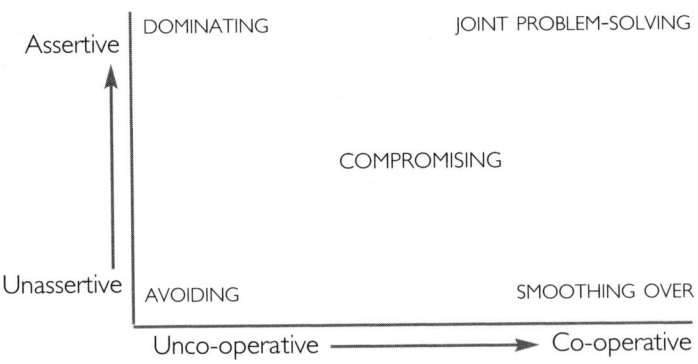

It is the ability to vary the style used — to choose the most appropriate style — that makes a person effective in dealing with conflict. We may each have our own preferred style/s, but we should also be flexible enough to use whichever style is going to be the most useful in the circumstances.

Adapted from unattributed secondary sources.

A. Avoiding Style (both lose)

This style attempts to 'get rid' of conflict by denying that it exists, or by post-poning any attempt to deal with it.

- A person using this style tends to withdraw or retreat from conflict.
- The style gives little importance to the task/s or the relationship/s involved.
- It may be associated with low levels of involvement and commitment, as well as low levels of co-operation and assertiveness.
- The person using it ignores his/her own needs and the needs of the other party, so no one's needs will be met.
- The main disadvantage of this style is that if conflict is neglected, it does not go away but tends to grow and become more and more unmanageable.

Some possible uses of this style are:

- as a temporary response if an issue is not urgent or important;
- for a 'cooling down' period;
- while collecting more information and making further analysis;
- if other people can resolve the conflict satisfactorily;
- if the issue is only a symptom of a wider problem;
- if other people are likely to be hurt by the use of other styles.

B. Smoothing Over Style (you lose, the other gains)

This style tends to emphasize the areas of agreement and play down the areas of disagreement.

- It puts others' needs and concerns above your own; if you use it you may be giving too little attention to your own goals and needs.
- This style tends to be co-operative, but not assertive.
- The person using it tends to yield to others, to give more importance to the harmony and relationship than the task or the real issues.
- He/she may not recognize the positive aspects or possible advantages of handling conflict openly; but this may be preferred in some cultures.

- Those who tend to 'accommodate' others are often seen as 'quiet'. If already perceived that way, when they do make their contribution it may not be heard, and they may lose recognition and influence.

- Conflicts dealt with in this way may not be resolved; or they may be resolved without either party's view being effectively presented or understood meaningfully.

Some possible uses of this style are:

- when goodwill and preserving a relationship is more important than dealing with the conflict;

- when one party is much more concerned about the issue/problem than the other;

- when one party is much more powerful than the other;

- to give the other party an experience of 'winning';

- to make the other party more receptive to a more important issue.

C. Compromising Style (both gain, but both lose too)

This style attempts to reach or negotiate a midway position.

- It is searching for solutions that bring some satisfaction to both parties; but it expects concessions on both sides.

- Both parties expect to gain a bit, but also to lose a bit: 'you give a little and I'll give a little;' 'let's split the difference'.

- There may be acceptance of a compromise agreement on both sides, but it gives limited satisfaction to either party.

- The process of bargaining may encourage both sides to take up inflated positions; it may be associated with positional bargaining.

- In the search for an agreement and compromise, both parties may lose sight of their own values.

- Any agreement reached may be weak, mediocre and ineffective; and there may be a lack of commitment to it.

- This style allows a more thorough exploration of the conflict than avoidance, but less thorough than collaboration.

- Overall more needs can be met through this style than through competition, but less than through collaboration.

- This style may not be ideal, but it is often expedient and practicable. It often fits the realities of management and organizations.
- It is important for everyone/every organization to use this style sometimes, i.e. to be able to negotiate, to make concessions, to extricate themselves from difficulty, etc.

Some possible uses of this style are:
- as an alternative, if collaboration fails;
- if time is short;
- if the goals of both parties in the conflict are not very important;
- if both parties are equally powerful and equally strongly committed.

D. Dominating Style (you gain: the other loses)

In this style one party imposes its own views or meets its own needs at the expense of the other.
- This style represents a high level of assertion but a low level of co-operation.
- Dominating, imposing one's views, or 'winning', is more important than preserving the relationship.
- It involves the use of authority or power (from position, rank, information, supervision, 'the system', expertise, etc.) to overcome the other party.
- It leads to 'winners' and 'losers'. The losers often do not support the decision/agreement which has been imposed, and the 'struggle' is taken forward into the future.
- The losers may be suppressed, coerced, hurt, damaged.
- This style tends to be used in competitive societies and cultures.
- Persistent users of this style may be seen as aggressive, and may be cut off by other people from interaction and information.
- Those who never use this style may feel powerless in conflicts, especially against those who often use it.

Some possible uses of this style:
- when a quick decision is essential;
- when an unpopular decision is necessary;
- in situations where life is threatened e.g. military, children in danger, emergen cies, disasters etc;

- when applying 'the law' or 'the rules';
- where decisions are made by majority vote.

E. Joint Problem-Solving Style (both gain)

Here the emphasis and energy is given to analyzing and jointly solving the problem, not on defending a position or defeating the other party.

- The aim is to meet the needs of both parties. Both parties recognize the needs and concerns of the other as legitimate.

- Both parties acknowledge that there is conflict. They identify each others' needs; and together identify alternative solutions and their consequences.

- Both parties expect to modify their views in order to reach agreement but both expect to gain from agreement.

- This style represents a high level of both assertion and co-operation.

- It gives importance both to the task and to the relationship.

- It may be associated with principled bargaining.

- This style is more creative and innovative; it leads to personal, group or organizational growth.

- The style calls for time, understanding, energy and commitment; some issues may not be worth so much if other work has to be neglected.

- It requires trust on both sides. If there is trust on one side only, that party may be taken advantage of.

- It is appropriate when both parties agree that the conflict is important and is worth the resources needed to solve it, and are committed to a joint resolution.

Adapted in part from: Donald T. Simpson, 'Handling Group and Organizational Conflict', *The Sixth Annual*, (eds. Jones and Pfeiffer), pages 120—121; Martin B. Ross, 'Coping with Conflict', *The Eleventh Annual* (eds. Pfeiffer and Goodstein), pages 135—139; Gordon Lippitt, 'Managing Conflict in Today's Organizations', *Management Development and Training Handbook*, (eds. Taylor and Lippitt) pages 67—68.

A and B are colleagues in a development organization. They work at the same level, and have similar responsibilities. The Head of their Department has just asked A to represent their organization at a meeting in a village 150 miles away next weekend. This will mean that A will be away from home for the whole of the weekend.

A went for a similar meeting a couple of weekends ago, and feels that it is now B's turn. Also A has been working very hard recently, and feels tired and in need of a rest at the weekend. When A told this to the Head of Department, the Head replied that A could see if B is willing to go to the meeting, but if not then A must go.

B has a heavy work load, and is feeling under a lot of pressure and strain. He/she also has many family responsibilities, especially at weekends. It seems to B that A is the obvious person who should attend the village meeting.

Now A has come to talk to B about the village meeting.

10.9 Approaches to Planning

This event uses a questionnaire which contains 25 statements about planning in community development programmes. Responding to these statements helps to direct members' minds towards the topic, and stimulates thinking about it. Discussion of their responses helps members to compare their own, and their organization's, attitudes and experiences with those of others.

Four additional statements under the heading Planning for Yourself can be added to the main questionnaire and dealt with at the same time. These statements explore the link between members' attitudes towards planning in their professional work and planning in their personal lives.

As a topic, planning is beyond the scope of this manual. The questionnaire can only be a starting point. Allow one session altogether.

Objectives

- to introduce the topic and processes of planning for development in a community;
- to raise issues related to planning and participation;
- to provide an opportunity for members to discuss their previous experience of planning, and to share their assumptions;
- to encourage members to reflect on whether their personal attitudes to planning are consistent with practice in their professional work.

 Using the Questionnaire

■ Distribute the questionnaire to each member and ask them to complete it individually without discussion. This may take 30 minutes.

Ask the members to form small groups of four or five. Separate colleagues from the same organization. Ask the small groups to work through the questionnaires, statement by statement, sharing their individual responses with others in their group and explaining their reasons. The task is not to reach consensus, but to uncover differing assumptions, approaches and experience. The discussion may take a further 30 minutes.

Bring the members back into the larger group, and take up any statement that you want to emphasize, or which members want to discuss further. Remember that the purpose is to stimulate thinking rather than to reach conclusions.

Avoid repeating the discussions which have already taken place in the small groups.

■ Some responses may depend on how members interpret the wording of statements. For example, in number 15, the word 'fully' can be understood in different ways. The words 'a part' in number 16 can also be contentious. Accept members' different assumptions and draw attention to them.

Statements in the main questionnaire that may be worth emphasis are numbers 4, 5, 14—19, 21 and 22. In the supplementary questionnaire statement 4 may be worth emphasis.

The statements which mention some of the advantages and benefits of planning are numbers 5, 10—13, 20 and 21.

<table>
<tr><td></td><td></td></tr>
</table>

Questionnaire: Approaches to Planning

Below are 25 statements about planning and plans. Read the statements and indicate whether you agree or disagree with them. Add comments if you wish.

	Agree	Disagree	Comments
1. Working without plans is like using a canoe without a paddle. The canoe drifts according to the winds and currents, instead of going on a chosen course.	☐	☐	
2. Planning is a specialized process which should be left to professional experts.	☐	☐	
3. Planning is a Western idea. It is not so appropriate or welcome in other cultures.	☐	☐	
4. Planning is basically a common-sense, natural activity. All people everywhere can and do plan.	☐	☐	
5. Planning allows us to use our imagination about possibilities for the future.	☐	☐	
6. Planning is a process of making decisions about the future.	☐	☐	
7. A plan puts us into a rigid framework and reduces our flexibility.	☐	☐	

8. The situation in many areas is so unpredictable
   that it is pointless to plan. ☐ ☐

9. When resources and skills are scarce,
   planning is a luxury. It is too expensive
   and takes too much time. ☐ ☐

10. A plan is necessary for work to be
    co-ordinated, and for tasks to be delegated. ☐ ☐

11. A plan provides the basis for day-
    to-day decisions, and helps to make
    consistent action possible. ☐ ☐

12. A plan helps in gathering and
    mobilizing resources. ☐ ☐

13. Planning helps us to foresee both
    problems and opportunities. ☐ ☐

14. As long as the planners are clear about
    about their plan, it doesn't matter if other
    people understand it or not. ☐ ☐

15. All the people who will be affected by a
    development plan must be fully involved in
    the process of planning. ☐ ☐

16. Those who are paying for a development
    programme should have a part in planning it. ☐ ☐

17. Much of the work of planning is convincing
    people to accept the plan. ☐ ☐

18. Much of the work of planning is listening
    to what people want in the plan. ☐ ☐

19. Effective planning includes giving attention
    to peoples' feelings. ☐ ☐

20. An effective plan helps to increase people's
    commitment and morale. ☐ ☐

21. Being involved in planning helps people
    prepare themselves for change. ☐ ☐

22. Planning for the future is an essential element in the process of development itself. ☐ ☐

23. The main reason for planning is that it helps us get support from donor agencies. ☐ ☐

24. If we have a good plan there won't be any problems in implementation. ☐ ☐

25. One of the 'inputs' for planning is evaluation. ☐ ☐

After you have responded to the statements:

(i) Indicate any statements that have given you a new thought or insight into planning, or which have raised a question in your mind.

(ii) Indicate the statements that mention advantages and benefits of planning.

(iii) Indicate any statement that you think you or your organization should give more attention to in future.

Planning for Yourself

Consider the additional statements below:

1. Planning may be necessary in my development work, but it is not necessary to the same extent in my personal life. ☐ ☐

2. Planning our personal future helps us to sort out what is important to us in our own lives. ☐ ☐

3. New opportunities and unexpected challenges constantly arise in real life. It is more important to be able to respond to these as they arise than to follow a previous plan. ☐ ☐

4. Planning is a tool. We should be able to use it when it is helpful and discard it when it is not. ☐ ☐

Is your attitude towards planning in your own life generally the same as, or different from, your attitude towards planning in your professional work?

John Staley, *Enticing the Learning: Trainers in Development*, University of Birmingham, pages 443—445

An Experience of Planning

> ▶ *We found ourselves sitting separately as planners and implementers, and before coffee break three nice mobiles (moving decorations) were hanging in the classroom. ... we shared our feelings and attitudes towards the other group. ... we also thought "how does this exercise relate to our work back at home?" We concluded that what happens in exercises — the same happens in real life.*

> ▶ *Such a simple exercise as in building a mobile but how much we learnt about planning, our colleagues and ourselves.*

This simulation provides experience of the processes of planning, and raises some central issues of planning, communication and participation. In particular it focuses on the roles of planners and of those who are expected to implement plans, and opens up the issue of participation.

Members work in roles, some as small teams of development workers engaged in planning, and others as small groups representing people from a local community who are expected to implement plans. The task in the simulation is to plan and make a hanging decoration capable of movement, known as a 'mobile'. The word mobile is now often applied to telephones, but the general meaning is any item or body capable of being moved.[1]

The simulation follows conveniently after Approaches to Planning (page 442), and can be seen as another contribution to the topic of planning; although that topic, as such, cannot be dealt with in this manual.

Two consecutive sessions are required, preferably a whole morning. The first session is for the simulation itself, and the second for reflection on the experience. It will help the discussion afterwards if the difference between reflection and evaluation has already been clarified.

Objectives

- to experience and identify processes in planning and in implementing a plan;

- to reflect upon the relationship between those whose role is planning and those whose role is implementing, and to raise awareness of the dynamics of planning and participation;

- to consider alternative approaches to planning, alternative styles of leadership, and alternative understandings of the roles involved;

- to reflect upon personal role, and upon interpersonal and inter-group process.

---

1. The use of mobiles in a planning exercise is taken from *A Handbook of Management Training Exercises*, Volume 1, BACIE, London, pages 14—16

Preparation

Allocating Members to Small Groups

Each planning group has three members. Less than three will be too few to support each other, and they may be unable to generate enough material for reflection. If the numbers make it necessary there could be four in the group, although this is unwieldy.

Each planning group works with a corresponding group from the community. The community or implementing groups have from three to five members each. So, for example, a course group of 20 could have three planning groups of three members each, one implementing group of three, and two implementing groups each of four.

In a homogeneous course group the small groups could be formed at random. In a heterogeneous group the learning may be clearer and stronger if members are allocated to roles and groups. Some criteria for this are given below.

- The task in the simulation is to make a hanging decoration capable of movement, known as a 'mobile.' Such mobiles are better known in some cultures, and among those who have had arts and crafts teaching. Put members who are more likely to be familiar with this idea of a mobile among the planners.

- The planners may want to write instructions, or draw a plan, with measurements and specifications. It will help if at least one of their members has some technical experience. So allocate engineers, mechanics or others familiar with plans and measurement to the planning groups.

- If you want to focus on participation, allocate members whose style may be more authoritarian to the planning groups. Allocate members with democratic, participative or 'radical' inclinations to the implementing groups.

- Mobiles should be visually appealing, so creativity, artistic ability and decorative skills are also important. Allocate such talents and skills to different groups.

Rooms

The simulation is introduced to the whole group in the course room, and discussion takes place there afterwards. During the simulation itself each small group, both planners and implementers, requires its own room with a table and chairs. These rooms should be within reach of each other. If there are not enough separate rooms, a group of planners and the corresponding group of implementers can work from opposite corners of the course room.

By the end of the simulation each implementing group produces a mobile. Make some arrangement to suspend these mobiles in the course room, preferably from the ceiling, for at least as long the experience is being discussed. The mobiles are often attractive and may be kept as decorations.

Tools and Materials

Each pair of groups will need:

- pliers;
- scissors;
- ruler or tape measure;
- 6 ft (2m) of stiff wire which can be cut by the pliers (such as wire coat hangers);
- a reel of white cotton thread;
- decorative items. (Coloured plastic balls or baubles, such as those used to decorate Christmas trees, are suitable. Each pair of groups should be given a dozen.)

Alternative materials are coloured paper, card, foil, sequins, buttons, cones, flowers, and leaves. If paper and card are used, glue and sticky tape are also needed. If sequins, buttons or leaves are used, needles are needed. Time in the simulation is limited, so give ample materials, but of limited kinds.

Before the simulation lay out a set of tools and materials on the table in each room where the planning groups will work. The tools and materials represent the 'technology and resources' for such a project.

Copies of the appropriate instructions will be needed for each small group.

Introducing the Simulation

■ If this happens to be the first simulation of the course introduce the method in general. (See Introducing the Method to the Course Group, page 230) This may take 5—10 minutes.

Then go on to introduce this particular simulation. This may take another 5—10 minutes.

Explain that the simulation will give members an experience of planning. Explain that some will be in the role of development workers engaged in planning, and others will be in the role of people from a local community who are expected to implement plans.

Tell them that they will shortly be dividing into small groups in separate rooms. They will work in the small groups during the simulation itself. This will take the rest of the session. After a break they will return to the course room to reflect on the experience.

Tell the members that the task in the simulation is to plan and make a mobile. Explain the general meaning of this word as necessary. If you have a ready-made mobile available as a demonstration, you can make the idea clear to members who are not familiar with it. At least you should show them illustrations or diagrams of mobiles.

Members may wonder what mobiles have to do with the practicalities of development work. Anticipate this and explain that the answer is nothing. The task is meant to seem 'neutral'. It is deliberately disconnected from development work and from back home preoccupations, so that members will be able to focus directly on the simulation. However

■ they should assume that mobiles represent development and are wanted in every community.

Check if there are questions before the group divides. Then tell each member which room he/she is to use, but without designating the small groups as planners or implementers at this stage. Tell them that they will receive further instructions in their rooms. Ask them to move to those rooms. Moving to the rooms may take another five minutes.

Instructing the Small Groups

The next stage is to give instructions to the small groups in their own rooms. Begin with the planning groups and instruct all of them before visiting any of the implementing groups.

To ensure that each group receives the same information, read the appropriate instructions out to them. Take your time and read slowly and clearly. The other groups which are waiting will be pleased to have an interlude! (Or, if additional trainers are available, arrange for them to instruct other groups. If so, make sure that they too stick to the instructions.) Do not elaborate on the instructions or the roles. If any member asks you how to play a role just reply 'be yourself'. As you finish instructing each group of planners they will start on their task. You should therefore note the beginning of the 30 minute planning period as you leave each group. You can also leave a copy of the instructions with the group.

Then instruct the implementing groups.

If two small groups have to use the same room they should be in opposite corners. The planners should sit at a table with the tools and materials. If it seems appropriate, tell the implementing group to sit on the floor. The instructions are the same as for separate rooms, except for small adjustments to the wording. Read the instructions for each group so that the other group can overhear it, even if they choose not to listen.

Depending on the number of groups, instructing the planning groups may take 5—10 minutes. Instructing the implementers may take a further 5—10 minutes, but this comes out of the planning period.

Instructions for Planning Groups

(The group should be seated at a table with a set of tools and materials.)

1. You are a team of development workers engaged in planning.
2. There is a group of people from the community in another room (in another part of this room) who are expected to implement plans.
3. The task during the next 30 minutes is to design and plan the making of a mobile, so that the other group can implement the plan and make the mobile within 20 minutes. You should assume that a mobile is developmental and desirable.
4. The materials and tools available are being given to you now so that you know what is available; but the materials and tools cannot actually be used during this 30 minute planning period.
5. Before the end of the 30 minutes the plan, with the materials and tools, must have been communicated and handed over to the other group for them to implement.

6. You will then become *silent* observers: you may not intervene or assist while the other group is implementing the plan and making the mobile.

7. You can choose whether you do the planning without consulting the other group, or whether you consult and involve them. Either way, the planning period is 30 minutes, and the implementing period will be 20 minutes.

(If the Planning Group ask — but only if they ask — they can be told which room the Implementing Group is in.)

Instructions for Implementing Groups

1. You are a group of people from the community. There is a team of planners in another room (in another part of this room).

2. The team of planners has been told that a plan for a mobile has to be made within 30 minutes.

3. After that, you are expected to implement the plan, that is, to make the mobile. 20 minutes will be available for implementation. You should assume that a mobile is developmental and desirable.

4. Tools and materials will be brought to you sometime during the 30 minutes; but you should not start to use them until the 30 minutes planning period is over.

5. The team of planners have also been told that they can decide whether to come and consult you about the plan or not.

6. While you are implementing the plan, the planners will be silent observers. They may not intervene or assist in the implementation.

7. If you have to wait for the planners you should discuss:
   a) how you feel about other people making plans for you to implement;
   b) how you would understand participation in this situation;
   c) what you would like to happen in this situation, and why.

(If the groups are in separate rooms the Implementers should not be told where the Planners are working. If they ask, reply that the Planners are in their office. If both groups are working in the same room, and if the Implementers ask if they may approach the Planners, tell them that they should decide that for themselves.)

 Conducting the Simulation

■ Once the members take up their roles in the small groups, and begin on the task, the situation becomes more fluid and less predictable. For example, a planning group may do any (or none) of the following:

- plan for most of the 30 minutes without meeting the implementing group;
- send a representative to the implementing group;
- invite the implementing group to send a representative;

- go as a group to visit the implementing group;
- invite the implementing group to come to their room;
- move out of their own room and shift to the implementing group's room.

■ Parallels with back home may become increasingly obvious. For example, if the planners go to the implementing group's room, this is equivalent to 'visiting the community'. When the planners invite the implementing group to their room, they are 'calling them to the development agency's office'. Such parallels are helpful during the discussion afterwards, but do not draw attention to them during the simulation as members may then enact 'stories' from back home instead of working with the dynamics of the simulation itself.

The behaviour of the implementing groups also varies. Some may sit and wait for the planners; some may decide to go and look for the planners; others may barricade the door and refuse to allow the planners in!

Be prepared for any outcome, and allow matters to take their course, provided there is no threat to members' safety. Your role at this stage is to visit the groups and observe both the process within groups and the relations between groups. Remember that your observations should be factual and not evaluative — what happened, in what sequence, who did what, who said what, and so on.

Remember too that the purpose of the simulation is learning. Whether the groups produce fine mobiles is not important. Do not let anxiety about the product disturb your attention on the process.

As you visit them, you can remind the groups about the timing, and warn them when 20 or 25 minutes of the planning period have elapsed. By this time some of the planning groups may already be working with their implementing groups. By the end of the 30 minutes, the planning groups must hand over completely to the implementing groups and then become silent observers themselves.

Continue to observe the groups during the implementing period. Twenty minutes are allowed for this, but some groups ask for extra time. If they have not yet made much progress, or if you judge that extra time will enable them to finish, you can extend the implementing period by 10 or 15 minutes.

When the time is up, or when the task is finished, ask each group to bring their mobile to the course room and suspend it there. Notice who carries it and suspends it.

The simulation itself ends with the display of the finished mobiles. As each small group gets to this point, invite its members to take a break. This allows the later groups to catch up. By now a session of 1½ hours will probably have elapsed.

Discussion and Reflection

A great deal happens during this simulation — for individuals, for the small groups, and for the course as a whole. The members of each small group have experience in their group to reflect upon. Each group also has experience with its corresponding group, so some discussion and reflection must be with that group. In addition the experience and conclusions of the small groups must be shared in the whole group so that there can be common learning for all. If discussions at so many levels are to be practicable and fruitful, a framework is necessary.

■ When the course group re-assembles, tell the members to sit again in their small groups. The planning groups should be on one side of the room, and each group should be opposite its corresponding implementing group.

Some members may be anxious about whether the mobiles meet the trainer's expectations, and you may want to start by congratulating the whole group on the mobiles. Then explain that each group of planners had the same task, with the same instructions and the same tools and materials. Similarly each group of implementers. Explain any difference due to the availability of rooms.

Remind members that in a simulation action is followed by reflection. Stress that the purpose is discussion and learning, but not evaluation of performance. Then tell the members that you will give them questions, each of which they will discuss before moving on to the next. The sequence of the questions will lead them through the different stages and aspects of the simulation. These explanations may take ten minutes.

Before giving the first question invite them to share in their small groups whatever is already on their minds. Allow as long as they seem to need — perhaps five minutes — and then begin the questions.

In Separate Small Groups

The first question, for discussion in the original small groups, is:
    'How did you, as members of your own small group, work together?'
Clarify and elaborate this with related questions, such as:
    'How did your group make its decisions?'
    'How did you divide up the work within the group?'
    'Who did what, and why?'

After a few minutes of discussion add further questions about the original groups:
    'What was the pattern of participation and leadership?'
    'What was the mood in your group?'
    'What was it like for you, being a planner or an implementer?'
    'What was your individual role in the group? What did you yourself do?'

The purpose of these additional questions is not to seek an answer to each one, but to encourage the members to discuss widely and thoroughly.

As the discussion proceeds, visit the groups, monitor their discussion, and clarify the task if necessary. Some members and groups may be absorbed at first with the technical aspects, and may need to discuss these before they are ready to think about the process. Do not criticise this, but repeat and elaborate the questions. Allow as long as the groups seem to need, probably about ten minutes, before raising the second question.

■ The second main question, also for discussion in the original small groups, is:
'How much was your small group aware of the other group?'

Elaborate with related questions, such as:
'Did your group have a view of the other group?'
'What were your assumptions about the planners or the implementers?'
'What was your attitude towards them?'
'Did you trust them?'
'Did you perceive them as people, or just as a category?'

After a few minutes of discussion elaborate further:
'What kind of relationship was there between your group and the other group?'
'Who had control? Which group had power?'
'Was it a developmental relationship?'
'Was it empowering, or was it a relationship of dependency?'

Allow another 10—15 minutes altogether.

The third main question is:
'Does your small group have a sense of accomplishment and satisfaction?'

Elaborate by also asking:
'Whose are these mobiles?'
'Do you feel that the finished work is yours or the other group's?'
'Were the implementers' human resources utilized in the work?'

Allow at least five minutes, and ask some small groups to share their conclusion — but not their discussion — with the whole group.

A short break at this point may be helpful.

Planners and Implementers Together

Ask the groups to sit with their corresponding group for the next stage in the discussion. Allow a few minutes for the groups to say whatever they want to each other.

The next main question for the combined groups is:
'The exercise allowed the planners to invite participation by the implementers — what were the factors which encouraged participation?'
'What were the factors which discouraged participation?'

As the discussion proceeds, add related questions, such as:
'What did each of you do, as individuals in your roles, to affect participation?'
'Did the planners need to keep complete control over all the planning?'
'Could the planning role have been stretched, and the role boundaries changed?'

This part of the discussion may take 10—15 minutes. Then tell the planners and implementers to separate and return to their small groups on each side of the room.

Inter-Group Feedback

The next task is for each group to give feedback to its corresponding group.

■ Explain that the task for each group is to share some learning from its own experience in the simulation. The purpose is to say something which will be helpful to the other group.

Each group is now to draft one or two short statements which they would like to make to the other group.

Go on to say that the statements should not be evaluative, and should not blame the other group for anything that happened. Each group must take responsibility for its own experience, and for its statements. All the statements are to begin with the words:

'We would have liked it if you ...'

Write these words on the board.

Visit the groups as they work on this task and monitor their drafts. Ensure that statements are directly addressed to the corresponding group, and begin with the words given. Statements which convey experience, feeling, insight or humour will be helpful. If you find that a draft is evaluative, or goes beyond the simulation, point this out and ask the group to work further. Some groups may like to make several statements. All this is valuable practice in giving feedback. Drafting the statements may take 10—15 minutes.

When the statements are ready, and you are satisfied that they are appropriate, invite the whole group to listen. Tell the members of each small group to face the corresponding group, and ask for one member to make the statement/s directly to the other group. Begin with a group of planners, followed by their corresponding implementers. As each statement is made, check for understanding and clarification but do not allow discussion or defence. Reading all the statements may take ten minutes.

In the Whole Group

The final work is done in the whole group in the usual horseshoe.

Some questions to raise now are:

'Is this what happens in the wider world?'
'How does this relate to our work back home?'
'How flexible are we when we are in a particular role?'

'What can we learn from this experience?'
'What is our personal learning?'

Bring the session to an end with any conclusions that emerge from this part of the discussion. This discussion in the whole group may take ten minutes.

Finally, encourage members to go on thinking about the processes in the simulation, and about the role they themselves played. Allow time for further discussion, perhaps during the next day's diary session.

Planners

▶ *I was in the planning group. In my group we had different opinions regarding consultation with implementors. Finally, we decided, we will do our plan without consulting implementors and we will see what happens during the implementation ...*

454

Reflecting on an experience of planning

▶ *... the implementers had different ideas of the plan altogether. What was produced at the end was not complete or correct according to the planners' ideas. This happens in real situation also, where villagers are busy with their normal activities and suddenly planners come with a ready-made plan for them and expect to get good results.*

▶ *The real emphasis of the exercise, however, was not on the quality of the mobile, but on the process that went on within and between individuals and groups. Time was devoted to reflection — not evaluation, as we were gently reminded by J. The findings were, in theory, not so new to us, but the difference was that in this exercise we actually experienced and felt them, e.g. what it means and how it feels, in planning with or planning for others. It struck me that the role playing — and my own work and group reactions — were very real, and am left with big questions, e.g. how would I act as a planner? What are my own needs as a planner?*

▶ *We need to plan our development work as we need to plan our daily life. But who is the planner? For whom is he planning?*

▶ *We came to see that increasing participation for the community means increasing power for them and conversely decreasing power for us as the development workers. I think the practice of allowing ourselves to be disempowered is not something we will adjust to easily, if the feelings revealed in simulations are anything to go by.*

Implementers

▶ *We didn't know who the planners were or what we were supposed to do. We felt a little frustrated and outside without possibilities to participate. We were not involved in the planning. After a few minutes we decided not to bother — this was not our project, so why should we take any responsibility?*

▶ *Our experts are not communicating with us. They are very strict to work for themselves. They seem as doctors doing operation in the theatre. I wonder why they are not communicating to us if they are planning for us. I now remember my work at home, where I write letters in my office without going to listen to the people. This is wrong. Then the planners called us and gave us the materials to implement the project. The plan and description were good: we didn't find it difficult to make. But that plan was not ours.*

▶ *... even in the midst of boredom and desperation in our small group of five implementers there were delightful moments of creativity, when each of us worked on unique designs — of birds and butterflies, moons and stars as well as beautiful trees — true pieces of artistry. It's just a pity you can't see them on our mobile, as they were not in the plan!*

▶ *I found myself in an implementer group, shunted into a corner of the room, while instructions were being given to the planners sitting officiously at the table. Although we could overhear the instructions, we were told to wait ... It was the first time during the course that I felt 'second class'. The other three in my group were more accepting and smiled at my proposal of a revolution. Before I could cause trouble, C came over to ask about our skills ... soon the planners and workers were jointly planning ... We were finished in good time ... the upstairs group had not come down ... we learned that a strike of the implementers had occurred ...*

▶ *The planning and participation exercise produced a lot more than fun ... It amazed me that we had so much to talk about and so many lessons to learn ... Chief among these lessons was for the implementors to be consulted early in the process. As our group waited, we discussed how it felt to hear rumours of plans being made, and saw parallels in our own situations. Our meeting with the planners got off to a rocky start. We had to visit them in their office, and we thought about reacting as communities often do and refusing to go, although we didn't go as far as demanding transport. It was important that the participation we were offered was a real chance to influence the outcome, and not just a bland promise.*

▶ *Whilst M, E and I waited we began to discuss our feelings of helplessness, weakness and frustration at being excluded from the planning process. Our discussion was interrupted by the arrival of our 'planners', who instantly declared, "We're not bosses, we thought it better to come and discuss it with you." At first I was overwhelmed ... A turning point came when our planners asked us "What do you want to do?" Suddenly the whole situation changed. It was no longer 'them' and 'us' ... I no longer felt helpless. We were not going to be presented with a plan from outside. We were participants.*

▶ *For the record ...*

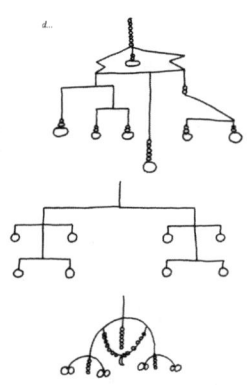

456

An Experience of Programming

▶ *The groups solved the exercise in quite different ways — and I don't know which would have been the most successful in real life.*

This simulation provides experience of working out the details of an overall plan. Such a level of planning and decision-making is often referred to as programming. The simulation uses the example of a rural literacy scheme.

Members work in small groups or teams and undertake the programming for this scheme. At the end of the task there are visits between groups and feedback on each other's work. The learning relates not only to programming and to schemes of the kind in the example, but also to decision-making, to interpersonal work, to greater awareness of content and process, and to inter-group feedback.

The simulation follows and complements An Experience of Planning (page 446), and can be seen as a further contribution to the topic of planning; although that topic, as such, cannot be dealt with in this manual.

It requires at least two consecutive sessions, and works best when course members have become accustomed to simulation as a method.

Objectives

- to experience and identify processes in the detailed preparation which is necessary before an overall plan can be implemented;
- to raise awareness of the dynamics of programming, participation, and decision-making;
- to recognize that there are alternative solutions to most problems, each having advantages and disadvantages;
- to provide an opportunity to explore role, process and feedback within and between small teams;
- to encourage members in using the imagination, as well as giving attention to detail.

 ## Preparation

Small Groups

Members work in small groups of 4 or 5 members (not more then 5) all sharing the same role. After it has completed the task, each group exchanges a visit with another group and gives feedback on that group's work. It is easier to organize the visits if the number of groups is two, four or six.

Within the small groups there is a natural tendency to rely on members who have previous experience of literacy schemes, or whose organizations have a comparable approach to work in the community. It is useful, at least for the task, if members with such experience are allocated to each group. It further assists work on the task if members who interact well together are allocated to the same group.

Rooms and Materials

Each small group will require its own room for the simulation itself. Most of the work is done on the floor, so rooms should not be filled with furniture. Each small group will require a 'time-line'. This is a length of string, preferably contrasting with the floor colour, about 15 ft (5 m) long. The string should be knotted at one foot (30 cm) intervals, and laid in a straight line across the floor. The intervals represent successive months.

Each group also needs a set of 40 cards. Each card represents a possible decision or action in the programming of such a literacy scheme. A list of the possible actions is included at the end of this section (pages 461—462). Another 15—20 blank cards should be added to each set. If each set is a different colour it becomes convenient to distinguish the groups as the 'yellow group', the 'pink group', and so on.

Before starting each member will require a copy of the Role Outline, and during the discussion each will require a copy of the Questions for Discussion (see pages 462—464).

Introducing the Simulation

■ Explain in the whole group that the simulation is principally about planning and programming, but it is also about a literacy scheme, and about working together.

Tell members that they will be working in small groups. Each member will have the same role and the same task. The role will be a staff-member in a rural development organization. The organization is well-established, and is somewhat conventional. Within this organization the staff have been given responsibility for setting up a new literacy programme. Give them a brief summary of the background and situation described in the Role Outline, without the details, and explain that you will give them all this information as a handout.

Show the members a time-line and explain it. Show them a set of cards, and explain that each card represents one decision or one action. Explain that their task in the simulation is to imagine the background and situation, and to place the cards in a sequence along the string to represent what has to be done in each of the forthcoming months, starting from the beginning of the next month.

Tell them to regard the cards as examples of decisions and actions. In a real life programme there may be many more decisions and actions which have to be taken.

■ Conversely, some of the actions on the cards may be dismissed as unnecessary or inappropriate. Make it clear that not all the cards have to be used. The decisions and actions on the cards represent what might be done, but the small groups can leave cards out, replace them, or add to them. Additions and alternatives can be written on the blank cards. Ask the groups to leave their sequence of cards on the floor at the end of the exercise so that another group can come and see their work.

Distribute the Role Outline, and ask members to read it through in the small groups. Tell them which small groups and which rooms they will work in, and ask the small groups to move to their own rooms.

The introduction in the whole group may take 15 minutes.

Visit all the groups and clarify anything not understood. If members ask for additional information such as, 'Who should be on the committee of advisors?' tell them it is for them to decide.

The time available for the task in the small groups is 1¼ hours. Visit the groups as they work on the task, and if necessary remind them about the timing. Some groups may want more time, so if the task is followed by a break it allows them extend their work into the break if they wish.

It is left to the members of each group to imagine the background and situation, and to decide how they will 'programme' the literacy scheme. Many of the decisions which have to be made are debatable. For example, are general objectives to be set before beginning any work, or only after survey and discussions in the villages? Is the Committee of Advisors to be at expert level, or at village level, or at both? When should it first meet? What assumptions — about the villages, about the local leaders, about their own organization — is the group making? What additional decisions and actions, if any, does the group choose to include?

Each small group will arrange their cards in a different sequence, yet each sequence may be valid, each with advantages and disadvantages. Seeing and understanding this can itself be a rich source of learning.

Conducting the Feedback

As the small groups finish the task they should take a break. After the break they exchange visits, look at each other's sequence or programme, and give each other feedback on it. This is done while the small groups are still based in their own rooms.

■ Visit all the groups as they are completing the task and explain the procedure. Tell each group that they will exchange visits and give feedback on the other group's work. Each visit will last for ten minutes.

Explain the rules for the visits. The visiting group's task is to look at the receiving group's programme, and to compare that work with their own. They are then invited to make comments, criticisms and suggestions, but whatever they say must be audible, and must be intended as helpful to the receiving group. Any criticism must be constructive.

■ Members of the receiving group should listen carefully to this feedback. If time permits they may respond briefly and explain their assumptions and decisions, but if time is short they will have to remain silent.

Then the visiting group will return to its own room and briefly discuss the visit, while the receiving group discusses what they have heard from their visitors. After five minutes the groups exchange tasks and the visit is returned, using the same procedure.

Tell each group which room to visit, and exactly when the visits will start.

If the number of small groups is even, they can exchange visits in pairs, but if there are three or five small groups the visits have to be rotated, which is more complicated. It is helpful if additional trainers are available to organize the visits and keep the groups to the timing and to the rules for feedback. To make one visit and to receive one may be all that is possible if the overall time is limited to two sessions. However, if more time is available, further visits between groups — or even a visit to each of the other groups — can be made, and the pros and cons of more programmes can then be considered.

Conducting the Reflection

There are several levels to this simulation — programming, literacy schemes, decision-making related to the content and the process, interpersonal work, and inter-group feedback — and so there is much to discuss. An hour is required. If less than an hour is available, the final reflections in the whole group may be left until the beginning of the next session.

■ After the visits between the small groups, ask all members to return to the course room, but to sit and work in their small groups.

Point out that there are many aspects to the simulation, and that the small groups have had different experiences.

A general discussion in the whole group would be unwieldy, at least to start with. Distribute the web chart with Questions for Discussion (page 464), which provides a structure for reflecting on both content and process.

Ask the small groups to work through the questions. Monitor their discussions, and check that they give attention to the process questions as well as to the content.

Conclude the event in the whole group with sharing and reflections from the small groups.

▶ *I found it a rather difficult task to establish a literacy programme ... The amount of cards was overwhelming ... We stuck too much to the 'prescription' and were not creative enough to use our own judgement ... There is no doubt that space was a problem. Our room was small and from the beginning we had difficulties to display our cards ...*

▶ *Your group thinks carefully on the most logical arrangement of the cards. When you are through, another group of colleagues come to look at your work and they speak out their constructive criticisms. You hold yourself, even when some of the comments really touch you!*

▶ *I was not sure how easy it would be to organize the men in my group but we worked well as a team and finished in time, satisfied that we had done a good job. We then visited W, A, M and O who had planned very differently but also thought theirs was good ... Before lunch I made a quick trip to see how F, Sa, C, E and Sh had done their planning. If I was employed by their organization I'm sure I would have suffered a breakdown by March because of the amount of work I would have done in January and February ...*

▶ *We were proud of our work and eager to defend it in the following discussion with the other groups. The other groups had come to other results ... We were not invited to choose the winner. In development work you will not find the champions. We tried to see the strength and weakness in each scheme.*

Decisions and Actions for Each Set of Cards

Advertise co-ordinator's post

Appoint co-ordinator

Arrange a meeting of teachers to discuss the programme

Arrange for first meeting of committee of advisers

Arrange public meetings in each village to explain programme and invite people to join in

Buy teachers' bicycles

Choose six villages for the programme

Consult the district adult education officer

Consult villagers (or their leaders) over objectives for the programme

Decide criteria for choosing villages for the programme

Decide how programme is going to be evaluated

Decide salary level for co-ordinator

Decide to whom the programme co-ordinator will be responsible

Discuss what the villagers who attend the programme will be asked to contribute

Discuss with villagers their seasonal and daily schedules. When can they find time to attend classes?

Evaluation

Form committee of advisers for programme

Identity possible programme advisers

Identify possible teachers

Identify possible villages for programme

Interim discussion with the teachers and villagers on the progress and impact of the programme

Interview candidates for co-ordinator's post

Invite District Adult Education Officer to visit

Invite the Chief of Police to tea

Make formal survey of literacy in the area

Make informal visits to 'possible villages' to get an informal impression of local conditions

Meet the leaders of the chosen villages

Organize a seminar

Place an order for a motor-cycle for the co-ordinator
Prepare budget for programme
Prepare job description for co-ordinator
Prepare teaching materials for the programme
Recruit teachers for the programme
Set general objectives
Set 'operational' objectives (measurable, precise, time-bound, etc.)
Set up accounting procedures for the co-ordinator and teachers
Start programme
Start training course for teachers
Take a holiday
Visit literacy programme in next district.

Role Outline: An Experience of Programming

You are a staff-member in a well-established rural development organization. The organization has a good relationship with the surrounding communities and with local leaders. The local leaders have requested the organization to start some adult literacy work in the area.

The organization has agreed in principle to set up a literacy programme, initially in six villages, but no detailed planning or programming has yet been done. The six villages have not yet been identified; and there is no detailed information about the existing level of literacy in the area but it is generally low.

You have been asked to take all the necessary steps to get the programme started. After the programme has started, you will take up some other work in the organization. So you can think of yourself as a temporary manager of the programme, but not as a full-time permanent staff-member of the programme.

Your organization has enough funds for all the preparatory and planning work (i.e. for the costs incurred by you), but no funds for the programme itself. The intention is to approach the donor agencies which are already supporting the work of the organization to see if any of them will offer funds. You have been asked to prepare the plan and budget, and to write applications for funding.

It is your organization's policy to set up a committee of advisers for each programme which the agency takes up. You have been asked to form a committee of advisers for this literacy programme.

The staffing proposed for the programme itself is one full-time co-ordinator (a new appointment), and one part-time teacher in each village. It is proposed that the co-ordinator should be paid a salary, and that the teachers should be paid a nominal amount only. The co-ordinator is to be provided with a motor-cycle, and the teachers with a bicycle each. You have been asked to take the necessary steps to recruit and train the co-ordinator and the teachers.

The villages are expected to make rooms available for the classes. Your organization is expected to provide lamps and teaching materials. The teaching materials have not yet been prepared.

John Staley, *Enticing the learning: Trainers in Development,* University of Birmingham, pages 462—463

Questions for Discussion: An Experience of Programming

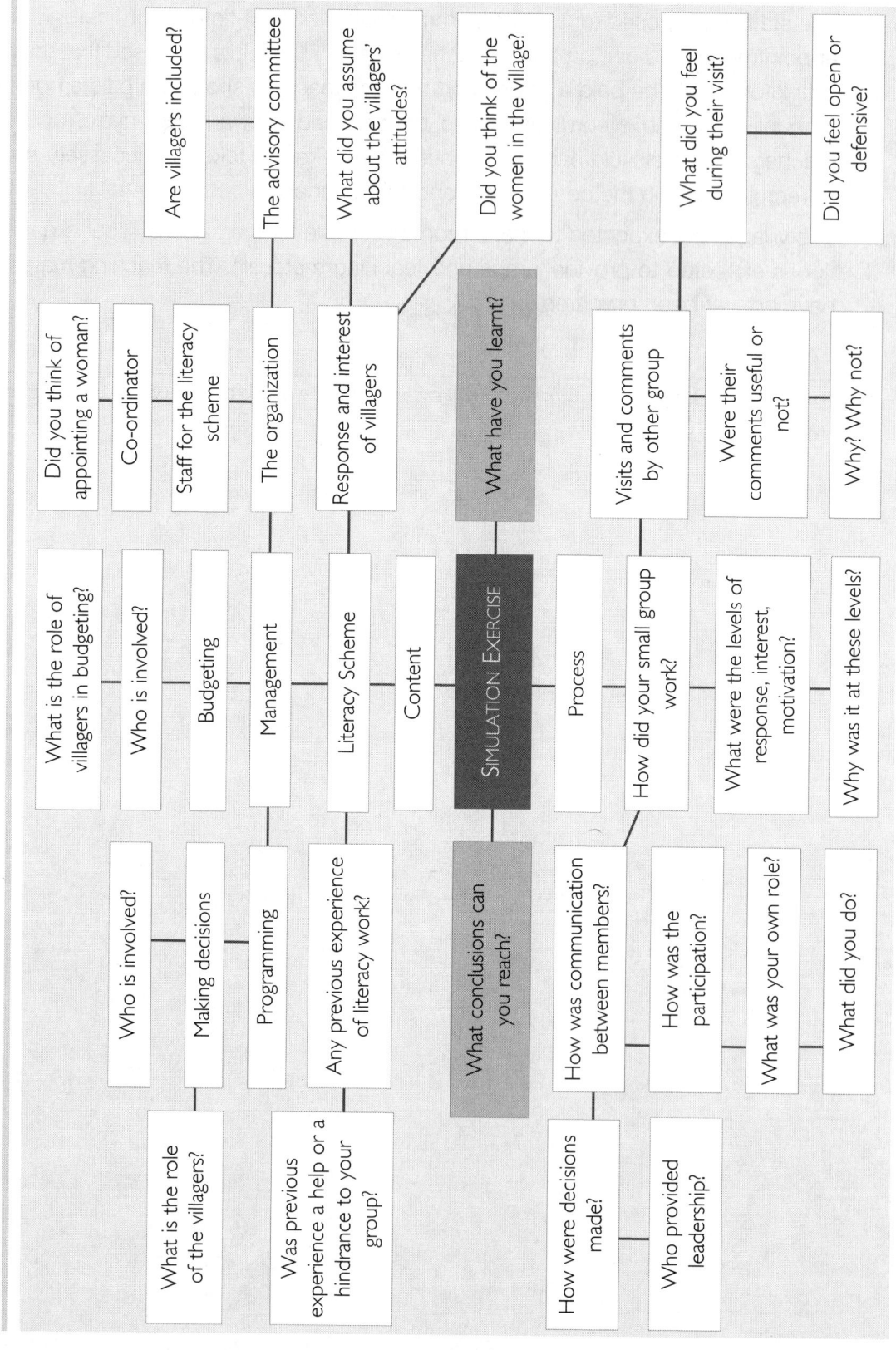

Are villagers included?

The advisory committee

What did you assume about the villagers' attitudes?

Did you think of the women in the village?

What did you feel during their visit?

Did you feel open or defensive?

Did you think of appointing a woman?

Co-ordinator

Staff for the literacy scheme

The organization

Response and interest of villagers

What have you learnt?

Visits and comments by other group

Were their comments useful or not?

Why? Why not?

What is the role of villagers in budgeting?

Who is involved?

Budgeting

Management

Literacy Scheme

Content

SIMULATION EXERCISE

Process

How did your small group work?

What were the levels of response, interest, motivation?

Why was it at these levels?

Who is involved?

Making decisions

Programming

Any previous experience of literacy work?

What conclusions can you reach?

How was communication between members?

How was the participation?

What was your own role?

What did you do?

What is the role of the villagers?

Was previous experience a help or a hindrance to your group?

How were decisions made?

Who provided leadership?

CHAPTER 11

Time To Move On

▶ *... all people found different ways of expressing their learning experience. We didn't confine ourselves to giving and receiving speeches, but were presented with visual aids, role play and acting.*

▶ *... members were reflecting on their learning from the course, bringing me to the understanding that quite a lot of development had been going on within the group.*

A course can be concluded by giving attention to three inter-related tasks. The first is evaluation (see page 243). The second is for members to identify and speak about their learning from the course. The third and final task is to bid each other farewell.

This section deals with the second task. It is directed to individual members in their roles as development workers. Details of the task are set out in the handout on page 467.

The purpose is to help the members consolidate their learning and prepare themselves for the return to work. Members take turns in the whole group to present their principal learning from the course, and to describe how they expect to apply this learning in their future work.

This requires reflection and preparation but is not a big task. During the last days of a course the attention and energy of members is drawn towards going home. It is not a suitable time for big tasks or lengthy assignments. Ten minutes for each contribution may be enough, with a little extra time for clarifications, and perhaps for other members' challenges. Members take turns to moderate the contributions of others.

A variety of methods can be encouraged, both to support members' individuality and creativity, and to make the presentations more lively and interesting. This also allows for the heterogeneity of members' roles back home. Some suggestions about methods are included in the handout.

The contributions should be separated by short breaks, so six members can make their contributions in one session.

The procedure for this task, with members taking turns to make presentations about their work back home, is a reminder of Me and My Work. However the purpose of this task is different: the direction here is forwards, beyond the course, into the future.

▶ *T started with a role play ... J showed us what she will carry in her bag after this course ... L explained to us the tension he is living in with the method of force field analysis. I surprised us with a poem ... D presented his organisation and how he now understands its motto ... T's story told us how 'Coconut' learnt about the world and became 'pregnant' ...*

▶ *... the role-play took us to S's home situation, first before leaving and then after returning home. It was clear for all of us that S had changed a lot, not only in management-style but also in the way he was working and his view of himself, the development process and the role of aid. I assume that some of the same changes have taken place in most of us ...*

▶ *I think the questions I have now are very different from the ones I had at the beginning of the course.*

▶ *At the end of the course I have more questions than answers, but this will not stop me acting.*

Guidelines: Possibilities for Change

The task is to make a short presentation based on the understanding and learning you have gained from the course. In this you are asked to explain or explore how you think your learning can be put to use in your work situation back home.

It is left to you to decide which learning or conclusions you would like to present and discuss. For example, you might:

- summarise your overall learning from the course, and discuss how you plan to use this learning in your own roles and work in the future;
- share particular insights, attitudes and understanding which you have gained, and how you think these will contribute to your effectiveness;
- speak about themes or topics from the course that have been especially important in your situation, or to you personally;
- analyse your new understanding on particular issues or problems, and share how this understanding will assist you or your organization;
- share your ideas for the future of your own work, or of your organization;
- share some enabling questions you are taking back to ask your colleagues or your organization;
- emphasize what you yourself will do differently in future.

The method of making your presentation is also left to you. You might:

- make a spoken statement;
- use visual materials as well: diagrams, posters, pictures, symbols, collage etc;
- involve others to set up a dramatic skit or use mime, sculptures, exercises or role-play;
- use interviews, story-telling, song or dance.

All of these methods have been used for the task. Creativity in method is welcome!

Contributions which arise from your own experience and learning in the course, and which relate in a clear, specific and concrete way to the situation back home, will be more useful. General resolutions and good intentions, however deep, will be less useful. We are calculating the time on the basis of ten minutes each. About half of this time may be for the presentation itself, leaving the remainder for questions, comments and discussion in the group.

Please be ready to take turns in moderating and keeping time for the presentations of others.

Finally please note that these presentations are not intended to be an evaluation of the course itself: that is a separate task.

John Staley, *Enticing the Learning: Trainers in Development*, University of Birmingham, pages 467—468

11.2 Saying Farewell

▶ *People sitting in a circle look inwards. Now we have to turn to look outwards ...*

▶ *I looked around me. These are not indifferent colleagues with whom I have my lectures. No! They are brothers and sisters, they are friends with whom I shared my anxieties, hopes and expectations; who have enriched me with their experiences and who I will always remember.*

This is the final session of a course. Members and trainers sit together in a circle for the last time. Their task, and opportunity, is to say whatever remains to be said to each other within the group, and as human beings rather than as development workers.

The session begins with each person speaking in turn. It ends with farewells, embraces, tears and departures.

Members may find some preliminary guidelines helpful (see page 470). The session itself is unstructured, and individuals speak one by one as the mood and moment take them. Some may share final reflections, some may express appreciation, some may attend to 'unfinished business,' some may voice anxieties about the future. Some make revelations, and some declare resolutions. Many reveal strong emotions.

Some training manuals recommend structures and ceremonies for the final closure of a course, but this seems unnecessary for a person-centred course.[1] The relationships between members, and the life they have shared in the group, will give shape to this session. It is a final expression of the life of the group.

▶ *In the session where we ended we all felt able to be honest. Some of us were feeling very sad, some of us showed it and some of us held it in. The spirit of sharing was a commentary in itself on how we have grown together as a group of friends.*

▶ *Finally E pulled the chairs into a tighter circle for the last session. It started quietly, but soon there were deep words and tears from the heart. This sort of sharing and 'farewelling' was very painful, but there was also a joy in completion and an assurance of continuing friendships ...*

---

1. The only 'ceremony' at the end of the DSC was the participatory distribution of certificates. At the end of the session each member was given a certificate which was not theirs, and was asked to present it to the rightful recipient as a final contribution in the life of the group.

The purpose of the last course session is to bring the life of the group to a close. This session will be a quiet sharing of personal thoughts and feelings before we separate and depart.

It will be an opportunity to sum up new perceptions and insights we have gained about ourselves; to redefine some of our deep concerns and commitments; to share the hopes and anxieties we may have about going back home; to express the feelings we have as the course comes to its end; to say the things we want to say to each other within the group; and to share our final opinions about the group and our life together before we disperse.

If each member comes ready to contribute such personal thoughts, our last session together can be one where we quietly listen to each other, receiving each other's contributions without challenge or discussion, in a final act of sharing.

GLOSSARY

Certain words tend to be used during experience-based training, and may have a particular meaning in that context. It is likely that some users of this manual will be working in English as a second or foreign language, so definitions and clarifications of such words may be helpful. A selection of these words is given below. A few terms from development work, which occur in the handouts and elsewhere in the manual, are also included for those who are unfamiliar with this kind of work.

Analyse: to examine (an object, a statement, a situation, a problem) in order to learn about it; to study what it consists of and to identify essentials; to divide into component parts and to study the nature, function and effect of every part.

Animator: literally, one who gives life to, or makes lively; used in development work of those who raise awareness and enthusiasm and inspire people to action.

Assertive: showing confidence in oneself; insisting on one's rights; stating one's beliefs, claims, needs or views clearly and strongly.

Assumption: something accepted as true although not proved; something taken for granted; something regarded as likely to happen although not certain.

Attitude: way of thinking, feeling, or behaving; behaviour that shows an opinion or a feeling towards an object, an event or a person/people.

Authoritarian: favouring authority; expecting or enforcing strict obedience to authority; concentration of authority in a person, role or group; dominating.

Authority: the right to make decisions or to take action in order to discharge a responsibility; legal power to control, to give orders and to make others obey; power derived from position, prestige or character.

Awareness: having knowledge of; informed about; consciousness of; being sensitive to.

Back home: this refers to a trainee's normal working situation in his/her home place; work and professional circumstances in the place where a person usually lives; the job a person was doing before training and/or will return to afterwards.

Bureaucratic: literally, ruled from the bureau or desk; governed by written or established rules and regulations; bound by 'red tape'; typical of officialdom.

Challenge: as a verb, to call into question; to call on to settle a matter; to ask someone to justify his/her statement; to make an objection to. As a noun, a difficulty or difference that stimulates interest or effort; an obstacle to be overcome.

Commitment: something for which one makes oneself responsible; an undertaking to which one is bound; a declared attachment to a course of action, a cause or a belief.

Communication: the act of transmitting, imparting, conveying or revealing information, ideas, messages, instructions, feelings, etc., together with the acceptance and understanding of the recipients.

Community: people living in one place considered as a whole; people linked together by common conditions of life; people organized under one authority.

Conflict: be in opposition; disagreement; quarrel; struggle; fight; a process that begins when one of the parties perceives that another has frustrated — or is about to frustrate — one of his, her or its needs or concerns.

Confrontation: to bring face to face; to face boldly; to face with criticism or opposition.

Congruent: when thought, feeling, expression and action are consistent with each other. To speak one's mind, state one's feelings, and act authentically without internal contradiction or concealment.

Constraint: an obstacle or barrier to action; a limiting force which restricts or prevents; being kept within bounds.

Content: a word with several meanings, depending on where the stress is placed. Here it is on the first syllable. In training the word refers to the substance, the task, the topic or the subject. When we observe what a group is working at, or listen to what a group is discussing, we are focussing on the content. When we observe how the group is working or discussing, we are focussing on the 'process'.

Control: literally, to be in command, in charge of; to exercise power or authority to direct, order or restrain. In management it can mean the setting up of standards, making regular comparisons of actual events with those standards, and taking corrective action.

Co-operate: being willing to take action together; agreement to produce a result; working together to achieve a result; being helpful and doing as one is asked.

Co-ordination: bringing into correct relationship; adjusting parts so that they work efficiently together; unification of effort; action to ensure different parts of an organization or enterprise follow the same policy.

Creativity: ability to bring into existence; ability to make something new and constructive; use of inventiveness and imagination; bringing something into being by imaginative thought or artistic ability.

Culture: patterns of thinking which distinguish the members of one group — or community or nation — from those of another; patterns of thinking that parents transfer to their children, teachers to students, leaders to followers, etc. Culture is reflected in the meanings people attach to aspects of life; and in what they consider good and evil, true and false, beautiful and ugly.

Decision-making: the process of reaching a decision; choosing among alternatives where there is a degree of uncertainty about the results of the decisions; a choice between dissenting opinions.

Democratic: literally, ruled by the people, directly or through representatives. In training the word means that authority is shared between trainers and trainees, and among trainees.

Dependence: depending upon others; relying on those in authority; real or perceived state of subordination; real or perceived lack of freedom to choose for oneself; being supported or controlled by others; not independent.

Dependency theory: an explanation for underdevelopment. It states that underdevelopment results from inequalities of power and wealth — local, national and international — and is an active process of impoverishment caused by exploitative relationships and systems.

Dialogue: an alternating conversation between two parties, talking to one another, an exchange of views.

Environment: the physical surroundings or external conditions in which people live. The word usually refers to the physical environment together with plants and aninmals, but can be used in other ways, e.g. social environment, childhood environment.

Experience-based: arising from first-hand or direct experiences. Experience-based learning arises from such experiences. Experience-based training offers appropriate experiences for learning.

Exploitation: when used of people, utilizing a person or people for one's own ends; taking advantage of another person or other people; making unfair or selfish use of other people for one's own benefit or profit; using people as objects.

Facilitate: literally, to make easier; to help forward; to help a group to achieve its own goal/s through better understanding of the process in the group; to support the members of a group in making their contributions to achieve those goals. Facilitator is a leadership role concerned with process rather than content.

Feedback: information about the result of a process or the effects of certain activity; reaction by others about how one's role and behaviour is perceived by them or is affecting them.

Feelings: 'feeling' is literally the sense of touch. Feelings generally refers to the emotional side of a person's nature; affections or emotions; the consciousness of pleasure or pain. Happiness, anger and sadness are examples of feelings.

Gender: the differences between men and women which are not biological; the characterisitics, activities and roles assigned to men and to women by culture and society; conventions and practices considered to be masculine and feminine.

Group: literally, a number of persons (or things) together; in a training situation it means two or more people in face-to-face interaction, each aware of the others, and each aware of his/her own membership of the group.

Group Dynamics: the interaction among members of a group; the study of the functioning of a group, usually in order to improve its effectiveness.

Idealism: a standard of perfection that exists in the imagination only; highest and best that can be thought of; an idea of what would be perfect, and can be striven for, but which is not likely to be achieved.

Ideology: way of thinking or collection of ideas which form the basis of a political, economic or social system; comprehensive theory based on certain ideas, values or assumptions; manner of thinking characteristic of a person or group.

Interdependence: depending on each other; mutual dependence.

Iterative: a repeated cycle; doing or saying repeatedly; adjusting up to the last minute. An approach to planning which makes continuous adjustment to a plan as a situation evolves, as further experience is gained, and as more information becomes available.

Laissez-Faire: French word meaning 'Let it Happen' or 'Let it Be'; not intervening; withdrawn or passive authority; abstention from active leadership or initiatives.

Leadership: literally, showing the way by going in front; ability to lead; characteristics of a leader; the exercise of authority; the use of influence within a group to help it achieve its goal.

Management: manner of directing or using anything; mobilising resources (human and material) towards a purpose; those concerned in managing an activity or an enterprise. To manage is to control, guide, direct, deal with or succeed in the running of an enterprise.

Managerialism: the assumption that political, social, economic — and developmental — difficulties in society can be solved by more effective management; optimism about the potential of management to resolve problems and issues in human life and society; ideology that relies upon improvements in management.

Marginalized: pushed to the outside edge or margin (of society, the community or group); those furthest from the 'centres' of power, wealth and influence.

Moderate: literally, to make less violent. In training, to lead an exploratory discussion, mediating between opinions and testing for consensus. A moderator is someone in a leadership role in a group or assembly, more concerned with content than a facilitator is, less concerned with decision-making than a chairperson.

Motivation: the cause of action; the incentive or inducing force; the factor that decides the direction of an individual's behaviour or actions. 'Motive' literally means causing motion or movement.

Multiple identity: recognizing and accepting two or more identities at the same time; for example being a member of a community, a national of a country and a citizen of the world simultaneously.

NGO: abbreviation for Non-Government Organization; self-directed organizations which exist in their own right independently of governments, often with socially responsible objectives and charitable status; voluntary agencies.

Norm: what is normal and expected; the ordinary or standard practice; a rule, often unstated and sometimes unconscious, that specifies acceptable behaviour in a group.

Objective: a word with several meanings: literally, relating to an object. As an adjective, having a real existence outside the mind; a statement or assessment not influenced by personal bias, opinion or feeling; contrasted with 'subjective'. In planning it refers to something aimed at; the result one expects to take place as a result of one's efforts; the specific end being sought.

Oppressed: kept down by tyranny; pressed upon; made subservient; crushed by those with greater power.

Organization: arranged in a system; organized body of people with a common purpose; differentiation of parts and functions and their integration into a systematic and interconnected whole.

Participation: taking part in; having a share in; being actively involved in.

Perception: act or process of becoming aware through the senses or through insight; intuitive recognition of a truth or quality; combining of sensations and impressions into recognition of an object or a concept; seeing, apprehending, understanding.

Perspective: view, viewpoint; perception of the relative importance of facts, ideas, etc;

apparent relation between different aspects of a situation or theory; relation in which parts of a problem or situation are viewed in the mind.

Power: in development work, the ability to do or to act; strength, force, energy; ability to impose one's will and control on others; an organization or nation having authority or influence.

Power Horizon: the boundary of an individual's perception of the workings of power. With a limited horizon we recognize power relationships that affect us immediately and personally — for example, with our supervisor at work, or with a local official — but we do not perceive the wider forces beyond. With a more distant horizon we perceive that organizational, economic, political and other wider forces are also affecting relationships at every level.

Practice: in development work and training, of the nature of action; the act of doing something; action related to — or contrasted with — a theory; something done regularly as part of a profession.

Process: connected series of actions or events, deliberate or unconscious; chain of interactions; sequence of operations or changes undergone; how things and people function; method by which something is done. In training the 'process' is often contrasted with the 'content'.

Realism: actually existing rather than imaginary; the tendency to see and accept things as they really are; taking a view that is based on the real world or on real facts, even when these are unpleasant.

Reflection: literally, to send back. In training, to think about an experience; to analyse what has happened; to consider — or reconsider — meditatively.

Review: literally, to see again. In training, to look back over what has happened; to reconsider something; to 'play back' events in one's mind or in discussion with others.

Responsibility: something for which a person is responsible; the extent of work for which one is accountable; being accountable for one's own behaviour; being obliged to bear the blame for others' mistakes.

Role: behaviour associated with a person's position in a group, family, organization or community; the part a person plays in life or in any event, action, situation or relationship.

Self-reliance: literally, relying upon oneself; having confidence in one's own abilities; not being dependent on others; having and using one's own resources; being able to look after oneself. Often used in development work as an ideal for organizations, communities and countries, and contrasted with reliance (dependence) on outside support, typically aid.

Sensitivity Training: a type of training, especially for managers, intended to make them more perceptive and sensitive towards other people.

Simulation: literally, a pretence or imitation. In training, a simulation is a simplified 'model' of an aspect of the real world. Trainees enter into and interact with the model, and so gain experience, by analogy, with an aspect of the real world.

Social Justice: equality within a society of persons and communities; justice between the component parts of a society; equality of opportunity and also of access to resources and services.

Society: a word with several meanings. In development it refers to the total membership and social organization of a nation; people collectively at the national level; the national social community.

Solidarity: standing together; mutual dependence; commonality of interests; held together by a shared commitment or conviction.

Structure: a word with several meanings. In development work it refers to the way in which something is put together or organized; the way in which essential parts of a complex whole are inter-related; set of interconnected parts; framework.

Subjective: arising from one's own mind, values, attitudes and feelings; influenced by personal perception or preference; not corresponding to or caused by external reality; not 'objective'.

Subversive: tending to weaken or undermine authority or loyalty; person seeking to disturb or destroy an established system, government or ideology.

Superordinate goal: an overall goal; a wider and longer-term purpose which transcends more immediate objectives and intentions; an overarching and enduring purpose.

Support: a word with several meanings. In development work and training it means to hold up; to keep going; to be-friend; to strengthen, encourage, help or sustain.

Sustainable: literally, able to be continued, supported, kept going, kept up, etc. Development of a kind that can be continued without long-term damage or deterioration to the environment. 'Sustainable development' attempts to meet the needs of the present generation without spoiling the opportunities of future generations to meet their needs.

Team: a group of individuals who share a common purpose, and who need to work together to achieve it.

Theory: principle or principles that are offered to explain observed facts or events; speculation as opposed to facts; ideas as contrasted with practice.

Trust: confidence in the strength, truth, effectiveness, competence, reliability of a person or thing; belief in the honesty, loyalty, goodwill of other people; confident expectation.

Underdevelopment: economic impoverishment and powerlessness, often combined with social, psychological and cultural deprivation; lacking control over the future; vulnerable to the control and exploitation of others; living below human potentials.

Values: moral or ethical standards; behaviour and goals that are esteemed and sought after; enduring beliefs that particular kinds of conduct (e.g. honest, kind) or states of being (e.g. security, safety, peace) are preferable to their opposites.

Voluntary Agency: organization existing in its own right independently of government; organization arising from a shared concern, and set up to work accordingly; having a voluntary status, as opposed to statutory (or government) status; often with socially responsible objectives and charitable status. Similar to NGO.

INDEX